THE SKILLED HELPER
A Systematic Approach to Effective Helping

About the Author

Gerard Egan, Ph.D., Professor of Psychology and Organizational Studies at Loyola University of Chicago, is Program Coordinator in the Center for Organization Development. He has written over a dozen books, including *The Skilled Helper, Interpersonal Living, People in Systems, Change Agent Skills in Helping and Human Service Settings, Change Agent Skills A: Designing and Assessing Excellence*, and *Change Agent Skills B: Managing Innovation and Change*. He currently writes and teaches in the areas of communication, counseling, counselor education, business and organization effectiveness, management development, leadership, and the management of innovation and change. He also conducts workshops in these areas both in the United States and abroad and consults to a variety of companies and institutions worldwide. In 1989 he received an award from University Associates for outstanding contributions to the field of Human Resource Development.

FOURTH EDITION

THE SKILLED HELPER
A Systematic Approach to Effective Helping

Gerard Egan
Loyola University of Chicago

Brooks/Cole Publishing Company
Pacific Grove, California

Brooks/Cole Publishing Company
A Division of Wadsworth, Inc.

Printed in the United States of America
10   9   8   7   6   5   4   3

Library of Congress Cataloging-in-Publication Data

Egan, Gerard.
    The skilled helper : a systematic approach to effective helping /
Gerard Egan. — 4th ed.
        p.   cm.
    Includes bibliographical references.
    ISBN 0-534-12138-1
    1. Counseling.   2. Helping behavior.   I. Title.
BF637.C6E39   1990
158'.3—dc20   89-38002
                                                                    CIP

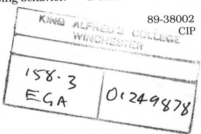

Sponsoring Editor: *Claire Verduin*
Marketing Representative: *Thomas L. Braden*
Editorial Assistant: *Gay C. Bond*
Production Coordinator: *Fiorella Ljunggren*
Production: *Nancy Sjoberg, Del Mar Associates*
Manuscript Editor: *John Bergez*
Permissions Editor: *Carline Haga*
Cover Design and Illustration: *Roy R. Neuhaus*
Interior Illustration: *Kristi Mendola*
Typesetting: *TypeLink, Inc.*
Printing and Binding: *Arcata Graphics/Fairfield*

Preface

The Skilled Helper presents a three-stage problem-management model of helping and the methods and skills helpers need to make it work. It is, therefore, a basic text for counselor and therapist training programs. While the model it describes is a "stand alone" model, its principles and methods can also be incorporated into other approaches to helping. Further, ideally the model can be used, not just by helpers, but by clients themselves. Ultimately, no matter what school or approach to helping is used, clients need to manage their own lives more effectively. The effective helper not only helps clients manage problems and develop unused resources and opportunities but also, at least indirectly, helps clients learn a *process* for managing their concerns better. *The Skilled Helper* model is just such a process.

While the 1990 edition keeps the basic model, methods, and skills intact, there have been a number of changes. For instance, Steps B and C of Stage I have been reversed. The logic here is that counselors can help clients focus on key issues better if they first challenge the kinds of blind spots that keep clients mired down in their problems. However, as in previous editions, the emphasis continues to be on doing what a particular client's needs call for. The model provides helpers with a wide range of possible interventions. Client need determines precisely which set of interventions is actually used.

This edition focuses even more strongly than its predecessors on the issue of client action. I have become more and more convinced, both as a counselor and as a consultant, that the primary problem in helping is not the lack of good problem- and opportunity-focused analysis, goal setting, and strategy formulation. The cognitive part of helping is, in the main, healthy. But too little of what is planned gets translated into problem-managing and opportunity-developing action.

Two correctives are needed. First, we need to find more effective ways of helping clients own the helping process. Second, the tempo of client action, both covert cognitive or internal action and overt action in the everyday settings of life, needs to be raised. The cognitive part of helping helps clients make sure that their actions will have direction and be prudent. But actions cannot have direction or be prudent if they do not take place.

In this edition further work has been done in the area of the values that underlie helping and the client–helper relationship. Novice counselors cannot wait for others to hand them the "correct" value list. Rather, they must actively determine the set of values that will guide them in their practice and then make sure that these are not just espoused values but values-in-use.

There are other new accents in this edition as well. Since the helping professions are in constant movement, new examples from different settings complement the old. The use of imagination in applying the helping model is stressed even more than previously because the "psychopathology of the average" (Maslow, 1968) afflicts not just individuals but also professions, including the helping professions. The social challenge of the helping professions is to get the kinds of skills discussed in these pages into the formal and informal education system of society. We still have not found effective ways of giving the best practice of psychology away (see Larson, 1984; Miller, 1969).

A new principle has emerged in these pages—or a new way of stating an old principle: The helping model, through its stages and steps, provides principles rather than formulas. These principles serve as guidelines for helper and client alike; the "right formula," that is, the most effective application of these principles, must be found in the interactions with each client. Books like this one are not cookbooks. The older I get, the more I realize that the technology of helping needs to be rinsed through with the wisdom of helping. This is a lifelong task.

Although this edition of *The Skilled Helper* represents a significant revision, I have resisted the temptation to add too much to the text. Many of the things I am asked to add are what I would call case-management issues. Although a good text on case management would be a welcome addition to the literature, case-management issues are better dealt with in experiential training and in supervised practice. Furthermore, a text that tries to do justice both to a helping process and to case-management principles and practices would, in my view, become too bloated to be practical.

Finally, this edition relies a little more on the clinical instincts of its author and a bit less on microresearch. Research findings are often so tentative and contradictory that it is difficult to formulate a coherent approach to practice based on them. After reading the research, the discussions, and the summaries in the journals, you may well shake your head and repeat what Carl Rogers said in 1958: "[I have] never learned much from controlled studies of therapy" (quoted in Rubenstein & Parloff, 1959, p. 313). Research that is statistically significant but meaningless in terms of practice (Paquin, 1983) still plagues us. It will probably plague us till the end. Morrow-Bradley and Elliott (1986) put it succinctly:

With virtual unanimity, psychotherapy researchers have argued that (a) psychotherapy research should yield information useful to practicing therapists, (b) such research to date has not been done, and (c) this problem should be remedied. (p. 188)

Their study showed that therapists report low rates of psychotherapy research utilization and state that they get more useful information from colleagues. Fortunately, there are many excellent helpers in the field, willing to learn and to share their learnings with the rest of us.

The point is not that we should give up on research; Gendlin (1986) has come up with an 18-point plan to make psychotherapy research more effective and relevant. As you will note, there are many new citations in this edition. But wherever possible I have tried to blend research findings with clinical insight in the constant search for best practice. Since the needs of clients are urgent, the practice of both formal and informal helping will always move ahead of its empirical research base. In my mind the best helpers are also "translators" (Egan, 1984; Egan & Cowan, 1979), people who stay in touch with the best in current theory and research, who constantly update their practice through ongoing action research with their clients, and who then share their findings, formally or informally, with others.

For offering their comments and suggestions for this edition of *The Skilled Helper*, I would like to thank the following reviewers: Frank Asbury of the University of Georgia, John H. Childers of the University of Arkansas, Ursula C. Gerhart of Rutgers–The State University of New Jersey, Lizabeth Gray of Oregon State University, Michael A. Greenwald of the University of Pittsburgh, Robert Masson of West Virginia University, Peter Maynard of the University of Rhode Island, John M. McGuire of the University of Central Florida, Bruce Palmer of Washington State University, Charles Mack Porter of Slippery Rock University, Wade Rowatt of Southern Baptist Theological Seminary, Laurie Wilson, a student reviewer from Washington State University, and David J. Zinger of the University of Manitoba. Renewed thanks, as well, to all those who have contributed to previous editions of this work.

Gerard Egan

Contents

Chapter Four   Action I: Helping Clients Act   84

Chapter Five   Communication Skills I: Attending and Listening   106

Chapter Six   Communication Skills II: Empathy and Probing   122

PART TWO THE STAGES AND STEPS OF THE HELPING MODEL 151

STAGE I: HELPING CLIENTS DEFINE AND CLARIFY PROBLEM SITUATIONS 153

Chapter Seven Step I-A: Helping Clients Tell Their Stories 155

Chapter Eight Step I-B: Challenging—New Perspectives at the Service of Action 183

Chapter Seventeen   Action II: Helping Clients Put Strategies to Work   370

Chapter Eighteen   Time and Termination   395

Epilog   408

PART ONE

LAYING THE GROUNDWORK

Chapter One

Introduction

FORMAL AND INFORMAL HELPERS

Throughout history there has been a deeply embedded conviction that, under the proper conditions, some people are capable of helping others come to grips with problems in living. Today this conviction is institutionalized in a variety of formal helping professions. Counselors, psychiatrists, psychologists, social workers, and members of the clergy are expected to help people manage the distressing problems of life.

There is also a second set of professionals who deal with clients in times of crisis and distress. Included here are organizational consultants, dentists, doctors, lawyers, nurses, probation officers, teachers, managers, supervisors, police officers, and the like. Although these people are specialists in their own professions, there is still some expectation that they will help their clients or staff manage a variety of problem situations. For instance, teachers teach English, history, and science to students who are growing physically, intellectually, socially, and emotionally and struggling with normative developmental tasks and crises. Teachers are, therefore, in a position to help their students, in direct and indirect ways, explore, understand, and deal with the problems of growing up. Managers and supervisors help workers cope with problems related to work performance, career development, interpersonal relationships in the workplace, and a variety of personal problems that affect their ability to do their jobs.

To these can be added any and all who try to help relatives, friends, acquaintances, strangers (on buses and planes), and even themselves come to grips with problems in living. Indeed, only a small fraction of the help provided on any given day comes from helping professionals. Friends often help one another through troubled times. Parents must manage their own marital problems while helping their children grow and develop. And all of us must help ourselves cope with the problems and crises of life. In short, the world is filled with informal helpers.

Since helping and problem solving are such common human experiences, training in both solving one's own problems and helping others solve theirs should be as common as training in reading, writing, and math. Alas, this is not the case. Therefore, although this book focuses specifically on those for whom helping is a formal part of their role—counselors, social workers, ministers, psychologists, psychiatrists, and the like—it is assumed that it will be useful for informal helpers, too.

THE GOAL OF HELPING

Many clients become clients because, either in their own eyes or in the eyes of others, they are involved in problem situations they are not handling well. These clients need ways of dealing with, solving, or transcending their problem situations. In other words, they need to manage their problems in living more effectively.

Problem situations arise in our interactions with ourselves, with others, and with the organizations, institutions, and communities of life. Clients—whether they are hounded by self-doubt, tortured by unreasonable fears, grappling with cancer, addicted to alcohol or drugs, involved in failing marriages, fired from jobs because they do not have the skills needed in the "new economy," suffering from a catastrophic loss, jailed because of child abuse, wallowing in a midlife crisis, lonely and out of community with no family or friends, battered by their spouses, or victimized by racism—all face problem situations that move them to seek help or move others to send them for help.

Some clients come for help, not because they are dogged by problems like those listed above, but because they are not as effective as they would like to be. They have resources they are not using or opportunities they are not developing. People who feel locked in dead-end jobs or bland marriages, who are frustrated because they lack challenging goals, who feel guilty because they are failing to live up to their own values and ideals, who want to do something more constructive with their lives, or who are disappointed with their uneventful interpersonal lives—such clients come to helpers, not to manage their problems, but to live more fully.

Given these needs of clients, we can state the goal of helping in terms of helpers' effectiveness in meeting these needs:

Helpers are effective to the degree that their clients, through client-helper interactions, are in a better position to manage their problem situations and/or develop the unused resources and opportunities of their lives more effectively.

Notice that I stop short of saying that clients actually end up managing both problems and opportunities better. The reason is that, in the end, clients can choose to live more effectively or not. Of course, the truth is that many clients, because of their interactions with helpers, are not only in a better position to manage the ups and downs of their lives, but actually do so.

Even devastating problem situations can often be handled more effectively. Consider the following example.

Fred L. was thunderstruck when the doctor told him that he had terminal cancer. He was only 52; death *couldn't* be imminent. He felt disbelieving, bitter, angry, and depressed. After a period of angry confrontations with doctors and members of his family, in his despair he finally talked to a clergyman who had, on a few occasions, gently and nonintrusively offered his support. They decided to have some sessions together, but the clergyman also referred him to a counselor who worked in a hospice for the dying. With their help Fred gradually learned how to manage the ultimate problem situation of his life. He came to grips with his religious convictions, put his affairs in order, began to learn how to say goodbye to his family and the world he loved so intensely, and, with the help of the hospice in which the counselor worked, set about the process of managing physical decline. There were some outbursts of anger and some brief periods of depression and despair, but generally, with the help of the clergyman and the counselor, and with the support of his family and the hospice workers, he managed the process of dying much better than he would have done without their help.

This case demonstrates in a dramatic way that the goal of helping is not to "solve" everything. Fred did die. Some problem situations are simply more unmanageable than others. Helping clients discover what kind and degree of problem management or opportunity development is possible is, as we shall see, a central part of the helping process.

The following case deals with a person who came for help because she wanted to identify opportunities and resources and exploit them more creatively.

> After ten years as a helper in several mental health centers, Carol was experiencing burnout. In the opening interview with a counselor, she berated herself for not being dedicated enough. Asked when she felt best about herself, she said that it was on those relatively infrequent occasions when she was asked to help another mental health center to get started or reorganize itself. The counseling sessions helped her explore her potential as a consultant to human-service organizations and make a career adjustment. She enrolled in courses in the Center for Organization Development at a local university. Carol stayed in the helping field, but with a new focus and a new set of skills.

In this case the counselor helped the client manage her problems (burnout, guilt) more effectively and at the same time develop her potential more fully.

Helping as an Education Process

Another way of looking at the goal of helping is client learning. As Strupp (1986) puts it, helping "typically involves learning (unlearning, relearning, new learning), which may take many different forms. . . . The outcomes may manifest themselves as changes in cognitions, feelings, or behavior (or some combination of these)" (p. 124).

Helping is thus an education process whose goal is learning. An excellent definition of learning is this: *Learning takes place when options are increased.* If the collaboration between helpers and clients is successful, clients learn in very practical ways. They have more "degrees of freedom" in their lives as they open up options and take advantage of them.

> Tom, a farmer in a midwestern state, lost his farm during a downturn in the economy. At first he was devastated. He did not see himself as a victim of economic forces and government policies beyond his control. He took it personally. In counseling sessions provided by the county, he first worked through his anger at "them" and his guilt about himself. Then he began to learn about himself. He had always believed that he was "meant for the

earth," that farming was in his bones. As he was helped to take a closer look at trends in society, he discovered that what he really wanted was not necessarily farming but to be on his own. He got a part-time job, took advantage of some retraining opportunities in computers, and went on to set up a business helping farmers use computers in their work. He started being what he had always wanted to be without knowing it—an entrepreneur.

Every helping interview can be seen as an opportunity to help clients develop more options in their lives. A poet once described the lot of people to be "cabined, cribbed, and confined." At its best, helping enables clients to learn to open doors, to throw off chains, to stretch.

Activity versus Outcomes

Counseling is an "-ing" word: it denotes an *activity* or series of activities in which helper and client engage. The activity, however, has value only to the degree that it leads to *valued outcomes* in the client's day-to-day life. Feeling good about a counseling session, while sometimes useful, is not the kind of valued outcome meant here. Ultimately, statements such as "We had a good session," whether spoken by the helper or client, must translate into more effective living on the part of the client. If a helper and client engage in the counseling process effectively, something valued will be in place that was not in place before the helping sessions: unreasonable fears will disappear or diminish to manageable levels, self-confidence will replace self-doubt, addictions will be conquered, an operation will be faced with a degree of equanimity, a better job will be found, new life will be breathed into a marriage, a battered wife will find support and the courage to leave her husband, self-respect will be restored to the person embittered by institutional racism.

Consider the case of a battered woman outlined by Driscoll (1984, p. 64). The mistreatment has caused her to feel that she is worthless even as she develops a secret superiority to those who mistreat her. These attitudes contribute in turn to her continuing passivity and must be challenged if she is to become assertive about her own rights. Through the helping interactions, she develops a sense of worth and self-confidence. This is the first outcome of the helping process. As she gains some confidence in herself, she becomes more assertive; she sees that she has the right to take stands and chooses to challenge those who take advantage of her instead of taking the safer course of merely resenting them. This is a second outcome: a pattern of assertiveness, however tentative in the beginning, takes the place of a pattern of passivity. When her assertive stands are successful, her rights become established, her social relationships improve, and her confidence in herself increases, thus further altering the original self-defeating pattern. This is a third set of outcomes. As she sees herself becoming more and more an agent rather than a patient in her everyday life, she finds it easier to relinquish the resentments and other satisfactions of the passive-victim position and to continue asserting herself. This constitutes a fourth set of outcomes. The activities in which she engages, either within the helping sessions or in her day-to-day life, are valuable *because* they lead to these valued outcomes.

Helping—A Collaborative Enterprise

Counseling, as we shall see, is a peculiar kind of service. It is a *collaborative* process between helper and client. The problem-management and opportunity-development model described in this book is not something that helpers do to clients; it is a process that helpers and clients work through together. In many ways, helpers stimulate clients to provide services *to themselves.* It is the clients who achieve the goals of helping, through the facilitation of the helper. It follows that, while counselors help clients achieve outcomes, they do not control outcomes. When all is said and done, clients have a greater responsibility for both the production and the quality of outcomes.

In talking about outcomes of the collaborative helping process, Eckert, Abeles, and Graham (1988) draw a distinction between "perceived gain" and "raw" (or real) gain. An example of perceived gain is that the client feels good about the helper and the helping sessions. Real gain occurs when the client makes actual progress in managing problem situations and developing opportunities. Some clients, when they think of whether helping has been successful, focus on what happened during the helping sessions—especially the warmth, respect, and interest of the helper and the good feelings they experienced as a result. Such good feelings are not to be downplayed, because they can stimulate clients to act on their own behalf; nevertheless, good feelings are not the same as the "raw gain" of problems managed and opportunities developed.

It is much better if clients feel good because of what they accomplish in their day-to-day lives rather than because of what happens in the helping sessions themselves. Indeed, as we shall see later, helping sessions may at times be painful. In counseling, pain is often the price of gain. The battered woman mentioned a moment ago found many of her helping sessions painful. If she had stopped with the good feelings she experienced in the first couple of sessions because of the helper's care and respect, the series of outcomes listed earlier might never have taken place. At its best, helping leads to outcomes with substance, outcomes that add up to a positive impact on the client's life.

Customer Satisfaction

Fisch, Weakland, & Segal (1985) suggest that the most important indicator of success in helping "is the client's statement that he or she is reasonably or completely content with the outcome of treatment, either because the behavior complained about has changed or because his or her evaluation of the behavior has changed so that he or she no longer perceives it as a significant problem" (pp. 122–123). Note that they do not say that "customer satisfaction" is the *only* indicator of success. It is not that simple. First of all, clients who are referred to a helper because their behavior is unacceptable to *others*—for instance, the alcoholic parent or the manager who destroys the quality of work life for her subordinates—may end up saying, "*I* am no longer bothered by this problem," but this does not mean that the problem has been successfully managed in the *social* context in which it is played out. Second, an I'm-not-bothered-anymore statement may mean that the client has merely accepted mediocrity. In this case, is it still the helper's job to, within reason, challenge the client to live more fully? Third, the client may be saying, "The pain is still here, but now I am living with it better." If the counselor can still help the client get at the roots of the pain, is customer satisfaction enough? Don't get me wrong. Client satisfaction is very important, but is it everything? I don't think so.

DOES HELPING HELP?

Before embarking upon a career in counseling or psychotherapy, you should know that a debate about the usefulness of the helping professions has been going on for at least 35 years (Hariman, 1984). Can and do helpers achieve the goals we have outlined? The disturbing question "Does professional helping really help?" is still being asked. Cowen (1982) expressed the problem with literary flair.

> Once upon a time, mental health lived by a simple two-part myth. Part 1: People with psychological troubles bring them to mental health professionals for help. Part 2: One way or another, often based on verbal dialogue, professionals solve these problems and the people live happily ever after.
>
> And sometimes the cookie does indeed crumble according to the myth. But events of the past several decades suggest that the "marriage-in-heaven" script is not nature's only, or even most frequent, way. In real life the idyllic myth breaks down at several key points.
>
> Let's talk first . . . about Part 2. Heresy though it may have been 20 years ago, it is now permissible to say that not all problems brought to mental health professionals are happily adjudicated. How much of the shortfall is due to the imprecision of our professional "magic," or even to the lack of skill of our magicians, and how much to the selectively refractory nature of the problems that professionals see remains unclear. Much clearer is a sense of mounting dissatisfaction with the reach and effectiveness of past traditional ways, a dissatisfaction that has powered active new explorations toward a more promising tomorrow in mental health. (p. 385)

As I read the literature on the efficacy of helping, whether it is called counseling or psychotherapy, I find a continuum. At the left end of the continuum is the position "Helping is never helpful"; at the right, "Helping is always helpful." As usual, truth seems to stand somewhere in the middle.

The Nay-Sayers and Yea-Sayers

Some critics express grave doubts about the legitimacy of the helping professions, even going so far as to claim that helping is a fraudulent process, a manipulative and malicious enterprise (see, for example, Eysenck, 1984; Masson, 1988; Rimland, 1979; Tennov, 1975). Masson claims that in the United States helping is a $2.5 billion business that does no more than profit from people's misery. He believes that devaluing people is part and parcel of all therapy and that the helper's values and needs are inevitably imposed on the client.

At the other end of the continuum are those who imply that helping, noble profession that it is, almost always works. Some of these seem more intent on defending the helping industry than taking a good, critical look at it in the service of making it better.

Many yea-sayers base their judgment on empirical studies of helping outcomes. However, Paquin (1983) rightly cautions us against research that is statistically significant but meaningless in terms of practice. For those with doubts about the meaningfulness of individual outcome studies, an approach to reviewing the evidence called meta-analysis has proved to be both helpful and controversial. The conclusions of meta-analysis are based on a review of many micro-studies. Smith, Glass, and Miller (1980), through a meta-analysis of hundreds of outcome studies, found convincing evidence of the efficacy of psychotherapy. However, the validity of meta-analysis itself has been debated ever since their first report.

The Caution Group: Helping CAN Help, BUT . . .

There is too much evidence that helping works to side with the nay-sayers (see London, 1986) and too much evidence that helping often falls short of the mark to side with the pure yea-sayers (see Mays & Franks, 1985). Like most practitioners, I side with those who, after reviewing the evidence, say that helping can be helpful. Empirical studies aside, my own experience, together with the experience of colleagues I trust, makes it quite clear to me that helping can help. However, the operative work is "can." The American Psychiatric Association Commission on Psychotherapies (1982) stated:

> Although research in psychotherapy is still plagued by many problems connected with assignment of patients, use of statistics, outcome measures, and experimental design, the data have shown empirically that

psychotherapy is effective with some populations with some problems. (p. 226)

This is obviously a guarded conclusion drawn from a complex study of the helping process. It is another way of saying "can." Let's consider two possible reasons why the evidence is not more unambiguously supportive of the efficacy of helping.

The Collaborative Nature of Helping

One reason it is difficult to give a clear-cut answer to the question "Does helping help?" is the collaborative nature of the enterprise. Helping is not like fixing a car or removing a tumor. Helpers do not "cure" their patients. Helping is a team effort in which helpers need to do their part and clients theirs. If either party refuses to play the game or play it well, then the enterprise can fail. For their part, helpers need to give their best to the enterprise. But giving their best means, to a great extent, helping clients tap their own resources—not just getting clients to play the game, as it were, but helping them to *want* to play the game. And helpers must do all of this in a moral, ethical, and professional way (see Chapter 3).

Providing counseling or psychotherapy is not the same as giving the client a pill, though sometimes researchers talk as if it were. Outcomes depend on the competence and motivation of the helper, on the competence and motivation of the client, on the quality of their interactions, and often on a host of environmental factors over which neither helper nor client has control. Determining what makes helping effective, then, is messier than determining whether or not a pill works.

The Competence and Commitment of the Helper

Another reason it is difficult to give a clear-cut answer to the question "Does helping help? is the fact of individual differences among helpers. As noted by Luborsky et al. (1986):

- There are considerable differences between therapists in their average success rates.
- There is considerable variability in outcome within the caseload of individual therapists.
- Variations in success rates typically have more to do with the therapist than with the type of treatment.

While helping can and often does work, there is plenty of evidence that ineffective helping also abounds, not because helpers are malicious or frauds but because they are not as competent as they might be. Helping is a powerful process that is all too easy to mismanage. It is no secret that because of inept helpers some clients get worse from treatment. Helping is not neutral; it is "for better or for worse." Ellis (1984) claims that inept helpers are either ineffective or inefficient. While the inefficient may ultimately help their clients, they use "methods that are often distinctly inept and that consequently lead these clients to achieve weak and unlasting results, frequently at the expense of enormous amounts of wasted time and money" (p. 24). There is growing evidence that the consumer movement is hitting the helping professions (Laungani, 1984; Lebow, 1982; Lorefice & Borus, 1984). Clients are beginning to speak out about the treatment they receive. And well they should: Every profession has its effective and its ineffective practitioners, but incompetence seems more deplorable in people professions like medicine and helping.

Since studies on the efficacy of counseling and psychotherapy do not usually make a distinction between high-level and low-level helpers, and since the research on deterioration effects in therapy suggests that there are a large number of low-level or inadequate helpers, the negative results found in many studies are predictable.

In the hands of skilled and socially intelligent helpers, people whom Gilbert (1978) and Carkhuff (1985) call "exemplars," helping can do a great deal of good. Norman Kagan (1973) suggested that the basic issue confronting the helping professions is not validity—that is, whether helping helps or not—but reliability:

> Not, can counseling and psychotherapy work, but does it work consistently? Not, can we educate people who are able to help others, but can we develop methods which will increase the likelihood that most of our graduates will become as effective mental health workers as only a rare few do? (p. 44)

To improve the reliability of helping, more effective training programs for helpers are needed. The negative studies mentioned earlier suggest that, while there are many professionals with the proper credentials, not all of them have and use essential helping skills. Carkhuff (1971a) calls helpers "functional" professionals if they have and use the skills needed for effective helping. There is a great need for functional helpers, whether they are "credentialed" or not. The model of helping presented in this book, together with the skills and techniques that make it work, is designed precisely to increase both the validity and the reliability of the helping process. This book is aimed at enabling helpers of all sorts "deliver the goods" consistently and ethically to clients who seek out or accept the services of helpers in order to manage their lives more effectively.

You are encouraged to acquaint yourself with the ongoing debate concerning the efficacy of helping. Study of this debate is not meant to discourage you, but to help you (1) appreciate the complexity of the helping process, (2) acquaint yourself with the issues involved in evaluating the outcomes of helping, (3) appreciate that, poorly done, helping can actually harm others, (4) make you reasonably cautious as a helper, and (5) motivate you to become a high-level helper, learning and using practical models, methods, skills, and guidelines for helping.

MODELS OF HELPING: RICHNESS OR CLUTTER?

What method helps counselors and psychotherapists, in collaboration with their clients, achieve the broad goals we have outlined? Well, as I write this, I glance up at my bookcase. It is filled with books on counseling and psychotherapy, books dealing with theory, research, and practice. Even a cursory investigation will reveal that the number of models or approaches to helping is staggering. If you were to leaf through books that are compilations of the different schools or approaches to counseling and psychotherapy (Belkin, 1987; Braswell & Seay, 1984; Burke, 1989; Corey, 1986; Corsini & Wedding, 1989; Kutash & Wolf, 1986; Patterson, 1986, to name but a few) or if you were to keep abreast of the fairly steady stream of books on new or reformulated approaches (Burke, 1989; Carkhuff, 1987; Cattell, 1987; Confer, 1987; Ellis & Dryden, 1987; Epting, 1984; Gerber, 1986; Howard, Nance, & Myers, 1987; Ivey, 1986; Propst, 1987; Robinson, 1988; Van Deurzen-Smith, 1988, to name but a few), you would soon discover a bewildering number of schools, systems, methods, and techniques, all of which are proposed with equal seriousness and all of which claim to lead to success.

Do all these approaches constitute richness, clutter, or a bit of both? They are a resource if helpers, especially novice helpers, have an *integrative model* or framework that helps them borrow from all these models and then organize what they borrow. There are two broad and overlapping approaches to this task of integration: *systematic eclecticism* and *systematic integration*, or the "converging themes" approach.

Systematic Eclecticism

The eclectic helper borrows good ideas from a variety of approaches and molds them into his or her own approach to counseling. Most helpers borrow in this way to a greater or lesser extent; indeed, research shows that most counselors and psychotherapists like to consider themselves eclectic (Norcross & Prochaska, 1988). However, an effective eclecticism must be more than a random borrowing of ideas and techniques from here and there. Helpers need a conceptual framework that enables them to borrow ideas, methods, and techniques systematically from all theories, schools, and approaches and integrate them into their own theory and practice of helping.

Integration: Converging Themes in Helping

There is a movement afoot to pool all the good ideas found in the many different forms of counseling and psychotherapy in order to identify a set of "converging themes," that is, principles, approaches, and methodologies that constitute the essence of helping (Erskine & Moursund, 1988; Goldfried, 1982; see also *Journal of Integrative and Eclectic Psychotherapy*, 1982 to the present). This approach moves one step beyond eclecticism, even systematic eclecticism, because it focuses on the "essence" of helping.

> When I think of eclecticism I think of a menu of different orientations from which one can make selections, and what bothers me about this is the implication that the menu will always be there. My own hope is that at some point in the future we will have a more comprehensive conceptualization that will allow us to function under a *common* paradigm—which is not to say a single method, but rather a meaningful structure that can guide us in what we do. (Goldfried & Wachtel, 1987, pp.131–132)

Subsequent articles in the same journal (1987) take exception to Wachtel's notion of integration. The fear is that one helping system would be developed and then imposed on everyone, with the result that the richness that comes with diversity would be lost. The real losers, it is said, would be the clients.

The integration movement is still in its infancy, and, as you can imagine, it involves a process plagued with professional politics (Prochaska & Norcross, 1986). It is an important movement, however, one worth watching.

A PROBLEM-MANAGEMENT APPROACH TO HELPING

In the face of all this diversity, helpers, especially beginning helpers, need a practical, working model of helping that enables them to learn

- what to do to help people facing problems in living,
- how to help clients develop unused resources and opportunities,
- what specific stages and steps make up the helping process,
- what techniques aid the process,
- what communication skills are needed to interact with clients,
- how these skills and techniques can be acquired,
- what clients need to do to collaborate in the helping process and to manage their problems and develop their opportunities more effectively, and
- how to evaluate their efforts.

For me, a flexible, humanistic, broadly based *problem-management* and *opportunity-development* model or framework meets all of these requirements. As Kanfer and Schefft (1988) note, "There are only a few books that offer [helpers] a conceptually consistent framework for structuring each step of the change process, regardless of the specific treatment method used" (p. xvi). It is precisely such a model that is presented in the pages of this book—a model that espouses a straightforward approach without ignoring the complexities of the helping process (Jones, Cumming, & Horowitz, 1988).

Common sense suggests that problem-solving models, techniques, and skills are important for all of us, since all of us must grapple daily with problems in living of greater or lesser severity. Ask anybody whether problem-solving skills are important for day-to-day living, and the answer inevitably is "certainly." Talk about the importance of problem solving is everywhere. Yet if you review the curricula of our primary, secondary, and tertiary schools, you will find that talk outstrips practice.

There are those who say that formal courses in problem-solving skills are not found in our schools because such skills are picked up through experience. To a certain extent, that's true. However, if problem-solving skills are so important, I wonder why society leaves the acquisition of these skills to chance. A problem-solving mentality should become second nature to us. The world may be the laboratory for problem solving, but the skills needed to optimize learning in this lab should be taught; they are too important to be left to chance. Indeed, you will soon discover that most of the clients you see are ineffective problem solvers.

Mahoney and Arnkoff (1978) recognized the value of a problem-management approach to helping when they said:

> Among the cognitive learning therapies, it is our opinion that the problem-solving perspectives may ultimately yield the most encouraging clinical results. This is due to the fact that—as a broader clinical endeavor—they encompass both the cognitive restructuring and the coping skills therapies (not to mention a wide range of "noncognitive" perspectives). With the problem-solving approaches, clients are not only taught specific coping skills, but also the more general strategies of assessment, problem definition, and so on. (p. 709)

The value of problem-management approaches to helping is being recognized more and more, and helpers, either directly or indirectly, are increasingly adopting a problem-management approach (see Burke, Haworth, & Brantley, 1980; Carkhuff, 1987; Held, 1984; Heppner, 1978; Heppner & Reeder, 1984; Ivey & Matthews, 1984; Janis, 1983b; Kanfer & Schefft, 1988; Livneh, 1984; Mahoney, 1977; Mahoney & Arnkoff, 1978; Nezu, 1987; Prochaska & Norcross, 1982; Schwebel, Schwebel, & Schwebel, 1985; Scott, 1979; Searight & Openlander, 1984; Sweeney, Clarkin, & Fitzgibbon, 1987; Wagman, 1979, 1980a, 1980b; Wasik & Fishbein, 1982; Watson & Tharp, 1989; Wheeler & Janis, 1980; Zins, 1984). Most crisis-intervention models have a strong problem-solving component (Janosik, 1984). In addition, a problem-management model in counseling and psychotherapy has the advantage of the vast amount of research that has been done on the problem-solving process itself. The model, techniques, and skills outlined in this book tap that research base.

The Problem-Management Model as Organizer

Many books on helping are filled with good ideas. To the novice helper, however, these ideas can seem like a hodgepodge, and even the advanced helper can benefit greatly from a model or framework of helping that puts some order in these ideas. A comprehensive problem-solving or problem-management model can be used to make sense of the vast literature in counseling and psychotherapy in at least three ways—mining, organizing, and evaluating:

1. Mining. First, helpers can use the problem-management model to mine any given school or approach, "digging out" whatever is useful without having to accept everything else that is offered. The stages and steps of the model serve as tools for identifying methods and techniques that will serve the needs of clients.

2. Organizing. Second, since the problem-management model is organized by stages and steps, it can be used to organize the methods and techniques that have been mined from the rich literature on helping. For instance, a number of contemporary therapies have elaborated excellent techniques for helping clients identify blind spots and develop new perspectives on the problem situations they face. These techniques can be organized, as we shall see, in Step I-B, the "new perspectives" step of the problem-management model.

3. Evaluating. Since the problem-management model is pragmatic and focuses on outcomes of helping, it can be used to evaluate the vast number of helping techniques that are constantly being devised. The model enables helpers to ask in what way a technique or method contributes to the "bottom line," that is, to outcomes that serve the needs of clients.

In sum, using an integrative framework helps reduce the amount of clutter found in the literature.

An Open-Systems Model

The problem-management model is an open-systems model, not a closed school. While it takes a stand on how counselors may help their clients, it is open to being corroborated, complemented, and challenged by any other approach, model, or school of helping. In this respect it fits the description of efficient therapy advanced by Ellis (1984):

> Like the scientific method itself, efficient therapy remains flexible, curious, empirically-oriented, critical of poor theories and results, and devoted to effective change. It is not one-sided or dogmatic. It is ready to give

up the most time-honored and revered methods if new evidence contradicts them. It constantly grows and develops; and it sacredizes no theory and no methodology. (p. 33)

The needs of clients must remain central to the helping process, not the egos of model builders.

A PRACTICAL CURRICULUM FOR HELPER DEVELOPMENT

Clients are our customers and have every right to expect the best of service from us. What kind of training will enable us to "deliver the goods" to our clients? I have some misgivings that the needs of clients are not "center stage" enough in the current debate on the training of psychologists (see Fox & Barclay, 1989). A practical curriculum is one that enables helpers to understand and work with their clients in the service of problem management and opportunity development. What follows is a brief overview of what I think belongs in the curriculum, whether it is offered by a university or through some other program.

The curriculum includes both working knowledge and skills. "Working knowledge" is the translation of theory and research into the kind of applied understandings that enable helpers to work with clients. "Skill" refers to the actual ability to deliver services. The broad content areas of the curriculum include the helping model itself, a working knowledge of applied psychology, an understanding of basic health principles, a people-in-systems framework that includes the life skills needed to participate fully in relationships and in the social settings of life, an understanding of the helping profession, and the helper's self-understanding. Let's look briefly at each of these categories.

A Comprehensive, Client-Oriented Model of Helping

Little needs to be said here, since the purpose of this book is to provide such a model. Chapter 2 presents an overview of the model; the rest of the book is devoted to the stages, the steps of the model, and the methods and communication skills that make it work.

As the title of this book suggests, you will need a range of skills to deliver to clients the help envisioned by the model. They include basic and advanced communication skills, establishing working relationships with clients, helping clients challenge themselves, problem clarification, goal setting, program development, program implementation, and ongoing evaluation. The only way to acquire these skills is by learning them experientially, practicing them, and using them until they become second nature. Therefore, a full program for learning the problem-management model includes the following stages:

1. A conceptual understanding of the steps of the model. Reading this book, reviewing examples, and listening to lectures will give you a conceptual or cognitive understanding of these skills.

2. A behavioral understanding of the helping model. By watching instructors model these skills, by watching videotapes of effective helpers, and by doing the exercises in the manual that accompanies this book, you will develop a behavioral rather than just a conceptual feeling for these skills.

3. Initial mastery. You will begin to master these skills by actually practicing them with your fellow trainees under the supervision of a trainer. In this stage you will at times feel awkward using your newly learned skills.

4. Further mastery. You will strengthen your hold on these skills by using them in practicum or internship experiences under the supervision of skilled and experienced helpers. Lipovsky (1988) has called internship experiences a time of professional adolescence in which trainees develop a sense of identity as helpers. Awkwardness in the use of helping skills lessens as they begin to become part of you.

5. Lifelong learning. The best helpers continue to learn throughout their careers—from their own experiences, from the experiences of their colleagues, from reading, from seminars, and, perhaps most importantly, from their interactions with their clients. In this sense, full mastery is a journey rather than a destination.

Therefore, reading this book, discussing it, learning the model, and doing the exercises in the accompanying manual are not enough. You need the competence that comes from supervised practice.

A Working Knowledge of Applied Psychology

Included here are developmental psychology, cognitive-behavioral psychology, the psychology of personality, and abnormal psychology. When I use the term "applied" psychology in a helping context, I mean psychology that is translated into understandings and tools that serve clients' needs in pragmatic ways.

Developmental Psychology

A solid working knowledge of applied developmental psychology will help you distinguish between the normal developmental problems all of us face over the life span and more serious social-emotional problems and disorders. A developmental framework—one that deals with the normative stages, tasks, and crises of the entire life span (Levinson & associates, 1978; Newman & Newman, 1984)—will help you listen to your clients more effectively and better understand their concerns. For instance, I worked with a man going through what Levinson and his associates call the age-30 transition. Without pigeonholing my client, I did use an understanding of this stage of human development to help him understand what he was going through better and to make a useful career change. Indeed, a number of helpers have based their approaches to helping, at least in part, on life-cycle realities (Blocher, 1966; Dinkmeyer, 1970; Ivey, 1986; Orr & Adams, 1987). Understanding healthy development (Burke, 1989; Heath, 1980a, 1980b) is the essential background for understanding and treating problems and deviations.

Cognitive and Behavioral Psychology

A great deal of attention in the helping professions is currently focused on both cognitive and behavioral psychology and the models of helping based on them. The framework presented in this book is a cognitive-behavioral approach in the humanist tradition. To explain what this means, let me say a word here about cognitive psychology, behavioral psychology, and their integration in the helping process.

Cognitive psychology. At one time in the history of modern psychology, the inner world of "thought" was banned from psychological study because it could not be observed. One had to focus on observable behavior to be credible. But psychologists have rediscovered the mind, the world of thought, the inner life that can dramatically affect both internal and external behavior. Cognitive psychology deals with this inner world and includes such areas of study as memory, perception, problem solving, language, information processing, attitudes, thoughts, ideas, prejudices, misconceptions, appraisal, attributions, beliefs, and expectations, as well as the influence of these inner processes on behavior and emotions. It is now commonly assumed that, since cognition is a powerful element in creating and dispelling emotional and behavioral disturbance, cognitive restructuring is an essential part of the helping process. Indeed, problem management includes learning how to exercise control over these inner processes. Controlling one's thoughts, getting rid of prejudices, paying attention to this but not to that, evoking useful images, engaging in beneficial daydreaming, changing the tenor of internal dialogues—all of these can contribute to both problem management and opportunity development (Dryden & Trower, 1988).

Behavioral psychology. Both self-enhancing and self-defeating patterns of behavior are influenced by the principles of behavior. A simple A-B-C framework can serve as an introduction to these principles. It deals with the antecedents (A) and the consequences (C) of behavior (B). The sequence is shown in Figure 1-1.

The feedback loop from consequences to behavior indicates that behavior in a situation can be influenced or controlled by both antecedents and consequences. Human behavior is stimulated by its antecedents and

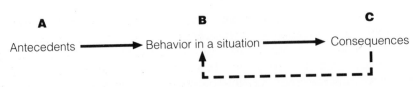

FIGURE 1-1   The ABC's of Behavioral Psychology

modified by its consequences. Cross and Guyer (1980), in a sobering book, point out how ignoring the consequences of behaviors can lead clients (and helpers, too) into "social traps."

> Put simply, a social trap is a situation characterized by multiple but conflicting rewards. Just as an ordinary trap entices its prey with the offer of an attractive bait and then punishes it by capture, so the social situations which we include under the rubric "social traps" draw their victims into certain patterns of behavior with promises of immediate rewards and then confront them with consequences that the victims would rather avoid. On the level of the individual person, examples are easy to think of. In the case of smoking . . . we find the cigarette smoker enjoying at first the repeated gratification of smoking, and only after a long delay, when it is much too late, does he find himself faced with the disagreeable consequences. . . . All [examples] involve individuals who use reinforcements like road signs, traveling in the direction of rewards and avoiding the paths marked by punishments. . . . Occasionally, these road signs lead to unfortunate destinations. (pp. 4, 12–13)

The clients we see are often people who have arrived at these "unfortunate destinations," like the married couple who are continually led on by the reward of avoiding small problems and annoyances only to find, down the road, that their relationship has fallen apart.

I think that acquiring an understanding of the principles of behavior and the ability to use them should be a goal of general education, not just part of a curriculum for helpers. The reason is simple: The principles of behavior are at work even when we ignore them or know nothing about them. We should learn about them and use them before, as Cross and Guyer's work shows, they use us.

Cognitive-behavioral integration. Most helpers do not refer to themselves as belonging to either the cognitive or the behavioral camp but rather adopt a cognitive-behavioral approach to helping (Bandura, 1986; T. W. Smith, 1982; Trower, Casey, & Dryden, 1988). It is silly to see the cognitive and the behavioral people at odds with each other. The principle is simple: People's thinking influences how they act, and how they act influences how they think. For instance, Sue, in her internal dialogues with herself, says in a variety of ways that she won't amount to much (thinking). Therefore, in school she does not do very well because she does not really try (behavior). This leads to a self-fulfilling prophecy. Tom continually gives in to short-term rewards in terms of drugs and sexual involvements (behavior). He comes to think of himself as a "free spirit" not bound like other people by rules (thinking). His "unfortunate destination" includes being out of community with an addiction he cannot manage. Here is one way of looking at cognitive-behavioral integration: Some clients need to think themselves into more effective ways of acting, while others need to act themselves into better ways of thinking. Maybe most need to do both.

Applied Personality Theory

A working knowledge of applied personality theory will give you ways of understanding your clients and their behavior better. For instance, a company counselor is helping Ken, a computer programmer, with problems of job dissatisfaction. A simple personality test indicates that Ken clearly falls on the extrovert side of the introvert-extrovert continuum and that he prefers working on imaginative projects rather than detailed ones. While he has all the skills needed to do the programming, the fact that he works on his own all day on very exacting tasks runs counter to his personality. Ken learns that to remain in that job requires him to swim against the current of his personality. Perhaps he can stay in the computer field, but get a job more in keeping with the kind of person he is.

Over the years researchers have learned a great deal about the structure and functioning of human personality. You will gradually learn how to turn their insights into action-oriented understandings of your clients.

Abnormal Psychology

Abnormal psychology is usually part of the curriculum for helpers. Courses in abnormal psychology can be of use to helpers, even though real life does not always stick to the categories outlined in the manuals. More to the point, the categorizations in the manuals are ultimately valuable only if they enable helpers to intervene more effectively. A working knowledge of these categories can enable helpers both to understand their clients better and to spot problems that are beyond their reach. Clients can then be referred to someone with greater expertise. For example, Carol, a psychologist in a college counseling center, had helped any number of students with reactive depression. Some incident—a soured relationship, failing a course, trouble at home—usually triggered the depression, and most students could be helped through it. When she met David, however, she knew that he was depressed, but her knowledge of abnormal psychology enabled her to spot a different and much more serious kind of depression. She provided David with a great deal of support until he made contact with a psychiatrist at a local hospital who specialized in patients with severe depression.

There are what I call both broad-band and narrow-band frameworks for understanding and working with clients. In my training in clinical psychology, narrow-band assessment frameworks based on abnormal psychology were stressed. There were some unfortunate consequences of this emphasis. Like other novices, I tended to see psychopathological symptoms everywhere, both in myself and in others. When I interviewed clients and wrote reports based on diagnostic tests, too often I focused on the category and missed the client. The very fact that clients were called patients made me look for illness; I was sensitized to illness, open to finding it wherever I could. I am not suggesting that books and courses on psychopathology, diagnostic frameworks, and batteries of tests designed to identify emotional illness cannot be of some service to clients. But I am convinced that most diagnostic procedures are narrow-band frameworks that can actually distort the helper's attempt to listen to and work with clients unless they are tempered by broad-band frameworks. Developmental psychology provides helpers with some excellent broad-band frameworks. Many of the clients counselors encounter are people with "normal" developmental problems rather than abnormal people. But perhaps the most important broad-band filter is common sense.

A Basic Understanding of Health Principles

Without becoming medical doctors, helpers need to develop a working knowledge of clients as psychosomatic beings. Many psychological problems—eating disorders, for instance—involve the body directly, and many more involve at least vague physical symptoms. Effective helpers take a broad-band or holistic view of their clients. On the one hand, we know that over half the complaints patients bring to their doctors are psychological in nature. Indeed, if helpers could "cut off at the pass" even a small percentage of those who visit doctors with vague physical complaints but whose problems are mainly psychological, billions of dollars in medical expenses could be saved.

On the other hand, it would be irresponsible for helpers to assume that even vague physical complaints are psychological in nature. If in doubt, the ethical thing to do is to refer the client to a physician. Therefore, it is useful for helpers to have a working knowledge of physical health and illness so that they can spot possible physical conditions and refer clients to a physician.

Another reason for being knowledgeable about health and illness is that physical conditions can have psychological consequences. For example, helpers working with psychiatrists need to understand the main and side effects of the drugs being prescribed. Some diseases, such as AIDS, have profound physical, psychological, social, and economic impact on clients (see American Psychological Association, 1988, and the *American Psychologist*, November 1988, an issue devoted to AIDS).

It is especially helpful for counselors to understand the basic principles of the wellness movement. Helpers can include such things as good nutrition and exercise in strategies for improving both physical and psychological health. Moreover, counselors can do a great deal in helping clients become responsible for their physical health.

An Understanding of Clients in Context: A People-in-Systems Framework

Professionals, especially those who deal with more serious disorders, can become increasingly remote from the everyday life of normal people (Jones, 1986). Egan and Cowan (1979; Egan, 1984) have developed a broad-band "people-in-systems" model to help counselors understand their clients and their problems in the context of the social settings in which they live. Over 20 years ago, Goldstein, Heller, & Sechrest (1966) demonstrated how much social psychology can offer helpers. Unfortunately, not enough helpers have listened to their advice.

The Egan-Cowan model deals with the different levels of social systems or settings in which people grow, develop, and live out their lives. As Hiltonsmith & Miller (1983) put it:

> Psychologists have long acknowledged that complete understanding of a given individual's behavior depends on knowledge of the attributes of both the individual and the setting in which that individual's behavior is occurring. This sounds simple enough in theory, yet in practice most professional psychologists appear to have gathered little information on the setting aspect of assessment. (p. 419)

Their sentiments have been echoed by Kanfer and Goldstein (1986; see also Conyne, 1987; Conyne & Clack, 1981; Fine, 1985; Herr, 1989; Stadler & Rynearson, 1981):

> Both research publications and other articles emphasize the need to treat each client, not for a specific symptom or behavioral problem, but with careful attention to his or her life setting, personal values, and biological and sociopsychological characteristics. . . . Social conditions are constantly altering the nature of psychological problems. (p. ix)

We live in a society in which change has become a constant. Social changes affect the way we develop across the entire life span.

> [S]ocial experiences, in interaction with individual development, have consequences for individuals' worldviews when they are experienced in childhood, for their identities when they are experienced in late adolescence and the transition to adulthood, and for their behavior when they are experienced in mature adulthood. (Stewart & Healy, 1989)

Understanding the contexts in which our clients live can add to the value of the services we are providing. "Blaming the victims" of social, economic, and cultural injustice (Caplan & Nelson, 1973; Ryan, 1971) was and is the fruit of a narrow view of the human condition.

The people-in-systems model also deals with the kinds of life skills people need to pursue developmental tasks and involve themselves in, contribute to, and cope with the various social systems of life (Adkins, 1984; Gambrill, 1984; Gazda, 1984; Goldstein, Gershaw, & Sprafkin, 1984). An important part of counseling process is helping clients identify their life-skills strengths and deficits. Clients often fail to manage problem situations and develop opportunities because they do not have the kinds of life skills they need to do so. Training in required skills, then, can become part of the helping process. As an example, one of my clients came to counseling because his angry outbursts were getting him in trouble. When he got angry, he would antagonize people; once or twice he actually progressed to physical assault. People became afraid of him, and he grew quite isolated. Since his interpersonal communication skills were poor, I included skills training as part of the overall helping program. He greatly benefited from this, especially from training in listening and empathy. As he began to see the world from others' points of view, he became more tolerant, and his overall "anger level" decreased. On occasion, however, he still relapsed. Further training in cognitive-relaxation coping skills helped him deal more effectively with specific anger-provoking situations.

An Understanding of the Helping Professions

The helping professions, like many others, are constantly changing and therefore challenging. In the field of counseling, work settings are expanding, counselors are assuming new roles, traditional definitions of counseling are being challenged, counselor education and training are being reformulated, and there is more and more talk about the rapprochement between, or the integration of, clinical and counseling psychology. Counselors are pushing into new areas: hospitals, community mental health centers, business, consulting firms, and correctional facilities. All of this can be both exciting and bewildering. As you learn more about the helping professions, you will need to develop a set of career-oriented values to guide you as you take charge of your own career.

Self-Knowledge

Effective helpers undertake the lifelong task—perhaps struggle is a better word—of fulfilling the ancient Greek injunction "Know thyself." Since helping is a two-way street, understanding clients is not enough. It is essential to understand your own assumptions, beliefs, values, standards, skills, strengths, weaknesses, idiosyncrasies, style of doing things, foibles, and temptations, and the ways in which these permeate your interactions with your clients. The adage "He who knows not and knows not he knows not is a fool—shun him" is relevant here: Helpers who do not understand themselves can inflict a great deal of harm on their clients.

Skilled helpers have their own human problems, but they do not retreat from the problematic in their own lives. They explore their own behavior and know who they are. They know what it means to be helped, and they have a deep respect for the helping process and its power for better or for worse. Their self-knowledge can also help them avoid or cope with burnout, a common problem in the helping professions. Forewarned is forearmed. It is easy for novices to say, "It won't happen to me; I'm too dedicated." While that kind of idealism is refreshing, it needs to be tempered by the realities of day-in-and-day-out service.

Self-knowledge, however, is not the same thing as self-preoccupation. Solid training programs in helping models, methods, and skills should provide ample opportunity for you to reflect on yourself in a healthy, upbeat way. The workbook that accompanies this text is designed to help you engage in this self-reflection and to get feedback from both instructors and peers.

Meier (1989; see pp. 55–62) suggests that helpers learn early on how to ask themselves questions such as the following—and, of course, to answer them honestly:

• How did you decide to be a helper?
• Why do you want to be a helper?
• With what emotions are you comfortable?
• What emotions—in yourself or others—give you trouble?
• What are your expectations of clients?
• How will you deal with your clients' feelings toward you?
• How will you handle your feelings toward your clients?
• To what degree can you be flexible? accepting? gentle?

I have always seen training as an opportunity for helpers-to-be to grapple with personal issues that will affect their ability to deliver services to clients. Effective training programs with high standards of quality are a better way of "licensing" helpers to practice than the written exams that allow helpers to practice in most states. But self-knowledge doesn't end with training: The best helpers learn constantly, both from successes and from failures.

These, then, are some of the things I highlight in training helpers (see the summary diagram in Figure 1-2). Others, working from a different philosophy of helping, might come up with a different package. Ultimately, you, the helper, will choose your own philosophy. My advice: Whatever you do, get good at it. This advice is based on the research finding that

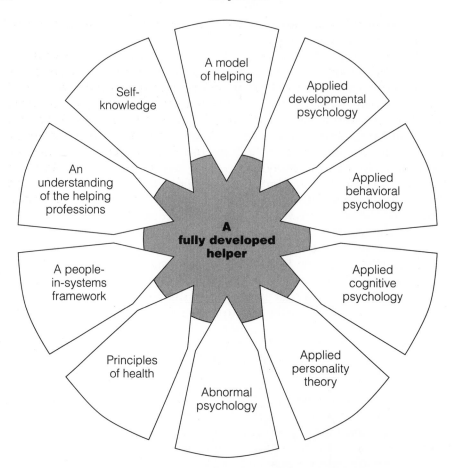

FIGURE 1-2 A Curriculum for Developing Helpers

successful helpers look more like one another than their less successful colleagues of the same ideological persuasion. Perhaps, in the long run, common sense wins out.

WHAT THIS BOOK IS—AND WHAT IT IS NOT

"Beware the person of one book," we are told. For some people the central message of a book becomes a cause; religious books such as the Bible or the Koran are examples. Although causes empower people, we should beware when a person believes that all he or she needs to know is in one book. Such a person remains closed to new ideas and growth. Certainly all truth about helping cannot be found in one book. Therefore, *The Skilled*

Helper is not and cannot be "all that you've ever wanted to know about helping."

Since this book cannot do everything, it is important to state what it *is* meant to do. Its purpose is to provide helpers—whether novices or those with experience—a practical framework or model of helping and some of the methods and skills that make the model work. It is designed to enable helpers to *do* something that will help their clients manage their lives more effectively. The kinds of working knowledge and skills described in our discussion of a curriculum for helpers will be referred to throughout this book and embodied in many of the examples, but the book does not pretend to deal with these areas directly. In short, this book is part of the curriculum—in my eyes, an extremely important part—but it is not the whole. Other books and other experiences must provide the rest.

Chapter Two

Overview of the Helping Model

A helping model is like a map that helps you know what to do in your interactions with clients. At any given moment, it also helps you to orient yourself, to understand "where you are" with the client and what kind of intervention would be most useful.

THE STARTING POINT: CLIENTS WITH PROBLEM SITUATIONS AND UNUSED OPPORTUNITIES

Clients constitute the starting point of the helping process. However, since they come for help because of problems and unused opportunities or potential, these, too, constitute the starting point. Focus on the person first and then the problem or opportunity.

Problem Situations

Clients come for help because they have crises, troubles, doubts, difficulties, frustrations, or concerns. These are often called, generically, "problems," but they are not problems in a mathematical sense, because often emotions run high and often there are no clear-cut solutions. It is probably better to say that clients come, not with problems, but with *problem situations* (D'Zurilla & Goldfried, 1971), that is, with complex and messy problems in living they are not handling well. They come for help on their own or because third parties, concerned about or bothered by their behavior, send them. While even those who come on their own may be resistant to help, involuntary clients—who "may well account for the majority of caseloads throughout the land" (Dyer & Vriend, 1975, p. 102)—are especially difficult to deal with, since they are both reluctant and resistant. Wife batterers might not see their violence as problematic, but their wives and society do. Dealing with reluctant and resistant clients is one of the principal challenges helpers face.

Missed Opportunities and Unused Potential

Clients' missed opportunities and unused potential constitute a second starting point for helping. In this case, it is a question not of what is going wrong, but of what could be done better. It has often been suggested that most of us use only a fraction of our potential. We are capable of dealing much more creatively with ourselves, with our relationships with others, with our work life, and, generally, with the ways in which we involve ourselves with the social settings of our lives. Counselors can help their clients empower themselves by helping them identify and develop unused or underused opportunities and potential.

In most cases, counselors interact with clients who are both grappling with difficulties and failing to take advantage of opportunities. Even when

The skilled helper model

I. Present scenario   II. Preferred scenario   III. Strategy: Getting there

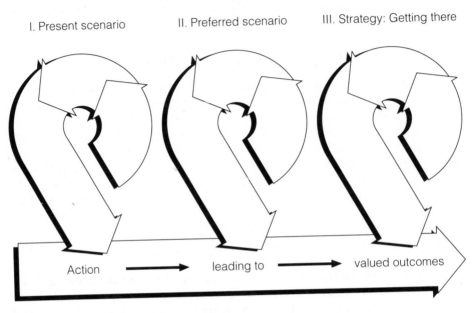

Action ———————▶ leading to ———————▶ valued outcomes

FIGURE 2-1   Overview of the Helping Model

clients talk about problems, effective helpers listen for missed opportunities and unused potential. A woman filled with self-doubt because of her sheltered upbringing and the obstacles presented by a male-dominated culture is probably also a woman who has missed opportunities and failed to develop many of her own resources. She may well be a victim of society, but she may also be a victim of her own unexploited potential.

THE STAGES OF THE HELPING PROCESS

The helping framework used in this book has three major stages. Each stage has its own set of client-focused outcomes. Figure 2-1 shows an overview of the entire model; the specific steps will be filled in as we go along.

Stage I: The Present Scenario

Help clients identify, explore, and clarify their problem situations and unused opportunities. Clients can neither manage problem situations nor develop opportunities unless they identify and understand them. Initial exploration and clarification of problems and opportunities takes place in Stage I. As indicated in Figure 2-1, Stage I deals with the present scenario—a state of affairs that the client or those who send the client for help find unacceptable. Problem situations are not being managed and opportunities are not being developed.

Stage II: The Preferred Scenario

Help clients develop goals, objectives, or agendas based on an action-oriented understanding of the problem situation. Once clients understand either their problem situations or opportunities for development more clearly, they may need help in determining what they would like to do differently. Involuntary clients need to understand and buy into the changes others are demanding. As indicated in Figure 2-1, Stage II deals with the preferred scenario, that is, with *what* needs to be done or put in place. What would things look like if they were better than they are now?

Stage III: Getting There

Help clients develop action strategies for accomplishing goals, that is, for getting from the current to the preferred scenario. Clients may know what they want to accomplish and where they want to go, but still need help in determining *how* to get there. Stage III is a transition stage, dealing with ways of moving from the current to the preferred scenario.

Outcome-Producing Action: All Stages

Last, but in no way least, help clients act on what they learn throughout the helping process. In many helping or problem-management models, action or implementation is tacked on at the end. In this model, as indicated in Figure 2-1, all three stages sit on the "action arrow," indicating that clients need to act in their own behalf right from the beginning of the counseling process. As we shall see, clients need to act both within the helping sessions themselves and in their real day-to-day worlds. Involuntary clients especially need to see that it is in their own interest to act. They often need to be helped or even urged to act.

This model can be called developmental in that it is systematic and cumulative. The success of Stage II often depends on the quality of work in Stage I. Success in Stage III often depends on the quality of work in both Stages I and II. Just why this is so will become clear as we move through the model.

Each stage of the model, as we are about to see, has three "steps." I put the word steps in quotation marks for at least two reasons. First, in practice the problem-management and opportunity-development process is not as clean, clear, and linear as the stages and steps described here. Second, some steps—for instance, the "step" of helping clients manage blind spots and develop new perspectives—refer to processes that apply to the entire model. Remember that the model is a framework or map to help you find your way as a helper. It is also an outline of this book.

STAGE I: IDENTIFYING AND CLARIFYING PROBLEM SITUATIONS AND UNUSED OPPORTUNITIES

Most people live without professional help. They handle their problems in living, whether successfully or unsuccessfully, by themselves or with the informal help of family, associates, and friends. On the other hand, people who find that they are not coping with their problems in living, and who either do not want to share them with family or friends or feel that family and friends are not competent enough to help them, might turn to a professional or paraprofessional helper—if not a psychologist, psychotherapist, or psychiatrist, then perhaps a minister, teacher, coach, supervisor, doctor, nurse, counselor, or social worker. Often they will turn to such a person (1) if the problem is serious or disturbing enough, (2) if they are serious about managing problems or developing opportunities, and (3) if they believe that the person can actually help them.

Step I-A: The Story

Help clients tell their stories. Helpers cannot be of service if clients fail to develop an understanding of the difficulties and possibilities of their lives. Therefore, as indicated in Figure 2-2, clients need to tell their stories, that is, reveal and discuss their problem situations and their missed opportunities. Some clients are quite verbal, while others may be almost mute. Some clients easily reveal everything that is bothering them, while others are quite reluctant to do so. You need only examine your own experience to discover how reluctant you are at times to share your problems with others. Involuntary clients often prefer to talk about the failings of those who sent them. Therefore, helpers need skills that enable them to help clients tell the "real" story and to provide support for them as they do so. As we shall see, these communication skills are central to the entire helping process. The outcome of this step, then, is a frank discussion of the "facts of the case." The story needs to be told, whether it comes out all at once at the beginning of the helping process or only in bits and pieces over its entire course. If this and other outcomes are to take place, helpers need to establish effective relationships with their clients.

In this overview, the highlights from an actual case will be used to illustrate each step of the model. The case has been simplified. It is presented here in bare outline and in a step-by-step way to illustrate the stages of the helping model. The client is voluntary, verbal, and, for the

I. Present scenario   II. Preferred scenario   III. Strategy: Getting there

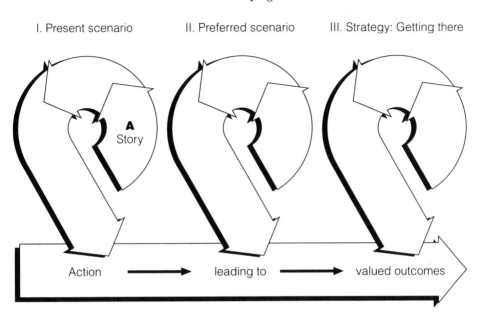

A
Story

Action ⟶ leading to ⟶ valued outcomes

FIGURE 2-2   The Helping Model: Step I-A

most part, cooperative. It goes without saying that in actual practice cases do not flow as easily as this one.

> Ray, 41, is a middle manager in a manufacturing company located in a large city. He goes to see a friend of his, an older woman whom he trusts and who happens to be a counselor, because he is experiencing a great deal of stress. She is supportive and helps Ray tell his story, which proves to be somewhat complex. He is bored with his job, his marriage is lifeless, he has poor rapport with his two teenage children, he is drinking heavily, his self-esteem is low, and he has begun to steal small things, not because he needs them but because he gets a kick out of taking them. He tells his story in a rather disjointed way, skipping around from one problem area to another. His agitation in telling the story reflects the anxiety he is experiencing. The counselor's nonjudgmental attitude and facilitative communication style help Ray overcome the unease he is experiencing in talking about himself and his problems. Since Ray is a talented person, the counselor assumes that missed opportunities for growth also form part of the overall picture, even though he does not talk about this point directly.

Since Ray is quite verbal, a great deal of the story comes tumbling out in a spontaneous way, and its telling is merely supported by the helper. However, involuntary clients, clients with poor verbal skills, or clients who are hostile, confused, ashamed, or highly anxious provide a much greater challenge for helpers in this first step.

I. Present scenario   II. Preferred scenario   III. Strategy: Getting there

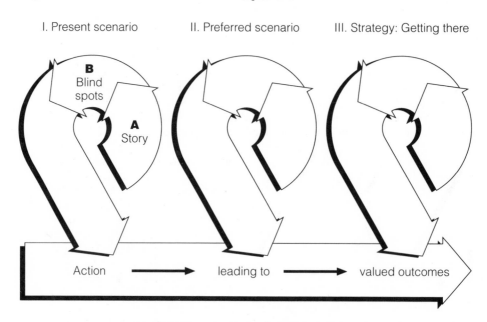

FIGURE 2-3   The Helping Model: Step I-B

As helpers listen, they need to assess rather than judge their clients. They assess such things as the nature and severity of the problem situation, hints at further problems that are not being discussed, the impact of clients' environment on their problems, the personal, interpersonal, and environmental resources to which clients have access, and the ways in which problems might be, paradoxically, opportunities (as in the Zen saying, "The obstacle is the path"). This kind of assessment, as we shall see later, is not limited to Stage I.

Step I-B: Identifying and Challenging Blind Spots

Help clients become aware of and overcome their blind spots and develop new perspectives on themselves and their problem situations. One of the most important things counselors can do is help clients identify blind spots and develop new, more useful perspectives on both problem situations and unused opportunities. As shown in Figure 2-3, this is the second step of Stage I.

Most clients need to move beyond their initial subjective understanding of their problem situations. Many people fail to cope with problems in living or to exploit opportunities because they do not see them from new perspectives. Comfortable but outmoded frames of reference keep them locked into self-defeating patterns of thinking and behaving. Helping clients unfetter their imaginations in the service of problem management and opportunity development is one of the major ways in which counselors can empower clients. Challenging blind spots is not the same as telling people what they are doing wrong; rather, it is helping people see themselves, others, and the world around them in more creative ways.

> At one point, the counselor asks Ray to describe his drinking behavior a bit more fully. Ray, pointing out that his drinking is "problematic" rather than a problem in itself, does so only reluctantly. With a bit of probing, the counselor soon discovers that he drinks not only excessively but also secretly. When he complains that she is accusing him of being an alcoholic, she replies that she isn't interested in labels but in lifestyle. She explores with him the impact his drinking has on him and on his relationships with others, his work, and his leisure. It is soon evident to her that his drinking is far more than problematic. He is an alcoholic who is reluctant to admit his alcoholism. In the course of their dialogue he does admit that his drinking is "a bit" more problematic than he had thought. Furthermore, as Ray tells his story, he describes himself at one time as "underemployed" and at another as "over the hill." The counselor helps him confront the discrepancy between these two descriptions of himself. Ray has always disliked people he sees as overly ambitious, but now he begins to see himself at the other end of the continuum, as underambitious in self-defeating ways. As she listens to Ray's story, the counselor also listens carefully for indications of his degree of commitment to working with these issues.

The counselor is very supportive as Ray explores his concerns. She realizes that support without challenge is often superficial and that challenge without support can be demeaning and self-defeating. It is important to understand the client's frame of reference or point of view even when it is evident that it needs to be challenged or at least broadened. Note that challenge in the service of new perspectives, though presented here as a "step," is best woven into the fabric of the entire helping process. The need for new perspectives does not stop with Stage I.

Step I-C: The Search for Leverage

Help clients identify and work on problems, issues, concerns, or opportunities that will make a difference. In Figure 2-4 the term *leverage* is used as the generic name of this third step. It includes three related activities. First of all, since helping is an expensive proposition, both financially and psychologically, some kind of *screening* is called for: Is the problem situation, at least as stated, worth the time and effort that is about to be spent in managing it? Second, if clients, in telling their stories, reveal a number of problems at the same time or if the problem situation discussed is complex, then criteria are needed to determine which concern is to be dealt with first. In other words, counselors help clients establish priorities and search for some kind of *leverage* in dealing with complex problem situations. For instance, they help them work on a problem which, if managed successfully, will contribute to the management of a number of other problems. Counselors are most useful when they help clients deal

I. Present scenario   II. Preferred scenario   III. Strategy: Getting there

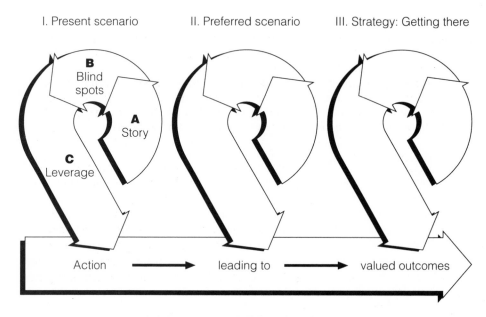

FIGURE 2-4   The Helping Model: Step I-C

with issues that can make a difference in their lives. If one of the themes that underlies or runs through a number of a client's problems is a lack of discipline, then self-discipline might well be an issue with leverage. Finally, once an issue is chosen for further exploration, counselors need to help clients *clarify* the problem, issue, or concern in terms of specific experiences, behaviors, and feelings. The process of clarification can help clients determine what needs to be changed.

> As to screening, it is obvious from the beginning that all of Ray's problems and unused opportunities merit serious consideration. The counselor, wanting Ray to take the lead, asks him which of the concerns he has mentioned bothers him the most and which he would like to work on. After some discussion, Ray decides that he would like to tackle the job problem, but he also makes some vague comments about the need to manage his drinking better. Through a combination of careful listening, empathic responding, and judicious probing, the counselor helps Ray spell out concretely his concerns about his job and, to a lesser degree, about his drinking, since he is somewhat reluctant to talk about the latter. The counselor makes sure that she understands Ray's point of view, even though she feels at times that it needs to be challenged, supplemented, or transcended. Some of the principal work-related issues are clarified: Ray sees himself in a dead-end job, that is, one in which there is no chance for promotion. He feels, on reflection, that he has always been underemployed, that his talents have never been significantly challenged. His dislike for his job is contaminating his interpersonal relationships at work and adding to his stress. He admits that his negative feelings about his job

probably carry over into his home life. He has been in the same job for 14 years and has never thought about changing. He believes that he may be "over the hill" when it comes to getting a different job. As to alcohol, he thinks he drinks "a bit too much" as a way of handling his stress and frustration, though he does not see his drinking as a central problem. As Ray discusses specific problems in greater detail, it is clear to the counselor that he is sometimes uncomfortable with what he is hearing himself saying. That is, he is beginning to understand that he needs to challenge some of the assumptions he has about himself.

Helping clients identify key issues—issues that, if managed, will make a difference in their lives—and commit themselves to clarifying them is a form of challenge in itself.

These three steps constitute the cognitive part of Stage I. If they are done well, then the problem situation, together with overlooked or unexploited opportunities, can be identified and explored to the point where it makes sense to look beyond the present unacceptable scenario to a preferred scenario. But the cognitive part of helping—discussing and planning—needs to be linked to client action right from the start.

Client Action: The Heart of the Helping Process

Help clients act both within and outside the counseling sessions. Helping is ultimately about problem-managing and opportunity-developing change. As the poet says, "There's the rub." There is nothing magic about change; it is work. If clients do not act in their own behalf, nothing happens. Two kinds of client action are important here: actions within the helping process itself and actions "out there" in the client's day-to-day world.

Ideally, clients by their actions come to "own" the helping process instead of being the objects of it.

The fact that Ray has come on his own is a good sign; he is acting in his own behalf. He is in pain and wants to do something about it. His willingness to explore problem situations and respond fairly nondefensively to challenges on the part of the counselor are indications that he is owning the interactions.

But taking an active role within sessions is only the first step. One reason that Ray is in trouble is that he has consistently failed to act in his day-to-day world. He has let life pass him by in a variety of ways—in his work life, for instance—and now is angry with himself and his world. The stages and steps of the helping process are, at best, *triggers and channels* for client action. Client actions between sessions—not random actions, obviously, but actions leading to client-enhancing *outcomes*—are the best indicators of how effective the sessions are. It makes no sense to say "We really had a good session today!" if the session bears no fruit in real life.

Planning makes action intelligent, but without real-life action, discussing, gathering insights, and planning tend to be aimless.

> After his first session with the counselor, Ray sits down one evening, writes "drinking" at the top of a piece of paper, and jots down, randomly, whatever thoughts come to his mind. The paper begins to fill up with such things as money spent on liquor, times he drinks, attempts to keep others from knowing, occasions when drinking has kept him from work or led to family fights, and so forth. He finds all of this painful and eventually rips the page up and throws it into a wastebasket, saying to himself that drinking is probably no more a problem for him than for anyone else "in his situation" and that it is silly to pick on himself like this.

This is not a dramatic act with a dramatic outcome, but at least Ray does *something*. He takes one somewhat ambiguous and abortive step in the direction of doing something about his drinking. In the beginning some client actions may be merely symbolic (Ray's list comes close to that). They may be internal (like Ray's mulling over issues that have been pushed to the side before) or external (on occasion his *not* having the usual two-drink nightcap), but they are of the essence of change. Any step of the helping process can both trigger and provide direction for goal-directed client action. Ray's abortive work on his "drinking" list was triggered by his telling his story and some gentle challenging on the part of the counselor. Helping him identify blind spots or focus on issues that capture his attention can, or rather *should*, trigger action.

Helping can seem to be all about talking when, in reality, it is all about *acting*—from subtle internal actions, such as gradual changes in attitudes about oneself and others, to "dramatic" external actions, such as stopping drinking "cold turkey." Counseling is successful only to the degree that it leads to problem-managing action, whether internal or external. Assessment for the sake of assessment, exploration for the sake of exploration, and insight for the sake of insight are all forms of whistling in the wind.

STAGE II: DEVELOPING A PREFERRED SCENARIO

People often take what I might call a "one-stage" approach to managing their problems. That is, when something goes wrong, they act, or rather, they react. For instance, Troy, a college student, found himself lonely, frustrated, and depressed during his first week away from home. When another student, noting his misery, not only expressed some concern but also intimated a sexual attraction, Troy was confronted with his own sexual ambiguity. He "solved" this complex problem situation by running away and getting a job in a hotel in another city. Obviously his action, however understandable because of his panic, solved nothing.

Others take a two-stage approach to managing their problems. The first stage is an analysis of the problem; the second is the discovery of solutions, that is, actions that need to be taken to manage the problem or develop the opportunity. The term "solution," however, is ambiguous. It usually refers to the strategies or courses of action designed to achieve a certain outcome. However "solution" in its most complete sense means what will be *in place* once these actions are taken; that is, it refers not just to actions, but to the outcomes of these actions.

This observation leads to the three-stage model of problem solving. Both research and everyday experience show that very few of us, when confronted by a problem or an unexploited opportunity, ask ourselves such questions as "What would this problem situation look like if managed? What would be in place that is not now in place? What would this opportunity look like if it were developed? What would exist that does not exist at this moment?" Yet these prove to be powerful questions, because they help clients use their imaginations and provide direction by helping them focus on a better future rather than a frustrating present.

Stage II of our model is based on these questions. It has three steps.

Step II-A: Preferred-Scenario Possibilities

Help clients develop a range of possibilities for a better future. If a client's current state of affairs is problematic and unacceptable, then he or she needs to be helped to conceptualize or envision a new state of affairs— that is, alternate, more acceptable possibilities. As indicated in Figure 2-5, this is the first step in Stage II. In Step II-A, helpers, against the background of the problem identification and clarification of Stage I, help clients develop answers to the question: "What would it look like if it looked better?" A new scenario is not a wild-eyed, idealistic state of affairs, but rather a conceptualization or a picture of the problem situation as it would be if improvements were made. For instance, for a couple whose marriage is coming apart and who fight constantly, one of the elements of the new scenario might be fewer and fairer fights. "Given the range of problems you've mentioned, what would your marriage look like if it were a little better?" is the kind of question that can be asked at this point. The possibilities discovered constitute the raw materials of what will ultimately be a preferred scenario. In marriage counseling, the preferred scenario could be divorce if differences are irreconcilable and if the couple's values system permits such a solution. Or it could be, generically, a better marriage. Some of the possible elements of this better marriage might be greater mutual respect, fewer fights, more openness, more effectively managed conflicts, a more equitable distribution of household tasks, the elimination of extramarital encounters, doing more things together, surrendering past animosities, greater mutuality in sexual relationships, more effectively managed emotions (especially jealousy and hurt), decreased game

I. Present scenario   II. Preferred scenario   III. Strategy: Getting there

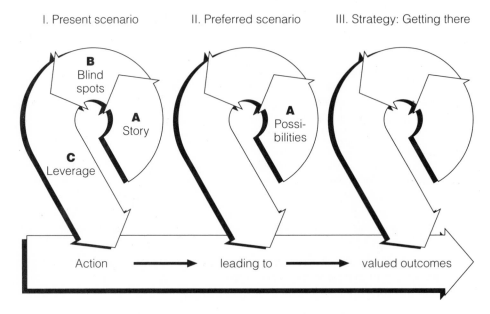

FIGURE 2-5   The Helping Model: Step II-A

playing, and so forth. In a better marriage these are the kinds of things that would be in place instead of what is actually in place now. Let's see how this step might apply to Ray.

> Ray believes that one preferred-scenario possibility is getting a new job. The counselor helps him review the kinds of jobs he might like. Ray identifies five or six possibilities and even some of the companies in which they might be found. He wants a job in a different company, one smaller than the one where he is currently employed. He wants a challenging job, but in a company where there is a sense of camaraderie. If he does move to a different kind of job, he still wants one in which he can use his technical expertise and experience, even though he realizes that some of his skills need updating.
>
> Second, although Ray does not admit that he is an alcoholic, he does think that he should stop drinking. Otherwise, he says, drinking will interfere with the work that needs to be done to get a new job. The counselor thinks it is a good sign that Ray says drinking "will" interfere, instead of saying merely that it "could" or "might" interfere.
>
> Therefore, Ray's preferred scenario might well include a new, more satisfying job and some form of alcohol-free living.

Galbraith (1979) suggests that one of the reasons (but hardly the only or even the principal one) why poor people remain mired in their poverty is that they get caught up in what he calls the culture of poverty. That is, they accept themselves as poor and do not even imagine themselves as not poor. In my estimation, this failure to imagine scenarios different from the pres-

I. Present scenario   II. Preferred scenario   III. Strategy: Getting there

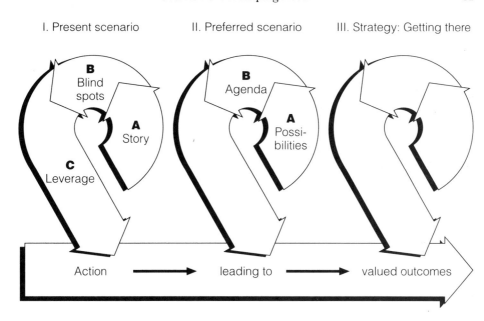

FIGURE 2-6   The Helping Model: Step II-B

ent one contributes a great deal to clients' remaining mired in their problem situations. In helping clients challenge their blind spots in order to develop new perspectives (Step I-B) and develop a range of preferred-scenario possibilities (Step II-A), helpers enable clients to empower themselves by tapping unused imaginal resources.

Step II-B: Creating Viable Agendas

Help clients translate preferred-scenario possibilities into viable agendas. The variety of preferred-scenario possibilities developed in Step II-A constitute possible goals or desired outcomes of the helping process. Once they have been generated, it is time to help clients choose the possibilities that make the most sense and turn them into an agenda. Figure 2-6 adds this step to the helping model.

The agenda put together by the client needs to be viable, that is, capable of being translated by the client into action. It is viable to the degree that it is stated in terms of clear and specific outcomes and is a substantive response to the presenting problem or opportunity, realistic, in keeping with the client's values, and capable of being accomplished within a reasonable time frame. For instance, if a couple want "better communication" as part of the renewal of their marriage, they need to spell out specifically what better communication means in their marriage. What undesirable patterns of communication are now in place? What kinds and patterns of communication are preferred? Suppose the couple say, "When we experience small annoyances in our relationships, we tend not to share them with each other. We swallow them. Well, we think we swallow them, but in reality we save them up and let them eat away at us inside. It seems that we could discuss our annoyances as they arise, and do so without being petty or without playing put-down games. If we were to manage little problems better, we could avoid the bigger ones." Such a statement is at least a first step toward spelling out more concretely what "better communication" means. Often helpers need to challenge clients to make vague goals or agendas more specific. If a client says, "I guess I should be a better father in a lot of ways," the counselor needs to ask, "What are some of these ways?"

Helping clients set outcome priorities includes reviewing with them the consequences of their choices. For instance, if a client sets her sights on a routine job with minimally adequate pay, this outcome might well take care of some of her immediate needs but prove to be a poor choice in the long run. Helping clients foresee the consequences of their choices may not be easy. I remember one woman with cancer who felt she was no longer able to cope with the sickness that came with her chemotherapy treatments. She decided abruptly one day to end the treatment, saying that she didn't care what happened. Eventually, when her health deteriorated, she had second thoughts about the treatments, saying, "There are still a number of things I must do before I die." But it was too late. Some challenge on the part of a helper might have helped her make a better decision.

What are some of the things Ray does to develop a preferred scenario for himself?

> The counselor helps Ray expand his list of job possibilities and then review each in terms of its pros and cons, conformity to his criteria, and realism. She encourages him to imagine himself as clearly as possible in each job. Ray is a bit impatient in discussing the pros and cons of each job, but she challenges him to do so, helping him see the consequences of making a poor choice at this juncture in his life. By scrutinizing each possibility, Ray soon realizes that at least four of the jobs he has been thinking about do not meet his criteria. For instance, one would entail his becoming a manager. He has no managerial experience and is resistant to the idea of developing managerial skills. Like many people, he has been assuming that the skills will come with his appointment to a managerial position.
>
> Ray is less enthusiastic about exploring his tentative decision to stop drinking. He refers to it somewhat guardedly as an "experiment." He is still having trouble seeing himself as a problem drinker and resists discussing what an alcohol-free life might look like concretely. The counselor decides not to push him further at this point but notes that there is serious work still to be done in this area.

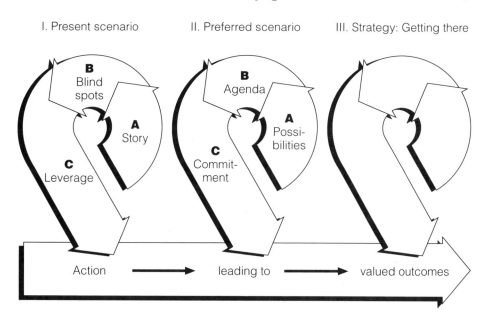

I. Present scenario   II. Preferred scenario   III. Strategy: Getting there

B Blind spots   **A** Story   **C** Leverage

B Agenda   **A** Possi-bilities   **C** Commit-ment

Action → leading to → valued outcomes

FIGURE 2-7   **The Helping Model: Step II-C**

Note that challenge is not relegated to Step I-B. Choosing from among preferred-scenario possibilities can be difficult for clients, because it often involves painful self-scrutiny and choices. Sometimes the choices themselves may be severely limited. Choices between almost certain death and agonizing chemotherapy sessions are not easy to make. Truants may have to choose between going back to a school they hate or being locked up in a detention center. Even before they are sent for counseling, they probably suspect that their options are limited, and this contributes to their reluctance to go to counseling and their resistance when there.

Step II-C: Choice and Commitment

Help clients identify the kinds of incentives that will enable them to commit themselves to the agendas they fashion. Ideally the agendas a client chooses are, on their face, appealing. If not, then incentives for commitment need to be discovered. Figure 2-7 adds this choice-and-commitment step to the helping model.

Effective helpers leave the responsibility for choice with clients. However, while they realize that they are not responsible for their clients' sense of commitment, they can help clients commit themselves by helping them search for incentives for commitment. This is especially true when the choices are hard. How are truants with poor home situations to commit themselves to returning to school? What are the incentives for such a choice? Ray, too, must struggle with commitment.

> Ray commits himself to getting a new, more challenging job. Having reviewed the possibilities, he now commits himself to his top priority, getting a professional/technical job in a high-tech company. If this kind of job is not available, he will move to the second choice on his list. His incentives include a strong desire to get rid of the pain he is currently experiencing and a more positive desire to develop some of the talents that have remained dormant over the past years. A third incentive is his conviction that getting a more fulfilling job will lead to his managing some of the other problems of his life a little better. A final incentive is his need to regain his self-esteem.
>
> Ray also decides to stop drinking—cold turkey. His desire to make a go of it in a new job and his desire for self-esteem are both incentives. He also realizes that stopping drinking will give him a new image at home and give him the kind of credibility he will need to start managing his home life better. His decision to stop drinking, however, appears a bit too facile to the counselor. Ray's "no problem" and "no need for discussion" attitude seems to be part of the problem rather than part of the solution.

If Stage II is done well, clients will have a clear idea of *what* they would like to accomplish without necessarily knowing *how* they will accomplish it. Once Ray says, "I want a professional/technical job in a high-tech firm," he must figure out just how he is going to get such a job. The goal is clear; the means to achieve the goal need to be developed. This brings us to Stage III of the helping process.

Client Action in Stage II

Each of the three steps of Stage II can be stimuli to action. Ray continues his discussion of career possibilities outside the counseling sessions with a couple of friends. He begins reading trade journals again. He makes an informal visit to one company and chats about job possibilities with a friend of a friend. He buys a workbook on résumé writing.

As to alcohol, even before his decision to go cold turkey, he declares some days "no drinking" days and feels good about himself when he is successful. In summary, thinking about and discussing future possibilities stimulate a range of informal actions that help him point himself in the right direction.

STAGE III: FORMULATING STRATEGIES AND PLANS

Discussing and evaluating preferred-scenario possibilities and making choices determine the *what*. Stage III deals with *how* goals are to be accomplished. Some clients know what they want to see in place but can use

I. Present scenario   II. Preferred scenario   III. Strategy: Getting there

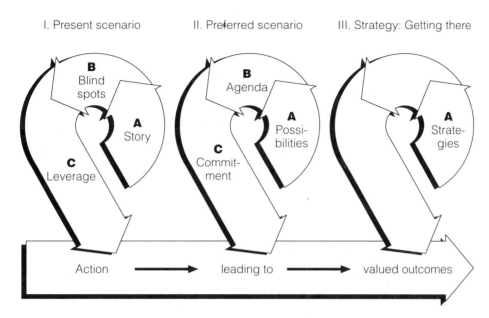

FIGURE 2-8   The Helping Model: Step III-A

help in determining how to make it happen. Rusty imaginations need stimulating. Other clients make the mistake of acting without knowing what they want. In this case action lacks direction and is both impractical and imprudent.

Step III-A: Brainstorming Strategies for Action

Help clients brainstorm a range of strategies for implementing their agendas. In this step, added in Figure 2-8, clients are helped to ask them-selves (with apologies to the poet), "How can I get where I want to go? Let me count the ways!" The principle is simple: Strategies tend to be more effective when chosen from among a number of possibilities. Some cli-ents, when they decide what they want, engage in the first action or imple-ment the first strategy that comes to mind. While the bias toward action may be laudable, the strategy may be ineffective, inefficient, imprudent, or a combination of all three.

A preferred scenario is a goal, an end, an accomplishment, an outcome (or a group of outcomes); a strategy is a set of actions designed to achieve the goal. If a preferred scenario is complex, then it needs to be divided into a number of interrelated outcomes or accomplishments. Each of these subgoals will then have its own set of strategies. This divide-and-conquer process can lead to accomplishments that at first blush seem impossible—whether it's placing a person on the moon or even salvaging a marriage.

One reason people fail to achieve goals is that they do not explore the different ways in which the goal can be accomplished. They choose one means or strategy without a great deal of exploration or reflection, try it, and when it fails, conclude that they just can't achieve that particular goal. Coming up with as many ways of achieving a goal as possible raises the probability that one of these ways, or a combination of several, will suit the resources of a particular client. At this stage of the problem-managing process, as many strategies as possible (within time and other constraints) should be uncovered. At first, time need not be wasted criticizing the options for action. Even seemingly outlandish strategies can provide clues for realistic action programs. Techniques such as brainstorming and fantasy often help clients identify different ways of achieving goals. Let us return to Ray.

> Since Ray has been in the same job so long, he is not familiar with the ways in which people look for new jobs. The counselor gives him a short article on career development that includes a section entitled "Fifty-Four Ways to Get a Job." Ray finds the article very useful. He checks the ways that make sense to him, adds some of his own, and combines some of these options into innovative groups. Just being aware of so many possibilities gives him a sense of freedom and hope.
>
> However, Ray is still somewhat defensive about his drinking problem. He says that the only way to stop drinking is to stop drinking. He indicates that he is not at all interested in any of the groups, such as Alcoholics Anonymous, that deal with drinking problems. The counselor challenges him a bit. He need not go to any group, but it might help to review some of the typical strategies people use to stop drinking, just as he has reviewed ways of getting a job. She gives him a photocopy of a page from a book that outlines two dozen ways to stop drinking and asks him to use his imagination to expand the list. He does this in private. He admits to himself that reviewing the list and adding to it give him a feeling for the pitfalls facing a person who has been drinking heavily as well as some strategies for coping with them. He still thinks he can cope with his drinking on his own. After all, he *has* made his decision.

Some counselors never get to Stages II or III with their clients, on the assumption that these stages are the client's responsibility. It is true that some clients, once they have a clear idea of what is going wrong or a clear picture of some undeveloped opportunity, set goals, devise programs, and act. However, many do not accomplish these steps on their own and therefore can profit from the support and challenge helpers can provide.

Step III-B: Choosing the Best Strategies

Help clients choose a set of strategies that best fit their environment and resources. Once a number of different options for action have been identified, then client and helper collaboratively review them and try to

I. Present scenario   II. Preferred scenario   III. Strategy: Getting there

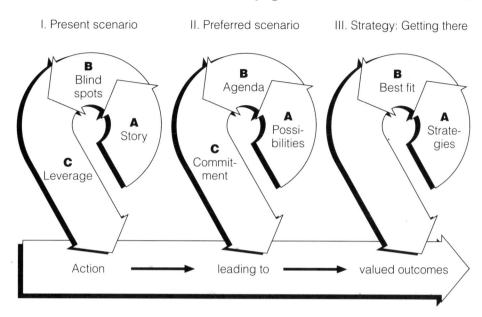

FIGURE 2-9   The Helping Model: Step III-B

choose the "best fit"—either the best single option or the best combination. Figure 2-9 adds this step to the helping model.

"Best" here means the single strategy or combination of strategies that best fits the client's needs, preferences, and resources and that is least likely to be blocked by factors in the client's environment. Strategies, in other words, need to be evaluated in terms of their realism. The options chosen must also be in keeping with the values of the client. For instance, even though one of the ways a young woman can afford to stay in college for the coming year is to accept a gift from a close relative, she might reject that option because developing a healthy independence from family may be more important to her. In that case, she will either have to put off going to school this year or find other sources of money.

> Ray takes a critical look at his short list of "ways to get a new job" and eliminates some of the options because of their lack of realism, because of time constraints, or because they do not fit his style. He puts an asterisk next to the options that seem to have the greatest potential for success. These include such things as joining a job-search group, making use of business contacts he has made over the years, telling selected friends of his availability, getting copies of the professional journals that list the kinds of jobs he is looking for, and even "cold canvassing" by telephone, that is, calling selected companies to see whether they have any vacancies that fit his criteria. Because of the high probability of rejection, the counselor is surprised that Ray chooses cold canvassing. Ray says that he does not mind being rejected when he is the instigator and there are no face-to-face contacts involved.

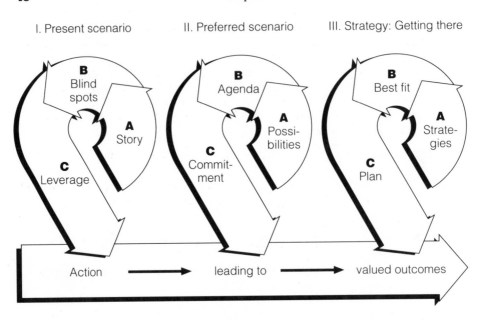

I. Present scenario   II. Preferred scenario   III. Strategy: Getting there

FIGURE 2-10   The Helping Model: Step III-C

Realism is important because there is no sense choosing strategies that can lead only to failure. Helpers need to be careful at this point, however. Sometimes clients choose strategies that make them stretch. Such a choice is fine, provided that the stretch is within reason. Cold canvassing is a strategy that makes Ray stretch, and, after years of passivity, stretching is one thing he needs to do.

Step III-C: Turning Strategies into a Plan

Help clients formulate a plan, that is, a step-by-step procedure for accomplishing each goal of the preferred scenario. The strategies that are chosen need to be translated into a step-by-step plan. Figure 2-10 adds this step to the helping model.

Clients are more likely to act if they know what they are going to do first, what second, what third, and so forth. Realistic time frames for each of the steps are also essential. Part of the challenge of this helping model is the demand for discipline that it places on clients. Let's see how this step applies to Ray.

Ray draws up a tentative plan. For instance, now that he has sorted out his priorities as to the kinds of job he wants, the first order of business is to draw up a résumé. He does this on a word processor so that he can easily tailor the résumé to the specific organization and job in question. He outlines the steps in the job search process—canvassing, getting interview offers, choosing among the offers, preparing for interviews, engaging in the interviews, follow up, and so forth—and sets up a flexible schedule. For instance, he outlines the kinds of canvassing he will do, the order in which he will canvass companies, and the time frame. Ray is not nearly as systematic in setting up a program for keeping away from alcohol. After all, he says, he has stopped drinking. One thing he instinctively does, however, is to begin a moderate exercise program. He says to himself that he might be old-fashioned, but in his mind physical fitness and heavy drinking do not go together.

Self-responsibility is still a key value in Stage III. Goals must be the client's goals, strategies must be the client's strategies, and action plans must be the client's plans. The helper's job is to stimulate the client's imagination and to help him or her in the search for incentives.

Client Action in Stage III

Each step of Stage III can act as a stimulus for informal action on the part of the client. Again, Ray provides an illustration.

With little prompting from his counselor, Ray uses his résumé-writing workbook to complete his résumé. He has it reviewed by a few friends, makes a few revisions, and has it printed. He also tries a few cold-canvassing telephone calls. He makes himself try a couple more before evaluating the experience. Of the five companies he contacts, three tell him right away that there are no jobs to be had. One personnel worker interviews him informally and then tells him that his skills are out of date and that he'll need to upgrade them before applying at that company. The last contact produces a second informal interview and an invitation to start a more formal process. The upshot is that Ray says to himself that he dislikes cold canvassing a great deal but that it is probably an efficient use of time. He keeps the strategy on his list even though he dislikes it.

Action Revisited: Preparing and Supporting Clients

The function of planning is to institute and give direction to problem-managing and opportunity-developing action. The actions clients must take to implement programs constitute the transition phase of counseling. This is illustrated in Figure 2-11, where the action arrow is now called transition.

There are a number of things counselors can do to help clients prepare themselves for the implementation of action programs. First, counselors can help clients in their immediate preparation for action. This may be called the "forewarned is forearmed" phase. Effective counselors help clients foresee difficulties that might arise during the actual carrying out of their plans. There are two extremes here. One is pretending that no difficulties will arise. The client optimistically launches into a program and then runs headlong into obstacles and fails. The other is spending too

I. Present scenario   II. Preferred scenario   III. Strategy: Getting there

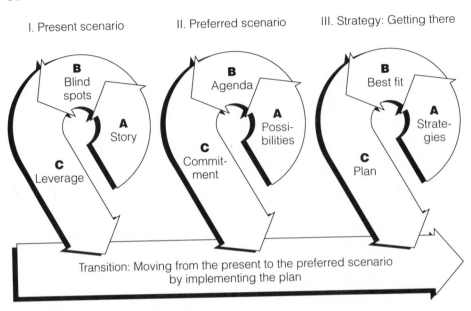

FIGURE 2-11 The Transition from the Present to the Preferred Scenario

much time anticipating obstacles and figuring out ways of handling them. This can be just another way of delaying the real work of problem management and opportunity development.

A reasonable consideration of obstacles that might well arise during the implementation of a program can be most useful. One way of doing this is to consider the principal *facilitating forces* and the principal *restraining forces* that will most likely be operative in the client's environment, including the client's inner environment of thoughts, feelings, imaginings, attitudes, and the like. For instance, if a person is trying to stop smoking, one facilitating force is thinking about the increased amount of aerobic energy that will be available for exercise. A principal restraining force will probably be the longing that comes from withdrawal from a pleasurable habit. Another will be the envy the person will experience when in the company of his or her friends who are still smoking.

Second, helpers can provide support and challenge for clients as they act. Clients need both to support and challenge themselves and to find support and challenge from others. The counselor can also challenge the client to mobilize whatever resources are needed to stick to a program. If a wife unilaterally institutes a program of more decent communication with her husband (who refuses to see the counselor either with his wife or alone), she may have a rough time in the beginning. She may find it extremely discouraging when he does not appreciate her attempts at a more caring kind of communication and even makes fun of them. But if there is a reasonable probability that her patience will eventually pay off, then she needs support and challenge to stick to the program. Support and challenge can come from herself, from her friends, and from the counselor.

At this point in the process, helpers do not act for clients but rather help them mobilize their resources in order to increase the strength of facilitating forces and decrease the strength of restraining forces. How does this process apply to Ray?

> Ray draws up a résumé and implements his plan of canvassing for a job. The counselor asks him two questions as he launches his program. (1) "In what ways might this plan fall apart?" (2) "What incentives and resources are available to keep you working at it?" Ray discusses some possible pitfalls. One he sees as quite serious: He wants something to happen quickly. He fears that if results are not quick in coming, he might get frustrated and quit. He might also begin drinking again. He and the counselor discuss ways of handling this possible pitfall. One of his best resources is the feeling he has of a new lease on life. It feels too precious to let it slip out of his hands. He contracts with the counselor to call her when he first begins to feel frustrated, even though he would prefer to "tough it out" himself.
>
>   Ray's spirits have been raised by this entire process. He and his wife go to a party at a neighbor's house, and he lets his guard down. Telling himself that it will be all right to take a couple of drinks in order to be sociable and to celebrate the new course he is on, he gets drunk. Out of shame and desperation, the next day he gets drunk again. On Sunday morning he calls the counselor. They decide to take a closer look at his "problematic" drinking.

The example of Ray is necessarily sketchy and perhaps overly sanguine in that it may make the helping process, which takes a great deal of work and certainly has its frustrating moments, seem too pat. The sole purpose of this example, however, is to give you a picture of the model in action and some idea of how you can use it to give direction to the entire process. In the best of worlds, Ray will get a more challenging job and manage his drinking problem more effectively and then move on to renewing his home life. But we do not live in the best of worlds. Clients may disappoint helpers, and helpers may disappoint clients; they may both disappoint themselves. In my experience the best helpers have an optimism tempered by realism.

Ongoing Evaluation of the Helping Process

In many helping models, evaluation is presented as the last step in the model. However, if evaluation occurs only at the end, it is too late. Therefore, in Figure 2-12, an "E" is placed in the center of every stage to indicate that the helping process needs to be evaluated at every step along the way. As we will explore in a later chapter, evaluation is not the last step; it is an ongoing process. At each step helpers and clients need to ask themselves

I. Present scenario   II. Preferred scenario   III. Strategy: Getting there

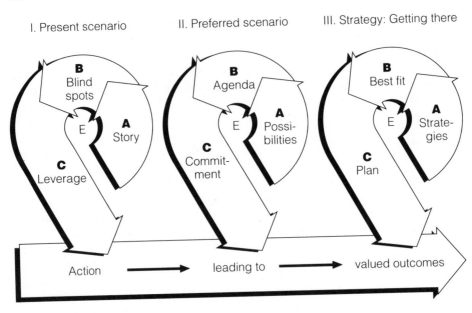

FIGURE 2-12   Evaluation in the Helping Model

such questions as, In what ways are the counseling sessions contributing substantially to problem management and opportunity development? To what degree is the client "owning" the helping process itself? In what ways is the client acting on what he or she is learning in the helping interviews?

OVERCOMING AWKWARDNESS

As a beginner, you can expect to experience some awkwardness as you learn to use the model and the skills and techniques it calls for. You need both practice and experience to be able to put all the elements of the model together smoothly. The following steps will help you achieve this integration.

   1. Modeling of extended counseling sessions by skilled helpers. It helps to watch someone who can "put it all together." Live sessions, training films, and videotapes all help. You can read and listen to lectures about the helping process, but then you need to watch someone actually do it. Modeling gives you the opportunity to have an "aha" experience in training; that is, as you watch someone competent, you say to yourself: "Oh, that's how it's done!"

   2. Step-by-step supervised practice. Watching someone else do it well will help you develop a behavioral feeling for the model and its skills, but it will not, of itself, dissipate your feelings of awkwardness. The next step is to learn and practice the stages, steps, and skills under supervision. A supervisor, in this instance, is someone who can tell you what you are doing right, so that you can keep on doing it and celebrate your success, and what you are doing wrong, so that you can correct it. If you have a clear understanding of the requirements of the helping process, you can also give yourself feedback and get feedback from your fellow trainees. Once you learn basic skills, then you can begin to practice short counseling sessions with your fellow trainees. As you become more and more self-assured, the length of these helping sessions can be increased.

3. Extended practice in individual skills outside the training sessions. The problem-management model and the skills you will be learning are the skills needed for effective living. Perhaps a "violin lesson" analogy can be used here. If you were taking violin lessons from an instructor, you would be introduced gradually and systematically to the skills of playing during the lesson itself. There would also be some minimal time for practice during the lesson, because the instructor would want to make sure that you had the right idea about each technique. However, once you learned the basics, it would be essential to go off and practice in order to master what you had learned. It would be a waste of time to return for a second lesson without having practiced what you had learned in the first. The same holds true in learning how to be a helper. In the classroom or training group, you will learn the basics of the model and the skills and techniques that make it operative, and you will have time for some practice. However, since the skills you will be learning are skills important for everyday living and relating, you will have ample opportunity to practice them outside the training sessions themselves. For instance, you can sincerely and genuinely practice the communication skills that serve the model in your daily interactions with others, and you can do so without making yourself an amateur psychologist. Furthermore, since planning and problem solving are part of everyday life, you will have ample opportunity to practice the stages and steps of the model. With enough practice, this model and its skills can become second nature, and your feelings of awkwardness will lessen. They will be part of your humanity and not something tacked on to it.

4. Supervised practice of the entire model. Learning microskills is a segmental process. The skills of helping are not helping itself. They all have to be integrated into that human encounter called helping, counseling, or psychotherapy. Supervised practicum experience is an essential step toward such integration.

FLEXIBILITY IN APPLYING THE MODEL

A beginning helper, or even an experienced but unskilled one, can apply the helping model too rigidly. Helping is for the client; the model exists only to aid the helping process. Flexibility is essential.

Sequence and Overlap

The overview in this chapter has presented the *logic* of the helping model. The "literature" of the model, that is, the model in actual use, is not as neat and clean. One form of rigidity is to progress mechanically through the stages of the model. The phases of helping are not always as differentiated and sequential as they are in our presentation of them. For instance, since clients do not always present all their problems at once, it is impossible to work through Stage I completely before moving on to Stages II and III. New problems must be explored and understood whenever they are presented. The same is true of any model of helping:

> [T]he process is not that simple! We know that we do not follow such a simple linear or one-way procedure—we double back and repeat ourselves many times. Indeed, we cannot truly separate the processes at times. Sometimes we seem to be doing two of the functions simultaneously. (Robertshaw, Mecca, & Rerick, 1978, p. 3)

The problem-solving model gives form and direction to the helping process, but it must also respond to the realities of the actual helping situation. This means that helpers will often enough find themselves moving back and forth in the model. A client might actually try out some problem-managing strategy even before the problem situation is adequately defined and some definite goal has been set. Action sometimes precedes understanding. If the action is not successful, then the counselor helps the client return to the tasks of clarifying the problem situation and setting some realistic goals. Similarly, clients set goals and develop strategies to achieve them at the same time. New and more substantial concerns arise while goals are being set, and the process moves back to an earlier exploratory stage. Step I-B, which involves challenging blind spots, can overlay and mingle with all the other steps. In practice, then, both the stages and the steps in the model overlay and mingle with one another, as illustrated in Figure 2-13.

The "Stage-Specific" Specialist

A general rule is that the helper should move as quickly through the stages and steps needed by the client as the client's resources permit. The client should not be penalized for the helper's lack of skills. Beginning helpers often dally too long in Stage I, not merely because they have a deep respect for the necessity of relationship development and problem clarification, but because they either do not know how to move on or fear doing so. High-level clients may be able to move quickly to action programs. The helper, obviously, should be able to move with them.

Some helpers tend to specialize in the skills of a particular step or stage of the model. Some specialize in problem exploration; others claim to

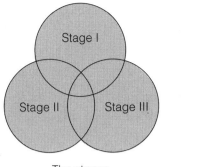 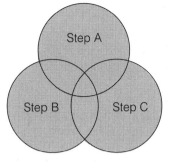

The stages   The steps of any given stage

FIGURE 2-13   Overlap of Stages and Steps

be good at confrontation; others want to move immediately to action programs. Helpers who specialize not only run the risk of ignoring client needs but often are not very effective even in their chosen specialties. For example, the counselor whose specialty is confrontation is often an ineffective confronter. The reason is obvious: Confrontation is poor if it is not based solidly on an understanding of clients. Effective counselors have a wide repertory of skills and use them in a socially intelligent way. These skills enable them to respond spontaneously to a wide variety of client needs. In sum, counseling is for the client; it is not a virtuoso performance by the helper.

Principles, Not Formulas

The model discussed and illustrated in this book provides the basic *principles* of helping others manage their lives more effectively. It does not provide easy *formulas*. As I have already indicated, the model itself is not a linear formula; nor is any one step or skill. One of the principles we will discuss, for example, is that self-defeating forms of thinking and self-talk need to be challenged. That is, we often say to ourselves, however covertly, "I can't," when in reality we can. Counselors can challenge their clients to replace such thinking with more creative and action-oriented forms of internal dialogue. However, there is no easy formula for doing so. Precisely what kind of self-defeating self-dialogue needs to be challenged in the case of any given client, how this can be done without alienating the client, and how the client can be helped to replace self-defeating ruminations with more creative thoughts—all of this has to be formulated during the helper's interactions with *this* client, in *these* circumstances. Clients and helpers collaboratively translate principles into formulas tailored to the specific case.

Chapter Three

Building the Helping Relationship: Values in Action

The Steps of the Helping Model as Ways of Being with Clients
The Working Alliance
    The Relationship Itself
    The Relationship as a Means to an End
    Individual Differences
Humanizing the Helping Process
Values in Helping
    Pragmatism
    Competence
    Respect
    Genuineness
    Client Self-Responsibility
    Ethics
Helping as a Social-Influence Process
    Current Views of Social Influence in Counseling and
      Psychotherapy
    Reconciling Self-Responsibility and Social Influence
The Client-Helper Contract
    The Content of the Contract
    Sharing the Helping Model with Clients as Part of the
      Contract

THE STEPS OF THE HELPING MODEL AS WAYS OF BEING WITH CLIENTS

Helping, at its best, is a deeply human venture. Models, methods, techniques, and skills are tools at the service of this venture. They are not meant to "technologize" the process. The relationship between helper and client is extremely important, but, in the end, it is a relationship of service, not an end in itself.

The steps of the helping model, reviewed in Chapter 2, are themselves ways in which helpers can "be with" their clients humanely and productively:

Stage I

- You can be with clients by helping them tell their stories, especially when these stories are difficult to tell.
- You can be with clients by helping them identify and overcome blind spots, by helping them reconceptualize problems and opportunities, and by helping them develop new, action-serving perspectives.
- You can be with clients by helping them find starting points in complex problem situations, by helping them find signs of hope, and by helping them clarify problem situations from their own point of view.

Stage II

- You can be with clients by helping them see and develop hopeful alternatives to their problem situations; you can be with them by helping them tap their conceptual and imaginal resources in the creation of new scenarios.
- You can be with clients by helping them create realistic and meaningful agendas; you can be with them by helping them set goals that make them stretch.
- You can be with clients by helping them make choices, even painful choices, and by helping them find the incentives that enable them to commit themselves to these choices.

Stage III

- You can be with clients by helping them brainstorm options for action.
- You can be with clients by helping them find strategies that fit them and their resources.
- You can be with clients by helping them turn viable strategies into meaningful plans.

All Stages and Steps

- You can be with clients by providing both support and challenge for them as they act to involve themselves more fully in the helping process and in translating the give-and-take of the helping interviews into problem-managing and opportunity-developing action.

You will not be with all clients in each of these ways, because you will tailor your active, involving, caring presence to each client's particular needs.

THE WORKING ALLIANCE

In a review of research findings, Goleman (1985) discovered that the best predictor of success in the helping process—a better predictor than the kind of therapy used, the qualities of the helper, or the problems of the client—is the quality of the relationship between the client and the counselor. It is essential, therefore, to understand what is meant by a quality helping relationship and what helpers need to do to develop and maintain such relationships. The relationship is the heart of the helping process; it is the carrier of its values.

While all agree that the helping relationship is very important (Highlen & Hill, 1984), not all agree why. Some stress the relationship in itself, while others stress the work to be done through the relationship.

The Relationship Itself

Patterson (1985) makes the relationship itself central:

> Counseling or psychotherapy is an interpersonal relationship. Note that I don't say that counseling or psychotherapy involves an interpersonal relationship—it *is* an interpersonal relationship. (p. 3)

Deffenbacher (1985) stresses the kinds of things helpers do to develop and foster the relationship:

> Good . . . therapists work to build rapport, lessen interpersonal anxiety in the relationship, increase trust, and build an interpersonal climate in which clients can openly discuss and work on their problems. Their clients need to perceive that they have a caring, positive, hopeful collaborator in understanding and making changes in their world. Good listening in an open, nondefensive manner, careful attention and tracking of client concerns, direct, honest feedback, and the like are not only important for assessment, but also create the context in which further exploration and [helping] strategies may be implemented. Clients . . . need to feel cared for, attended to, understood, and genuinely worked with if successful therapy is to continue. (p. 262)

Stressing the relationship itself is especially important when helping is seen as a *forum for social-emotional reeducation.* The kind of social-emotional reeducation that takes place through the interactions between helpers and their clients is sometimes the most significant outcome of the helping process. Clients begin to care for themselves, trust themselves, and challenge themselves more because of what they learn through their interactions with helpers. For instance, a helper at the termination of the helping process might be able to say of her client, "Because I trusted him, he trusts himself more; because I cared for him, he is now more capable of caring for himself; because I invited him to challenge himself and because I took the risk of challenging him, he is now better able to challenge himself. Because of the way I related to him, he now relates better both to himself and to others. Because I respected his inner resources, he is now more likely to tap these resources."

The Relationship as a Means to an End

Others see the helping relationship primarily as a means to an end. A good relationship enables the counselor to collaborate with the client in the use of the helping model and the methods that make it work (Driscoll, 1984; Gelso & Carter, 1985). The relationship is subservient and instrumental to achieving the goals of the helping process.

I have trouble with those who imply that the importance of the relationship cannot be overstressed. Before long, "deep and mythical" things are being said about the relationship that, in my view, obscure the ultimate goal of helping: clients' managing their lives better. The goal won't be achieved if the relationship is poor, but if too much focus is placed on the relationship itself, both client and helper are distracted from the real work to be done.

Individual Differences

Furthermore, the idea of the one perfect kind of helping relationship is a myth. Different clients have different needs, and these needs are best met through different kinds of relationships. For instance, one client may work best with a helper who expresses a great deal of warmth, while another might work best with a helper who is more objective and businesslike. Some clients come to counseling with a fear of intimacy. If helpers, right from the beginning, communicate a great deal of empathy and warmth, these clients might be put off. Effective helpers use a mix of skills and techniques tailored to the kind of relationship that is best for each client.

One way of viewing the helping relationship is to focus on the values that should permeate it. And so we turn our attention to these values.

HUMANIZING THE HELPING PROCESS

What follows is my view of the values that should define and permeate the helping relationship. The focus is on the beliefs, assumptions, values, norms, and standards that serve as the philosophical and moral foundations of helping. To be fair to myself, many other helpers might well buy much of the package outlined here. However, values cannot be handed to prospective helpers on a platter. What is written here is meant to stimulate your thinking about values. In the final analysis, as you sit with your clients, only those values that you have made your own will make a difference.

You need to be proactive in your search for the beliefs, values, and norms that will govern your interactions with your clients. This does not mean that you will invent a set of values different from everyone else's. We all learn from the tradition of the profession and the wisdom of others. The set of values you come up with will certainly be influenced by the values of your clients, of the helping profession, and of society, together with whatever transcendent values you see governing interactions among people. Ultimately, however, you must commit yourself to your own "package."

Values are not just ideals. In the pragmatics of helping others, they are a set of criteria for making decisions. For instance, a helper might say to himself or herself, "The arrogant I'm-always-right attitude of this client needs to be challenged. How to challenge her is another story. Since I respect the client, I do not want to challenge her by putting her down. On the other hand, I value openness. Therefore, I can challenge her by describing the impact she has on me and do so without belittling her." Working values enable the helper to make decisions on how to proceed. Helpers without a set of working values are adrift.

A distinction can be made among beliefs, values, and norms. Consider the following example:

- *Belief:* I believe that people are free, that they can determine much of what they do.
- *Value:* I prize self-responsibility, both in myself and in my clients.
- *Norm:* I will not make decisions for clients; rather, I will do what I can to help them find their own solutions to their problems.

In practice, however, the term "value" is used to refer to all three. In these pages, values will often be cast in terms of norms, because norms point directly to behavior. In the final analysis, what helpers and clients *do* or *fail to do* determines the success or failure of the enterprise. Espoused values are "nice." Values-in-use make a difference.

Helpers, like other professionals, sometimes have problems wedding values to practice. In studying helpers' perceptions of good and poor practices in psychotherapy, Pope, Tabachnick, and Keith-Spiegel (1988) find a house in some disorder:

> There is an absence of comprehensive, systematically gathered data about psychologists' beliefs about what constitutes good practice in regard to the wide range of possible behaviors associated with professional practice. We know relatively little about the degree to which such notions of good practice coincide with or diverge from professional behavior, formal ethical principles, legal standards, and assertions by professional committees, authors, and expert witnesses about those notions. (p. 551)

This chapter is a first step in helping you put your own house in order.

VALUES IN HELPING

Values that guide transactions between helpers and their clients can be packaged in a variety of ways. The five major sets I will address are pragmatism, competence, respect, genuineness, and client self-responsibility.

Pragmatism

Any kind of helping worth its salt is useful—right from the start. A humane pragmatism can be expressed in a variety of ways.

Keep the client's agenda in focus. We live in an era when customer service is getting a great deal of attention. Your clients are your customers, and they deserve the best you can give. In particular, helpers should pursue their clients' agendas, not their own. Paar (1988) recalled, painfully, an early attempt at helping. The client was a young man who was being beaten up by his lover. Paar, focusing more on the theories he had learned in graduate school than the client's pain, talked to the client about his "real" problem, the dynamics of his sexual orientation. Paar's elation over his success in pinpointing the dynamics correctly turned sour when the young man did not return. A customer focus means, in part, appealing to what matters to the client (see Driscoll, 1984).

Maintain a real-life focus. If clients are to make progress, they must "do better" in their day-to-day lives. The focus of helping, then, is not narrowly on the helping sessions and client-helper interactions themselves, but on clients' managing their day-to-day lives more effectively. A friend of mine, again in his early days as a helper, exulted in the "solid relationship" he was building with a client until in the third interview she stopped, stared at him, and said, "You're really filled with yourself, aren't you?" He had become lost in the "solid relationship" he had been building.

Stay flexible. This book suggests a framework, principles, methods, and skills, but *no formulas*. As I have emphasized, the entire process of helping needs to be adapted to the status and needs of the client. This is not the same as saying that the client dictates the process. Often enough, as we will see later, the client needs to be challenged. The flexibility principle is: Do whatever is ethical and works. Howard, Nance, and Myers (1987) have adapted an approach called "situational leadership"—in which managers and supervisors adapt their style to the individual needs of the people being supervised—to the helping process. They demonstrate how helpers can "pitch" the helping process to the status of the client.

Develop a bias toward action. As we shall see in greater detail in the next chapter, a pragmatic bias toward acting—rather than merely talking about acting—is an important helping value. I am active with clients and see no particular value in mere listening and nodding. I engage clients in a dialogue. During that dialogue, I constantly ask myself, "What can I do to raise the probability that this client will act in her own behalf intelligently and prudently?" I know a man who years ago went "into therapy" (like into another world) because, among other things, he was indecisive. Recently he has become engaged several times. He has broken off each engagement. So much for decisiveness.

Do only what is necessary. Helping is an expensive proposition, both monetarily and psychologically. Even when it is "free," someone is paying for it through tax dollars, insurance premiums, or free-will offerings. Therefore, without rushing nature or your clients, get to the point. Do not assume that you have a client for life. A colleague of mine experimented, quite successfully, with shortening the counseling "hour." I do not assume that the average helper will get to the point he did with his experimental subjects when he would begin by saying, "We have five minutes together. Let's see what we can get done." He was very respectful, and it was amazing how much he and his clients could get done in a short time. (On the other hand, a friend of mine knew a helper who said, as he glanced at his Mercedes, that he could not "afford" such an approach.) As we shall see, you need not drag each client kicking and screaming through every stage and step of the model described in the previous chapter. Do only what is necessary.

Avoid generating resistance. More will be said about managing client resistance later. However, as Driscoll (1984; see pp. 184–193) notes, clients tend to resist when they think they are being *coerced* in some way:

When resistance occurs, assess what you are doing which is seen by the client as coercive, and then alter or avoid it in order to maintain a co-operative relationship in which issues can be dealt with productively. (pp. 189–190)

This in no way means that good helpers are conflict-avoiding wimps. It does mean, as Dimond and his associates (1978) suggested, that helpers do whatever is necessary to "dissolve, to avoid, or to take advantage of, rather than to break down, resistance" (p. 245). As we have already seen, some clients come resisting because they have been coerced into coming.

Do not offer helping as a panacea. Part of pragmatism is realizing the limitations of your profession. For one thing, realize that clients can "get better" in a variety of ways, even without your help. For instance, some people get depressed during winter. This affliction, called "seasonal affective disorder" (SAD), is fairly prevalent in climates with short days and little sun. It has been discovered that exposure to two hours of bright, full-spectrum light each day helps many of these sufferers regain their zest for life (Hellekson, Kline, & Rosenthal, 1986) without any counseling. Stressed managers use a variety of strategies to cope—rest and sleep, exercise, time with family and friends, getting away from it all on weekends, and the like. In one study, only 6% resorted to counseling.

I often show a popular series of videotaped counseling sessions in which the client receives help from a number of helpers, each with a different orientation. Once the course participants have seen the tapes, I ask, "Does this client need counseling?" They all practically yell, "Yes!" Then I ask, "Well, if this client needs counseling, how many people in the world need counseling?" Then there is a great deal of retreating from the word "needs." That a person might well benefit from counseling is not the same thing as needing counseling.

Competence

In Chapter 1 we asked the question "Does helping really help?" As I noted then, studies show that competent helpers do help, while incompetent helpers are often not neutral. They actually do harm. Competence in helping is not a goal to be achieved; it is a lifelong pursuit.

Become good at helping. In the context of this book, this means becoming proficient in delivering the helping model described and illustrated here. Being able to deliver the goods to clients goes far beyond merely understanding models and having an intellectual understanding of what needs to be done. Helpers need plenty of supervised experience in real-life helping situations. Counselor training programs should, in my opinion, be competency-based. Certificates and degrees should be awarded only if the helper can deliver the goods.

One way of becoming good is practice. The problem-solving model can be used every day in your own life. The best learners immerse themselves in it until it becomes second nature.

Continue to learn. I once gave a talk to a professional psychology club in a large city. Since most of the people there were professionals, I did not want to talk down to them. During the question period, however, it soon became apparent that many of them had not been keeping up with the profession. This does not automatically mean that they were incompetent. But look at it this way: How comfortable would you feel going to a doctor who had not read a medical journal for years? The curriculum outlined in Chapter 1 is not just for school but for life.

Use modeling. One way you can demonstrate your competence is to model the kinds of things you challenge clients to do. If you want them to be open, be open. If you want them to act, do not be afraid to be active in the helping sessions. One client told me that she was not going to go back to her counselor at the university counseling center: "He just sits there and nods. I can get anyone to do that." Effective helpers use the tools of their trade on their own problems. Some (see Berenson & Mitchell, 1974) say that only those helpers who are committed to living fully themselves deserve to help others.

Be assertive. If you are good at what you do, don't apologize for it. Do it. I find that one of the cardinal problems with many trainees in the helping professions is that they are afraid to assert themselves. Some want to settle for a caricature of "nondirective counseling" as a helping model, not necessarily because they espouse the theory underlying it but because their interpretation (or misinterpretation) of this approach is what they are most comfortable with. You will do little to help clients if all you do is sit there and say, "Uh-huh." Learn to do many things that can help clients, and then don't be afraid to do them. Most clients are less fragile than helpers make them out to be.

Find competence, not in behavior, but in outcomes. According to Gilbert (1978), competence does not lie principally in behaviors but in the accomplishments toward which these behaviors are directed. If Brenda comes to a helper with persistently high levels of free-floating anxiety, then "anxiety reduced" is one of the hoped-for accomplishments of the helping process. If a year later she is still as anxious as ever despite weekly visits to a professional helper, then that helper's competence—other things being equal, such as Brenda's commitment to change—is in question. Trust in a helper can evaporate quickly if little or nothing is accomplished through the helping sessions. And yet, too often, it would seem, clients persist in trusting helpers even though they fail to demonstrate competence through verifiable accomplishments.

Respect

In a book on the social nature of humankind, Harre (1980) contends that the deepest human need is the need for respect. Respect is such a fundamental notion that, like most such notions, it eludes definition. The word comes from a Latin root that includes the notion of "seeing" or "viewing." Indeed, respect is a particular way of viewing oneself and others. Respect means prizing people simply because they are human.

Respect, if it is to make a difference, cannot remain just an attitude or a way of viewing others. As Mayeroff (1971) puts it, it is "more than good intentions and warm regards" (p. 69). In helping situations, respect is communicated principally by the ways in which helpers orient themselves toward and work with their clients.

Do no harm. This is the first rule of the physician and the first rule of the helper. Yet some helpers do harm either because they are unprincipled or because they are incompetent. There is no place for the "caring incompetent" in the helping professions. Helping is practically never a neutral process; it is for better or for worse.

In a world in which child abuse is much more common than we care to think, it is important to emphasize a nonmanipulative and nonexploitative approach to clients. Studies show that some instructors do exploit helpers in training sexually and that some helpers do the same with their clients. This behavior obviously breaches the codes of ethics espoused by all the helping professions.

Nor do I believe that clients should be manipulated into more effective living. In the late 1960s, helping communities sprang up where clients with certain problems such as drug addiction struggled to live more effectively. Very often these communities imposed very strict regimes. Strict regimes do not bother me. Failing to be transparent with clients about what they are getting into does. Duping clients into living more effectively is, from a values perspective, a contradiction in terms.

Treat clients as individuals. Respect means prizing the individuality of clients, supporting each client in his or her search for self, and personalizing the helping process to the needs, capabilities, and resources of this client. Effective helpers do not try to make clients over in their own image and likeness. On the other hand, respect does not mean encouraging clients to develop or maintain a kind of individualism that is either self-destructive or destructive of others.

Suspend critical judgment. You are there to help clients, not to judge them. Rogers (1961, 1967), following Standal (1954), calls this kind of respect "unconditional positive regard," meaning that "the therapist communicates to his client a deep and genuine caring for him as a person with potentialities, a caring uncontaminated by evaluations of his thoughts, feelings, or behaviors" (Rogers, 1967, p. 102). Consider the differences in the following counselors' remarks.

Client: I am really sexually promiscuous. I give in to sexual tendencies whenever they arise and whenever I can find a partner. This has been the story for the past three years at least.

Counselor A: Immature sex hasn't been the answer, has it? Ultimately it is just another way of making yourself miserable. These days, it's just asking for AIDS.

Counselor B: So, letting yourself go sexually is also part of the total picture.

Counselor B neither judges nor condones because *she is not there as a judge.* This does not mean that she is naive. She realizes that some of the client's experiences must be transcended and that some of his behaviors must change, but she respects the client as the subject of these experiences and behaviors. She gives the client room to move.

Driscoll (1984) goes a step further. He suggests that helpers can show clients that they are *already* acceptable in a variety of ways. Some of clients' problems are a misuse of strengths that are quite acceptable in themselves. A client's angry outbursts can manifest a willingness to stick up for his rights. The way he does it may need to be reformulated, but the basic instinct is healthy.

Be "for" the client. The counselor's manner indicates that he or she is "for" the client, that he or she cares in a down-to-earth, nonsentimental way. Being for the client is not the same as taking the client's side or acting as the client's advocate. Being for means taking clients' interests seriously enough to challenge them when they do things that are not in their own interest. Respect often involves placing demands on clients or helping them place demands on themselves. This "being for," then, can refer to clients' potential to be more than they are right now. Respect is both gracious and tough-minded. As Fisher and Ury (1981) suggest, "Be soft on the person, hard on the problem."

Be available. You should be able to say: "Working with this client is worth my time and energy." Effective helpers are ready to commit themselves to their clients and are available to them in reasonable ways. "Reasonable" seems to differ from helper to helper. I have talked to helpers who are more available than I would be and to helpers who are less available than I would be. However, whenever you are with your clients, you should be all there, psychologically available. This often means putting your own concerns aside for the time being.

Understand and communicate understanding to clients. One of the best ways of showing respect is by working to understand clients—their experiences, their behavior, their feelings. People generally believe that people respect them if they spend time and effort trying to understand them. In a later chapter the skills needed both to understand and to communicate understanding to clients are discussed in some detail.

Assume the client's good will. Work on the assumption that clients want to work at living more effectively, at least until the assumption is proved false. The reluctance and resistance of involuntary clients is not necessarily evidence of ill will. Respect means entering the world of the clients in order to understand their reluctance and a willingness to help clients work through it. The best helpers ask themselves whether they are contributing in any way to the failure of the counseling relationship. Some counselors abandon "unmotivated" clients too easily. On the other hand, respect does not call for continuing a relationship that is going nowhere.

Be warm within reason. Research findings indicate that some clients expect a professional, and not an idealized, friendly relationship with the helper (Reisman, 1986). On the other hand, research also shows that clients are not looking for a cold, aloof, "objective" helper. Indeed, when helpers themselves seek help, they look for competence, experience, good reputation, *and* warmth in their counselors (Norcross, Strausser, & Faltus, 1988). Baekeland and Lundwall (1975) reported evidence that approximately half of those who attend an initial psychotherapy interview do not return. Dembo, Weyant, and Warner (1982) found that clients' initial perceptions of the therapist were significantly related to dropping out of treatment. Specifically, the degree to which the therapist in the first interview met the client's expectations that he or she would be warm and friendly versus businesslike was predictive of whether the client would return for treatment.

Gazda (1973) sees warmth as the physical expression of understanding and caring, which is ordinarily communicated through nonverbal media such as gestures, posture, tone of voice, touch, and facial expression. Warmth is only one way of showing respect. It is not necessarily the best way, and it can be misused. The helper can express initial warmth through friendliness, which is not the same as either "role" warmth (standard counselor warmth) or the warmth he or she would accord a good friend. The client is simply not a good friend. Warmth is not an end in itself, but a natural part of the relationship.

Individual clients differ in their expectations and needs with respect to warmth. Effective counselors, without being phony, gear their expressions of warmth to the needs of the client and not to their own need to either express or withhold warmth. Further, there are limits to warmth. Clements (1985) discusses the case of an internist in a small town who practiced humanistic theories that called for a loving, concerned doctor-patient relationship. Some patients got the wrong message, and one committed suicide.

Help clients utilize their own resources. The helper's basic attitude is that clients have the resources to manage their lives more effectively. These resources may be blocked in a variety of ways or simply unused. The counselor's job is to help clients free and cultivate these resources. They also help clients assess their resources realistically so that aspirations do not outstrip resources. Respect includes helping clients use their resources to participate as fully as possible in the helping process.

Client: There are a lot of things I find really hard to talk about. I would rather have you ask questions. That would be easier for me.

Counselor A: Okay. You mentioned that you got in trouble in school. What kind of trouble was it? How did it all start?

Counselor B: Well, let's talk about that for a moment. I feel that if I ask a lot of questions, I'll get a lot of information that I might think important, but I'm not convinced that it would be important for you. Putting yourself on the line like this is really new to you, and it seems you're finding it quite painful.

Counselor A responds immediately to the client's request. And, at this stage, that might not be a bad thing to do. Counselor B, on the other hand, assumes that the client does have the resources necessary to engage in self-exploration. She tries to help the client move beyond his reluctance to explore himself.

Driscoll (1984) affirms clients' strengths by showing them the sense they make:

> There are ways in which clients are rational and make sense in what they do, and ways in which they are confused and mistaken. . . . There are important reasons to begin with and emphasize the ways our clients do make sense, and to use these as a foundation to troubleshoot and resolve the mistakes and errors. (pp. 98–99)

One client so loved his work that he spent most of his waking time either doing it or thinking about it. On weekends he would involve his wife in some work-related task. He could not understand why she resented the amount of time he spent at work and talked about work. Work, after all, was his passion. The counselor affirmed his work-as-cause philosophy and the many ways in which this helped him mobilize and use his resources. After all, why not? However, she then used this as a basis for helping him develop some new perspectives. For instance, he believed that one of the best compliments he could pay his wife was to involve her in the business. He did not realize that she needed or wanted some attention *separate* from the business.

Help clients through the pain. Clients might well find the helping process or parts of it painful. Counselors show respect by helping clients through their pain, not by helping them find ways to avoid it. That is, respect includes an assumption on the part of the counselor that the client, right from the beginning, is willing to pay the price of living more effectively. Respect, then, places a demand on the client at the same time that it offers him or her help to fulfill the demand. For instance, let's assume that a voluntary client has been manifesting a great deal of reluctance to talk about substantial issues and even changes the topic when the helper gets too close. Finally, the helper says something like this:

Counselor: I'd like to share with you my perception of what's happening between you and me and get your reaction. The way I see it, you come close to discussing problems that are quite important for you, but then you draw back. It's almost as if you were saying, "I'm not sure whether I can share this part of my life here and now." My hunch is that exploring yourself and putting all the cards on the table can be quite painful. It's like writing a blank check; you don't know how high a figure is going to be written in.

This counselor's understanding is gently demanding. Respect and challenge are not enemies.

Genuineness

Like respect, genuineness, as it is discussed here, refers to both a set of attitudes and a set of counselor behaviors. Some writers call genuineness "congruence." Genuine people are at home with themselves and therefore can comfortably be themselves in all their interactions. Being genuine has both positive and negative implications; it means doing some things and not doing others.

Do not overemphasize the helping role. Genuine helpers do not take refuge in the role of counselor. Relating deeply to others and helping are part of their lifestyle, not roles they put on or take off at will. MacDevitt (1987) points out the negative effects of helpers' overemphasizing their role or being too rigid in the helping role. Gibb (1968, 1978) suggests ways of being "role-free." He says that helpers should learn how to

• express directly to another whatever they are presently experiencing,
• communicate without distorting their own messages,

- listen to others without distorting the messages they hear,
- reveal their true motivation in the process of communicating their messages,
- be spontaneous and free in their communications with others rather than use habitual and planned strategies,
- respond immediately to another's need or state instead of waiting for the "right" time or giving themselves enough time to come up with the "right" response,
- manifest their vulnerabilities and, in general, the "stuff" of their inner lives,
- live in and communicate about the here and now,
- strive for interdependence rather than dependence or counterdependence in their relationships with their clients,
- learn how to enjoy psychological closeness,
- be concrete in their communications, and
- be willing to commit themselves to others.

Gibb does not think that counselors should be "free spirits" who inflict themselves on others. Indeed, "free spirit" helpers can even be dangerous to their clients (see Lieberman, Yalom, & Miles, 1973, pp. 226–267). Being role-free is not license; freedom from role means that counselors should not use the role or facade of counselor to protect themselves, to substitute for competence, or to fool the client.

Be spontaneous. Many of the behaviors suggested by Gibb are ways of being spontaneous. Effective helpers, while being tactful as part of their respect for others, do not constantly weigh what they say to clients. They do not put a number of filters between their inner lives and what they express to others. On the other hand, Rogers (1957) notes that being genuine does not mean verbalizing every thought to the client. For instance, he suggests that helpers express negative feelings to clients only if these feelings persist or if they are interfering with their ability to move with the client through the helping process.

Avoid defensiveness. Genuine helpers are nondefensive. They know their own strengths and deficits and are presumably trying to live mature, meaningful lives. When clients express negative attitudes toward them, they examine the behavior that might cause the client to think negatively, try to understand the clients' points of view, and continue to work with them. Consider the following example:

Client: I don't think I'm really getting anything out of these sessions at all. I still feel drained all the time. Why should I waste my time coming here?
Counselor A: I think you are the one wasting time. You just don't want to do anything. Have you thought of that?

Counselor B: Well, that's your decision.

Counselor C: So from where you're sitting, there's no payoff for being here. Just a lot of dreary work and nothing to show for it.

Counselors A and B are both defensive. Counselor C centers on the experience of the client, with a view to helping the client explore his responsibility for making the helping process work. Since genuine helpers are at home with themselves, they can allow themselves to examine negative criticism honestly. Counselor C, for instance, would be the most likely of the three to ask himself or herself whether he or she is contributing to the apparent stalemate.

Be consistent. Genuine helpers are consistent. They do not think or feel one thing and say another—or at least they are able to identify any discrepancies that may arise, especially those affecting their ability to help others, and are willing to deal with them. Consider this example.

Client: Frankly, I don't think you like me. I think you're working hard with me, but I still don't think you like me.

Counselor A: I'm not sure what liking or not liking you has to do with what we're doing here. I'm here to help you. Liking you or not liking you is not the issue.

Counselor B: I'm not sure that makes any difference . . . (Pause) . . . Wait a minute. Let me catch myself here. Last session we talked about your being more assertive in our relationship. I think that right now you are being more assertive with me, and I'm brushing you aside. You seem to be saying that it's time that we take a look at how we're relating to each other here. My seeming not to like you even though I work hard with you bothers you.

Counselor A brushes aside the client's challenge as irrelevant. Counselor B catches herself in a discrepancy. She wants the client to be more assertive toward her and catches herself in the act of brushing this behavior aside.

Be open. Genuine helpers are capable of deeper levels of self-disclosure. They do not see self-disclosure as an end in itself, but they feel free to reveal themselves, even intimately, when and if it is appropriate. Being open also means that the helper has no hidden agendas: "What you see is what you get."

Work at becoming comfortable with behavior that helps clients. In my experience, clients become annoyed when counselors seem so relaxed that their ease can be interpreted as lack of interest. On the other hand, it is not helpful for clients to experience helpers as uptight. Ultimately, genuine helpers are comfortable with what they are doing because they are good at what they're doing. Over time many helpers need to become comfortable with behaviors that help clients but that are not a natural part of their style. In order to deliver the helping model described in this book, you might well have to learn new behaviors. For instance, you might have to become more assertive. Don't say, "Gee, I'm just not warm or I'm just not assertive." Work on making these behaviors second nature if they are not first nature.

Client Self-Responsibility

Client self-responsibility is a core value of the helping process. It is assumed that, within limits, women and men are capable of making choices and, to some degree, controlling their destinies.

Freedom versus Determinism

For years many psychologists took a deterministic stance and considered the issue of freedom versus determinism a non-question. Harcum (1988) notes that the authors of introductory psychology texts "appear to have largely ignored the specific issue of free will and determinism; most merely adopt a deterministic viewpoint without verbalizing it" (p. 483). Howard and Conway (1986) see a bias against empirical research on volition in psychology despite the fact that concepts such as self-control and self-determination have a long history in Western thought.

There is no doubt that social, political, economic, and cultural forces can limit people's ability to exercise self-responsibility. We cannot pretend that helping takes place in an idealized society. It does not. Sometimes counseling others means helping them exercise self-responsibility in settings in which the odds are overwhelmingly against them. Sometimes counseling means challenging clients to develop a sense of self-responsibility in a society that unwittingly rewards dependency and helplessness. Helping those who have few incentives to exercise self-responsibility is not easy.

Nevertheless, Bandura (1986) finds strict determinism contrary to human experience:

> Theories that seek to explain human behavior as solely the product of external rewards and punishments present a truncated image of human nature because people possess self-directive capabilities that enable them to exercise some control over their thoughts, feelings, and actions by the consequences they produce for themselves. (p. 335)

Murray's (1988) research shows that a whole range of thinkers from different ideological backgrounds, from Aristotle to Karl Marx, agree that happiness includes the self-respect that comes from accepting responsibility for one's own life and earning one's way in the world. Wise men and women agree that happiness flows from realizing one's innate capacities by doing productive work and overcoming obstacles. In this sense, no one can provide happiness for someone else. Like freedom, it cannot be conferred; it must be seized.

Currently there is a renewal of interest in psychology in human freedom (see Harcum, 1988; Kimble, 1984; Howard, DiGangi, & Johnson, 1988; Lazarick, Fishbein, Loiello, & Howard, 1988; Murray, 1988; Perloff, 1987; Pollio, 1982; Westcott, 1988). Whether the capacity in question is called free will or volition or self-determination or something else does not matter. Perloff, going one step further, proposes that personal responsibility, in the service of enlightened (rather than mean-spirited) *self-interest*, is an effective tool for enhancing both personal well-being and the public good. Driscoll (1984) translates theory into practice when he claims that an important task in counseling is helping clients pursue enlightened self-interest through self-control:

> We must confirm the ways in which the client is not undirected, but misdirected; not weak, but inept in how he is using his strengths; not adrift in life, but paddling crosswise and backwards against the current. (p. 113)

If clients are not urged to explore and assume self-responsibility, they may not do the things needed to manage their lives better, or they may do things that aggravate the problems they have.

The Pragmatics of Self-Responsibility

Farrelly & Brandsma (1974) outlined a number of hypotheses about client self-responsibility that still ring true:

- Clients can change if they choose.
- Clients have more resources for managing problems in living and developing opportunities than they or most helpers assume.
- The psychological fragility of clients is overrated both by themselves and by others.
- Maladaptive and antisocial attitudes and behaviors of clients can be significantly altered no matter what the degree of severity or chronicity.
- Effective challenge can provoke in the client a self-annoyance that can lead to a decision to change.

Hines (1988a), in recalling a critical incident in his helping career from which he learned some invaluable lessons, describes how he was so "wiped out" by his failure to help a married couple work out their difficulties that he threw up. Luckily he found a supervisor ready to listen. The supervisor said that Hines was hogging responsibility to the point that his clients were left with little or none.

> As I gained experience and continued to receive high quality supervision, I recognized a pattern of taking too much responsibility for my clients. The harder I worked, the less my clients worked. The more responsibility I took, the less I helped them take responsibility. . . . My clients and I now engage in the counseling process together, share responsibility, and work as a team to accomplish their goals. (p. 106)

Schmitt (1985) believes that understanding where clients are in terms of assumed self-responsibility enables helpers to tailor their responses to them. For instance, he says that early in therapy, when clients are anxious and confused about their behavior, they may need more support. However, as they come to see themselves as responsible for their behaviors, they may need to be challenged more.

Ultimately, if clients choose to live less effectively than they might, counselors, after helping them challenge such choices, can only respect their clients' right to determine their own fate. It may be that a client's values differ from those of the helper to the point that the helper finds it impossible to work with the client. If this is the case, the relationship should be terminated.

Ethics

Unethical behavior dogs the helping professions just as it does any other. The Ethics Committee of the American Psychological Association (1987) notes that the number of complaints against psychologists has risen 56% over the past few years.

> It is important that all psychologists become active in APA's attempts to protect consumers from both unintentional and intentional unethical behavior. In part, this means maintaining awareness of the evolving ethical standards and sensitivity to the harm that can befall consumers when we psychologists engage in substandard practices. In part, this means making ethical concerns prominent in our day-to-day discussions with our colleagues. In two recent national studies psychologists indicated that colleagues were their most useful resource for information and guidance concerning ethical issues. In part, it means improving the formal mechanisms, such as ethics committees, by which we hold ourselves formally accountable for our behavior. (p. 564)

In particular, sexual misconduct with clients remains one the profession's perplexing problems.

The focus of this chapter is on the values that need to permeate the helper/client relationship rather than on ethics. Ethics and ethical issues are too important to be treated in a summary way. It is assumed that, if helpers translate the values reviewed in this chapter into practice, they will be more than ethical. However, helpers' attempts to make their behavior legal, moral, ethical, and caring do not automatically empower them to deal with ethical dilemmas. Consider the following case posed by Lamb and his associates (1989).

> Susan is a 29-year-old married woman who recently entered psychotherapy for assistance with a moderate depression related to the inability to become pregnant. She is distraught because she has learned that a man with whom she had an affair 3 years ago has just died of AIDS. They did not use [safe-sex] techniques, and she realizes that it is possible that

she has contracted the virus. She refuses to be tested, to inform her husband, or to discontinue active attempts to become pregnant. (p. 37)

Does the woman have a moral obligation to protect her husband or the child that might be conceived? Does the helper have an obligation to discuss these issues with her? At what point do obligations to others or to society take precedence over protecting a client?

Clearly, it is important for helpers to know the ethical standards of their profession and the principles needed to cope with such dilemmas. However, Eberlein (1987) claims that mere exposure to professional guidelines is inadequate. Learning ethics must be a practical exercise. He outlines a practical, problem-solving approach to learning ethical principles. Case studies can help flesh out the principles (American Psychological Association, 1987; see Corey, Corey, & Callanan, 1988).

Finally, since we live in a society addicted to litigation, helpers must understand not just their ethical and moral obligations but also their legal ones. In the United States, these may differ from state to state. An acquaintance told me recently that fighting a malpractice suit was the worst experience of his life, even though he won.

HELPING AS A SOCIAL-INFLUENCE PROCESS

It is assumed that helping is in part a process of social influence. Social influence in the helping professions has a long history. Many cultures have stories about how people suffering from a variety of emotional disturbances and a variety of physical ailments of psychogenic origin have been "cured" by their belief in the curing powers of a helper (Frank, 1973; Kottler, 1986). Very often such cures have taken place in religious contexts, but they have not been limited to such contexts. In the average case, people come to see a certain person as being a healer with great powers. This person might be a tribal shaman or a Western helper with a good reputation. Prospective clients hear that such healers have cured others with ailments similar to theirs. They generally see these healers as acting, not in their own interests, but in the interests of the afflicted who come to them. This belief enables the afflicted person to place a great deal of trust in the healer. Finally, in a ceremony that is often public and highly emotional, the healer in some way touches the afflicted person either physically or metaphorically, and the person is "healed." The tremendous need of the afflicted person, the reputation of the healer, and the afflicted person's trusting belief in the healer all heighten the person's belief that he or she will be cured. In fact, in cases where sufferers are not cured, the failure is often attributed to their lack of belief or to some other evil within them (for instance, possession by a demon or poor motivation). Then they not only remain with their afflictions but also lose face in the community, becoming outcasts or "crazies."

The dynamics of such "cures" are hard to explain empirically. It is obvious that elements of the healing process help marshal the emotional energies and other resources of the afflicted. For instance, sufferers experience hope and other positive emotions, which they perhaps have not experienced for years. The whole situation both mobilizes their resources and places a demand on them to be cured. It presents them with what the Greeks called *kairos*—an opportune, acceptable, favorable, legitimate *moment in time* to leave their old way of life behind and take up a new one. The power of suggestion in such cases can be great, even overwhelming. Skilled helpers are aware of and have a deep respect for such "arational" factors in the helping process.

In developed societies, Kottler (1986) sees the magic in the person of the helper.

> Lock a person, any person, in a room alone with Sigmund Freud, Carl Rogers, Fritz Perls, Albert Ellis, or any other formidable personality, and several hours later he will come out different. It is not what the therapist does that is important—whether she interprets, reflects, confronts, or role plays—but rather who she is. A therapist who is vibrant, inspirational, charismatic; who is sincere, loving, and nurturing; who is wise, confident, and self-disciplined will have a dramatic impact by the sheer force and power of her essence, regardless of her theoretical allegiances. (pp. 2–3)

Both Frank and Kottler are talking about dramatic forms of *social influence*. Most, if not all helping encounters, involve social influence, usually of a less dramatic kind.

Why study social influence? First of all, it is not possible for helpers to avoid influencing their clients (or being influenced by them), any more than it is possible to eliminate social influence as a part of everyday life. We are constantly influencing one another in many different ways. Driscoll (1984) puts it well:

> The obvious objective of [helping] is not merely to understand, but to benefit troubled persons. The emphasis is thus on *influence*, and on the concepts, understanding, procedures, and competencies used to generate . . . changes. (p. 5)

Helping as a social-influence process is a practical concept calling for study beyond what is presented here. The following general remarks may serve to provide a framework for further exploration.

Current Views of Social Influence in Counseling and Psychotherapy

In 1968 Stanley Strong wrote what proved to be a landmark article on counseling as an interpersonal-influence process. I use the word "landmark" because the article has stimulated a great deal of writing and research that continues to this day (Dorn, 1984; Strong & Claiborn, 1982).

Corrigan and his associates (1980) outlined the main points of Strong's argument:

> Strong postulated that the extent to which counselors are perceived as expert, attractive, and trustworthy would reduce the likelihood of their being discredited [by clients]. . . . From these hypotheses, Strong suggested a two-stage model of counseling. In the first stage, counselors enhance their perceived expertness, attractiveness, trustworthiness, and clients' involvement in counseling. In the second stage, counselors use their influence to precipitate opinion and/or behavior change in clients. (p. 396)

In this view, helpers establish a power base and then use this power to influence clients to do whatever is necessary to manage their lives more effectively. The strong personalities discussed by Frank and Kottler have precisely such a base. While subsequent research has shown that it is not quite as simple as this (Corrigan, Dell, Lewis, & Schmidt, 1980; Driscoll, 1984; Heppner & Dixon, 1981; Heppner & Heesacker, 1982; McNeill & Stoltenberg, 1988), few challenge the premise that helping is a social-influence process.

Goldstein (1980) describes the social-influence process in helping in a way that is complementary to Strong's. He calls behaviors by which helpers establish an interpersonal power base with their clients "relationship enhancers." In essence, these "enhancers" are the values we have just reviewed, put into practice. The "power base" of the helper, then, is what I have been calling a working alliance or relationship. In the Strong tradition, the power base of the helper is seen in terms of the attractiveness, trustworthiness, and competence of the helper, and much of the research that has been done relates to these three characteristics.

Reconciling Self-Responsibility and Social Influence

It is especially important for helpers to come to grips with helping as a process of social influence in view of the unilateral nature of helping.

> It is . . . agreed, explicitly or implicitly, that the focus of the relationship and all its activities is on solving the problems of the client. In this respect, the change process is unlike most other interpersonal interactions. The personal problems, the private affairs, the worries, and the wishes of one person, the helper, are intentionally not focused upon. Treatment, therapy, or whatever the helping relationship may be called, is one-sided and concentrates exclusively on the client. (Goldstein, 1980, p. 2)

It goes without saying that the client is not there to help the helper. But this does not make the relationship itself lopsided. Here are ways, not of eliminating social influence, but of making it pay off for the client.

Imagine a continuum. At one end lies "telling clients what to do" and at the other "leaving clients to their own devices." Somewhere along that continuum is "helping clients make their own decisions and act on them."

Preventing a client from jumping off a bridge moves to the controlling end of the continuum, while accepting a client's decision to leave therapy even though he or she is "not ready" moves toward the other end. Most forms of helper influence will fall somewhere in between. As Hare-Mustin and Marecek (1986) note, there is a tension between the principle of autonomy, or the right of clients to determine their own interests, and the principle of beneficence, or the therapist's obligation to protect the client's welfare.

Use a participative rather than a directive model of helping. We have already discussed helping as a collaborative effort on the part of helper and client. Kanfer (1980) referred to a "participant model" of helping:

> A participant model emphasizes the importance of client responsibility in treatment. It represents a shift from the provision of a protective treatment environment toward the offering of rehabilitative experiences in which the client accepts increasing responsibilities for his or her own behavior, for dealing with the environment, and for planning the future. The therapeutic environment is viewed as a transitory support system that prepares the client to handle common social and personal demands more effectively. (p. 334)

Social influence and client self-responsibility are by no means contradictory terms. Client collaboration is to be encouraged at every stage and step of the helping process.

Empower clients. Helping can be dangerous if it increases clients' feelings of powerlessness (Stensrud & Stensrud, 1981). In a classic work, Freire (1970) warns helpers against making helping itself just one more form of oppression for the already oppressed. However, if the values outlined earlier in this chapter permeate the helping process, clients will become empowered—capable of doing what they could not do, or thought they could not do, before. The notion of empowerment in human-service professions is a powerful one (Berger & Neuhaus, 1977; Egan & Cowan, 1979; Egan, 1984; Kanter, 1983; Rappaport, 1981). Rappaport notes, "Prevention suggests professional experts; empowerment suggests collaborators" (p. 24).

Accept helping as a natural, two-way influence process. Kottler's (1986) premise is that clients and therapists change one another in the helping process. Even a cursory glance at helping reveals that clients can affect helpers in many ways. Helpers find clients attractive or unattractive and must deal with both positive and negative feelings about them as well as manage their own behaviors. For instance, they may have to fight the tendency to be less demanding of attractive clients or not to listen carefully to unattractive clients. On the other hand, some clients trip over their own distorted views of their helpers. For instance, a young woman who has had serious problems in her relationship with her mother might begin to have problems relating to a helper who is an older woman. Unskilled helpers can get caught up in both their own and their clients' games. Skilled helpers understand the "darker side" of the helping relationship and manage it.

The ways in which clients can influence helpers are endless. Furthermore, in these days of consumerism, many clients won't sit still for helpers who pretend to be omnipotent. Clients certainly expect competence from helpers, but they also expect give-and-take.

Become a consultant to clients. Helpers can be seen as consultants hired by clients to help them face problems in living more effectively.

> The therapist serves as a consultant and expert who negotiates with the client in how to go about change and to what end. The interactions are future oriented in that they focus on the development of general repertoires for dealing with problem situations. (Kanfer, 1980, p. 336)

Consultants in the business world adopt a variety of roles. They listen, observe, collect data, report observations, teach, train, coach, provide support, challenge, advise, offer suggestions, and even become advocates for certain positions. But the responsibility for running the business remains with those who hire the consultant. Therefore, even though some of the activities of the consultant can be seen as quite directive, the decisions are still made by managers. Consulting, then, is a social-influence process, but it is a collaborative one that does not rob managers of the responsibilities that belong to them. In this respect it is a useful analogy to helping.

Democratize the helping process. Tyler, Pargament, and Gatz (1983) move a step beyond consultancy in what they call the "resource collaborator role." Seeing both helper and client as people with defects, they focus on the give-and-take they believe should characterize the helping process. In their view, either client or helper can approach the other to originate the helping process. Both have equal status in defining the terms of the relationship, in originating actions within it, and in evaluating both outcomes and the relationship itself. In the best case, positive change occurs in both parties.

Focus on the client's enlightened self-interest. In one sense, the issue is not social influence but whether the communication between helper and client is meaningful to the client, whether it contributes to his or her enlightened self-interest (Perloff, 1987). McNeill & Stoltenberg's (1988) research suggests that clients are influenced by high-quality messages—messages that hit the mark (see Heesacker, 1986) and help them manage both themselves and problem situations better.

If social influence means pushing clients to accept the counselor's point of view, then clients will inevitably feel coerced and do what we all tend to do when coerced—resist actively or passively. Even worse, some clients might mindlessly accept what we say, even when it is not in their self-interest. Social influence at its best means that clients will listen to and *weigh* what helpers say to determine whether it will help them manage their lives better.

THE CLIENT-HELPER CONTRACT

Both implicit and explicit contracts govern the transactions that take place between people in a wide variety of situations, including marriage (where some but by no means all of the provisions of the contract are explicit) and friendship (where the provisions are usually implicit). Back in 1966, Goldstein, Heller, and Sechrest lamented the fact that many therapists fail to tell their clients much about the therapeutic process even though "ethical principles assert that therapists should inform clients about the purpose and nature of therapy and that clients have freedom of choice about their participation" (Hare-Mustin & others, 1979, p. 7). Goodyear and Bradley (1980) noted that, traditionally, virtually all counseling has been governed by *implicit* contracts that define both the treatment goals and procedures and the client-counselor relationship. In a sense, clients have been expected to buy a pig in a poke without much assurance that it will turn out to be a very succulent pig. Further, Wollersheim and her associates (1980) showed that contracts make clients more willing to enter counseling and help them develop a more accurate understanding of the requirements of treatment.

Today, implicit contracts are not enough. The helping professions are more mature, and clients are often more sophisticated (see Laungani, 1984). As Henig (1988) puts it:

> In this age of consumerism, a patient may demand to know more about what is happening or should be happening in therapy, and [be] less willing to sit back and accept the ultimate wisdom of the doctor. People now seem most comfortable with a counselor who will answer questions easily, directly, and honestly, who will say up front what the definition of success will be, who will apply common sense and logic to a problem, along with the special therapeutic skill and knowledge that come with training and experience. (p. 34)

If helping is to be a collaborative venture, then both parties must understand what their responsibilities are. The helping process needs to be "owned" by helper and client alike, and both should share a basic understanding about the major goals to be pursued and the procedures to be used in the helping process so that they both own the same thing. An explicit contract, whether verbal or written, can help achieve these goals.

The contract need not be too detailed, nor should it be rigid. It needs to provide structure for the relationship and the work to be done without frightening or overwhelming the client.

> Written or at least explicit verbal contracts can do much to clarify mutual expectations as to goals and methods, but inflexibility and irrevocable commitment to initial goals need to be avoided. An optimal form of contracting would involve making explicit mutual expectations, while allowing for periodic reassessment and revision. (Coyne & Widiger, 1978, p. 707)

Ideally, the contract is an instrument that makes clients more informed about the process, more collaborative with their helpers, and more proactive in managing their problems. At its best, a contract can help client and helper develop realistic mutual expectations, give clients a flavor of the mechanics of the helping process, diminish initial client anxiety and reluctance, provide a sense of direction, and enhance clients' freedom of choice.

The Content of the Contract

To achieve the objectives just outlined, there are a number of things the contract might include.

• *An overview of the helping process, including some of the techniques to be used:* "I don't want you to buy a pig in a poke. Helping should not be a 'black box.' Here is a pamphlet that outlines what counseling is about and gives examples along the way. I'd like you to read it between now and the next session and then we can discuss it."

• *What a client-helper relationship is like:* "I'd like us to be partners. But counseling is not about our relationship so much as your managing your problems better. I'd like our relationship to help you do just that."

• *The responsibilities of the helper:* "I want to make sure that I understand your concerns. If I do that, then you will come to understand them better and be in a better position to do something about them."

• *The responsibilities of the client:* "In the end, counseling is not about talking, but about acting. If people are to manage their lives better, they usually have to act differently. I'd like to help you do that, but, of course, I can't do it for you."

• *Certain limits* (for instance, how free the client is to contact the helper between sessions): "Ordinarily my clients don't contact me between sessions, unless we prearrange it for a particular purpose. However, . . ."

• *The kind of influence the helper will exert:* "If I see you trying to avoid doing something that is for your own good, I will challenge you. Or rather I will invite you to challenge yourself. But I will not force you to do anything."

• *An understanding of the flexibility of the helping process:* "I have outlined what the helping process might look like. But, in the end, everything we do here should help you manage your problems better. There are no rigid rules about the helping process. We can do anything that is ethical and useful."

Obviously, you may not use this specific list or these words. Different clients have different needs, and what you share with them should be geared to their ability to assimilate and use it. Some clients might be helped by a great deal of information up front. Others might appreciate getting information in stages. For them an outline up front is enough; they can learn the details as they go along. In sum, the contract between you and your clients needs to be explicit and clear, but there are many ways of accomplishing this.

Sharing the Helping Model with Clients as Part of the Contract

An explanation of the helping model itself can be the vehicle for establishing the contract. Some counselors are reluctant to let the client know what the process is all about. Others seem to "fly by the seat of their pants." They can't tell clients what it's all about simply because they don't know what it's all about. Still others seem to think that knowledge of helping processes is secret or sacred or dangerous and should not be communicated to the client.

In my opinion, clients should be told as much about the model as they can assimilate.

> Psychotherapy need not be a secretive or esoteric procedure which is conducted on clients without their understanding. Indeed, clients are generally appreciative when we share with them the secrets of what we are attempting to accomplish, and are in a better position from there to collaborate and contribute. (Driscoll, 1984, p. 84)

Obviously, highly distressed clients should not be told to contain their anxiety until helpers teach them the helping model. But, like helpers, clients can use the model as a cognitive map to give themselves a sense of direction.

Explaining the counseling process does not lock the helper rigidly into a single way of doing things.

> Explaining our rationales does not lock us to them or require that we never change our minds or never acknowledge misdirections. When we do change directions, we can explain whatever new considerations are operative so that the changes make sense, and such changes are generally ac-

cepted with few problems. Changing as we consider things further may itself improve our credibility because clients, like anyone else, have more respect for those who are flexible than for those who consider themselves infallible. (Driscoll, 1984, p. 84)

Flexibility at the service of the client is a value. Effective helpers are natural, and it is only natural to change things when they are not working: "If what we're doing together is not working, then we can change it. This is all about helping you manage your concerns better."

Beyond a discussion of the contract, some helpers use a variety of techniques to give clients the "flavor" of the helping process. Studies show that written contracts, books, and videotapes can help clients "hit the decks running" (see Heesacker, 1986). Books have been written to help clients understand and prepare for the helping process. For instance, three social workers (Bruckner-Gordon, Gangi, & Wallman, 1988) use a combination of explanation, exercises, and examples to explore the process of therapy from start to finish. Some helpers use the overview chapter (Chapter 2) of this book to orient some clients. Others write their own pamphlets tailored to the way they do counseling. Tinsley, Bowman, and Ray (1988) demonstrated that audiotaped and videotaped presentations on the nature of counseling helped clients more than verbal or written presentations. "Here it is in action" is their approach (see Thompson & Mountain, 1987; Zwick & Attkisson, 1985).

Whatever is used to orient clients to counseling should take into consideration the state of each client and his or her ability to assimilate the material. A client in crisis should not be asked to sit down and review a tape, and a highly anxious client might find a videotape even more anxiety-provoking. In short, in counseling common sense should never take a holiday.

Chapter Four

Action I:
Helping Clients Act

Too much thinking about things can paralyze us. Shakespeare, in the person of Hamlet, talks about important enterprises, what he calls "enterprises of great pith and moment," losing "the name of action." Helping is an enterprise "of great pith and moment." It, too, can lose the name of action. It is my conviction that one of the principal reasons clients do not manage the problem situations of their lives effectively is their failure to *act* intelligently and prudently in their own best interests. Counselors fail by not helping their clients act. Helping becomes a process of too much talking and too little action.

Many approaches to helping discuss the need for clients to act and suggest ways of helping them do so, but too often action is tucked away at the end of the model, after all the talking is over—as if it were an afterthought. Too many clients do poorly because they fail to act or act ineptly on the good ideas produced in the counseling sessions. Frese and Sabini (1985) have suggested that psychology return to the pre-Watsonian notion of action as its fundamental unit.

The lack of outcome-achieving is not just an individual problem; it is a social problem. Magaro (1985) claims that deinstitutionalizing mental patients hasn't worked because of the lack of emphasis on behavior change in the community mental health movement. This is economic madness. Helping will not be cost-effective until fees for service are established through performance contracts based on *demonstrable behavior change*. Magaro refers to this as a rehabilitation model. He predicts the end of state-supported practitioners who fail to be responsible for behavior change.

Howard, Nance, and Myers (1987) endorse Argyris's (1957, 1962, 1964) list of tasks to be accomplished in moving toward adult maturity. All of them require, directly or indirectly, a "bias toward action" in people's lives:

1. Change from a passive to a more active state.
2. Change from a state of dependency on others to relative independence.
3. Change from behaving in a few ways to acting in many ways.
4. Change in interests—with erratic, shallow, and casual interests giving way to mature, strong, and enduring interests.
5. Change from a present-oriented time perspective to a perspective encompassing past, present, and future.
6. Change from solely subordinate relationships with others to relationships as equals or superiors.
7. Change from lack of a clear sense of self to a clearer sense of self and control of self (Howard, Nance, & Myers, 1987, pp. 90–91).

Helpers see many clients who have difficulties in one or more of these areas, clients who need assistance in becoming agents in their own lives.

EXPERIENCES, ACTIONS, AND EMOTIONS

It is useful to distinguish action from experience in general and from that extremely important category of experience called *affect*.

- Clients talk about their experiences—that is, what happens *to* them. If a client tells you that she was fired from her job, she is talking about her problem situation in terms of an experience.
- Clients talk about their behavior—that is, what they do or refrain from doing. If a client tells you that he has sex with underage boys, he is talking about his problem situation in terms of his behavior.
- Clients talk about their affect—that is, the feelings and emotions that arise from or are associated with either experiences or behavior. If a client tells you how depressed she gets after drinking bouts, she is talking about the affect associated with her problem situation.

In practice, of course, clients talk about all three together. Consider this example. A client says to a counselor in the personnel department of a large company: "I had one of the lousiest days of my life yesterday." At this point the counselor knows that something went wrong and that the client feels bad about it, but she knows relatively little about the specific experiences, behaviors, and feelings that made the day a horror for the client. However, the client continues: "Toward the end of the day my boss yelled at me for not getting my work done [an experience]. I lost my temper [emotion] and yelled right back at him [behavior]. He blew up and fired me [an experience for the client]. And now I feel awful [emotion] and am trying to find out [behavior] if I can get my job back." Note that the problem situation is much clearer once it is spelled out in terms of specific experiences, behaviors, and feelings related to specific situations.

Experiences

Most clients spend a fair amount of time, perhaps too much time, talking about what happens *to* them.

- "I get headaches a lot."
- "My ulcers act up when family members argue."
- "My wife doesn't understand me."

In contrast, they often talk about what *other people* do or fail to do, especially when others' behavior affects them adversely:

- "She doesn't do anything all day. The house is always a mess when I come home from work."
- "He tells his little jokes, and I'm always the butt of them."

As these examples suggest, clients often see themselves, rightly or wrongly, as victims of forces not in their control. If these forces are described as being *outside* them, they are *external*, or *overt*, experiences:

- "She never calls."
- "Company policy discriminates against women."
- "The economy is so lousy that there are no jobs."
- "No innovative teacher gets very far around here."

However, the "controlling" forces may be *internal*, or *covert*:

- "These feelings of depression come from nowhere and seem to suffocate me."
- "No matter what I do, I always feel hungry."
- "I just can't stop thinking of her."
- "It's the way I was educated. I was always taught to think of ethnics as inferior, and now it's just the way I think."

One reason that some clients are clients is that they see themselves as victims, as adversely affected by other people, the immediate social settings of life, society in its larger organizations and institutions, or cultural prescriptions. They feel that they are no longer in control of their lives. Therefore, they talk extensively about these experiences.

- "He treats me like dirt. But that's the way he is. He just doesn't care about people and their feelings at all. He's totally self-centered."
- "I can't control my appetite. I've heard that some people are like that. They have a different sort of metabolism. I must be one of those."
- "I keep hearing voices. They tell me to harm myself. I think they're coming from the devil."

For some clients, talking constantly about experiences is a way of avoiding responsibility: "It's not my fault. After all, these things are happening *to* me."

Behaviors

Some clients talk freely about their experiences, but are much less willing to talk about their behaviors, that is, what they do and don't do. The reason for this is rather simple and relates to most of us. While we may not feel accountable for our experiences, what happens to us, we realize at some level of our being that we are responsible for what we do or actively refrain from doing. Or at least we sense that the possibility of accountability is much higher when it comes to behavior.

- "When he ignores me, I go off by myself and cry."
- "I haven't even begun to look for a job. I know there are none in this city."

- "When I feel the depression coming on, I take some of the pills the doctor gave me."
- "When I get bored, I find some friends and go drinking."

Note that in each of these examples, the behavior is a reaction to some experience. Whether or not it is a creative reaction is another matter.

Affect

Affect refers to the feelings and emotions that proceed from, lead to, accompany, underlie, or give color to a client's experiences and behaviors.

- "I finished the term paper that I've been putting off for weeks and I feel great!"
- "I've been feeling sorry for myself ever since he left me."
- "I yelled at my mother last night and now I feel pretty ashamed of myself."
- "I've been anxious for the past few weeks, but I don't know why. I wake up feeling scared and then it goes away but comes back again several times during the day."

Of course, clients often express feelings without talking about them. Some clients feel deeply about things, but do their best to repress their feelings. But often there are cues or hints, whether verbal or nonverbal, of the feelings inside. A client who is talking listlessly and staring down at the floor may not say, in so many words, "I feel depressed." A dying person might express feelings of anger and depression without talking about them.

Some clients imply that their emotions have a life of their own and that they can do little or nothing to control them. This includes describing others as the causes of their emotions:

- "Whenever I see him with her, I feel hurt."
- "She can get my goat whenever she wants. She's always making me angry."
- "I can't help crying when I think of what they did to her."

One goal of the helping process is to help clients get out from under the burden of disabling feelings and emotions. As we shall see later on, people *can* learn how to control their emotions. Usually feelings and emotions cannot be controlled directly. Controlling them indirectly means controlling what goes on inside one's head. If I let myself dwell on the ways in which you have wronged me, I will inevitably get angry. But I can actively *refrain* from dwelling on such thoughts. On the other hand, some clients need to learn how to *express* emotions as part of their humanity and as a way of enriching their interactions with themselves and others.

Helpers tend not to have enough working knowledge about human emotions and the skills to help clients manage the affective dimensions of life well (Greenberg & Safran, 1989). On the other hand, some helpers err by focusing too exclusively on clients' emotions instead of dealing with them in the context of experiences and behaviors. In the best case, helpers can assist clients to become more effective agents in all dimensions of their lives.

THE MANY FACES OF ACTION

Behavior, or action, comprises the things I *do* and the things I actively *refrain from doing*. Five ways of categorizing action are important in the helping process. First, actions can be *internal*, that is, "inside the head" of the client, or *external*, actions that can be seen by others (whether they are actually seen or not). Second, actions can take place *during* the helping sessions themselves or *outside* the sessions in the client's day-to-day life. Third, these actions may be *informal* (not part of an overall plan) or *formal* (part of an overall plan). Fourth, there are actions that clients take to *influence* existing realities and actions they take to *accommodate* themselves to these realities. Finally, actions can lead to *helpful* outcomes or *unhelpful* outcomes (in the latter category I would include actions that seem to lead nowhere in particular).

All these modes include both acting and actively refraining from action. The following case will help put some flesh and bones on these abstract categories.

> Ben, 48, lost his wife and daughter in a train crash. At the time he saw a counselor, more than a year later, he was still suffering from shock and blaming himself for letting them go on the trip without him. He lived in a cluttered house, found it difficult to focus on work, and had given up most social contacts. From time to time he got involved in drinking bouts, mostly on weekends. He suffered from depression running from mild to severe, falling on occasion "into the pit," as he put it, when he would sit in a dark room, steeped in his misery. When "in the pit" he was convinced that his life was over. Although he had been a churchgoer, he now alternated between "screaming at God," taking what had happened as punishment for his "sins and his life of selfishness," and believing in nothing. Thoughts of suicide arose from time to time, and once he found himself staring at a bottle of sleeping pills his wife had used on occasion. But he always dismissed suicidal thoughts as beneath him.
>
> 　Late one night Ben was found wandering the streets in a daze. Brought to a local hospital, he had a brief session with a counselor the next morning. He agreed to come back to see the counselor because, as he told someone later, he found that she was "compassionate but not sentimental" and "seemed to have a great deal of common sense." In the counseling sessions, Liz, the counselor, found Ben to be quite bright but with little ambition and a tendency to sell himself short.

The five ways of categorizing actions are all illustrated in Ben's story. As we discuss each in turn, we'll come back to Ben's case.

External versus Internal Action

External Actions

External action (overt behavior) is action that can be witnessed by others, whether it is actually witnessed or not. Some examples of overt behavior:

- "When he called me a name, I punched him."
- "I haven't told my husband about the affair."
- "I read pornography a lot."

In our example, Ben performed a number of external actions that moved him along. He agreed to a session with Liz, talked about himself during the session, and at the end made a second appointment. All these external actions related to the helping process itself. Eventually he needed to find new ways of acting in his everyday life. For instance, he had to come to grips with interactions with friends, relatives, and co-workers.

Internal Actions

Many cognitive processes, those things that go on inside our heads, are really forms of internal behavior. These include such actions as thinking, expecting, attending to things inside or outside oneself, registering information, daydreaming, rehearsing behaviors in one's mind, turning things over in one's mind, making associations, imagining, thinking about one's emotions, thinking about one's thoughts or inner life, remembering, planning, deciding, and permitting thoughts to hang around (see Martin, Martin, Meyer, & Slemon, 1986). Here are some statements by clients that describe internal actions:

- "When he called me a name, I began thinking of the ways I could get back at him."
- "I like to daydream about having a child."
- "I never let myself think bad things about another person."
- "When she left me, I decided I'd find some way of getting back at her."
- "I try not to let thoughts of sex enter my mind."

People who feel that they have little or no control over what is going on inside their heads often describe internal actions as experiences:

- "I try to get into my work, but I just can't stop thinking of her and how she played me for a fool."
- "Sexual fantasies seem to keep popping up all the time. I just don't seem to have any control."
- "I know I get depressed and cry when I think of John on his deathbed, but I can't help thinking of him."

Attitudes and prejudices, as ingrained ways of thinking about things, are more like experiences than actions, but—as we know well—they can lead to powerful and sometimes destructive actions.

Part of the counseling process can be to help clients see that they can control their experiences, especially their internal or covert experiences, more than they first think. We can exercise control over many internal actions just as we can over our external actions, and we can work at changing our attitudes and prejudices. Indeed, some forms of therapy, such as Ellis's (Ellis & Dryden, 1987), are based on learning how to control what goes on inside one's head. In our example, Ben discovered that he was allowing himself—almost *encouraging* himself—to dwell morbidly on the death of his wife and daughter. He dwelled on thoughts that made him feel guilty. Learning how to refrain from such thoughts became one of the goals of counseling. Liz helped him find ways of remembering and mourning his wife and daughter that uplifted his spirit instead of destroying it. He discovered that he had not really mourned their deaths. Instead, he had indulged in guilt and self-recrimination.

For most clients, managing problems and developing opportunities demand a combination of thinking right (doing the right things inside their heads) and doing right externally. Rusk (1989) put it this way:

> Deliberate self-change requires a willingness to: (a) stand back from yourself far enough to question your familiar beliefs and attitudes about yourself and others, and (b) persist at awkward and risky experiments designed to increase your self-respect and satisfy your needs.

To manage his life better, Ben needed both kinds of action.

Actions within the Helping Sessions versus Actions Outside

Inside Helping Sessions

Clients need to participate in and *own* their part of the helping process. It cannot remain something that is done to them, something they merely experience. Ben did a number of things during the first helping session. He risked telling his story for the first time since the accident. And, struck by Liz's non-pushy, commonsense approach, he even let himself cry. These actions made him feel relieved and prompted him to set up another appointment.

I have expressed reservations about the amount of talking and the lack of acting that characterizes too much of what passes for helping. Without taking that back, I also know that talking within the session can be a form of outcome-producing action. Clients who have kept problems to themselves for years can make significant breakthroughs just by talking about them. Moreover, as indicated earlier, helping can be, even principally, a social-emotional reeducation process. Many clients have changed their negative views of themselves and made improvements in their interpersonal styles through their interactions with me. For instance, one client significantly altered his bossy, confrontational style by first changing his style with me. In most cases, however, the ultimate fruits of social-emotional reeducation lie in changed behavior outside the helping sessions.

Outside Helping Sessions

I know someone who participated in a counseling group for over 15 years. He looked forward to the meetings and felt bad if he had to miss one. Indeed, the group was an important part of his social life. But there is some question as to how effectively he translated what he learned inside the group to his everyday life. Now, it was his life, and he could do what he wanted with it. For me, however, becoming dependent on the helping process is itself a problem.

When Ben left the hospital, he went home, and, after a great deal of hesitation, called a sister who he knew would soon find out about his hospital stay and be alarmed. The phone call was very brief, but he did think of someone outside himself and he did, at least for the moment, reestablish a social contact. He did not have a "grand plan," but his experience in the hospital promoted him to *do something useful* and to do it right away.

Formal versus Informal Action

As illustrated in the overview of the helping model, informal action—as opposed to action based on some specific plan—can start right from the first interview. In some cases, more is accomplished through informal action than through formal planning. A friend of mine who is highly successful did not set demanding career goals and then devise a plan for achieving them. Instead, he took an incremental approach. He said yes to offers that felt a little bit beyond his current level of expertise. He developed a pattern of stretching himself bit by bit. His approach to his career has been an informal, incremental approach, but it has been action-based and highly effective. Some clients prefer mostly informal actions and goals. Some are helped by formal planning involving explicit goals and action programs. Some need a combination of the two.

Ben began by doing a number of little things differently—things he didn't even discuss with the counselor. People at work had been very indulgent with him since the tragedy. They didn't expect him to be 100% himself. On his own, however, Ben, who had been coming to work late, started showing up on time. He still drank some, but not nearly as much as before. He took walks. Though solitary, these represented an advance over sitting in the dark of the house brooding. These actions and others were not part of a plan. In fact, Ben did not reflect on them a great deal. They were signs that something of the old Ben were beginning to stir. And his sessions with Liz helped trigger them.

On the other hand, actions that are part of a formal plan can be most useful. One of my clients, in rebuilding his life after a serious automobile accident, very deliberately planned both a rehabilitation program and a career change. Keeping to a schedule of carefully planned actions not only helped him keep his spirits up but also helped him accomplish a succession of goals.

Influencing Realities versus Accommodating to Them

Weisz, Rothbaum, and Blackburn (1984; also see Rothbaum, Weisz, & Snyder, 1982; Weisz, 1983) use the terms *primary* and *secondary control* to discuss the cultural bias found in North America related to people's ability to control their destinies.

> There are at least two general paths to a feeling of control. In primary control, individuals enhance their rewards by influencing existing realities (e.g., other people, circumstances, symptoms, or behavior problems). In secondary control, individuals enhance their rewards by accommodating to existing realities and maximizing satisfaction or goodness of fit with things as they are. American psychologists have written extensively about control, but have generally defined it only in terms of its primary form. (p. 955)

Helping is the art of the possible. While most clients can do more to control their lives than they actually do, this does not mean that clients must substitute taking charge of everything for passivity and dependency.

> Debbie learned, to her chagrin, that she and her husband had more areas of incompatibility than she had imagined. Though she knew that he liked his work, she had no idea that it was his passion. Work came before almost everything else. However, she did not think that she could make him change. A counselor helped her find ways of coping. Instead of feeling sorry for herself, she developed friends and interests outside the home, activities in which he did not participate. In her mind, this was not the perfect solution. But it certainly made life fuller and more livable.

For some clients, a great deal of primary control might be possible; for others, secondary control might be the only realistic option; for most, the best available course is a combination of the two. Clients, like ourselves, have limitations. Like ourselves, they are in many ways not captains of their own fates. Some would say that what Debbie did amounted to giving up. Others would see it as practicing the art of the possible.

Although Ben influenced many of the realities of his life, he accommodated to others. While he did reestablish better relationships at work and some minimal social interactions with closer relatives (an occasional dinner at his sister's, for example), he also accommodated to a more solitary life. Perhaps he believed that no one could take the place of the two people he had lost, or perhaps he had no desire to develop further relationships.

Or perhaps he found something satisfying in a life that was in fact more solitary than it was lonely. Instead of brooding, he became more meditative and came to enjoy his newfound inner life. He was neither a hermit nor the more social person he had been before the tragedy. Although Liz had noted his apparent lack of ambition, Ben did not want to discuss his job or career prospects. He admitted, at least to himself, that he could be more, but he also realized that he did not particularly want to be. Even though he was underemployed, he kept the same job, and the company was glad to keep him.

Liz did not push Ben to explore the areas of life with which he was satisfied. Could he have ended up living a "fuller" life had he accommodated less and exercised more influence on realities? Perhaps. But there are no formulas.

Action and Outcomes

To deserve the name of problem-managing or opportunity-developing action, action must lead to client-enhancing outcomes. What difference does it make if the clients leave helping sessions with smiles on their faces and songs in their hearts if their problems are not managed more effectively? (Unless the originating problem was the lack of a smile and the absence of a song.)

This issue has already been explored in Chapter 1 in the discussion on the goals of helping. Ideally, helping is both an effective and an efficient process. It is effective if clients manage problems and develop opportunities better. It is efficient if they do not waste a lot of energy getting to their goals. Thus, some client activities are a waste of time because they lead nowhere in particular. They may be *actions*, but they do not lead to helpful *outcomes*.

Early in my career, one of my clients kept a detailed record of everything that happened in the counseling sessions and everything outside that seemed in any way related. Good idea? Probably not. It took up a great deal of his time and in the end was probably his way of putting off problem-managing action. It made him focus excessively on the helping process itself instead of on behavioral change in his everyday life. He was spinning his wheels.

Even purposeful action can be relatively pointless in terms of the goals of helping. A client of a colleague of mine set goals and acted to accomplish them, but the goals had little to do with her principal concerns. For instance, she decided that looking more fashionable and getting a degree would help her with her self-image. She worked hard at both sets of goals and accomplished a great deal. But self-image was not one of her major problems. More significantly, her rather acerbic interpersonal style turned people off—family members, friends, co-workers. But she did not pursue any substantial goals in this area. Perhaps she thought, at some level of her being, that a better self-image would take care of everything. In fact, her stormy relationships persisted. Reflecting on this case some months after she terminated the helping process, my friend mused, "I let her get away with murder."

Ben was fairly efficient in the use of counseling time. There were not many sessions—perhaps eight in all, spread out over a year's time. In the sessions he saw many things as they really were—his morbidity, the stupidity of total social withdrawal, the corrosive nature of his guilt—and he worked gradually and quietly to reestablish his equilibrium. He did not pursue issues during the sessions just to talk. He did not spin his wheels. He learned a few things, and he acted on his learnings. As he left his eighth session, he somehow knew it would be his last. And it was.

THE MANY FACES OF INERTIA

What keeps clients from acting on their own behalf? In physics, the law of inertia states, in part, that a body at rest tends to stay at rest unless something happens to move it along. In counseling, inertia refers to clients' reluctance to act. Many clients are in trouble or stay in trouble because, for whatever reason, they are "at rest." The sources of inertia are many, ranging from pure sloth to paralyzing fear. In trying to help clients act, you will come up against the many faces of inertia. What is said here is meant to give you the flavor of inertia, not to exhaust its possibilities. Most of us can start by examining inertia in our own lives.

Let us not be quick to blame our clients for their inertia. Inertia permeates life and is one of the principal mechanisms for keeping individuals, organizations, and institutions mired in the psychopathology of the average. A friend of mine is a consultant to organizations. He told me about one larger organization in which he worked with senior managers to transform the place. They did it right: diagnosis, identification of key issues, establishment of objectives, formulation of strategies, drawing up of plans. My friend went away satisfied with a job well done. He returned six months later to see how the changes were working out. But there were no changes: No one from the president on down had acted on their plans. The managers looked sheepish and gave the excuses we all give—too busy, other things came up, couldn't get in touch with the other guy, ran into obstacles—the litany is endless. And this was a fairly successful company!

Earlier I noted that Howard, Nance, and Myers (1987) adapt a "situational leadership" model to counseling and therapy. The model identifies three sources of client inertia: lack of competence, lack of confidence, and lack of willingness. This in turn suggests three ways in which counselors can be helpful: by helping clients discover ways of developing competence, including training as a form of treatment (for instance, training in inter-personal skills); by providing support and helping clients find ways of bol-stering their confidence (for instance, through "little successes" related to the counseling process itself); and by challenging clients to act in their own behalf.

Often, clients are clients because they have problems with self-respon-sibility. The list of ways in which we avoid taking responsibility is endless. We'll examine several of them here: passivity, learned helplessness, dis-abling self-talk, and getting trapped in vicious circles.

Passivity

Early in the history of modern psychology, William James remarked that few people bring to bear more than about 10% of their human potential on the problems and challenges of living. Others since James, while changing the percentages somewhat, have said substantially the same thing, and few have challenged their statements (Maslow, 1968). It is prob-ably not an exaggeration to say that unused human potential constitutes a more serious social problem than emotional disorders, since it is more widespread. Maslow (1968) suggests that what is usually called "normal" in psychology "is really a psychopathology of the average, so undramatic and so widely spread that we don't even notice it ordinarily" (p. 16). Many clients you will see, besides having more or less serious problems in living, will also probably be chronic victims of the psychopathology of the average.

One of the most important ingredients in the generation and perpetu-ation of the psychopathology of the average is passivity, the failure of peo-ple to take responsibility for themselves in one or more developmental areas of life or in various life situations that call for action. Schiff (1975) discusses four kinds of passivity: (1) *doing nothing*, that is, not respond-ing to problems and options; (2) *overadapting*, or uncritically accepting the goals and solutions suggested by others; (3) engaging in *random* or *agitated behavior*, or acting aimlessly; and (4) *becoming incapacitated or violent*, that is, shutting down or blowing up.

> When Zelda and Jerzy first noticed small signs that things were not going right in their relationship, they did nothing. They noticed certain inci-dents, mused on them for a while, and then forgot about them. They lacked the communication skills to engage each other immediately and to explore what was happening.

Zelda and Jerzy had both learned to remain passive before the little crises of life, not realizing how much their passivity would ultimately contribute to their downfall (see Egan, 1985, pp. 167–170). Endless unmanaged problems led to major blow-ups until they decided to end their marriage.

Learned Helplessness

Seligman's (1975) concept of "learned helplessness" and its relationship to depression has received a great deal of attention since he first introduced it. Clients may have learned to believe from an early age that there is nothing they can do about certain life situations. Obviously there are degrees in feelings of helplessness. Some clients feel minimally helpless (and minimally depressed) and come to a helper primarily because they believe that getting help will be a more effective or efficient way of facing some problem or difficulty. Other clients feel totally helpless and overwhelmed by the difficulties of life and fall into deep, almost intractable depression.

Bennet and Bennet (1984) see the positive side of hopelessness. If the problems clients face are indeed out of their control, they say, then it is not helpful for them to have an illusory sense of control, unjustly assign themselves responsibility, and indulge in excessive expectations. Somewhat paradoxically, they found that challenging clients' tendency to blame themselves for everything actually fostered realistic hope and change. The trick is helping clients learn what is and what is not in their control. A man with a physical disability may not be able to do anything about the disability itself, but he does have some control over how he views his disability and the power to pursue certain life goals despite it. One answer to learned helplessness, as Simons and her colleagues (1985) have suggested, is "learned resourcefulness."

Disabling Self-Talk

As has been shown by Ellis (1974, 1979; Ellis & Dryden, 1987) and others (Grieger & Boyd, 1980), people often get into the habit of engaging in disabling self-talk, thus talking themselves into passivity. They say to themselves such things as

- "I can't do it."
- "I can't cope."
- "I don't have what it takes to engage in that program; it's too hard."
- "It won't work."

Such self-defeating conversations with themselves get people into trouble in the first place and then prevent them from getting out. Ways of helping clients to manage their disabling self-talk will be discussed in later chapters.

Vicious Circles

Pyszczynski and Greenberg (1987) developed a theory about self-defeating behavior and depression. They said that people whose actions fail to get them what they want can easily lose a sense of self-worth and become mired in a vicious circle of guilt and depression.

> Consequently, the individual falls into a pattern of virtually constant self-focus, resulting in intensified negative affect, self-derogation, further negative outcomes, and a depressive self-focusing style. Eventually, these factors lead to a negative self-image, which may take on value by providing an explanation for the individual's plight and by helping the individual avoid further disappointments. The depressive self-focusing style then maintains and exacerbates the depressive disorder. (p. 122)

It does sound depressing. One client, Amanda, fit this theory to a tee. She had aspirations of moving up the career ladder where she worked. She was very enthusiastic and dedicated, but she was unaware of the "gentleman's club" politics of the company in which she worked and didn't know how to "work the system." She kept doing the things that she thought should get her ahead. They didn't. Finally, she got down on herself, began making mistakes in the things that she usually did well, and made things worse by constantly talking about how she "was stuck," thus alienating her friends. By the time she saw a counselor, she felt defeated and depressed. She was about to give up.

Inertia as Staying Disorganized

I once knew someone who lived out of his car. No one knew exactly where he spent the night. The car was chaos, and so was his life. He was always going to get his career, family relations, and love life in order, but he never did. Living in disorganization was his way of putting off life decisions.

Like my acquaintance, some people seem to choose to remain disorganized. Ferguson (1987b) paints a picture that may well remind us of ourselves, at least at times.

> When we saddle ourselves with innumerable little hassles and problems, they distract us from considering the possibility that we may have chosen the wrong job, the wrong profession, or the wrong mate. If we are drowning in unfinished housework, it becomes much easier to ignore the fact that we have become estranged from family life. Putting off an important project—painting a picture, writing a book, drawing up a business plan—is a way of protecting ourselves from the possibility that the result may not be quite as successful as we had hoped. Setting up our lives to insure a significant level of disorganization allows us to continue to think of ourselves as inadequate or partially-adequate people who don't have to take on the real challenges of adult behavior. (p. 46)

Many things can be behind this unwillingness to get our lives in order, like defending ourselves against a fear of succeeding.

Driscoll (1984, pp. 112–117) has provided us with a great deal of insight into this problem. He sees inertia as a form of control. He uses a car rental agency's motto—"Let us put you in the driver's seat"—to make the point of client action. He says that if we tell some clients to jump into the driver's seat, they will compliantly do so—at least until the journey gets too rough. The most effective strategy, he says, is to show clients that they have been in the driver's seat right along: "Our task as therapists is not to talk our clients into taking control of their lives, but to confirm the fact that they already are and always will be." That is, inertia, in the form of staying disorganized, is a form of control. The client is actually *successful*, sometimes against great odds, at remaining disorganized and thus preserving inertia.

Given the many faces of inertia, we cannot assume that clients will take action. In collaboration with them, we need to build action into the helping process right from the start.

SELF-EFFICACY

The opposite of passivity is "agency" (Egan, 1970), "assertiveness," or "self-efficacy" (Bandura, 1977a, 1980, 1982, 1986; Bandura & Schunk, 1981; Bernier & Avard, 1986; Clifford, 1983; Devins & Edwards, 1988; Lee, 1983; Strauss & Ryan, 1987). Bandura has suggested that people's expectations of themselves have a great deal to do with their *willingness* to put forth effort to cope with difficulties, the *amount* of effort they will expend, and their *persistence* in the face of obstacles. In particular, people tend to take action if two conditions are fulfilled:

1. They see that certain behavior will most likely lead to certain desirable results or accomplishments (outcome expectations).
2. They are reasonably sure that they can successfully engage in such behavior (self-efficacy expectations).

For instance, Yolanda not only believes that participation in a rather painful and demanding physical rehabilitation program following an accident and surgery will literally help her get on her feet again (an outcome expectation), but also believes that she has what it takes to inch her way through the program (a self-efficacy expectation). She therefore enters the program with a very positive attitude. Yves, on the other hand, is not convinced that an uncomfortable chemotherapy program will prevent his cancer from spreading and give him some quality living time (a negative outcome expectation), even though he knows he could endure it, so he says no to the doctors. Xavier *is* convinced that a series of radiation and chemotherapy treatments would help him (a positive outcome expectation), but he does not feel that he has the courage to go through with them (a negative self-efficacy expectation). He, too, refuses the treatment.

People's sense of self-efficacy can be strengthened in a variety of ways:

- *Success.* They act and see that their behavior actually produces results. Often success in a small endeavor will give them the courage to try something more difficult.
- *Modeling.* They see others doing what they are trying to do and are encouraged to try themselves. For example, a counselor in the hospital can get Xavier to talk to patients who are "toughing it out" in the treatments.
- *Encouragement.* Others exhort them to try, challenge them, and support their efforts.
- *Reducing fear and anxiety.* If people are overly fearful that they will fail, they generally do not act. Therefore, procedures that reduce fear and anxiety help heighten the sense of self-efficacy.

As a helper, you can do a great deal to help people develop a sense of agency or self-efficacy. First of all, you can help them challenge self-defeating beliefs and attitudes about themselves and substitute realistic beliefs about their ability to act. This includes helping them reduce the kinds of fears and anxieties that keep them from mobilizing their resources. Second, you can help them develop the working knowledge, life skills, and resources they need to succeed. Third, you can help them challenge themselves to take reasonable risks and support them when they do.

There is a rich and growing literature on self-efficacy. It makes sense to stay in touch with it since it deals with the most ticklish of all problems, clients' failure to act. There are critics of self-efficacy theory (Bandura, 1984; Eastman & Marzillier, 1984; Marzillier & Eastman, 1984), but both academicians and practitioners in general find it most helpful. The usefulness of the self-efficacy construct is not limited to counseling. O'Leary (1985) has noted that perceived self-efficacy can play a significant role in the control of smoking, the management of pain, control of eating, successful recovery from heart attack, and adherence to preventive health programs.

SELF-REGULATION

While self-efficacy deals with how clients think about action, self-regulation deals with how they go about it. There is a growing literature on self-regulation (Bandura, 1986, pp. 335–389; Kanfer & Schefft, 1988), including books on practical self-direction in everyday life (see Watson & Tharp, 1989; Williams & Long, 1988). Let's start with theory and move to practice.

Self-Regulation Theory

Bandura (1986) does not see self-regulation as a feat of will power. Rather, he focuses on a group of subprocesses that contribute to self-regulation. These include such things as

- *self-observation*, which provides the information necessary for setting realistic performance standards and for evaluating ongoing changes in behavior;
- setting *internal standards* for judging and guiding one's actions;
- identifying *incentives* for one's own actions;
- setting one's own *improvement goals*, even when not encouraged by others to do so;
- *recognizing* and *evaluating* one's accomplishments at the service of self-respect and self-satisfaction.

Kanfer and Schefft (1988), too, underscore the importance of learning the processes and skills of self-regulation:

> An effective therapy program has at its core the development of self-regulatory skills to help the client reach realistic and attainable goals that meet his needs and are acceptable to the society in which he lives. This presupposes the goal of changing regulatory processes rather than just behavioral outcomes or products in a specific situation. The effectiveness of self-management therapies must be judged on process measures, not just product or outcome measures. (p. 59)

In other words, counselors not only can help clients achieve therapeutic outcomes but also can change the way they go about getting to these outcomes. There are all sorts of benefits for those who exercise reasonable self-control. Their self-esteem goes up, they feel freer, they are motivated to try things, they discourage others in their attempts to exercise control over them, their sense of self-efficacy and of autonomy is increased, social acceptance follows, and control in one area tends to spread to control in other areas.

Self-Regulation Practice: Helping Clients Become Problem Solvers

The literature suggest a wide variety of ways in which counselors can help clients to become more effective in self-regulation. Counselors can help clients to

- become sensitive to cues indicating that some kind of self-regulation is called for,
- control inner behavior, such as resisting intrusive thoughts, self-doubt, and self-defeating urges and temptations,
- control emotions,
- identify problems as they begin to develop,
- set goals,
- establish a set of values to act as standards of evaluation,
- develop an effective planning style,

- turn good intentions into actions,
- engage in reasonable self-criticism, and
- learn the techniques of self-reward.

In short, counselors can help clients become better problem solvers—better problem managers and opportunity developers. Although this book is about a model and methods counselors can use to help clients, more fundamentally, it is about a problem-solving model and methods that clients can use to help themselves.

When people are presented with the basic steps of a problem-solving model, they tend to say: "Oh yes, I know that." Recognition of the logic of problem solving, however, is a far cry from using it.

> In ordinary affairs we usually muddle about, doing what is habitual and customary, being slightly puzzled when it sometimes fails to give the intended outcome, but not stopping to worry much about the failures because there are still too many other things still to do. Then circumstances conspire against us and we find ourselves caught failing where we must succeed—where we cannot withdraw from the field, or lower our self-imposed standards, or ask for help, or throw a tantrum. Then we may begin to suspect that we face a problem. . . . *An ordinary person almost never approaches a problem systematically and exhaustively unless he has been specifically educated to do so.* (Miller, Galanter, & Pribram, 1960, pp. 171, 174; emphasis added)

Over the past few years there has been a great deal of interest in the problem-solving abilities of people in general and of clients in particular (see Heppner, 1988; Heppner & Anderson, 1985; Heppner, Neal, & Larson, 1984). Furthermore, problem solving has been a useful approach with children as well as adults, and the technology for training children in problem-solving skills has been developed (Shure & Spivack, 1978; Spivack, Platt, & Shure, 1976; Spivack & Shure, 1974; Urbain & Kendall, 1980).

Clients often are poor problem solvers—or whatever problem-solving ability they have tends to disappear in times of crisis. The function of the helper is to get clients to apply problem solving to their current problem situations and, at the same time, help them adopt more effective approaches to future problems in living. So it is not just a question of using a problem-management framework to help clients work out *this* set of problem situations. Counseling can also be a training *process* whereby clients learn to do for themselves what counselors are helping them to do.

THE SELF-HELP MOVEMENT

We live in a society that has become somewhat suspicious of and confrontational toward professional help. Further, there is a growing realization that help must begin at home, that is, with the person with the problem. In medicine there is the wellness movement, which is based on the idea that we are in charge of our own bodies. The analog in mental health is the self-help movement: help can be found with your fellow sufferers. Since self-help methods tend to be pragmatic and action-oriented, it is only right to discuss them in a chapter on action.

Self-Help Books

Studies show that many helpers use self-help treatment books in conjunction with counseling. There are at least two schools of thought on clients' use of such books. One school is somewhat pessimistic about their value and strongly suggests caution (see Forest, 1988; Rosen, 1987). Another school suggests that many helpers believe that such books can, under certain circumstances, help clients a great deal (see Holtje, 1988; Starker, 1988a, 1988b). Mahalik and Kivlighan (1988) urge helpers to distinguish between "succeeders" and "failers" in the use of do-it-yourself manuals, while Holtje and Starker call for an evaluation of do-it-yourself manuals themselves so that the wheat can be separated from the chaff. The point to be made is this: If you use self-help books in conjunction with your counseling, make sure that you use tested materials and that your clients are likely to benefit from their use.

Self-Help Groups

Across the country groups have been established to help people cope with almost every conceivable problem. Twenty years ago, Hurvitz (1970, 1974) claimed that these groups were more effective and efficient than other forms of helping: "It is likely that more people have been and are being helped by [self-help groups] than have been and are being helped by all types of professionally trained psychotherapists combined, with far less theorizing and analyzing and for much less money" (1970, p. 48). His hypothesis probably still holds true today. A conservative estimate holds that over six million people are currently participating in such groups (Jacobs & Goodman, 1989). This figure might surprise a lot of professionals, Jacobs and Goodman say, because most groups are "quiet, small, and local" (p. 536). They range from such traditional groups as Alcoholics Anonymous to groups that help women cope with the aftermath of a mastectomy operation, from Weight Watchers to newly formed groups of people who are HIV positive but have not yet developed AIDS.

By definition these groups have the flavor of action. An issue of the *Self-Help Reporter* (Fall, 1985, p. 5) describes the elements of the pragmatic, democratic ethos of self-help groups:

1. A noncompetitive, cooperative orientation.
2. An anti-elite, antibureaucratic focus.
3. An emphasis on the indigenous—people who have the problem know a lot about it from the "inside," from experiencing it.

4. Do what you can do. One day at a time. You can't solve everything at once.
5. A shared, often circulating leadership.
6. Being helped through helping [others] . . . no necessary antagonism between *altruism* and *egoism.*
7. Helping is not a commodity to be bought and sold.
8. An accent on empowerment—control over one's own life.
9. A strong optimism regarding the ability to change.
10. Small . . . is the place to begin and the unit to build upon.
11. A critical stance toward professionalism, which is often seen as pretentious, purist, distant, and mystifying. Self-helpers like simplicity and informality.
12. An emphasis on the consumer. . . . The consumer is a producer of help and services.
13. Helping is at the center—knowing how to receive help, give help, and help yourself. Self-victimization is antithetical to the ethos.
14. The group is the key—de-isolation is critical.

The bias toward action of self-help groups might well be built in, because there is some evidence that those who join such groups are more motivated to take an active role in changing their lives (Levy, 1988). Self-help groups also use peer pressure to get passive group members to act.

Professional helpers tend to ignore self-help groups. Whether this is in reaction to the movement's suspicion of professionals is another matter.

> Lacking familiarity with the potential of the self-help groups to be a primary treatment of choice for any number of serious personal problems, the psychologist sometimes views them as mere inexpensive, naive adjuncts to therapy—hand-holding, morale-boosting, do-no-harm meetings of fellow sufferers. (Jacobs & Goodman, 1989, p. 536)

This, the authors say, is a mistake. There is a place for professionals, for the self-help movement, and for partnerships between the two.

> We will argue that self-help groups are well on their way to becoming a major and legitimate format for delivering mental health care in this country. If we psychologists do not play a significant part in this development, other professionals will, perhaps dropping our national relevance a notch. (p. 536)

Placing self-help groups in the context of the current health care revolution, the authors hypothesize that such groups will become a legitimate part of the overall mental and physical health-care scene, that they will grow and flourish, and that professionals will get involved with them without taking them over. I strongly urge helpers to stay in touch with developments in health care, in both the physical and social-emotional dimensions, and to learn about and get involved with the self-help movement. On the other hand, I do not encourage mindless referrals of your clients to any group whatsoever. As with self-help treatment books, it is a question of the right group for the right person. Riordan and Beggs (1987) lay down some commonsense criteria for helping clients find the group that makes sense for them. They also claim that not every client would profit from a self-help group and that for many clients the self-help group should be seen as an adjunct to rather than a replacement for personal counseling. This contention, of course, would be challenged by strict self-help group advocates.

HELPERS AS AGENTS

Driscoll (1984, pp. 91–97) discusses the temptation of helpers to respond to the passivity of their clients with a kind of passivity of their own, a "Sorry, it's up to you" stance. This, he says, is a mistake.

> A client who refuses to accept responsibility thereby invites the therapist to take over. In remaining passive, the therapist foils the invitation, thus forcing the client to take some initiative or to endure the silence. A passive stance is therefore a means to avoid accepting the wrong sorts of responsibility. It is generally ineffective, however, as a long-run approach. Passivity by a therapist leaves the client feeling unsupported and thus further impairs the already fragile therapeutic alliance. Troubled clients, furthermore, are not merely unwilling but generally and in important ways unable to take appropriate responsibility. A passive countermove is therefore counterproductive, for neither therapist nor client generates solutions, and both are stranded together in a muddle of entangling inactivity. (p. 91)

In order to help others act, helpers must be agents and doers in the helping process, not mere listeners and responders. In my opinion, the best helpers are active in the helping sessions. They keep looking for ways to enter the worlds of their clients, to get them to become more active in the sessions, to get them to own more of it, to help them see the need for action—action in their heads and action outside their heads—in their everyday lives. And they do all this without violating the values outlined in Chapter 3. They don't push reluctant clients, thus turning reluctance into resistance, but neither do they sit around waiting for reluctant clients to act. They take seriously the collaborative nature of helping without taking over what the client should do.

I have suggested that the helping model itself can provide clients with a means of taking action. Before turning to the elaboration and illustration of each step of the model, we next focus on the basic communication skills helpers need to deliver the model in interactions with clients.

Chapter Five

Communication Skills I: Attending and Listening

Since the helping process involves a great deal of communication between helper and client, it goes without saying that relevant communication skills are extremely important for the helper at every stage and step of the helping process. These skills are *not* the helping process itself, but they are essential tools for developing relationships and interacting with clients in helping them manage their problems in living. This chapter deals with the first set of these skills, attending and listening. Chapter 6 deals with a second set, empathy and probing. Chapter 9 deals with a third set related to helping clients identify blind spots and develop new perspectives.

These skills are not special skills peculiar to helping. Rather, they are extensions of the kinds of skills all of us need in our everyday interpersonal relationships. Ideally, helpers-to-be would enter training programs with this basic set of interpersonal communication skills in place, and training would simply help them adapt the skills to the helping process. Unfortunately, this is often not the case. That is why these skills are reviewed here before the helping process itself is explored in greater detail.

Since communication skills are not ends in themselves but means or instruments to be used in achieving helping outcomes, there has been a growing concern about the overemphasis of communication skills and techniques. Rogers (1980) spoke out against what he called the "appalling consequences" (p. 139) of an overemphasis on the microskills of helping. Instead of being a fully human endeavor, helping was, in his view, being reduced to its bits and pieces. Some helper training programs focus almost exclusively on these skills. As a result, trainees know how to communicate but not how to help.

Hills (1984) discussed an "integrative" versus a "technique" approach to training in communication skills. In an integrative approach:

- skills and techniques become extensions of the helper's humanity and not just bits of helping technology;
- communication skills and helping techniques serve the goals of the helping process;
- skills and techniques are permeated with and driven by the values discussed in Chapter 3.

Therefore, "communication skills learned, practiced, and used in a fully human way at the service of the helping relationship, process, and outcomes" is the goal of training in these skills.

In worthwhile helping interviews, attending, listening, responding with empathy, probing, and challenging skills are woven together at the service of the client. However, they are treated separately here to emphasize certain points.

To begin, we need to distinguish between attending and listening:

• *Attending* refers to the ways in which helpers can be with their clients, both physically and psychologically.
• *Listening* refers to the ability of helpers to capture and understand the messages clients communicate, whether these messages are transmitted verbally or nonverbally, clearly or vaguely.

Let's examine each of these skills in detail.

ATTENDING: ACTIVELY BEING WITH CLIENTS

At some of the more dramatic moments of life, simply being with another person is extremely important. If a friend of yours is in the hospital, sometimes just your presence there can make a difference, even if conversation is impossible. Similarly, simply being with a bereaved friend can be very comforting to him or her, even if little is said. By the same token, being ignored is often painful: The averted face is too often a sign of the averted heart. Given how sensitive most of us are to others' attention or inattention, it is paradoxical how insensitive we can be at times about attending to others.

Helping and other deep interpersonal transactions demand a certain intensity of presence. Attending, or the way you orient yourself physically and psychologically to clients, contributes to this presence. Effective attending does two things: It tells clients that you are with them, and it puts you in a position to listen.

Clients read cues that indicate the quality of your presence to them. Your nonverbal behavior influences clients for better or worse. For instance, attentive presence can invite or encourage them to trust you, open up, and explore the significant dimensions of their problems. Half-hearted presence can promote distrust and lead to clients' reluctance to reveal themselves to you.

There are various "levels" of attending to clients: (1) the *microskills* level, (2) the *body language* level, and (3) the *presence* level.

Level 1: Microskills

There are certain microskills helpers can use in attending to clients. While this microskills level is the most superficial level of attending, it does serve as a starting point. The microskills can be summarized in the acronym **S-O-L-E-R.**

• **S:** Face the client **Squarely**; that is, adopt a posture that indicates involvement. In North American culture, facing another person squarely is often considered a basic posture of involvement. It usually says: "I'm available to you; I choose to be with you." Turning your body away from another person while you talk to him or her can lessen your degree of contact with that person. Even when people are seated in a circle, they usually try in some way to turn toward the individuals to whom they are speaking. The word "squarely" here may be taken literally or metaphorically. What is important is that the bodily orientation you adopt convey the message that you are involved with the client. If, for any reason, facing the person squarely is too threatening, then an angled position may be called for. The point is the quality of your attention.

• **O:** Adopt an **Open** posture. Crossed arms and crossed legs can be signs of lessened involvement with or availability to others. An open posture can be a sign that you're open to the client and to what he or she has to say. In North American culture an open posture is generally seen as a nondefensive posture. It can say: "I'm open to you right now." Ridley and Asbury (1988) see it as a sign of confidence and involvement: "Perhaps clients view counselors with open posture as more secure and, therefore, more capable" (p. 257). Again, the word "open" can be taken literally or metaphorically. If your legs are crossed, this does not mean that you are not involved with the client. But it is important to ask yourself: "To what degree does my present posture communicate openness and availability to the client?"

• **L:** Remember that it is possible at times to **Lean** toward the other. Watch two people in a restaurant who are intimately engaged in conversation. Very often they are both leaning forward over the table as a natural sign of their involvement. The main thing is to remember that the upper part of your body is on a hinge. It can move toward a person and back away. In North American culture a slight inclination toward a person is often seen as saying, "I'm with you, I'm interested in you and in what you have to say." Leaning back (the severest form of which is a slouch) can be a way of saying, "I'm not entirely with you" or "I'm bored." Leaning too far forward, however, or doing so too soon, may frighten a client. It can be seen as a way of placing a demand on the other for some kind of closeness or intimacy. In a wider sense, the word "lean" can refer to a kind of bodily flexibility or responsiveness that enhances your communication with a client. Hermansson and his associates (1988, p. 152) suggest that leaning forward or backward provides "subtle adjustments toward maintaining an equilibrium of involvement" with the client.

• **E:** Maintain good **Eye** contact. In North American culture, fairly steady eye contact is not unnatural for people deep in conversation. It is not the same as staring. Again, watch two people deep in conversation. You may be amazed at the amount of direct eye contact. Maintaining good eye contact with a client is another way of saying, "I'm with you; I want to hear what you have to say." Obviously this principle is not violated if you occasionally look away. But if you catch yourself looking away frequently, your behavior may give you a hint about some kind of reluctance to be with this person or to get involved with him or her. Or it may say something about your own discomfort.

• **R:** Try to be relatively **Relaxed** or natural in these behaviors. Being relaxed means two things. First, it means not fidgeting nervously or engaging in distracting facial expressions. The client may wonder what's making you nervous. Second, it means becoming comfortable with using your body as a vehicle of contact and expression. Being natural in the use of skills helps put the client at ease.

These "rules" should be read cautiously. People differ both individually and culturally in how they show attentiveness. The main point is that an internal "being with" a client might well lose its impact if the client does not see this internal attitude reflected in the helper's nonverbal communication. It is not uncommon for helpers in training to become overly self-conscious about their attending behavior, especially in the beginning and perhaps even more especially if they are not used to attending carefully to others. However, the guidelines just presented are just that—guidelines. They should not be taken as absolute rules to be applied rigidly in all cases.

Level 2: Nonverbal Communication

What is much more important than a mechanical application of micro-skills is an awareness of your body as a source of communication. Effective helpers are mindful of the cues and messages they are constantly sending through their bodies as they interact with clients. Reading your own bodily reactions is an important first step. For instance, if you feel your muscles tensing as the client talks to you, you can say to yourself: "I'm getting anxious here. What's causing my anxiety? And what cues am I sending the client?" Once you read your own reactions, you can use your body to communicate appropriate messages. You can also use your body to censor messages that you feel are inappropriate. For instance, if the client says something that instinctively angers you, you can control the external expression of the anger (for instance, a sour look) to give yourself time to reflect. This second level of attending does not mean that you become preoccupied with your body as a source of communication. It means rather that you learn to use your body instinctively as a means of communication. Being aware of and at home with nonverbal communication can reflect an inner peace with yourself, the helping process, and this client.

Level 3: Social-Emotional Presence

What is most important is the quality of your total presence to your clients. Both your verbal and your nonverbal behavior should indicate a clear-cut willingness to work with the client. If you care about your clients and feel

---

BOX 5-1   Questions on Attending

- What are my attitudes toward this client?
- How would I rate the quality of my presence to this client?
- To what degree does my nonverbal behavior indicate a willingness to work with the client?
- What attitudes am I expressing in my nonverbal behavior?
- What attitudes am I expressing in my verbal behavior?
- To what degree does the client experience me as effectively present and working with him or her?
- To what degree does my nonverbal behavior reinforce my internal attitudes?
- In what ways am I distracted from giving my full attention to this client?
- What am I doing to handle these distractions?
- How might I be more effectively present to this person?

---

committed to their welfare, then it is unfair to yourself to let your nonverbal behavior suggest contradictory messages. On the other hand, if you feel indifferent to them and your nonverbal behavior suggests commitment, then you are not being genuine. Effective helpers stay in touch with how they present to clients without becoming preoccupied with it.

Box 5-1 summarizes, in question form, the main points related to attending, especially in terms of social-emotional presence. Obviously, helpers are not constantly asking these questions of themselves as they interact with clients, but they are in touch with the quality of their presence to their clients.

ACTIVE LISTENING

Effective attending puts helpers in a position to listen carefully to what clients are saying both verbally and nonverbally. Listening carefully to a client's concerns seems to be a concept so simple to grasp and so easy to do that one may wonder why it is given such explicit treatment here. Nonetheless, it is amazing how often people fail to listen to one another. How many times have you heard someone exclaim, "You're not listening to what I'm saying!" When the person accused of not listening answers, almost predictably, "I am, too; I can repeat everything you've said," the accuser is not comforted. What people look for in attending and listening is not the other person's ability to repeat their words. A tape recorder could do that perfectly. People want more than physical presence in human communication; they want the other person to be present psychologically, socially, and emotionally.

In a tongue-in-cheek essay, Hines (1988b) outlines 13 ways to fail in private practice. One way of failing is not to listen:

> You can start by bypassing the client's perception of the problem(s). You are the trained professional counselor, and the client knows little in comparison. Feel free to define problems where the client does not see any. Then insist that the client work on what you perceive as the problems. . . . This procedure is designed to get clients to work on problems they did not even think existed for them, thereby increasing your income. (p. 253)

Of course, what Hines is implying in a backhanded way is that the goal of listening is the kind of understanding that can serve the *client's* concerns.

Complete listening involves four things: first, observing and reading the client's nonverbal behavior—posture, facial expressions, movement, tone of voice, and the like; second, listening to and understanding the client's verbal messages; third, listening to the whole person in the context of the social settings of life; fourth, tough-minded listening.

1. Listening to and Understanding Nonverbal Behavior

Nonverbal Behavior as a Channel of Communication

We are only beginning to realize the importance of nonverbal behavior and to make a scientific study of it. The face and body are extremely communicative. We know from experience that, even when people are together in silence, the atmosphere can be filled with messages. Knapp (1972) defines nonverbal behavior as "all human communication events which transcend spoken or written words" (p. 20). Sometimes the facial expressions, bodily motions, voice quality, and physiological responses of clients communicate more than their words.

Mehrabian (1971) wanted to know what cues people use to judge whether another person likes them or not. He and his associates discovered that the other person's actual words contributed only 7% to the impression of being liked or disliked, while voice cues contributed 38% and facial cues 55%. They also discovered that when facial expressions were inconsistent with spoken words, facial expressions were believed more than the words (see Mehrabian, 1971, p. 43).

What is significant in Mehrabian's research is not the exact percentages but rather the clear importance of nonverbal behavior in the communication process. Effective helpers learn how to listen to and read

1. *bodily behavior*, such as posture, body movements, and gestures,
2. *facial expressions*, such as smiles, frowns, raised eyebrows, and twisted lips,
3. *voice-related behavior*, such as tone of voice, pitch, voice level, intensity, inflection, spacing of words, emphases, pauses, silences, and fluency,

4. *observable autonomic physiological responses*, such as quickened breathing, the development of a temporary rash, blushing, paleness, and pupil dilation,

5. *physical characteristics*, such as fitness, height, weight, complexion, and the like, and

6. *general appearance*, such as grooming and dress.

We will use the following case to help you get a better behavioral feeling for both attending and listening.

> Jennie, a black college senior, was raped by a "friend" on a date. She received some immediate counseling from the university Student Development Center and some ongoing support during the subsequent investigation. But while she knew she had been raped, it turned out that it was impossible for her to prove her case. The entire experience—both the rape and the investigation that followed—left her shaken, unsure of herself, angry, and mistrustful of institutions she had assumed would be on her side (especially the university and the legal system). When Denise, a counselor for a health maintenance organization (HMO) sponsored by Jennie's employer, first saw her a few years after the incident, Jennie was plagued by a number of somatic complaints, including headaches and gastric problems. At work she engaged in angry outbursts whenever she felt that someone was taking advantage of her. Otherwise she had become quite passive and chronically depressed. She saw herself as a woman victimized by society and was slowly giving up on herself.

When Denise said to Jennie, "It's hard talking about yourself, isn't it?" Jennie said, "No, I don't mind at all." But the real answer was probably in her nonverbal behavior, for she spoke hesitatingly while looking away and frowning. Reading such cues helped Denise understand Jennie better. A person's nonverbal behavior has a way of "leaking" messages to others (Ekman, 1982). The very spontaneity of nonverbal behaviors contributes to this "leakage" even in the case of highly defensive clients.

Nonverbal Behavior as "Punctuation"

Besides being a channel of communication in itself, such nonverbal behavior as facial expressions, bodily motions, and voice quality can punctuate verbal messages in much the same way that periods, question marks, exclamation points, and underlinings punctuate written language. Nonverbal behavior can punctuate or modify interpersonal communication in the following ways (see Knapp, 1978, pp. 9–12):

• *Confirming or repeating.* Nonverbal behavior can confirm or repeat what is being said verbally. For instance, when Denise hit the mark and Jennie felt understood, her eyes would light up (facial expression), she would lean forward a bit (bodily motion), and she would say animatedly (voice quality), "Yes, that's exactly it!" Her nonverbal behavior confirmed her verbal message.

• *Denying or confusing.* Nonverbal behavior can deny or confuse what is being said verbally. When challenged by Denise once, Jennie denied that she was upset, but her voice faltered a bit (voice quality) and her upper lip quivered (facial expression). Her nonverbal behavior carried the real message.

• *Strengthening or emphasizing.* Nonverbal behavior can strengthen or emphasize what is being said. When Denise suggested to Jennie that she might discuss the origin of what her boss saw as erratic behavior, Jennie said, "Oh, I don't think I could do that!" while slouching down and putting her face in her hands. Her nonverbal behavior underscored her verbal message. Nonverbal behavior adds emotional color or intensity to verbal messages. Once Jennie told Denise that she didn't like to be confronted without first being understood and then stared at her fixedly and silently with a frown on her face. Jennie's nonverbal behavior told Denise something about the intensity of her feelings.

• *Controlling or regulating.* Nonverbal cues are often used in conversation to regulate or control what is happening. If, in group counseling, one participant looks at another and gives every indication that she is going to speak to this other person, she may hesitate or change her mind if the person she intends to talk to looks away. Skilled helpers are aware of the ways in which clients send controlling or regulating nonverbal cues.

Of course, helpers can "punctuate" their words with the same kind of nonverbal messages. Denise, too, without knowing it, sent "silent messages" to Jennie.

In reading nonverbal behavior—"reading" is used here instead of "interpreting"—caution is a must. We listen in order to understand clients rather than to dissect them. There is no simple program available for learning how to read and interpret nonverbal behavior (I have reservations about claims that neurolinguistic programming does precisely that). Once you develop a working knowledge of nonverbal behavior and its possible meanings, you must learn through practice and experience to be sensitive to it and read its meaning in any given situation.

Since nonverbal behaviors can often mean a number of things, how can you tell which meaning is the real one? The key is context. Effective helpers listen to the entire context of the helping interview and do not become overly fixated on details of behavior. They are aware of and use the nonverbal communication system, but they are not seduced or overwhelmed by it. This is the integrative approach. Sometimes novice helpers will fasten selectively on this or that bit of nonverbal behavior. For example, they will make too much of a half-smile or a frown on the face of a client. They will seize upon the smile or the frown and in overinterpreting it lose the person. Denise, an effective helper, did not become a victim of her skills of reading nonverbal cues.

2. Listening to and Understanding Verbal Messages

Beyond nonverbal cues and messages, what do helpers listen to? As outlined in Chapter 4, they listen to clients' verbal descriptions of their experiences, behaviors, and affect. A problem situation is clear if it is understood in terms of specific experiences, specific behaviors, and specific feelings and emotions. The counselor's job is to help clients achieve this kind of clarity. However, to do so he or she must first listen carefully to what the client has to say. Denise listens to what Jennie has to say early on about her past and present experiences, actions, and emotions: "I had every intention of pushing my case, because I knew that men on campus were getting away with murder. But then it began to dawn on me that people were not taking me seriously because I was a black woman. First I was angry, but then I just got numb. . . ."

Later, Jennie says, "I get headaches a lot now. I don't like taking pills, so I try to tough it out. I'm also very sensitive to any kind of injustice, even in movies or on television. But I've stopped being any kind of crusader. That got me nowhere."

Denise hears Jennie's disillusionment. She wonders whether Jennie is disillusioned not only with society and its institutions but also with herself. She listens very carefully, because she realizes that people had not listened to and believed Jennie when she was telling the truth. She listens for verbal and nonverbal messages. She listens to the feelings and emotions that permeate Jennie's words and nonverbal behavior. As she listens to Jennie speak, she constantly asks herself: "What are the *core* messages here? What *themes* are coming through? What is Jennie's point of view? What is most important to her? What does she want me to understand?" That is, she listens *actively*. Her first instinct is not to formulate responses to what Jennie is saying, but just to listen.

3. Listening to and Understanding Clients in Context

People are more than the sum of their verbal and nonverbal messages. Listening in its deepest sense means listening to clients themselves as influenced by the contexts in which they "live, move, and have their being." Denise tries to understand Jennie's verbal and nonverbal messages, even the core messages, in terms of the people-in-systems model described briefly in Chapter 1. As she listens to her client's story, Denise says to herself: "Here is an intelligent black woman from a conservative Catholic background. She is very loyal to the church because it proved to be an inner-city refuge. It was a gathering place for her family and friends. It meant a decent primary- and secondary-school education and a shot at college. Initially college was a shock. It was her first venture into a predominantly white and secular culture. But she chose her friends carefully and carved out a niche for herself. Studies were much more demanding, and she had to come to grips with the fact that, in this larger environment, she was closer to average. The rape and investigation put a great deal of stress on what proved to be a rather fragile social network. Her life began to unravel. She pulled away from her family, her church, and the small circle of friends she had at college. At a time she needed support the most, she cut it off. After graduation, she continued to stay 'out of community.' She got a job as a secretary in a small company and has remained underemployed."

Denise strives to listen to and understand Jennie's verbal and nonverbal messages against this social background. She listens to Jennie's discussion of her headaches (experiences), her self-imposed social isolation (behaviors), and her chronic depression (affect) against the background of her social history—the pressures of being religious in a secular society, the problems associated with being an upwardly mobile black woman in a predominantly white male society. She sees the rape and investigation as social, not merely personal, events. She listens actively and carefully, because she knows that her ability to help depends, in part, on not distorting what she hears. She does not focus narrowly on Jennie's inner psychology, as if Jennie could be separated from the social context of her life.

4. Tough-Minded Listening

Clients' visions of and feelings about themselves, others, and the world are real and need to be understood. However, their perceptions of themselves and their worlds are sometimes distorted. For instance, if a client sees herself as ugly when in reality she is beautiful, her experience of herself as ugly is real and needs to be listened to and understood. But her experience of herself does not square with what is. This, too, must be listened to and understood. If a client sees himself as above average in his ability to communicate with others when, in reality, he is below average, his experience of himself needs to be listened to and understood, but reality cannot be ignored. Tough-minded listening includes detecting the gaps, distortions, and dissonance that are part of the client's experienced reality. This does not mean that helpers challenge clients as soon as they hear any kind of distortion. Rather, they note gaps and distortions and challenge them when it is appropriate to do so (see the chapter on challenging).

Denise realizes from the beginning that some of Jennie's understandings of herself and her world are not accurate. For instance, in reflecting on all that has happened, Jennie remarks that she probably got what she deserved. When Denise asks her what she means, she says, "My ambitions were too high. I was getting beyond my place in life." It is one thing to understand how Jennie might put this interpretation on what has happened; it is another to assume that such an interpretation reflects reality. To be client-centered, helpers must first be reality-centered.

OBSTACLES TO LISTENING TO AND UNDERSTANDING CLIENTS

Active listening is not as easy as it sounds. Obstacles and distractions abound. The following kinds of ineffective listening, as you will see from your own experience, overlap.

Inadequate Listening

In conversations it is easy for us to be distracted from what other people are saying. We get involved in our own thoughts, or we begin to think about what we are going to say in reply. At such times we may get the "You're not listening to me!" exclamation. Helpers, too, can become preoccupied with themselves and their own needs in such a way that they are kept from listening fully to their clients. They are attracted to their clients, they are tired or sick, they are preoccupied with their own problems, they are too eager to help, they are distracted because clients have problems similar to their own, or the social and cultural differences between them and their clients make listening and understanding difficult. The number of ways in which helpers can be distracted from listening to their clients is without end.

Evaluative Listening

Most people, even when they listen attentively, listen evaluatively. That is, as they listen, they are judging the merits of what the other person is saying in terms of good-bad, right-wrong, acceptable-unacceptable, like-dislike, relevant-irrelevant, and so forth. Helpers are not exempt from this universal tendency.

The following interchange took place between Jennie and a friend of hers. Jennie recounted it to Denise as part of her story.

Jennie: Well, the rape and the investigation are not dead, at least not in my mind. They are not as vivid as they used to be, but they are there.
Friend: That's the problem, isn't it? Why don't you do yourself a favor and forget about it? Get on with life, for God's sake!

This might well be sound advice, but the point here is that Jennie's friend listened and responded evaluatively. Clients should first be understood, then challenged. Evaluative listening, translated into advice giving, will just put clients off. Of course, understanding the client's point of view is not the same as accepting it. Indeed, a judgment that a client's point of view, once understood, needs to be expanded or transcended or that a pattern of behavior, once listened to and understood, needs to be altered can be quite useful. That is, there are productive forms of evaluative listening. It is practically impossible to suspend judgment completely. Nevertheless, it *is* possible to set one's judgment aside for the time being at the service of understanding clients, their worlds, and their points of view.

Filtered Listening

It is impossible to listen to other people in a completely unbiased way. Through socialization we develop a variety of filters through which we listen to ourselves, others, and the world around us. As Hall (1977) notes: "One of the functions of culture is to provide a highly selective screen between man and the outside world. In its many forms, culture therefore designates what we pay attention to and what we ignore. This screening provides structure for the world" (p. 85). We need filters to provide structure for ourselves as we interact with the world. But personal, familial, sociological, and cultural filters introduce various forms of bias into our listening and do so without our being aware of it.

The stronger the cultural filters, the greater the likelihood of bias. For instance, a white, middle-class helper probably tends to use white, middle-class filters in listening to others. Perhaps this makes little difference if the client is also white and middle class, but if the helper is listening to an Oriental client who is well-to-do and has high social status in his community, to a black mother from an urban ghetto, or to a poor white subsistence farmer, then the helper's cultural filters might introduce bias. Prejudices, whether conscious or not, distort understanding. Like everyone else, helpers are tempted to pigeonhole clients because of gender, race, sexual orientation, nationality, social status, religious persuasion, political preferences, lifestyle, and the like. In Chapter 1 the importance of self-knowledge was noted. This includes ferreting out the biases and prejudices that distort our listening.

Learnings as Filters

The curriculum outlined in Chapter 1 is meant to help you understand your clients. Sometimes, however, book learning can act as a distorting filter. Personality theories can easily become pigeonholes. Diagnostic categories such as "schizophrenia" can take precedence over the persons being diagnosed. If what you "hear" is the theory and not the person, you can be "correct" in your diagnosis and lose the client. In short, what you learn as you study psychology may help you to organize what you hear but it may also distort your listening. To use terms borrowed from Gestalt psychology, make sure that your client remains "figure" (in the forefront of your attention) and that models and theories about clients remain "ground" (learnings that remain in the background and are used only in the service of understanding and helping *this* unique client).

Fact-Centered Rather than Person-Centered Listening

Some helpers ask a lot of informational questions, as if the client would be cured if enough facts about him or her were known. It's entirely possible to collect facts but miss the person. The antidote is to listen to clients contextually, trying to focus on themes and key messages. Denise, as she listens to Jennie, picks up what is called the "pessimistic explanatory style" theme (Peterson, Seligman, & Vaillant, 1988). This is the tendency to attribute causes to negative events that are stable ("It will never go away"), global ("It affects everything I do"), and internal ("It is my fault"). Denise knows that the research indicates that people who fall victim to this style tend to end up with poorer health than those who do not. There may be a link, she hypothesizes, between Jennie's somatic complaints (headaches, gastric problems) and this explanatory style. This is a theme worth exploring.

Rehearsing

When beginning helpers ask themselves, "How am I to respond to what the client is saying?" they stop listening. When experienced helpers begin to mull over the "perfect response" to what their clients are saying, they stop listening. Helping is more than the "technology" found in these pages. It is also an art. Helpers who listen intently to clients and to the themes and core messages embedded in what they are saying, however haltingly or fluently they say it, are never at a loss in responding. They don't need to rehearse. And their responses are much more likely to help clients move forward in the problem-management process.

Sympathetic Listening

Often clients are people in pain or people who have been victimized by others or by society itself. Such clients can arouse feelings of sympathy in helpers. Sometimes these feelings are strong enough to distort the stories that are being told. Recall the case of Ben, the client who lost his wife and daughter, and his helper, Liz.

> Liz had recently lost her husband to cancer. As Ben talked about his own tragedy during their first meeting, she wanted to hold him. Later that day she took a long walk and realized how her sympathy for Ben distorted what she heard. She heard the depth of his loss but, reminded of her own loss, only half heard the implication that this now excused him from much of life.

Sympathy has an unmistakable place in human transactions, but its "use," if that does not sound too inhuman, is limited in helping. In a sense, when I sympathize with someone, I become his or her accomplice. If I sympathize with my client as she tells me how awful her husband is, I take sides without knowing what the complete story is. Helpers should not become accomplices in letting client self-pity drive out problem-managing action.

Interrupting

I am reluctant to add "interrupting" to this list of obstacles, as some do (see Seltzer & Howe, 1987). Certainly, by interrupting clients, the helper stops listening. But my reluctance comes from the conviction that helping goes best when it is a *dialogue* between client and helper. I seldom find monologues, including my own, helpful. Occasionally, monologues that help clients get their stories or significant updates of their stories out are useful. Even then, such a monologue is best followed by a fair amount of dialogue. Therefore, I see benign and malignant forms of interrupting. The helper who cuts the client off in mid-thought because *he* has something important to say is using a malignant form. But the case is different when a helper "interrupts" a monologue with some gentle gesture and a comment such as "You've made several points; I want to make sure that I've understood them." If interrupting promotes the kind of dialogue that serves the problem-management process, then it is useful.

LISTENING TO ONESELF

To be an effective helper, you need to listen not only to the client but to yourself. Granted, you don't want to become self-preoccupied and stop listening to the client, but listening to yourself on a "second channel" can help you identify what is standing in the way of your being with and listening to the client. It is a positive form of self-consciousness.

Some years ago, this second channel did not work very well for me. A friend of mine who had been in and out of mental hospitals for a few years and whom I had not seen for over six months showed up unannounced one evening at my apartment. He was in a highly excited state. A torrent of ideas, some outlandish, some brilliant, flowed nonstop from him. I sincerely wanted to be with him as best I could. I started by more or less naturally following the "rules" of attending, but I kept catching myself at the other end of the couch on which we were both sitting with my arms and legs crossed. I think that I was defending myself from the torrent of ideas. When I discovered myself almost literally tied up in knots, I would untwist my arms and legs, only to find them crossed again a few minutes later. It was hard work being with him. In retrospect, I realize I was concerned for my own security. I have since learned to listen to myself—to my nonverbal behaviors as well as my internal dialogues—so that these interactions might serve clients better.

Rogers (1980) talked about letting oneself get lost in the world of the other.

> In some sense [attending and listening] means that you lay aside your self; this can only be done by persons who are secure enough in themselves that they know they will not get lost in what may turn out to be the strange and bizarre world of the other, and that they can comfortably return to their own world when they wish. (p. 143)

This ability to focus almost exclusively on the client while forgetting oneself and then return to productive self-consciousness comes with both experience and maturity. Having a second ear lightly tuned to oneself is certainly a step short of the kind of total immersion Rogers described, but, as we shall see in greater detail later, it can serve the client's goals.

Box 5-2 summarizes, in question form, the main points related to effective listening.

BOX 5-2   Questions on Listening

- How well do I read the client's nonverbal behaviors and see how they modify what he or she is saying verbally?
- How careful am I not to overinterpret nonverbal behavior?
- How intently do I listen to what the client is saying verbally, noticing the mix of experiences, behaviors, and feelings?
- How effectively do I listen to the client's point of view, especially when I sense that this point of view needs to be challenged or transcended?
- How easily do I tune in to the core messages being conveyed by the client?
- How effective am I at spotting themes in the client's story?
- What distracts me from listening more carefully? What can I do to manage these distractions?
- How effectively do I pick up cues indicating dissonance between reality and what the client is saying?
- To what degree can I note the ways in which the client exaggerates, contradicts himself or herself, misinterprets reality, and holds things back without judging him or her and without interfering with the flow of the dialogue?
- How effectively do I listen to what is going on inside myself as I interact with clients?

Chapter Six

Communication Skills II: Empathy and Probing

As we have seen, attending and listening are not passive activities. But, since the fruit of attending and listening lies in the way the helper *responds* to the client, it is essential to move on to the responding skills of empathy and probing. Empathy as a form of human communication involves *both* listening and understanding *and* communicating understanding to the client. Empathy that remains locked up in the helper contributes little to the helping process.

Empathy continues to draw the attention of theoreticians and researchers (Bohart, 1988; Eisenberg & Strayer, 1987; Emery, 1987; Marks & Tolsma, 1986; Miller, 1989; Patterson, 1984, 1985, 1988; Rogers, 1986a). However, there is still some confusion as to just what empathy is. Some of the confusion comes from the distinction between empathy as *a way of being* and empathy as *a communication process or skill* and the way this distinction is played out in the helping process.

EMPATHY AS A WAY OF BEING

A helper cannot communicate an understanding of a client's world without getting in contact with that world. Therefore, a great deal of the discussion on empathy centers on the kind of attending, observing, and listening—the kind of "being with"—needed to develop an understanding of clients and their worlds. Empathy in this sense is primarily a mode of human contact.

Huxley (1963) noted the basic problem—the fact that it is metaphysically impossible to get inside another in such a way as actually to experience reality as the other does:

> We live together, we act on, we react to, one another; but always in all circumstances we are alone. . . . Sensations, feelings, insights, fancies— all these are private and, except through symbols and second hand, incommunicable.

And yet he believes that empathy is both possible and necessary in human relationships:

> Most island universes are sufficiently like one another to permit inferential understanding or even empathy or "feeling into." . . . To see ourselves as others see us is a most salutary gift. Hardly less important is the capacity to see others as they are themselves. (pp. 12–13)

Huxley, then, describes empathy as an attempt to penetrate the metaphysical aloneness of the other.

Mayeroff (1971) sees empathy as an essential part of caring.

> To care for another person, I must be able to understand him and his world as if I were inside it. I must be able to see, as it were, with his eyes

what his world is like to him and how he sees himself. Instead of merely looking at him in a detached way from outside, as if he were a specimen, I must be able to be with him in his world, "going" into his world in order to sense from the "inside" what life is like for him, what he is striving to be and what he requires to grow. (pp. 41–42)

Mayeroff goes on to describe caring as a tough and action-oriented, rather than a sentimental, value.

Rogers (1980) talks about basic empathic listening—being with and understanding—as "an unappreciated way of being" (p. 137) because, despite its usefulness in counseling and therapy, even so-called expert helpers either ignore it or are not skilled in its use. Rogers defines basic empathic listening, or being with, as follows:

It means entering the private perceptual world of the other and becoming thoroughly at home in it. It involves being sensitive, moment by moment, to the changing felt meanings which flow in this other person, to the fear or rage or tenderness or confusion or whatever that he or she is experiencing. It means temporarily living in the other's life, moving about in it delicately without making judgments. (p. 142)

In Rogers's (1986b) view, this way of being with clients is so powerful that it is almost a sufficient condition for client progress.

To my mind, empathy is in itself a healing agent. It is one of the most potent aspects of therapy, because it releases, it confirms, it brings even the most frightened client into the human race. If a person is understood, he or she belongs. (p. 129)

Indeed, Rogers never ceased to maintain that empathy, respect, and genuineness constituted the "necessary and sufficient conditions of therapeutic personality change" (Rogers, 1957).

This ability to enter another's world exacts a price of helpers. They must put themselves and their concerns aside as they listen to and are with their clients.

This negation of the self by the therapist involves a kind of self-aggression: to submerge oneself, to submit to not-knowing, and to put oneself aside. Perhaps it is one component of the sometimes exhausting nature of therapeutic work—the therapist not only bears intense affects but also denies the self in the pursuit of the other. (Margulies, 1984, p. 1030)

Margulies likens the helper to Keats's conception of the poet as a person without identity since he or she is so open and filled with the realities of the world and others. Indeed, authors who feel strongly about empathy as a way of being become almost lyrical in its praises. Kohut (1978) writes: "Empathy, the accepting, confirming, and understanding human echo evoked by the self, is a psychological nutrient without which human life, as we know and cherish it, could not be sustained" (p. 705). Empathy, then, becomes a value, a philosophy, a cause with almost religious overtones.

This exalted conception of empathy poses a number of problems. It can put an essential process—listening and responding to clients with understanding—beyond the capability of many helpers. It can so focus on one aspect of the helping process, however important it might be, as to distort the rest. Prospective helpers can be trained mainly in attending, listening, and empathy and not in the other skills needed to deliver a problem-management and opportunity-development model of helping. I have no problem with empathy as a way of being, and I acknowledge that too few helpers are capable of it. I do have problems with empathy as a cult and with exalting it so as to make everything else subservient to it.

Empathic Relationships

However deep one person's empathic understanding of another, it needs to be communicated to the other. This does not necessarily mean that understanding must always be put into words. Given enough time, people can establish what I call empathic relationships with one another in which understanding is communicated in a variety of rich and subtle ways without being put into words. A simple glance across a room as one spouse sees the other trapped in a conversation with a person he or she does not want to be with can communicate worlds of understanding. The glance says: "I know you feel caught. I know you don't want to hurt the other person's feelings. I can feel the struggle going on inside. I know you'd like me to rescue you, if I can do so tactfully." People with empathic relationships often express empathy in actions. An arm around the shoulders of someone who has just suffered a defeat can be filled with both support and empathy. I was in the home of a poverty-stricken family when the father came bursting through the front door shouting, "I got the job!" His wife, without saying a word, went to the refrigerator, got a bottle of beer with a makeshift label on which "CHAMPAGNE" had been written and offered it to her husband. Beer never tasted so good.

Empathic participation in the world of another person obviously admits of degrees. As a helper, you must be able to enter clients' worlds deeply enough to understand their struggles with problem situations or their search for opportunities with enough depth to make your participation in problem management and opportunity development valid and substantial. If your help is based on an incorrect or invalid understanding of the client, then your helping may lead him or her astray. If your understanding is valid but superficial, then you might miss the central issues of the client's life.

Some people do enter caringly into the world of another and are "with" him or her but are unable to communicate understanding, especially through words. Others develop the skill or technology of communicating empathic understanding but have little to communicate because their experiencing of or being with the other person is superficial. Helpers need both the depth of human contact and understanding and the ability to communicate this understanding in verbal and nonverbal ways. The following discussion of the microskills involved in the communication of empathy is based on the assumption that the helper enters the world of the client through attending, observing, listening, and "being with" deeply enough to make a difference.

Labels as a Perversion of Understanding

As suggested in Chapter 5, the very labels we learn in our training can militate against empathic understanding. Kleinman (1988) makes a useful distinction between illness and disease. Illness, he says, consists of patients' subjective experience of their distress and concerns and the ways they talk about them, express them, and try to cope with them. Disease, on the other hand, is a category more removed from the patient's immediate experience. It is the product of the minds of theorists and practitioners, a reworking and translation of the patient's experience into the language and terms of the profession. There is a tendency to strip away the "illness" in order to find the real "disease" underneath. The disease is understood, the patient is not. While helping is not a medical specialty (although medical personnel often engage in it), helpers, too, get caught in a similar bind, forgetting that their labels are *interpretations* rather than understandings of the client's experience. It is not that certain interpretations of the client's experiences are not helpful, as we shall see in a later chapter. Rather, problems arise when pre-cast interpretations drawn from our theories about people and their problems preempt our understanding of clients from *their* points of view.

EMPATHY AS A COMMUNICATION SKILL

If attending and listening are the skills that enable helpers to get in touch with the world of the client, them empathy is the skill that enables them to communicate their understanding of this world. A secure starting point in helping others is listening to them, struggling to understand their concerns, and sharing this understanding with them. Indeed, when clients are asked what they find helpful in counseling interviews, understanding gets top ratings (Elliott, 1985). Since empathy in this sense is a skill, it is something that can be learned.

As I have noted, you cannot respond empathically to clients unless you *are* empathic. Now, on the assumption that you are empathic, we turn to what needs to be done to *express* empathy to your clients.

The Three Dimensions of Communication Skills in the Helping Process

The communication skills involved in responding to and engaging in dialogue with clients have three components or dimensions: perceptiveness, know-how, and assertiveness.

Perceptiveness

Your communication skills are only as good as the accuracy of the perceptions in which they are based. If your perceptions are inaccurate, then your communication skills are flawed at the root.

> Jenny is counseling Frank in a community mental health center. Frank is scared about what is going to happen to him in the counseling process, but he does not talk about it. Jenny senses his discomfort but thinks that he is angry rather than scared. She says: "Frank, I'm wondering what's making you so angry right now." Since Frank does not feel angry, he says nothing. He's startled by what she says and feels even more insecure. Jenny takes his silence as a confirmation of his "anger." She tries to get him to talk about it.

Jenny's perception is wrong and disrupts the helping process. The kind of perceptiveness needed to be a good helper is based on the quality of one's "being with" clients and on practical intelligence. It can be developed through experience.

Know-How

Once you are aware of what kind of response is called for in the helping process, you need to be able to deliver it. For instance, if you are aware that a client is anxious and confused because this is his first visit to a helper, it does little good if your understanding remains locked up inside you.

> Frank and Jenny end up arguing about his "anger." Frank finally gets up and leaves. Jenny, of course, takes this as a sign that she was right in the first place. Frank goes to see his minister. The minister sees quite clearly that Frank is scared and confused. But he lacks the know-how to translate his perceptions into meaningful interactions with him. As Frank talks, the minister nods and says "uh-huh" quite a bit. He is fully present to Frank and listens intently, but he does not know how to respond.

Understandings are lost without the skill of delivering them to the client.

Assertiveness

Accurate perceptions and excellent know-how are meaningless unless they are actually used when called for. If you see that a client needs to be challenged and know how to do it but still fail to do so, you do not pass the assertiveness test. Your goodness remains locked up inside you.

> Edna, a young helper in the Center for Student Development, is in the middle of her second session with Aurelio, a graduate student. It soon becomes clear to her that he is making sexual overtures. In her training she did quite well in challenging her fellow trainees. The feedback she got from them and the trainer was that she challenged others directly and caringly. But now she feels immobilized. She does not want to hurt Aurelio or embarrass herself. She tries to ignore his seductive behavior, but Aurelio takes silence to mean consent.

In this case awareness and know-how are both lost because of a lack of assertiveness. The helper does not act when action is called for. This is not to say that assertiveness is an overriding value in itself. Certainly, to be assertive without perceptiveness and know-how is to court disaster. The counseling profession can do without bulls in the china shop.

The Know-How of Empathy

The remainder of this chapter focuses on the second aspect of empathy as a communication skill—know-how. Let's start with a few examples. A single middle-aged man who has been unable to keep a job shares his frustration with a counselor.

Client: I've been to other counselors, and nothing has ever really worked. I don't even know why I'm trying again. But things are so bad. . . . I just have to get a job. I guess something has to be done, so I'm trying it all over again.
Helper: You're here with mixed feelings. You're not sure that our sessions will help you get a job and keep it, but you feel you have to try something.
Client: Yes, "something," but I don't know what the something is. What can I get here that will help me get a job? Or keep a job?

The helper's nondefensive response helps diffuse the client's anger and refocus his energies.

In the next example, a woman who is going to have a hysterectomy is talking with a hospital counselor the night before surgery.

Patient: I'm just so afraid. God knows what they'll find when they go in tomorrow. You know, they don't tell you much. And that usually spells trouble.
Counselor: The uncertainty of the whole thing really gets to you.
Client: Yes, that's it—not knowing what's going to happen. I think I can take the pain. But the uncertainty drives me up the wall. . . . Well, I guess it's that way with everyone.

The accuracy of the helper's response does not solve all problems, but the patient does move a bit, recognizing her solidarity with others going through the same thing.

In the next example, a young woman visits the student services center at her college.

Client: And so here I am, two months pregnant. I don't want to be pregnant. I'm not married, and I don't even love the father. To tell the truth, I don't even think I like him. Oh, Lord, this is something that happens to other people, not me! I wake up thinking this whole thing is unreal.
Helper: You're still so amazed that it's almost impossible to accept that it's true.
Client: Amazed? I'm stupefied! At my own stupidity for getting myself into this. Maybe that's it. And I feel so alone.

After the helper's empathy, self-recrimination and the feeling of being alone emerge as perhaps deeper concerns for the client.

The skill of communicating understanding, then, is critical in moving clients forward. Let's now examine in greater detail what the helpers are doing in these examples.

ELEMENTS OF EMPATHIC UNDERSTANDING AND RESPONDING
Experiences, Behaviors, Feelings

To begin with, the technology of empathy involves translating your understanding of the client's *experiences, behaviors,* and *feelings* into a response through which you share that understanding with the client. If a student comes to you, sits down, looks at the floor, hunches over, and haltingly tells you that he has just failed a test, that his girlfriend has told him she doesn't want to see him anymore, and that he might lose his part-time job because he has been "goofing off," you might respond to him by saying something like this:

Helper: That's a lot of misery all at once.
Client: I'm not even sure who I'm mad at the most. Damn!

You see that he is both agitated and depressed (affect), and you understand in some initial way what has happened to him (experiences) and what he has done (behaviors) to contribute to the problem situation, and then you communicate to him your understanding of his world. This communication is *basic empathy.* If your perceptions are correct, then it is *accurate empathy.* In this example, the helper might notice that the client talks about getting angry with the people involved, but does not take much responsibility himself. But at this point she "files" this observation because this is not the time to offer it. For the moment, basic empathy is what is called for.

Another client, after a few sessions with you spread out over six months, says something like this:

Client (talking in an animated way): I really think that things couldn't be going better. I'm doing very well at my new job, and my husband isn't just putting up with it. He thinks it's great. He and I are getting along better than ever, even sexually, and I never expected that. We're both working at our marriage. I guess I'm just waiting for the bubble to burst.

Helper: You feel great because things have been going better than you ever expected—it's almost too good to be true.

Client: What I'm finding out is that I can make things come true instead of sitting around waiting for them to happen as I usually do. I've got to keep making my own luck.

Helper: You've discovered the secret!

This client, too, talks about her experiences and behaviors and expresses feelings, the flavor of which you capture in your empathic response. The response seems to be a useful one, because the client moves on.

Core Messages

In order to respond empathically, you can ask yourself, as you listen to the client: "What *core message* or messages are being expressed in terms of feelings and the experiences and behaviors that underlie these feelings? What is most important in what the client is saying to me?" Once you feel you have identified the core messages, then you check out your understanding with the client. The formula *"You feel . . . because . . ."* (used in the preceding example) provides the essentials for an empathic response.

Feelings

"You feel . . ." is to be followed by the correct family of emotions and the correct intensity. For instance, the statements "You feel hurt," "You feel relieved," and "You feel great" specify different *families* of emotion. The statements "You feel annoyed," "You feel angry," and "You feel furious" specify different *degrees of intensity* in the same family.

The emotions clients express in the interview may or may not be the ones associated with the problem situation. For instance, a client may express anger over the fact that he gives in to fear when talking with his father. If your empathic response picks up the fear the client is describing but not the anger he is expressing now, the client may feel misunderstood. "You feel angry because you let fear get the best of you in your interactions with your father" is an accurate response. Notice that there is a difference between clients' talking about feelings and emotions experienced in the past and their expressing feelings and emotions in the interview.

Experiences and Behaviors

The *"because . . ."* in our formula is to be followed by an indication of the experiences and behaviors that underlie the client's feelings. "You feel angry because he stole your course notes and you let him get away with it" specifies both the experience and the behavior (in this case, a failure to act) that give rise to the feeling. Some additional examples:

- "You feel sad because moving means leaving all your friends."
- "You feel anxious because the results of the biopsy aren't in yet."
- "You feel frustrated because the social-service bureau keeps making you do things you don't want to do."
- "You feel annoyed with yourself because you didn't even reach the simple goals you set for yourself."
- "You feel hopeless because even your best efforts don't seem to help you lose weight."
- "You feel relieved because sticking to the regime of diet and exercise means that you probably won't need to go on the medicine."
- "You feel angry with me because you see me pushing all the responsibility on you."

Of course, the formula itself is not important; it merely provides a framework for communicating understanding to the client. Though many people in training use the formula to help themselves communicate understanding of core messages, experienced helpers tend to avoid formulas and use whatever wording best communicates their understanding.

Listening to the Context, Not Just the Words

As Berger (1984) noted, empathy is contextual and integrating. A good empathic response is not based just on the client's immediate words and nonverbal behavior. It takes into account the context of what is said, everything that "surrounds" and permeates a client's statement. You are listening to clients in the context of their lives.

Recall the people-in-systems framework mentioned in Chapter 1. For example, Jeff, a white teenager, is accused of beating a black youth whose car stalled in a white neighborhood. The beaten youth is still in a coma. When Jeff talks to a court-appointed counselor, the counselor listens to what Jeff says in terms of Jeff's upbringing and environment. The context includes the racist attitudes of many people in his blue-collar neighborhood, the sporadic violence there, the fact that his father died when Jeff was in primary school, a somewhat indulgent mother with a history of alcoholism, and easy access to soft drugs. The following interchange takes place.

Jeff: I don't know why I did it. I just did it, me and these other guys. We'd been drinking a bit and smoking up a bit—but not too much. It was just the whole thing.

Counselor: It's almost like it's something that happened rather than something you did, and yet you know, somewhat bitterly, that you actually did it.

Jeff: Bitter's the word! I can be screwed for the rest of my life. It's not like I got up that morning saying "I'm going to bash me a black today."

The counselor's response is in no way an attempt to excuse Jeff's behavior, but it does factor in some of the environment in which Jeff lives. Later on he will challenge Jeff to decide whether the environment is to own him or whether, to the degree that this is possible, he is to own the environment.

Selective Responding

In most of the examples given so far the helper has responded to both affect and content, that is, to both feelings and the experiences and behaviors underlying the feelings. While this might ordinarily be the best kind of response, helpers can respond selectively so as to emphasize feelings, experiences, or behaviors. Consider the following example of a client who is experiencing stress because of his wife's health and because of concerns at work.

Client: This week I tried to get my wife to see the doctor, but she refused, even though she fainted a couple of times. The kids had no school, so they were underfoot almost constantly. I haven't been able to finish a report my boss expects from me next Monday.

Counselor: It's been a lousy week all the way around.

Client: As bad as they come. When things are lousy both at home and at work, there's no place for me to relax. I just want to get the hell out of the house and find some place to forget it all.

Here the counselor chooses to emphasize the feelings of the client, because she believes that his feelings of frustration and irritation are what is uppermost in his consciousness right now. At another time or with another client, the emphasis might be quite different. In the next example, a young woman is talking about her problems with her father.

Client: My dad yelled at me all the time last year about how I dress. But just last week I heard him telling someone how nice I looked. He yells at my sister about the same things he ignores when my younger brother does them. Sometimes he's really nice with my mother and other times—too much of the time—he's just awful: demanding, grouchy, sarcastic.

Counselor: The *inconsistency* gets to you.

Client: Right; it's hard for all of us to know where we stand. I hate coming home when I'm not sure which "dad" will be there.

In this response the counselor emphasizes the client's experience of her father, for he feels that this is the core of the client's message. The point is that effective helpers do not stick to rigid formulas in using empathy.

For some clients, fear of intimacy makes the helping sessions difficult. Since empathy is a kind of intimacy, too much empathy too soon can inhibit rather than facilitate helping. Warmth, closeness, and intimacy are not goals in themselves. As we will see, the goal of Stage I is to help clients clarify their problems. If empathy, or too much empathy too soon, stands in the way of this goal, then it should be avoided.

Other clients are threatened by a discussion of their feelings. In this case it might be better to focus on experiences and behaviors and proceed only gradually to a discussion of feelings. The following client, an unmarried man in his mid-thirties who has come to talk about "certain dissatisfactions" in his life, has shown some reluctance to express or even to talk about feelings.

Client (in a pleasant, relaxed voice): My mother is always trying to make a little kid out of me. And I'm in my mid-thirties! Last week, in front of a group of my friends, she brought out my rubber boots and an umbrella and gave me a little talk on how to dress for bad weather (laughs).

Counselor A: It might be hard to admit it, but I get that down deep you were furious.

Client: Well, I don't know about that.

Counselor B: So she keeps playing the mother role to the hilt.

Client: And the "hilt" includes not wanting me to grow up. But I am grown up . . . well, pretty grown up.

Counselor A pushes the emotion issue and is met with mild resistance. Counselor B, choosing to respond to the "strong-mother" issue rather than the more sensitive "being-kept-a-kid" issue, gives the client more room to move. This works, for the client himself moves toward the more sensitive issue.

Accurate Empathy: Staying on Track

Although helpers should strive to be accurate in the understanding they communicate, all helpers can be somewhat inaccurate at times. But they can learn from their mistakes. If the helper's response is accurate, the client often tends to confirm its accuracy by a nod or some other nonverbal cue, or by a phrase such as "that's right" or "exactly." Then the client goes on to give more specific details about the problem situation.

Helper: So the neighborhood in which you live pushes you toward a whole variety of behaviors that can get you in trouble.

Client: You bet it does! For instance, everyone's selling drugs. You not only end up using them, but you begin to think about pushing them. It's just too easy.

When the helper again responds with empathy, this leads to the next cycle. The problem situation becomes increasingly clear in terms of specific experiences, behaviors, and feelings.

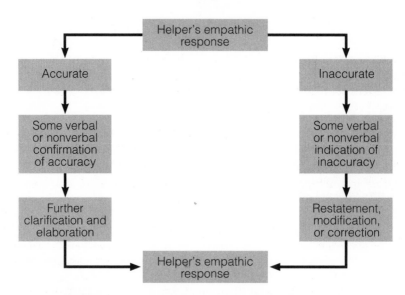

FIGURE 6-1   The Movement Caused by Accurate and Inaccurate Empathy

When a response is inaccurate, the client often lets the counselor know in any one of a variety of ways: he or she may stop dead, fumble around, go off on a new tangent, tell the counselor "That's not exactly what I meant," or even try to provide empathy for the counselor and get him or her back on track. But all is not lost. A helper who is alert to these cues can get back on track. Recall the case of Ben, the man who lost his wife and daughter; Liz is his helper. Ben has been talking about the changes that have taken place since the accident.

Liz: So you don't want to do a lot of the things you used to do before the accident. For instance, you don't want to socialize much any more.

Ben (pausing a long time): Well, I'm not sure that it's a question of wanting to or not. I mean that it takes much more energy to do a lot of things. It takes so much energy to phone others to get together. It takes so much energy sometimes being with others that I just don't try. It's as if there's a weight on my soul a lot of the time.

Liz: It's like the movie of a man in slow motion—it's so hard to do almost *anything.*

Ben: Right. I've been in slow motion, low gear in lots of things.

Ben says that it is not a question of motivation but of energy. The difference is important. By picking up on it, Liz gets the interview back on track.

Figure 6-1 indicates the movement both when helpers are on the mark and when they fail to grasp what the client has expressed. If you are empathic in your relationship with your clients, they will not be put off by occasional inaccuracies on your part.

THE USES OF EMPATHY

Empathy is not a miracle pill, but it can contribute to the overall helping process in a variety of ways. Other things being equal (such as the skill of the helper and the state of the client), empathy can help to do the following:

- *Build the relationship.* In interpersonal communication, empathy is a tool of civility. Making an effort to get in touch with another's frame of reference sends a message of respect. Therefore, empathy plays an important part in establishing rapport with clients.
- *Stimulate self-exploration.* Empathy is an unobtrusive tool for helping clients explore themselves and their problem situations. The understood client is influenced to move on, to explore more widely or more deeply. As Havens (1978) put it, the client's "narrative flow" is stimulated and deepened. Or in Driscoll's (1984) commonsense terms, "Empathic statements are those recurring nickle-and-dime interventions which each contribute only a smidgen of therapeutic movement, but without which the course of therapeutic progress would be markedly slower" (p. 90).
- *Check understandings.* In describing empathy as a response, Rogers (1986a) used the terms "testing understandings" and "checking perceptions." You may think you understand the client and what he or she has said only to find out, when you share your understanding, that you were off the mark. This gives you an opportunity to get back on track.
- *Provide support.* Since empathy is a way of staying in touch with clients and their experiences, behaviors, and feelings, it is a way of providing support throughout the helping process. It is never wrong to make sure that you are in touch with the client's frame of reference.
- *Lubricate communication.* Empathy acts as a kind of communications lubricant; it encourages and facilitates dialogue. It thus encourages collaboration in the helping process.
- *Focus attention.* Empathy helps client and helper alike understand the client's experiences, behaviors, and emotions. Core issues are held up to the light. As Driscoll (1984, pp. 88–90) noted, empathy has a way of focusing attention on an issue that encourages clients to understand and review important messages embedded in their experiences, behaviors, and feelings.
- *Restrain the helper.* Empathy keeps helpers from doing useless things such as asking too many questions and giving premature and inept advice. Empathy puts the ball back into the client's court and thus in its own way encourages the client to act.
- *Pave the way.* Empathy paves the way for the stronger interventions suggested by the helping model, including challenging a client's point of view, setting goals, formulating strategies, and moving to action.

Consider the following interchange between a trainee and her trainer.

Trainee: I don't think I'm going to make a good counselor. The other people in the program seem brighter than I am. Others seem to be picking up the knack of empathy faster than I am. I'm still afraid of responding directly to others, even with empathy. I have to reevaluate my participation in the program.

Trainer: You're feeling pretty inadequate and it's getting you down, perhaps even enough to make you think of quitting.

Trainee: And yet I know that giving up is part of the problem, part of my style. I'm not the brightest, but I'm certainly not dumb either. The way I compare myself to others is not very useful. I know that I've been picking up some of these skills. I do attend and listen well. I'm perceptive even though at times I have a hard time sharing these perceptions with others.

When the trainer "hits the mark," the trainee moves forward and explores her problem more fully.

Empathy as a way of "being with" others is a human value and needs no justification. Empathy as a communication skill, however, is instrumental; that is, it is good to the degree that it helps a client persist in the helping process and move on toward problem management. Asbury (1984) demonstrated that teachers can help students decrease disruptive classroom behaviors through empathy. The teachers involved in the study talked to the offenders for a couple of minutes each day, listening to each of them and responding with empathy. This should not be taken as proof that "empathy cures." Indeed, it might well have been the attention the offenders received that helped them change their behavior. Even so, empathy was part of whatever package did the trick.

DO'S AND DON'TS IN EXPRESSING EMPATHY

Here are a few hints to help you improve the quality of your empathic responses.

Some Things to Do

Give yourself time to think. Beginners sometimes jump in too quickly with an empathic response when the client pauses. "Too quickly" means that they do not give themselves enough time to reflect on what the client has just said in order to identify the core message being communicated. Even the experts pause and allow themselves to assimilate what the client is saying.

Use short responses. I find that the helping process goes best when I engage the client in a dialogue rather than give speeches or allow the client to ramble. In a dialogue the helper's responses are relatively frequent, but they should also be lean and trim. In trying to be accurate, the beginner may become long-winded, sometimes speaking longer than the client in trying to elaborate an adequate response. This often happens when the helper tries to respond too quickly. Again, the question "What is the core of what this person is saying to me?" can help you make your responses short, concrete, and accurate.

Gear your response to the client, but remain yourself. If a client speaks animatedly, telling the helper of his elation over various successes in his life, and she replies accurately, but in a flat, dull voice, her response is not fully empathic. This does not mean that helpers should mimic their clients. It means that part of being with the client is sharing in a reasonable way in his or her emotional tone.

Ten-Year-Old Client: My teacher started picking on me from the first day of class. I don't fool around more than anyone else in class, but she gets me anytime I do. I think she's picking on me because she doesn't like me. She doesn't yell at Bill Smith, and he acts funnier than I do.

Counselor A: You're perplexed. You wonder why she singles you out for so much discipline.

Counselor B: You're mad because she seems unfair in the way she picks on you.

It is evident which of these two helpers will probably get through. Counselor A's language is stilted, not in tune with the way a 10-year-old speaks. On the other hand, helpers should not adopt a language that is not their own just to be on the client's wavelength. For instance, in the next example a middle-class probation officer is responding to a client who is tempted to steal in order to pay off a debt to someone he fears:

Probation Officer: Unless you find some bread, man, that cat's going to get you wasted.

The probation officer is using the client's jargon. Helpers can use informal language without using adaptations that are simply not their own.

Some Things to Avoid Doing

There are a number of poor substitutes for empathy that are best avoided. Peter, the client in the next example, is a college freshman. This is his second visit to a counselor in the student-services center. After talking about a number of concerns, Peter speaks in a halting voice, looking at the floor and clasping his hands tightly between his knees.

Peter: What seems to be really bothering me is a problem with sex. I don't even know whether I'm a man or not, and I'm in college. I don't go out with women. I don't even think I want to. I may . . . well, I may even be gay. . . . Uh, I don't know.

The following are some examples of poor responses.

No response. First of all, the counselor might say nothing. Generally, if the client says something significant, respond to it, however briefly. Otherwise the client might think that what he or she has just said doesn't merit a response.

A question. The counselor might ask something like: "How long has this been bothering you, Peter?" This response ignores the emotion Peter is experiencing. Since a question elicits further information, it implies that Peter has not said anything worth responding to.

A cliché. The counselor might say: "Many people struggle with sexual identity throughout their lives." This is a cliché. It completely misses the feelings of the client and deals only with the content of his statement, and even then only in the vaguest way. The impact of such a response is "You don't really have a problem at all, at least not a serious one."

An interpretation. A counselor might say something like "This sexual thing is probably really just a symptom, John. I've got a hunch that you're not really accepting yourself." The counselor fails to respond to the client's feelings and also distorts the content of the client's communication. The response implies that what is really important is hidden from the client.

Advice. Another counselor might say: "There are a few videotapes on sexuality in the college years I'd like you to take a look at." This counselor also ignores Peter's feelings and jumps to an action program in sex education. It well may be that Peter could use some good input on sexual development, but this is neither the time nor the way to accomplish that.

Pretending to understand. Clients are sometimes confused, distracted, and in a highly emotional state; all these conditions affect the clarity of what they are saying about themselves. On the other hand, counselors themselves might become distracted and fail to follow the client. In either case, it's a mistake to feign understanding. Genuineness demands that counselors admit that they are lost and then work to get back on track again. A statement like "I think I've lost you. Could we go over that once more?" indicates that you think it important to stay with the client. It is a sign of respect. Admitting that you're lost is infinitely preferable to such clichés as "uh-huh," "ummmm," and "I understand." Peter is saying that he is having a problem with his sexual identity and finds it very difficult to talk about it. The mature counselor can take this in stride, even though it's an entirely new part of Peter's story.

Parroting. Empathy is not mere parroting. The mechanical helper corrupts basic empathy by simply restating what the client has said.

Counselor: So it's really a problem with sex that's bothering you. You're not sure of your manhood even though you're in college. You not only don't go out with women, but you're not even sure you want to. All this makes you think that you might be gay, but you're not sure.

Sounds awful, doesn't it? Here repetition is substituting for empathy. A tape recorder could do that perfectly.

Some people use the terms "empathy" interchangeably with "reflection" or "rephrasing." While rephrasing is not the same as parroting, I see a distinction between rephrasing and empathy. When I listen to clients and keep asking myself such questions as "What is this person's point of view?" and "What are the core messages in what this person is saying?" I am engaged in a process that is more than mere reflection. When I am empathic, I am sharing a part of myself, that is, my understanding of the other person.

Sympathy and agreement. Being empathic is not the same as being sympathetic. Sympathy, as Gill (1982) noted, has much more in common with pity, compassion, commiseration, and condolence than with empathy. While these are fully human traits, they are not particularly useful in counseling. Book (1988) spells out the reasons for this:

> Empathy is often confused with sympathy, kindness, and approval. Thus, it may come to mean behaving compliantly in response to the patient's behavior and [responding] sympathetically to his or her problems. It may evoke a stance of unquestioning acceptance of the patient's experiences by the therapist. . . . It leaves the therapist stuck in the participant [as opposed to observer] stance only. Bogged down in this stance, the therapist runs the risk of only identifying with and colluding with the patient's experience. (p. 422)

Sympathy, as the following example indicates, denotes agreement, whereas empathy denotes understanding and acceptance of the *person* of the client.

> A Holocaust survivor raged against the rudeness to which he felt subjected at work. His Jewish therapist responded, "It really makes me angry when I hear that. What the hell's the matter with them?" The patient responded, "That's what I'm telling you. They're all a bunch of butchers!" (Book, 1988, p. 422)

Here the counselor's collusion obscured the real issue: this client's aggressive and suspicious stance invited the very rudeness he complained about. Some clients fail to manage their lives better because they take an "Isn't it awful!" attitude toward their problems. Sympathy makes this worse. In our example of Peter, sympathy would not be of help ("Yes, isn't it awful, Peter!"). The objectivity of empathy rather than the collusion of sympathy will prove more useful:

BOX 6-1   Suggestions for the Use of Empathy

1. Remember that empathy is, ideally, a way of being and not just a professional role or communication skill.
2. Attend carefully, both physically and psychologically, and listen to the client's point of view.
3. Try to set your judgments and biases aside for the moment and walk in the shoes of the client.
4. As the client speaks, listen especially for core messages.
5. Listen to both verbal and nonverbal messages and their context.
6. Respond fairly frequently, but briefly, to the client's core messages.
7. Be flexible and tentative enough that the client does not feel pinned down.
8. Use empathy to keep the client focused on important issues.
9. Move gradually toward the exploration of sensitive topics and feelings.
10. After responding with empathy, attend carefully to cues that either confirm or deny the accuracy of your response.
11. Determine whether your empathic responses are helping the client remain focused while developing and clarifying important issues.
12. Note signs of client stress or resistance; try to judge whether these arise because you are inaccurate or because you are too accurate.
13. Keep in mind that the communication skill of empathy, however important, is a tool to help clients see themselves and their problem situations more clearly with a view to managing them more effectively.

Counselor: You've got a number of misgivings about just where you stand with yourself sexually, and it's certainly not easy talking about it.

Peter: I'm having a terrible time talking about it. I'm even shaking right now.

The counselor's empathy gives Peter the opportunity to deal with his immediate anxiety and then to explore his major concern.

Box 6-1 summarizes some of the main points about the use of empathy as a communication skill.

A Caution on Empathy

While some may expect too much of empathy in and of itself, others do not understand and respect its power. I personally prefer to see it integrated into a realistic helping model that provides both challenge and support at the service of both the client-helper relationship and problem-managing behavior change. Driscoll (1984), with his usual common sense, puts empathy in perspective.

> Showing that we understand should not be seen as incompatible in any way with any of the range of further interventions. The sequencing of therapeutic interventions is important. One who acknowledges another's position is more easily seen as an ally, and is in a better position from

there to challenge and restructure. Expressing an understanding is thus an initial intervention which prepares the groundwork for later, more forceful strategies for change. In general, as each issue is introduced, we should convey that we understand the client's position on that issue, and then continue from there to interpretation and redirection.

The empathic response is given an exalted position in classical client-centered counseling: it is the answer to everything, and anything else a counselor might do is just plain wrong. Most eclectics use empathic responses but reject the restrictive ideology. We see the empathic response as but one of a range of available therapeutic responses. (p. 90)

A further caution about the place of communication skills in the helping process is found at the end of this chapter.

THE ART OF PROBING

In most of the examples used in the discussion of empathy, clients have demonstrated a willingness to explore themselves and their behavior rather freely. Obviously, this is not always the case. While it is essential that helpers respond empathically to their clients when they do reveal themselves, it is also necessary at times to encourage, prompt, and help clients to explore problem situations when they fail to do so spontaneously. Therefore, the ability to use prompts and probes well is another important skill.

Prompts and probes are verbal tactics for helping clients talk about themselves and define their problems more concretely in terms of *specific* experiences, behaviors, and feelings. As such, they can be used in all the stages of the helping process.

Prompts and probes, therefore, are at the service of information generation. I don't mean mindless information gathering based on the unvoiced assumption that there is some kind of magic relationship between the amount of information gathered and the client's progress—that there is some magic *bit* of information that, once unearthed, will do the trick. This is the stuff of movies. Information gathering needs to serve the problem-management process, not lead it. In this sense, quality of information is much more important than quantity. Probing is the search for quality information, information on which the client can act.

Prompts and probes can take the form of questions, statements, or interjections. Let's look at examples of each.

Questions That Help Clients Talk More Freely and Concretely

I start with the premise that helpers often ask too many questions. If in doubt, they ask a question. For them, the question is the helping equivalent of talking about the weather. Questions can indeed be useful, but guidelines are called for.

1. Do not assault clients with volleys of questions. When clients are asked too many questions, they feel grilled, and this does little for the helping relationship.

> I feel certain that we ask too many questions, often meaningless ones. We ask questions that confuse the interviewee, that interrupt him. We ask questions the interviewee cannot possibly answer. We even ask questions we don't want the answers to, and, consequently, we do not hear the answers when [they are] forthcoming. (Benjamin, 1981, p. 71; the author devotes an entire chapter to the question, its uses, and his misgivings about it)

Let's assume, in the example of Peter, that the helper asks Peter a whole series of questions:

- "When did you first feel like this?"
- "With whom do you discuss sex?"
- "What kinds of sexual experience have you had?"
- "What makes you think you are gay?"

And so on and so forth. Peter might well say, "Goodbye, no thanks" in response to these intrusions. Heavy reliance on questions is a sign of ineptness, and it can turn helping interviews into boring question-and-answer sessions that go nowhere.

2. Ask questions that serve a purpose. Don't ask random, aimless questions. Ask questions that have teeth (but not barbs) in them, questions that help clients get somewhere. If the question is information-oriented, it should be information that is useful to the client. Some helpers mindlessly use questions to amass information, much of which proves to be irrelevant. Ask questions that challenge the client to think. Consider the following exchange between Peter and his counselor.

Peter: I've got moral principles. I can't be gay. . . . I might as well shut down my sex life. You know, forget about it.
Counselor: Is that what you want?
Peter (pausing): Well, no, of course not. Who would?

Here the counselor uses a question, not to gather information, but to challenge Peter to consider what he's saying. The question has a purpose.

Later, Peter is talking about his relationship with one of his best friends.

Peter: He has no idea that I'm attracted to him.
Counselor: What's the worst thing that could happen if he knew?

Peter is making all sorts of assumptions about how people would react to him if they knew he was ambivalent about his sexual identity. The helper uses the question to open up Peter's "assumptive world" for discussion.

Ask questions that help clients get into the stages and steps of the helping model. In the following example, the client has been talking about his dissatisfaction with his present job.

Counselor: If you had just the kind of job you wanted, what would it look like?
Client: Well, let me think. . . . It certainly would not be just the money. It would be something that interested me.

Note that the question puts the ball once more in the client's court and that it centers the discussion on Stage II, the preferred scenario.

3. Ask open-ended questions that get clients to talk about specific experiences, behaviors, and feelings. As a general rule, ask open-ended questions, that is, questions that require more than a simple yes or no or similar one-word answer. Not "Now that you've decided to take early retirement, do you have any plans?" but "Now that you've decided to take early retirement, what are your plans?" Counselors who ask closed questions—questions that invite one-word answers—find themselves asking more and more questions. This is often a problem for beginners. Of course, if a specific piece of information is needed, then a closed question may be used: "How many jobs have you had in the past two years?" Such a question could provide essential background information in a career-counseling session.

Ordinarily, however, prefer open-ended questions that help clients fill in things that are being left out of their story, whether experiences, behaviors, or feelings. Probes can keep clients from rambling and talking in generalities.

Client: I don't like doing those kinds of things.
Helper: What kinds of things?
Client: I don't enjoy cleaning the house, doing the laundry, picking up after the kids. . . . Cooking is about the only household task I enjoy.

Client: He treats me badly, and I don't like it!
Helper: What does he do?
Client: He laughs at me behind my back—I know he does.

Client: Coming home at night is a real downer for me.
Helper: What's a "downer" like for you?
Client: I see him sitting in that chair, helpless, and my heart goes out to him so much. Or I see him there and I get so angry because I'm trapped here with him.

In each case, the client's story gets more specific.

4. Keep the focus on the client. Questions should keep the focus on clients and their interests, not on the theories of helpers. One possibility is to have clients ask relevant questions of themselves. In the following example, Jill, the helper, and Justin, the client, have been discussing how Justin's disability—he has lost a leg to cancer—is standing in the way of his picking up his life again:

Jill: If you had to ask yourself one question right now, what would it be?
Justin (pausing a long time): "Why are you taking the coward's way out?" (His eyes tear up.)

Jill's question (or challenge) puts the ball in Justin's court. It's her way of asking Justin to take responsibility for his part of the session. Justin uses her challenge to challenge himself in a way he would never have done otherwise. Another example:

Counselor: What are some of the questions you need to ask yourself if you are to understand what's happening between you and your husband a little better?
Client: Hmmm. I think I'd have to ask myself: "What do *you* do that makes him want to drink all the time? What's your part in all this?" Those are unsettling questions for me.

Thus, another way to probe is to help clients ask relevant, even "impertinent," questions of themselves.

Statements That Encourage Clients to Talk and Clarify

Prompts and probes do not have to be questions. With the same guidelines in mind, counselors can use *statements and requests* to help clients talk and clarify relevant issues. For example, an involuntary client may come in and then just sit there and fume. The helper probes with a statement:

Helper: I can see that you're angry, but I'm not entirely sure what it's about.
Client: As if you didn't know. It's you—you're so damn smug.

Of their very nature, probing statements make some demand on the client either to talk or to become more specific. They are indirect requests of clients to elaborate on their experiences, behaviors, or feelings.

Helper: I realize now that you often get angry when your mother-in-law stays for more than a day. But I'm still not sure what she does that makes you angry.
Client: First of all, she throws our household schedule out and puts in her own.

In these examples, the helper's statement places a demand on the client to clarify the *experiences* that give rise to certain behaviors and feelings.
Consider another example.

Helper: The Sundays your husband exercises his visiting rights with the children end in his taking verbal pot shots at you, and you get these headaches. I've got a fairly clear picture of what he does when he comes over, but it might help if you could describe what you do.

Client: Well, I don't do anything.

Helper: Last Sunday, he just started making comments about you.

Client: I asked him about increasing the child support payments. And I might have asked him why he's dragging his feet about getting a better job.

Another example:

Helper: When the diagnosis of cancer came in two weeks ago, you said that you were both relieved—because you knew what you had to face—and depressed. You've mentioned that your behavior has been a bit chaotic since then. Tell me what you've been doing.

Client: I've been to the lawyer to get a will drawn up. I'm trying to get all my business affairs in order. I've been writing letters to relatives and friends. I've been on the phone a lot. . . . I've been burying my anger and fright by filling my days with lots of activity, from beginning to end.

In the last two instances the helper encourages the client to describe his or her *behavior* as a way of giving greater clarity to the problem situation.
    A final example:

Helper: When you talk about your wife and what she does, you use fairly positive emotions. For instance, you "appreciate" it when she points out the mistakes you make. I haven't heard any negative or mixed feelings yet. Maybe there are none.

Client: I think you probably know I get them buried. I see no advantage to blowing up and just making myself feel worse.

Here the helper's statement provides the client with an opportunity to discuss the *feelings* that go with his experiences and behaviors.

Interjections That Help Clients to Focus

A prompt or probe need not be a full question or a statement. It can be a word or phrase that helps focus the client's attention on the discussion.

Client: My son and I have a fairly good working relationship now, even though I'm not entirely satisfied.

Helper: Not entirely satisfied?

Client: Well, I should probably say "dissatisfied" because . . .

Another example:

Client: At the end of the day, what with the kids and dinner and cleaning up, I'm bushed.
Helper: Bushed?
Client: Tired, angry, hurt—he and the kids do practically nothing to help me!

In these cases the probe helps clients say more fully what they are only half saying.

Even such responses as "uh-huh," "mmm," "yes," "I see," "ah," and "oh," as well as nods and the like, can serve as prompts, provided they are used intentionally and are not a sign that the helper's attention is flagging.

Client: There are a lot of things I don't like about my lifestyle. (Pause)
Helper: Uh-huh.
Client: For instance, I spend too much time working and too much time by myself when I'm not working.

Interjections can also be nonverbal.

Client: I don't know if I can tell you this. I haven't told it to anyone.
(**Helper** maintains good eye contact and leans forward a bit.)
Client: Well, my brother had sexual relations with me a few times a couple of years ago. I think about it all the time.

In Chapter 5 I suggested that you become aware of the messages your non-verbal behavior communicates. With that awareness, you can progress to using nonverbal forms of communication to prompt the client to explore the problem situation in greater detail.

Some Cautions in the Use of Probes

It is probably clear that prompts and probes, both verbal and nonverbal, can be overused to the detriment of both the helping relationship and the steps of the helping process. In keeping with the values of Chapters 3 and 4, use probes to help increase rather than decrease the client's initiative. If you extort information with a constant barrage of probes and prompts, clients are unlikely to take more and more responsibility for problem solving and opportunity development. Therefore, after using a probe, use basic empathy rather than another probe or series of probes as a way of encouraging further exploration. After all, if a probe is effective, it will yield information that needs to be listened to and understood.

In the following example, the client is a young Chinese-American woman whose father died in China and whose mother is now dying in the United States. She has been talking about the traditional obedience of Chinese women and her fears of slipping into a form of passivity in her

American life. She talks about her sister, who, in traditional Chinese fashion, seems to give everything to her husband without looking for anything in return.

Counselor: Are these tendencies to passivity rooted in your genes?
Client: Sometimes I think so. They seem to be in my cultural genes. And yet I look around and see many of my American counterparts adopt a different style. Last year, when I took a trip back to China with my mother to meet my half-sisters, the moment I landed I wasn't American. I was Chinese again.

Counselor A: What did you learn there?
Client: That I was Chinese!

Counselor B: So part of it is, perhaps, being loyal to your heritage.
Client: While still being loyal to myself. Both are important. I don't want to be passive, but my trip told me I do not want to lose the values of my roots—at least not the best of them.

Counselor A, instead of responding with empathy to what the client has said, follows the probe with another question, and the client ends up repeating herself emphatically. Counselor B uses empathy to seize on a core message and so helps the client move forward.

Bob Carkhuff, in a workshop, suggested that if helpers find themselves asking two questions in a row, it might be that they have just asked two stupid questions. Prompts and probes are the salt and pepper of communication in the helping process. They should remain condiments judiciously used and not become the main course. Box 6-2 presents a checklist for effective probing.

THE LIMITS OF COMMUNICATION SKILLS

One of the reasons I have separated a discussion of the basic communication skills from the steps of the helping process is my feeling that helpers tend to overidentify the helping process with the communication skills that serve it. This is true not only of attending, listening, empathy, and probing, but also of the skills of challenging to be treated in Chapter 8. Being good at communication skills is not the same as being good at helping. Moreover, an overemphasis on communication skills can make helping a great deal of talk with very little action. Technique can replace substance. Communication skills are essential, of course, but they still must serve the outcomes of the helping process. As we proceed through the helping model, ways of using communication skills to produce these outcomes will be illustrated.

BOX 6-2   Suggestions for the Use of Probes

1. Keep in mind the goals of probing:
   a. To help nonassertive or reluctant clients tell their stories and engage in other behaviors related to the helping process.
   b. To help clients remain focused on relevant and important issues.
   c. To help clients identify experiences, behaviors, and feelings that give a fuller picture of the issue at hand.
   d. To help clients understand themselves and their problem situations more fully.
2. Use a mix of probing statements, open-ended questions, and interjections.
3. Do not engage clients in question-and-answer sessions.
4. If a probe helps a client reveal relevant information, follow it up with basic empathy rather than another probe.
5. Use whatever judicious mixture of empathy and probing is needed to help clients clarify problems, identify blind spots, develop new scenarios, search for action strategies, formulate plans, and review outcomes of action.
6. Remember that probing is a communication tool that is effective to the degree that it serves the stages and steps of the helping process.

Becoming Proficient at Communication Skills

Understanding communication skills and how they fit into the helping process is one thing. Becoming proficient in their use is another. Doing the exercises in the manual that accompanies this book and gaining practice in counselor-training groups can help, but these activities are not enough to incorporate empathy into your communication style. Empathy that is trotted out, as it were, for helping encounters is likely to have a hollow ring. These skills cannot be gimmicks. They must become part of your everyday communication style. After providing some initial training in these skills, I tell students, "Now, go out into your real lives and get good at these skills. I can't do that for you. But you cannot be certified in this program unless and until you demonstrate competency in these skills." Microskills training is just the first step in a process that must lead to these skills becoming second nature (Patterson, 1988).

Beyond Communication Skills: The Helping Process Itself

Some make too much of the communication skills needed in helping—especially empathy—expecting them to carry most of the helping burden. Kierulff's (1988) almost chilling experience reinforces this point.

A young man (whom I will call John) attempted to rob a bar. He and his older partner carried loaded shotguns, but the bartender was armed and quick on the draw, and John was shot. The . . . bullet severed John's spine; his legs collapsed under him, and he was left paraplegic. When he was taken to the hospital, he was assigned to me for psychotherapy.

John and I talked for hours, day after day, as he lay prone in his hospital bed. This 20-year-old armed robber fascinated me. He lied to me straightfaced. He portrayed himself as a victim. He changed his story whenever he thought he could gain an advantage. . . . He displayed no loyalty, no honor, no compassion. He trusted no one, and he displayed not even a crumb of trustworthiness. He used everyone, including me.

I had not dealt with any sociopaths before interacting with John. . . . I believed that Rogerian unconditional positive regard would eventually work its wonders and soften John's tough shell, allowing me to connect with him on a level of mutual empathy, caring, and respect.

"You can't change these people," my supervisor admonished. . . . I hoped that my supervisor was wrong. I kept on trying, but when the internship was over and I said goodbye to John, I could tell from the look in his eyes that in spite of the extra concern I had shown him, in spite of my warmth and care and effort, I was just another in the long list of people he had coldly manipulated and discarded. (p. 436)

In the ensuing article, Kierulff muses on the meaning of and the relationship between free will and determinism and what kind of treatment is needed to get through to "guiltless, manipulative people." His response is one that does not tolerate the helper's being conned and one that places demands for responsibility on such clients.

Johnson and Heppner (1989) are right in maintaining that effective counseling is more than the application of a range of skills. Counselors need to help clients process and use the information gathered through their dialogues at the service of problem-managing outcomes. The rest of this book provides that framework, that is, the problem-solving/opportunity-developing process itself. Like communication skills, the helping model, too, must become second nature. And so we turn now to its stages and steps.

PART TWO

THE STAGES AND STEPS OF THE HELPING MODEL

STAGE I: HELPING CLIENTS DEFINE AND CLARIFY PROBLEM SITUATIONS

Clients come to helpers because they need help in managing their lives more effectively. Stage I illustrates three ways in which counselors can help clients understand themselves and their problem situations with a view to setting goals and taking action.

Step I-A: Helping clients **tell their stories**.

Step I-B: Challenging—helping clients overcome blind spots and develop new perspectives.

Step I-C: Using leverage or focus to help clients **get the most out of helping** by working on issues that will make a difference.

These three "steps" are not restricted to Stage I. They are also processes to be used throughout the helping model.

Chapter Seven

Step I-A: Helping Clients Tell Their Stories

The Goals of Step I-A
Helping Clients Tell Their Stories
Clarity
    Talking about the Past to Clarify the Present
    The Overall Quality of a Client's Self-Disclosure
Assessment and Learning
    Initial Assessment
    Assessing and Promoting Clients' Ability to Learn
    Assessment as the Search for Resources
The Relationship: Social-Emotional Reeducation
Resistant and Reluctant Clients
    Resistance
    Reluctance
    Managing Resistance and Reluctance
Step I-A and Action
    The Sufficiency of Step I-A for Some Clients
    Action as a Means of Further Discovery
    Action as a Precondition for Helping
    Homework
Ongoing Evaluation
Evaluation Questions for Step I-A

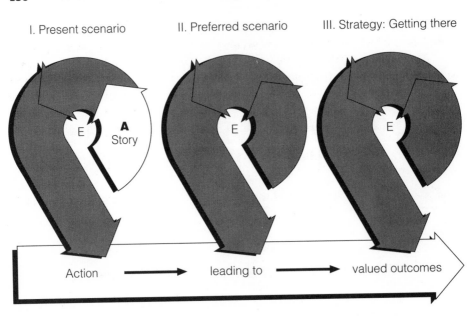

I. Present scenario   II. Preferred scenario   III. Strategy: Getting there

FIGURE 7-1   Step I-A: Helping Clients Tell Their Stories

Figure 7-1 highlights the first step in the helping process. Though "telling the story" may be first in a logical sense, it may not be first in time. As I mentioned in the overview of the helping model (Chapter 2), clients do not necessarily start at the beginning. For instance, I once counseled a man who had done all the steps by himself in managing the problems involved with restructuring his life after bypass surgery. He sought my help only because a few things were not going the way he wanted them to. We spent one session fine-tuning his goals and action program, and I never saw him again.

THE GOALS OF STEP I-A

Goals are desired outcomes, that is, those specific things you are trying to help your clients accomplish. If you are effective, Step I-A will result in clarity, learning, a developing relationship, and an orientation toward action.

• *Clarity:* Clients will spell out their problem situations and their unused opportunities in terms of *specific* experiences, behaviors, and feelings. Vague problems lead to vague solutions. The skills of empathy and probing help clients achieve clarity.

• *Learning:* Clients will begin to learn things about themselves and their world that will help them manage their lives better. Some helping models focus on assessment at this stage. In this model assessment is an ongoing process and is, potentially, one kind of learning.

• *Relationship:* The kind of relationship that serves helping outcomes (see Chapter 3) will develop and strengthen. I don't use the word "deepen" lest client-helper intimacy be seen as an end in itself. Helping *is* a kind of intimacy, but often it is more like the intimacy experienced by two people working together on a challenging project than the intimacy we associate with friendship or love.

• *Action:* Clients will begin to see that some kind of action on their part will be needed if problems are to be managed and opportunities developed. As we have seen in Chapter 4, this includes action inside and outside their heads, action inside and outside the helping sessions.

Since telling the story is not limited to Step I-A, the goals listed here will permeate the entire helping process.

HELPING CLIENTS TELL THEIR STORIES

Self-disclosure—its relationship to personality, its place in relationships, and its role in therapy—has attracted the attention of theoreticians, researchers, and practitioners alike (Derlega & Berg, 1987). Using the communication skills outlined in the previous chapter, counselors help clients engage in self-disclosure or, in the words of the helping model, tell their stories—that is, their concerns about problem situations that are not being managed well and/or opportunities that are not being developed. In the following example, the client, Louella, is a 34-year-old woman who is separated from her husband and living in public housing in a large city in the Midwest. This is her first session with a social worker.

Social Worker: You say that a lot of things are bothering you. What kinds of things?

Louella: Well, they don't take care of this building very well. It's actually dangerous to live here. I've got two children, and I'm always worried about them. I worry about myself, too, but mostly about them.

Social Worker: It's so bad that you fear for your safety, most of all the safety of your kids.

Louella: I think that the elevators scare me the most. . . .

Social Worker: The elevators?

Louella: Often they're broken down. But that's not the real scary part. . . . People that don't live here can get in, and women have been raped. . . . I'm afraid the kids could get hurt. That's the real scary part. . . . And no one seems to do anything about it. This building's not at the top of anyone's list, I can tell you that. I don't know whether to stay here or go, but I don't know where I'd go.

Social Worker: So you don't feel safe, but even worse is that no one seems to care. Plus, you're not sure you could move even if you wanted to.

Here attending, listening, empathy, and probing are all used to build a relationship with the client and help her tell her story.

If client and helper are sucessful in working together, the client will reveal the main features of the problem situation and, in telling the story, come to understand the problem situation more fully. Furthermore, the helper will develop an understanding of the client and his or her needs.

The stories clients tell often fall into the categories of choice issues, change issues, or a mixture of the two (Cormier & Cormier, 1986; Dixon & Glover, 1984; Tyler, 1969). In *choice* issues, clients have the resources to act on some problem, but do not feel ready to do so (Tyler, 1969). Or, as Cormier and Cormier (1986) put it, "Clients have prerequisite skills and opportunities but feel conflicted or uncertain about a particular option, choice, or decision" (p. 90). Louella's uncertainty about moving falls roughly into this category. Some clients don't have the information to make the decision. Others run into emotional blocks. Louella does not know whether she can go someplace else and also is not sure she wants to leave her friends.

In *change* issues, as Dixon and Glover (1984) noted, clients are dissatisfied with themselves or some situation and want to make modifications in themselves, the situation, or both. In change situations, deficits or excesses need to be remedied, or some kind of restructuring is called for. Louella is dissatisfied with her living conditions. She wants safer living conditions for herself and her children. Because of unsafe conditions (experience), she feels frightened and depressed (affect). She makes no mention of attempts on her part to remedy things (action). Thus, her situation involves change issues as well as choice issues.

Helpers deal with a wide variety of clients with a wide variety of concerns.

Martin, 24, asks a counselor in private practice for an appointment in order to discuss "a number of issues." Martin is both verbal and willing to talk, and his story comes tumbling out in rich detail. While the helper uses the skills of attending, listening, empathy, and probing, she does so sparingly. Martin is too eager to tell his story.

Martin tells a rather full story. Although trained as a counselor, Martin is currently working in his uncle's business because of an offer he "could not turn down." He is doing very well, but he feels guilty because service to others has always been a value for him. He both likes his job and feels hemmed in by it. A year of study in Europe has whetted his appetite for "adventure." He feels that he is nowhere near fulfilling the "great expectations" he has for himself.

He also talks about his problems with his family. His father is dead. He has never gotten along well with his mother, and now that he has moved out of the house, he feels that he has abandoned his younger brother, whom he loves very much.

Martin is also concerned about his relationship with a woman who is two years older than he. They have been involved with each other for about three years. She wants to get married, but he feels that he is not ready. He still has "too many things to do" and would like to keep the arrangement they have.

This whole complex story comes tumbling out in a torrent of words. Martin feels free to skip from one topic to another. The way Martin tells his story is part of his impulsive style. At one point he stops, smiles, and says, "Boy, I didn't realize that I had so much on my plate!" While all of these issues bother him, he does not feel overwhelmed by them.

Martin, too, has a mixture of choice and change issues.

Contrast this example with the following one of a woman who comes to a local mental health center because she feels she can no longer handle her 9-year-old boy.

> Edna is referred to the clinic because of the trouble she is having with her son. She has been divorced for about two years and is living on public assistance. After introductions and preliminary formalities have been taken care of, she just sits there and says nothing; she does not even look up. Since Edna offers almost nothing spontaneously, the counselor uses a relatively large number of probes to help her tell her story. Even when the counselor responds with empathy, Edna volunteers very little. Every once in a while, she begins to cry. When asked, she says she does not want to talk about the divorce. "Good riddance" is all she can say about her husband. Gradually, almost torturously, the story gets pieced together. Edna talks mostly about the "trouble" her son is getting into, how uncontrollable he seems to be getting, and how helpless she feels.

Consider a third example. Terry, a young woman in her late teens who has been arrested several times for street prostitution, is an involuntary client. She ran away from home when she was 16 and is now living in a large city on the East Coast. Like many other runaways, she was seduced into prostitution "by a halfway decent pimp." Now she is pretty street smart. She is also cynical about herself, her occupation, and the world. She is forced to see a counselor as part of the probation process.

> As might be expected, Terry is quite hostile during the interview. She has seen other counselors and sees the interview as a game. The counselor already knows a great deal of the story because of the court record.
>
> **Terry:** If you think I'm going to talk with you, you've got another think coming. What I do outside is my business.
>
> **Counselor:** You don't have to talk about what you do outside. You could talk about what we're doing here in this meeting.
>
> **Terry:** I'm here because I have to be. You're here either because you're dumb and like to do stupid things or because you couldn't get a better job. You people are no better than the people on the street. You're just more "respectable." That's a laugh.
>
> **Counselor:** So nobody could really be interested in you.
>
> **Terry:** I'm not even interested in me!
>
> **Counselor:** And if you're not, no one else could be, including me.

The counselor tries to help Terry tell, not the story "out there"—the story of the lifestyle that gets her in trouble—but rather the story that both of them are living right now "in here." Even though there are some explosive moments, Terry goes on to tell a story of her distrust of just about everyone, especially anyone connected with "the system." She emphasizes her contempt for the kind of people that try to "help" her.

Each client is different and will approach the telling of the story in different ways. Some of the stories you will help clients tell will be long and detailed, others short and stark. Some will be filled with emotion; others will be told coldly, even though they are stories of terror. Some stories will be, at least at first blush, single-issue stories—"I want to get rid of these headaches"—while others, like Martin's, will be multiple-issue stories. Some will be told readily, tumbling out with practically no help, while others will be told only haltingly or grudgingly. Some clients will tell the core story immediately, while others will tell a secondary story first in order to test the helper's reactions. Some stories will deal with the inner world of the client almost exclusively—"I hate myself," "I hear voices"—while others will deal with the outer world of interpersonal problems and the social settings of life. Still others will deal with a combination of inner and outer concerns. In all these cases the job of helpers is to be with their clients in such fully human and skillful ways that the clients are enabled to tell their stories. A story that is brought out in the open is the starting point for possible constructive change. Often the very airing of the story helps the client see it more objectively.

Some clients may pour out their stories if this is the first time they have had the opportunity to do so. If you judge that it is better for the time being to let the client pour everything out at once without much dialogue, then, as you listen, you should concentrate on identifying the core experiences, behaviors, and feelings and the core themes running through the story. When the client has finished, it will be impossible for you to respond empathically all at once to everything the client has said. But you do need some way of getting back to the most salient issues and of helping the client explore them further. Expressions like the following can be used to help the client review the core parts of the story.

- "There's a lot of pain and confusion in what you've just told me. Let's see if I've understood some of the main points you've made."
- "You've said quite a bit. Let's see if we can see how all the pieces fit together."

Your empathy will let the client know that you have been listening intently.

The telling of the story is not a goal in itself; it is a subgoal in the larger helping process. It is a means to help clients manage their lives more effectively. Just as some helpers mistakenly identify communication skills with helping, so others identify the telling of the story with helping. It is a step on the way. As I noted earlier, the goals of this step include achieving clarity, helping clients learn, building the relationship, and moving the client to an action orientation.

CLARITY

Clarity in terms of specific experiences, behaviors, and feelings is sought not for its own sake, but, as Mehrabian (1970) noted, to move the whole process forward.

> If we can find a way to expand the statement of a problem to a concrete list of specific behaviors which constitute it, one major obstacle to the solution of the problem will have been overcome. In other words, the initial ambiguity with which most people analyze their interpersonal problems tends to contribute to their feeling of helplessness in coping with them. Knowing which specific behaviors are involved, and thereby what changes in those behaviors will solve the problem, provides a definite goal for action—and having that goal can lend a great sense of relief. (p. 7)

What he says about behaviors can also be said about experiences and emotions.

Talking about the Past to Clarify the Present

Some schools of psychology suggest that problem situations are not clear and fully understood until they are understood in terms of their roots. However, the causes of things, especially the remote causes, are seldom evident. Deutsch (1954) noted that it is often almost impossible, even in carefully controlled laboratory situations, to determine whether event B, which follows event A in time, is actually caused by event A. Asking clients to come up with such causes often is inviting them to whistle in the wind.

Client: I think the problems between me and my husband have a lot to do with my relationship to my father. My husband is a lot like my father. I preferred being with my mother. He wasn't cruel or anything like that. It went much deeper . . .

Such talk is a bottomless pit. Very often it deals with what *happened* to clients (experiences) rather than what they *did* about what happened to them (behaviors).

A potentially dangerous logic can underlie discussions of the past. It goes something like this: "I am what I am today because of my past; I cannot change my past. So how can I be expected to change today?" Driscoll (1984) had a reply:

> "What you have learned from the past are ways of seeing and reacting to things, which are essentially habits. The habits exist not in your past but in your present, and can be changed. Change the habits, and the spell of your past is broken." (p. 68)

Indeed, breaking the spell of the past is one of the important tasks of helping.

This is not to say that a person's past does not influence current behavior. Nor does it imply that a client's past should not be discussed.

> The logic of this point need not be taken as a prejudice against talking about the past. We might investigate the past in order to make better sense of existing problems and to help the client restructure his (present) understanding of himself and of his relationships. Investigation of the past is thus a means to understand or try to change present viewpoints, but it is not a logical requirement for therapeutic changes and should not be seen as a necessary objective in and of itself. (p. 68)

Thus, *how* the past is discussed is more important than whether it is discussed. However, the focus must remain on action, not the investigation of causes.

> In clinical practice the issue is not so much how the person acquired a particular characteristic, but rather how he can alter or rearrange troublesome tendencies and acquire more constructive ones. The means by which present characteristics were acquired may be of some importance nonetheless, for they may give some leads to the means by which current changes may be made and more beneficial characteristics acquired. (Driscoll, 1984, p. 55)

Even with these reservations, Deutsch (1954) remained skeptical:

> This is not to deny the significance of the past in indirectly affecting behavior. However, even though the past can create a certain condition which carries over into the present, it is, nevertheless, the present condition which is influential in the present. Strictly considered, linking behavior with a past is an extremely difficult undertaking; it presupposes that one knows sufficiently how the past affected the psychological field at that time, and whether or not in the meantime other events have again modified the field. (p. 186)

In sum, if the past can add clarity to current experiences, behaviors, and emotions, then let it be discussed. If it can provide hints as to how self-defeating thinking and behaving can be changed now, let it be discussed. The past, however, should never become the principal focus of the client's self-exploration. When it does, helping tends to "lose the name of action."

The Overall Quality of a Client's Self-Disclosure

As I noted in Chapter 5, listening is both an empathic and a reality-checking activity. The categories indicated by the questions below can help you reality-check if they are triggered by what the client says or how the client acts. This is not to say that you should be consciously asking yourself these questions as the client talks. That would interfere with attending, listening, and empathy. Rather, these questions should be in the back of your mind.

- How appropriate is the client's self-disclosure?
- How informative is it in terms of quantity and quality of information related to problem situations?
- How easily does the client talk about self? How rewarding or punishing does this talk seem to be?
- To what extent does the client seem to get something out of telling his or her story?
- How truthful is the client?
- To what degree does the client seem to learn something from what he or she says?
- To what degree does the client relate his or her story to other parts of the helping process, such as goal setting or action?
- What signs, if any, are there that the client is trying to con or manipulate me?
- What is the client leaving out?
- To what extent does the client talk about experiences rather than his or her own behavior?
- To what extent does the client express or discuss feelings and emotions?

These are not cynical questions. If something the client says or does triggers one or more of these questions, it may be a sign that some intervention on your part would help him or her tell the story better at the service of higher-quality helping outcomes. For instance, suppose you notice that the client neither discusses nor expresses emotion. On the assumption that a problem situation is spelled out clearly when it is expressed in specific experiences, behaviors, and emotions, at some point you might remark: "I have a clear idea of what happened. I'm not sure, however, how you felt about all this." On the other hand, emotions, at least stronger emotions, might not play an important part in a specific problem situation, in which case there is nothing particularly sinister about their absence.

No claims are made here that self-disclosure in itself "cures." Nevertheless, it should be noted that, as Mowrer demonstrated (1968a, 1968b, 1973a, 1973b), in some cases self-disclosure can release "healing" forces or resources in the client. For instance, self-disclosure can help a client get out from under a burden of guilt and thus be the first solid step toward behavior change.

ASSESSMENT AND LEARNING

Learning is what the problem-management model is all about (Abbey, Hunt, & Weiser, 1985; Weinstein & Alschuler, 1985). Recall that *learning takes place when options are increased* (see Howell, 1982). Assessment, as part of the helping process, makes sense to the degree that it contributes to learning, to increasing the client's options. Hayes, Nelson, and Jarrett (1987) call this the "treatment utility of assessment." Unfortunately, while a great deal of work has been poured into assessment methods such as psychological tests, very little has been devoted to determining what payoff these methods have for clients. In terms of the helping model, assessment is the ability to understand clients, to spot "what's going on" with them, to see what they do not see and need to see, to make sense out of their chaotic behavior and help them make sense out of it—all at the service of helping them manage their lives and develop their resources more effectively. Assessment, then, is not something helpers do to clients: "Now that I have my secret information about you, I can fix you." Rather, it is a kind of learning in which both client and helper participate.

Assessment is a way of asking: What's really going on here? It takes place, in part, through the kind of reality-testing listening discussed in Chapter 5. As helpers listen to clients, even as they listen in intensely empathic ways, they hear more than the client's point of view. They listen to the client's deep conviction that he is "not an alcoholic," and at the same time they see the trembling hand, smell the alcohol-laden breath, and hear the desperate tone of voice. The purpose of such listening is not to place the client in the proper diagnostic category. The purpose is to be open to any kind of information or understanding that will enable them to help the client. Helping others is a profession for the open-minded and the broad-minded.

In medicine, assessment is usually a separate phase. In helping, as Driscoll (1984) noted, there is an interplay between assessment and intervention. Helpers who continually listen to clients in context and through the non-distorting filters discussed in Chapter 1—applied developmental psychology, cognitive psychology, the principles of behavior, applied personality theory, and the rest—are engaging in a kind of *ongoing assessment* that is in keeping with the clients' interests and need to act. Assessment is thus part and parcel of all stages and steps of the helping model. However, as in medicine, some initial assessment of the seriousness of the client's concerns is called for.

Initial Assessment

Clients come to helpers with problems of every degree of severity. Problems run, objectively, from the inconsequential to the life-threatening. Subjectively, however, even a relatively inconsequential problem can be experienced as severe by a client. If a client thinks that a problem is critical, even though by objective standards the problem does not seem to be that bad, then for him or her it is critical. In this case, the client's tendency to "catastrophize," to judge a problem situation to be more severe than it actually is, itself becomes an important part of the problem situation. One of the tasks of the counselor in this case will be to help the client put the problem in perspective or to teach him or her how to distinguish between degrees of problem severity.

Mehrabian and Reed (1969) suggested the following formula as a way of determining the severity of any given problem situation:

$$\text{Severity} = \text{Distress} \times \text{Uncontrollability} \times \text{Frequency}$$

The multiplication signs in the formula indicate that these factors are not just additive. Even low-level anxiety, if it is uncontrollable or persistent, can constitute a severe problem; that is, it can severely interfere with the quality of a client's life.

One way of viewing helping is to see it as a process in which clients are helped to control the severity of their problems in living. The severity of any given problem situation will be reduced if the stress can be reduced, if the frequency of the problem situation can be lessened, or if the client's control over the problem situation can be increased. Consider the following example.

> Indira is greatly distressed because she experiences migraine-like headaches, sometimes two or three times a week, and seems to be able to do little about them. No painkillers seem to work. She has even been tempted to try strong narcotics to control the pain, but she fears she might become an addict. She feels trapped. For her the problem is quite severe because stress, uncontrollability, and frequency are all high.
>
> Eventually Indira is referred to a doctor who specializes in treating headaches. He is an expert in both medicine and human behavior. He first helps her to see that the headaches are getting worse because of her tendency to "catastrophize" whenever she experiences one. That is, the self-talk she engages in ("How intolerable this is!") and the way she fights the headache actually add to its severity. He helps her control her stress-inducing self-talk and teaches her relaxation techniques. Neither of these gets rid of the headaches, but they help reduce the degree of stress she feels.
>
> Second, he helps her identify the situations in which the headaches seem to develop. They tend to come at times when she is not managing other forms of stress well, for instance, when she lets herself become overloaded and gets behind at work. He helps her see that, while her headaches constitute a very real problem, they are part of a larger problem situation. Once she begins to control and reduce other forms of stress in her life, the frequency of the headaches begins to diminish.
>
> Third, the doctor also helps Indira spot cues that a headache is beginning to develop. She finds that, while she can do little to control the headache once it is in full swing, there are things she can do during the beginning stage. For instance, she learns that medicine that has no effect when the headache is in full force does help if it is taken as soon as the symptoms appear. Relaxation techniques are also helpful if they are used soon enough. Indira's headaches do not disappear completely, but they are no longer the central reality of her life.

The doctor helps the client manage a severe problem situation much better than she has been doing by helping her reduce stress and frequency, while increasing control. In other words, he helps the client learn.

Assessing and Promoting Clients' Ability to Learn

William Miller (1986) talks about one of the worst days of his life. Everything was going wrong at work: projects were not working out, people were not responding, the work overload was bad and getting worse—nothing but failure all around. Later that day, over a cup of coffee, he took some paper, put the title "Lessons Learned and Relearned" at the top and put down as many entries as he could. Some hours and seven pages later, he had listed 27 lessons. The day turned out to be one of the best of his life. Both his attitude and his ability to come up with solutions to his problems helped so much that he began writing a "Lessons Learned" journal every day. He learned not to get caught up in self-blame and defeatism. Subsequently, on days when things were not working out, he would say to himself, "Ah, this will be a day filled with learnings!"

A similar process can be used when helping clients tell their stories, because most client stories are filled with learnings. The learnings are lost because they are not identified and captured.

> Elsa's husband had just died. The day of the funeral—there were just a few neighbors in the chapel—she was talking to her minister about the last couple of years. She and her husband had led a rather solitary life. They were childless, and neither had relatives in the area. Her husband had had Alzheimer's disease. Her story was a painful one: Misdiagnosis and misunderstanding early on. Gradual deterioration. No one to turn to. The pain and the relief of the end.
>
> Elsa and her husband had attended church only now and then. When the minister asked, "Is there anything to be learned from all this?" she looked at him and said, "Well, if you are looking for a theological treatise, you're not going to get one from me."
>
> "No," he said, "I'm not thinking about theology; I'm thinking of tomorrow."
>
> "Oh," she said, "tomorrow." After pausing for a while, she finally said, "Now that you ask, there are some lessons. I've learned that no matter what happens, you've got more resources inside yourself than you think. . . . A second one seems to contradict the first, but not really: Find a couple of good friends. They are like gold."

Clients' stories inevitably contain lessons. Your job is to help clients tap those lessons without becoming a preacher.

Assessment as the Search for Resources

Low-level helpers concentrate on clients' deficits. High-level helpers, as they listen to and observe clients, do not blind themselves to deficits, but they are quick to spot clients' *resources*, whether used, unused, or even abused. These resources can become the building blocks in whatever action program the client ultimately undertakes. For instance, Terry, the street prostitute, has obvious deficits. She is engaged in a dangerous and self-defeating lifestyle. But as the probation counselor listens to Terry, the counselor discovers a range of resources. Terry is a tough, street-smart woman. The very virulence of her cynicism and self-hate, the very strength of her resistance to help, and her almost unchallengeable determination to go it alone are all signs of resources. Many of her resources are currently being used in self-defeating ways, but they are resources nevertheless.

Helpers need a resource-oriented mind-set in all their interactions with clients.

Client: I practically never stand up for my rights. If I disagree with what anyone is saying—especially in a group—I keep my mouth shut. I suppose that on the rare occasions when I do speak up, the world doesn't fall in on me. Sometimes others do actually listen to me. But I still don't seem to have much impact on anyone.
Counselor A: It's depressing for you to keep backing away from saying what's on your mind, but you've learned to accept it.
Counselor B: Sometimes when you do speak up, you get a hearing. And so you're annoyed at yourself for getting lost in the crowd so often.

Counselor A misses the resource mentioned by the client. Although it is true that the client habitually fails to speak up, he has some impact when he does speak: Others do listen, at least sometimes, and this is a resource. Counselor A emphasizes the deficit; Counselor B notes the asset.

The search for resources is especially important when the story being told is bleak. I once listened to a man's story that included a number of bone-jarring life defeats—a divorce, false accusations that led to his dismissal from a job, months of unemployment, serious health concerns, and more. The only emotion the man exhibited as he told the story was depression.

Helper: Just one blow after another, grinding you down.
Client: Grinding me down, and almost doing me in.
Helper: Tell me a little more about the "almost" part of it.
Client: Well, I'm still alive, still sitting here talking to you.
Helper: Despite all these blows, you haven't fallen apart. That seems to say something about the fiber in you.

At the word "fiber," the client looked up, and there seemed to be a glimmer of something else besides depression in his face. I put a line down the center of a newsprint pad. On the left side I listed the life blows the man had experienced. On the right I put the word "fiber." Then I said, "Let's see if we can add to the list on the right side." We came up with a list of the man's resources—his "fiber," his musical talent, his honesty, his concern for and ability to talk to others, and so forth. After about a half-hour, he smiled—weakly, but he did smile.

Of course, this sensitivity to and search for resources is not limited to this step of the helping model. It belongs in every step. Assessment at its best is the continual search for anything that can be of use to the client. It includes problems the client is overlooking, but it also includes opportunities that can be seized. Assessment is not the search for things that can fit into the helper's models—or diagnostic categories. Models should be used to identify things that are useful to clients. Clients should not be forced into the models.

THE RELATIONSHIP: SOCIAL-EMOTIONAL REEDUCATION

The first interview is the time to start putting into practice what was outlined in Chapter 3 on the client-helper relationship and the values that need to permeate it. The relationship itself should contribute to the client's learning. Effective helpers are capable of identifying the relationship needs of clients and of adapting their style to these needs. Their relationships are characterized by the two elements that run through all effective helping—support and challenge, in whatever judicious mix of the two meets the needs of the particular client.

The social-emotional reeducation that takes place through the relationship between helpers and their clients is sometimes the most significant outcome of the helping process. Clients begin to care for themselves, trust themselves, and challenge themselves more because of what they learn through their interactions with helpers. Sometimes helpers overlook this critical outcome and, after a relationship is terminated, say to themselves, "Nothing much seemed to happen." But if they were to examine both process and outcomes more carefully, they might be able to say, "Because I trusted her, she trusts herself more, because I cared for her, she is now more capable of caring for herself, because I invited her to challenge herself and because I took the risk of challenging her, she is now more capable of challenging herself. Because of the way I related to her, she now relates better to herself and is in a better position to relate to others more effectively. She is now more likely to tap into her own resources."

RESISTANT AND RELUCTANT CLIENTS

It is impossible to be in the business of helping people for long without encountering both resistance and reluctance. Theoreticians, researchers, and practitioners are paying more and more attention to resistance and reluctance (Anderson & Stewart, 1983; Brehm, 1966; Cavanaugh, 1982; Chamberlain and others, 1984; Cormier & Cormier, 1985; Dyer & Vriend, 1975; Ellis, 1985b; Larke, 1985; Lewis & Evans, 1986; Medeiros & Prochaska, 1988; Ritchie, 1986; Spinks & Birchler, 1982; Stern, 1984;

Stream, 1985; Wachtel, 1982). As we will see, there is a difference between them, although in practice a mixture of reluctance and resistance as they are defined here can be found in the same client.

Resistance

I have reformulated my terminology on resistance and reluctance in this edition. Following the lead of Dimond and his associates (1978) and of Driscoll (1984), I now use the term *resistance* to refer to the reaction of clients who in some way feel *coerced*. It is their way of fighting back.

> Resistance . . . is active or passive opposition to something, not merely confusion, lethargy, or inertia. . . . The situation as perceived [by the client] has two aspects: it is seen as a force—an authority, power, or pressure to comply—and as unfair—as callous, intrusive, threatening, or otherwise unwarranted or unjust. (Driscoll, p. 185)

Resistance is the client's reaction to a power play. It may well arise because of a misperception—the client's seeing coercion where it does not exist. But, since people act on their perceptions, the result is still some form of fighting back. Resistant clients are likely to present themselves as not needing help, to feel abused, to show no willingness to establish a relationship with the helper, to con helpers whenever possible. They may be resentful, make active attempts to sabotage the helping process, terminate the process at the earliest possible moment, and be either testy or actually abusive and belligerent. In marriage counseling, one spouse might be there willingly while the other is there because he or she feels pressured by the helper, the spouse, or both. Resistance to helping is, of course, a matter of degree, and not all these behaviors in their most virulent forms are seen in all resistant clients.

Involuntary clients—"mandated" clients—are often resisters. Helpers can expect to find a large proportion of such clients in settings where clients are forced to see a counselor (a high school student is in trouble with a teacher, and going to a helper is a form of punishment) or in settings where a reward can be achieved only on the condition of being involved in some kind of counseling process (going to a counselor is the price that must be paid to get a certain job). Clients like these are found in schools, especially schools below college level; in correctional settings; in marriage counseling, especially if it is court-mandated; in employment agencies; and in welfare agencies, court-related settings, and other social agencies. Dyer and Vriend (1975, p. 102) suggest that involuntary clients constitute the majority of clients seen by helpers in North America.

Reasons for Resistance

There are all sorts of reasons for resisting—which is to say that clients can experience coercion in a wide variety of ways. The following kinds of clients are likely to be resistant:

- Clients who see no reason for going to the helper in the first place.
- Clients who resent third-party referrers (parents, teachers, agencies) and whose resentment carries over to the helper.
- Clients in medical settings who are asked to participate in "psychological therapies" (DeGood, 1983).
- Clients who feel awkward in participating, who do not know how to be "good" clients.
- Clients who have a history of being rebels against systems; they rock the boat, and boat-rockers are more likely to become involuntary clients.
- Clients who see the goals of the helper or the helping system as different from their own. For instance, the goal of counseling in a welfare setting may be to help the clients become financially independent, whereas some clients might be satisfied with the present arrangement. The goal of helping in a mental hospital may be to help the clients get out, whereas some clients might feel quite comfortable in the hospital.
- Clients who have developed negative attitudes about helping and helping agencies and who harbor suspicions about helping and helpers. Helpers are referred to in derogatory and inexact terms ("shrinks").
- Clients who believe that going to a helper is the same as admitting weakness, failure, and inadequacy. They feel that they will lose face by going. By resisting the process, they preserve their self-esteem.
- Clients who feel that counseling is something that is being done to them. They feel that their rights are not being respected.
- Clients who feel that they have not been invited by helpers to be participants in the decisions that are to affect their lives. This includes expectations for change and decisions about procedures to be used in the helping process.
- Clients who feel a need for personal power and find it through resisting a "powerful" figure or agency: "I may be relatively powerless, but I still have the power to resist." Riordan, Matheny, and Harris (1978) suggest that this can be a healthy sign in that "clients are grasping for a share in the control of their destiny" (p. 8).
- Clients who distrust helpers and need to test their level of support or their competence.
- Clients who dislike their helpers, but do not discuss their dislike with them.
- Clients who have a conception of the degree of change desired that differs from the helper's conception.

All these clients have in common a feeling of being coerced to engage in the process, even if they are not sure precisely of the source of the coercion.

This list is not exhaustive. Many sociopsychological variables—sex, prejudice, race, religion, social class, upbringing, cultural and subcultural blueprints, and the like—can play a part in resistance. For instance, a man might instinctively resist being helped by a woman, and vice versa. A black person might instinctively resist being helped by a white, and vice versa. A person with no religious affiliation might instinctively think that helping coming from a minister will be "pious" or will automatically include some form of proselytizing. Different schools of or approaches to counseling and psychotherapy identify causes of resistance that are derived from the theory of the particular school or approach (see Stream, 1985; Wachtel, 1982).

The fact that a client is not self-referred does not automatically mean that he or she will be a resister, even though the evidence seems to indicate that most are. If counseling is defined as a cooperative venture, Smaby and Tamminen (1979) wonder, does it make sense to talk about counseling involuntary clients? Perhaps not until the problem of coercion is faced and managed. Resistance can even be seen as something positive, a sign of life and struggle rather than surrender.

Reluctance

Reluctance—and some of it is found in everyone—refers to the ambiguity clients feel when they know that managing their lives better is going to exact a price. Clients are not sure whether they want to pay that price. Indeed, reluctance is "an unavoidable process in every effective treatment, for that part of the personality that has an interest in the survival of the pathology actively protests each time therapy comes close to inducing a successful change" (Redl, 1966, p. 216).

In contrast to resisters, reluctant clients are more likely to seem unsure of what they want, talk about only safe or low-priority issues, benignly sabotage the helping process by being overly cooperative, set unrealistic goals and then use them as an excuse for not working, not work very hard at changing their behavior, and be slow to take responsibility for themselves. While resisters make it clear that they want nothing to do with the process, reluctant clients may at times be indirectly uncooperative. They may tend to blame others or the social settings and systems of their lives for their troubles and play games with helpers. Reluctance, too, admits of degrees; clients come "armored" against change to a greater or lesser degree.

Some of the Roots of Reluctance

The reasons for reluctance are many. They are built into our humanity, plagued as it is by the "psychopathology of the average." Here is a sampling.

Fear of intensity. If the counselor uses high levels of attending, accurate empathy, respect, concreteness, and genuineness, and if the client cooperates by exploring the feelings, experiences, and behaviors related to the problematic areas of his or her life, the helping process can be an intense one. This intensity can cause both helper and client to back off. Skilled helpers know that counseling is potentially intense. They are prepared for it and know how to support a client who is not used to such intensity.

Lack of trust. Some clients find it very difficult to trust anyone, even a most trustworthy helper. They have irrational fears of being betrayed. Even when confidentiality is an explicit part of the client-helper contract, some clients are very slow to reveal themselves.

Fear of disorganization. Some people fear self-disclosure because they feel that they cannot face what they might find out about themselves. The client feels that the facade he or she has constructed, no matter how much energy must be expended to keep it propped up, is still less burdensome than exploring the unknown. Such clients often begin well, but retreat once they begin to be overwhelmed by the data produced in the self-exploration process.

Digging into one's inadequacies always leads to a certain amount of disequilibrium, disorganization, and crisis. But, just as disequilibrium for the child is the price of growth, so for the adult growth often takes place at crisis points. High disorganization immobilizes the client, while very low disorganization is often indicative of a failure to get at the central issues of the problem situation.

Shame. Shame is a much overlooked experiential variable in human living (Egan, 1970; Lynd, 1958). It is an important part of disorganization and crisis. The root meaning of the verb "to shame" is "to uncover, to expose, to wound," a meaning that suggests the process of painful self-exploration. Shame is not just being painfully exposed to another; it is primarily an exposure of self to oneself. In shame experiences, particularly sensitive and vulnerable aspects of the self are exposed, especially to one's own eyes. Shame often has the quality of suddenness: in a flash one sees heretofore unrecognized inadequacies without being ready for such a revelation. Shame is sometimes touched off by external incidents, such as a casual remark someone makes, but it could not be touched off by such insignificant incidents unless, deep down, one was already ashamed. A shame experience might be defined as an acute emotional awareness of a failure to be in some way.

Fear of change. The title of an article written by Bugental and Bugental (1986) says it all: "A fate worse than death: The fear of changing." Some people are afraid of taking stock of themselves because they know, however subconsciously, that if they do, they will have to change—that is, surrender comfortable but unproductive patterns of living, work more diligently, suffer the pain of loss, acquire skills needed to live more effectively, and so on. For instance, a husband and wife may realize, at some level of their being, that if they see a counselor they will have to reveal themselves and that, once the cards are on the table, they will have to go through the agony of changing their style of relating to each other.

In a counseling group I once dealt with a man in his sixties whose presenting complaint was a very high level of anxiety that was making his life quite painful. He told the story of how he had been treated brutally by his father until he finally ran away from home. We have already seen his logic earlier in this chapter: "No one who grows up with scars like mine can be expected to take charge of his life and live responsibly." He had been using his mistreatment as a youth as an excuse to act irresponsibly at work (he had an extremely poor job record), in his relationship with himself (he drank excessively), and in his marriage (he had been uncooperative and unfaithful and yet expected his wife to support him). The idea that he could change, that he could take responsibility for himself even at his age, frightened him, and he wanted to run away from the group. But, since his anxiety was so painful, he stayed. And he changed.

Each and every one of us needs only to look at our own struggles with growth, development, and maturity to add to this list of the roots of reluctance.

Managing Resistance and Reluctance

There are two problems with the distinction between resistance and reluctance. First, in popular and professional parlance the behavioral manifestations of both reluctance and resistance are called "resistance." Second, both reluctance and resistance can be found in the same client. Voluntary clients who are generally cooperative might become resistant whenever they feel that helpers are coercing them. Also, since most helpers tend to see natural reluctance as resistance, they describe all negative behaviors on the part of clients as resistance. This is unfortunate because clients become the "bad guys," and helpers fail to examine their own behavior to determine whether or not they are playing a power game.

Unhelpful Responses to Resistance and Reluctance

Helpers, especially beginning helpers who are unaware of the pervasiveness of reluctance and resistance, are often disconcerted by them. They may find themselves facing unexpected feelings and emotions in themselves when they encounter these behaviors in clients: they may feel confused, panicked, irritated, hostile, guilty, hurt, rejected, meek, or depressed. Distracted by these unexpected feelings, they may react in any of several unhelpful ways:

- They accept their guilt and try to placate the client.
- They become impatient and hostile and manifest these feelings either verbally or nonverbally.
- They do nothing in the hope that the reluctance or resistance will disappear.
- They lower their expectations of themselves and proceed with the helping process, but in a half-hearted way.
- They try to become warmer and more accepting, hoping to win the client over by love.
- They blame the client and end up in a power struggle with him or her.
- They allow themselves to be abused by clients, playing the role of a scapegoat.
- They lower their expectations of what can be achieved by counseling.
- They hand the direction of the helping process over to the client.
- They give up and terminate counseling.

In a word, when helpers engage "difficult" clients, they experience stress, and some give into self-defeating "fight or flight" approaches to handling it.

The source of this stress is not just the behavior of clients; it also comes from the helper's own self-defeating attitudes and assumptions about the helping process. Here are some of these attitudes and assumptions:

- All clients should be self-referred and adequately committed to change before appearing at my door.
- Every client must like me and trust me.
- I am a consultant and not a social influencer; it should not be necessary to place demands on clients or even help them place demands on themselves.
- Every unwilling client can be helped.
- No unwilling client can be helped.
- I alone am responsible for what happens to this client.
- I have to succeed completely with every client.

Effective helpers neither court reluctance and resistance nor are surprised by it.

More Productive Approaches to Dealing with Resistance and Reluctance

In a book like this it is impossible to identify every possible form of reluctance and resistance, much less provide a set of strategies for managing each. What I can do is provide you with some principles and a general approach to managing reluctance and resistance in whatever form they take.

See some resistance as normative. Help clients see that they are not odd because they are reluctant or resistant. Beyond that, help them see the positive side of resistance. It may well be a sign of their affirmation of self.

See reluctance as avoidance. Reluctance can be seen as a form of avoidance that is not necessarily tied to ill will on the client's part. Therefore, you need to understand the principles and mechanisms underlying avoidance behavior (which is often discussed in texts dealing with the principles of behavior; see Watson and Tharp, 1985). If clients are avoiding counseling or any part of it because they see it either as punishing or at least as lacking in suitable rewards, then helpers have to demonstrate to them in concrete and specific ways that engaging in the helping process can be rewarding rather than punishing and that change can be more rewarding than maintaining the status quo. Effective helpers realize that motivation usually has more to do with incentives than "motives" locked away in the hearts of clients (Gilbert, 1978). Ask yourself such questions as: What incentives move this client to engage in this form of reluctance? What incentives does this client need to move beyond resistance?

Explore your own reluctance and resistance. Examine reluctance and resistance in your own life. How do you react when you feel coerced? How do you resist personal growth and development? If you are in touch with the various forms of reluctance and resistance in yourself and are finding ways of overcoming them, you are more likely to help clients deal with theirs.

Examine the quality of your interventions. Without setting off on a guilt trip, examine your helping behavior. Ask yourself whether you are doing anything to coerce clients and therefore run the risk of provoking resistance. For example, you may have become too directive without realizing it. Furthermore, take stock of the emotions that are welling up in you because clients lash back or drag their feet and the ways in which you are communicating these feelings to them. Do not deny these feelings. Rather, own them and find ways of coming to terms with them. For instance, do not overpersonalize what the client does. If you are allowing a hostile client to get under your skin, you are probably reducing your effectiveness.

Accept and work with the client's reluctance and resistance. This is a central principle. Start with the frame of reference of the client. Accept both the client and his or her resistance. Do not ignore it or be intimidated by it. Let clients know how you experience it and then explore it with them. Model openness to challenge. Be willing to explore your own negative feelings. The skill of direct, mutual talk (called *immediacy*, to be discussed later) is extremely important here. Help clients work through the emotions associated with resistance. Avoid moralizing. In this sense, befriend the resistance instead of reacting to it with hostility or defensiveness.

Be realistic and flexible. Remember that there are limits to what a helper can do. Know your own personal and professional limits. If your expectations for growth, development, and change exceed the client's, you can end up in an adversarial relationship. Rigid expectations of the client and yourself become self-defeating. As Cormier and Cormier (1985) note, "Some of what gets labeled 'client resistance' is nothing more than the inflexibility of the therapist" (p. 577).

Establish a "just society" with your client. Deal with the client's feelings of coercion. Provide what Smaby and Tamminen (1979) call a "two-person just society" (p. 509). A just society is based on mutual respect and shared planning. Therefore, establish as much mutuality as is consonant with helping goals.

Invite participation. Invite clients to participate in every step of the helping process and in all the decision making. Share expectations. Discuss and get reactions to helping procedures. Have the clients help design a mini-contract that is related only to the first couple of sessions.

Help clients identify resistance-supporting incentives. Help clients see and appreciate the roots and even the legitimacy of their resistance. If they discover the payoff that is associated with and helps maintain their resistance, they may be open to finding other ways of getting the same kinds of payoff.

Search for incentives for moving beyond resistance. Help clients find incentives for participating in the helping process. Use client self-interest as a way of identifying these. Use brainstorming (see Chapter 14) as a way of discovering possible incentives. For instance, the realization that he or she is going to remain in charge of his or her own life may be an important incentive for a client.

Tap significant others as resources. Do not see yourself as the only helper in the life of your clients. Engage significant others such as peers and family members in helping clients face their resistance. For instance, lawyers who belong to Alcoholics Anonymous might be able to deal with a lawyer's reluctance to join a treatment program more effectively than you can.

Employ clients as helpers. If possible, find ways to get resistant clients into situations where they are helping others. The change of perspective can help clients come to terms with their own resistance. One tactic is to take the role of the client in the interview and manifest the same kind of resistance he or she is. Have the client take the counselor role and help you overcome your resistance. Group counseling, too, is a forum in which clients become helpers. One person who did a great deal of work for Alcoholics Anonymous had a resistant alcoholic go with him on his city rounds, which included visiting hospitals, nursing homes for alcoholics, jails, flophouses, and down-and-out people on the streets. The alcoholic saw through all the lame excuses other alcoholics offered for their plight. After a week he joined AA himself.

In summary, do not avoid dealing with reluctance and resistance, but do not reinforce them. Work with your client's unwillingness and become inventive in finding ways of dealing with it.

Using the Helping Model Itself to Deal with Resistance and Reluctance

The issues clients bring with them can be called "content" problems. The alcoholic talks about his drinking problem, the surgery patient talks about her fears of dying, a married couple talk about their seemingly irreconcilable differences. "Content" problems generally refer to clients' life "out there." But clients can also have problems with the helping process and sessions themselves. These can be called "process" problems. They include avoiding a frank discussion of a problem and all the other forms of reluctance, the muteness of the involuntary client and all the other forms of resistance, incompatibility with the helper, and difficulties engaging in any of the stages and steps of the helping model.

The tool that I use most frequently to manage reluctance, resistance, and process problems is the helping model itself. An example:

- *Current scenario:* The client is avoiding talking concretely about the principal issues related to her problem situation.
- *Preferred scenario:* The client is talking more freely and concretely about her principal concerns. This helps her begin to manage her problems.
- *Getting from the current scenario to the preferred scenario:* The helper brainstorms strategies for helping the client talk more freely and chooses the strategies that make most sense.

Again, be inventive in devising appropriate strategies. One client might respond to a direct challenge: "The issues you're talking about are very sensitive, and I appreciate how difficult it may be for you to talk about them in any detail. Is there anything that I can do to help you do this more easily?" Another might be helped by a more indirect strategy:

Helper: Let's change roles for a little while. If you were the counselor, what would you be saying to me right now?

Client: Let me think. . . . I'd say, "You seem to be stalling around. Not talking about the real issues seems to be a problem in itself."

Sometimes in frustration or even panic we can fail to use our own medicine in managing the problems we encounter as helpers. In training counselors, I inevitably run into what-if questions ("What if the client does *x, y,* or *z,* then what do I do?") or very real problems trainees have run into in practicum and internship situations ("The client did *x,* and I didn't know what to do"). When the trainee is challenged to apply the three-stage model to the process problem, almost inevitably she or he comes up with a number of strategies for handling it. There can be hundreds of different process problems, hundreds of different forms of reluctance and resistance. It is impossible to come up with a specific strategy for dealing with each, just as it is impossible to devise a single strategy for all the hundreds of content problems clients bring. The key is to use the problem-solving model to generate appropriate ways of getting to the preferred state of affairs.

STEP I-A AND ACTION

If what you do in Step I-A is worth its salt, clients will move closer to problem-managing action. There are a number of ways of looking at the relationship between this "first" step of the model and action.

The Sufficiency of Step I-A for Some Clients

Some clients seem to need only this first step of the helping model. That is, they spend a relatively limited amount of time with a helper, they tell their story in greater or lesser detail, and then they go off and evidently manage quite well on their own. Here are two ways in which clients may need only the first step of the helping process.

A Declaration of Intent and the Mobilization of Resources

For some clients the very fact that they approach someone for help may be sufficient to help them begin to pull together the resources needed to manage their problem situations more effectively. For these clients, going to a helper is a declaration, not of helplessness, but of intent: "I'm going to do something about this problem situation." Once they begin to mobilize their resources, they begin to manage their lives quite well on their own and no longer need the services of a helper.

Sometimes a client's story is about a "trigger event." DuBrin (1987) describes, mostly through examples, how frustrations, especially "last-straw" frustrations, can act as "trigger events" in people's lives, that is, events that finally trigger some action. In Ben's case (Chapter 4), being taken to the hospital acted as a trigger event, of course with some help from Liz. In cases like these, a problem can sometimes be turned into opportunity fairly readily.

Many different kinds of events, not just last-straw frustrations, can trigger action. For instance, Tess is in a dead-end job. When her boss leaves the company, a company counselor helps her use her boss's departure as a trigger event. As a result, Tess becomes much more proactive in finding a job with a career track within the same company. Any event that can point to meaning beyond itself can be a trigger event. The realization that a "friend" has canceled four dates in the last four months can trigger the rethinking of a relationship; getting a raise can trigger a rethinking of one's career; successful surgery can trigger a rethinking of one's values. Since serious rethinking leads to action, helpers sensitive to the power of trigger events can help clients galvanize themselves into action.

Coming Out from under Self-Defeating Emotions

Some clients come to helpers because they are incapacitated, to a greater or lesser degree, by feelings and emotions. Often, when such clients are shown respect, listened to, and understood in a nonjudgmental way, their self-defeating feelings and emotions subside. Once this happens, they are able to call on their own inner and environmental resources and begin to manage the problem situation that precipitated the incapacitating feelings and emotions. In short, they move to action. These clients, too, seem to be "cured" merely by telling their story. Once they get out from under the emotions that have been burdening them, they once more take charge of their lives. Such clients may even say something like "I feel relieved even though I haven't solved my problem." Often they feel more than relieved; they feel empowered by their interactions, however brief, with a caring helper.

It goes without saying that not all clients fall into the two categories just described. Those who do not move readily to action need further help. Skilled helpers, in collaboration with their clients, are able to help clients discover what further services they need beyond being helped to tell their stories.

Action as a Means of Further Discovery

Actions are heuristic: they can find more problems, they can uncover blind spots, they can help set priorities, they can discover preferred-scenario possibilities, they can help formulate agendas, they can test commitment, and they can point the way to viable strategies and plans. A young client of mine said that he had little problem with interpersonal relationships, and certainly none with women. Rather, he was simply too busy to have much of a social life. I encouraged him to try dating, and he discovered a few blind spots. Some weeks later his new story dealt with problems with social interactions, especially with women. In this case the client's action of dating helped him discover that he was not so at ease with women as he had thought. Action generated more of the story.

Action as a Precondition for Helping

Some helpers (see Omer, 1985) require prospective clients to complete certain tasks as a precondition for acceptance in therapy. They find that these tasks can increase clients' commitment to the helping process, help them get a running start, and improve their outlook. Researchers are not sure why this works, but often enough it does. One explanation is that the fulfillment of precondition tasks triggers a self-perpetuating, positive cycle.

Omer (1985) offers two guidelines for setting such precondition tasks. First, choose tasks that prepare the client for the helping process. Tasks with an air of finality to them might distract clients from the helping process. Second, choose tasks that clients can master and that consequently increase self-efficacy expectations.

Some helpers demand action on the part of clients as a condition for continuing the process. In Step I-A this would mean requiring the client to complete some kind of task before the next session. Here is a striking example of this approach, as applied to drug counseling. The helper first listens carefully to the addict's story. Then:

> Once the client is motivated to continue in the first session, I advise my client, to his or her amazement, that I will not make a second appointment until he or she is clean [drug-free]. For the heroin addict this means 3 days, for the alcoholic it means 14 days. . . . I say to them, "I will not even give you a second appointment until you call me up and say to me, 'Nick, I'm clean.'" (Cummings, 1979, p. 1123)

Here, client action literally buys the next session. A colleague of mine had a client who taped many of his conversations to get "evidence" on his enemies. He assured my friend that he had not taped any of *their* conversations. Since the client found coming to the helping sessions very rewarding, the helper laid down conditions for getting together. First, the client could come to the session only if he had not taped any conversations within a week of the appointment. Later, he had to buy sessions by erasing tapes he had previously made.

Homework

Sometimes I believe that the best predictor of whether helping is going to "work" is what the client *does* between the first and second sessions. If the client returns to the second session having done nothing, this does not bode well. Too many helping sessions begin with either the helper or the client saying, "Well, now let's see . . . where were we the last time?" The real work of helping is what the client does "out there." Even when the helping sessions focus mainly on social-emotional reeducation, little is gained if the changes in the client's perspective do not make a difference in his or her day-to-day life.

Therefore, Step I-A, like every other step, is best seen as a stimulus to action. It is as if the helper keeps asking, "What are you learning from the telling of your story? In what ways can you act on what you are learning?" These exact words might not be used, but the spirit behind them needs to inform the process, beginning with the first interview. The fact that some clients take so long to act may be due to timidity—the timidity of helper and client alike. Driscoll (1984) noted that too many helpers shy away from doing much more than listening early on. They are fearful of making some kind of irretrievable error if they don't go slow. Some caution is appropriate, but one can easily become overly cautious. He suggested that helpers *intervene* more right from the beginning, maintaining that most clients appreciate early interventions. Keep to the values outlined in Chapter 3, but get clients to act. Doing so makes them feel more confident about the helping process.

ONGOING EVALUATION

The "E" in the center of each of the stages of the helping process illustrated in Figure 7-1 (p. 157) reminds us that evaluation should be built into the entire model. Evaluation does not refer primarily to control. It does mean control of the helping process in the upbeat sense that both helper and client want to make sure that there are beneficial outcomes. These are "friendly" controls, not rigid attempts to make sure that everything goes "by the book." Evaluation in the best sense means making sure that helping remains a *learning* process in which counselor and client together learn about themselves and about the process of change.

Appraisal that comes at the end of the process is often quite judgmental: "It didn't work." Ongoing evaluation is much more positive. It helps both client and helper learn from what they have been doing, celebrate what has been going well, and correct what has been going poorly. Therefore, a series of evaluation questions will be listed for each of the nine steps of the helping model. In the beginning, you might well ask yourself these questions—at least the relevant ones—explicitly. If you do this, you will come to a point where you do not have to ask the questions explicitly because you will have developed an evaluative sense. That is, some part of you will always be monitoring your interactions with your clients in an unobtrusive and constructive way. It is this sense that will have you at times stop the interaction with the client and say something like "Let's stop a moment and take stock of how well we're doing here."

The following page lists evaluation questions for Step I-A. These questions serve as a summary of the main points of the chapter.

EVALUATION QUESTIONS FOR STEP I-A

How effectively am I doing the following?

The Telling of the Story

- Using a mix of attending, listening, empathy, and probing to help clients tell their stories in terms of specific experiences, behaviors, and feelings.
- Using probes when clients get stuck.
- Understanding blocks to client self-disclosure and providing a mix of support and challenge for clients having difficulty talking about themselves.

Establishing a Working Relationship

- Developing a collaborative working relationship with the client.
- Using the relationship as a vehicle for social-emotional reeducation.
- Not doing for clients what they can do for themselves.

Ongoing Assessment

- Using assessment as an instrument of mutual learning.
- Noting client resources, especially unused resources.
- Listening to clients through the larger contexts of their lives.
- Getting an initial feeling for the severity of a client's problems and his or her ability to handle them.

Managing Client Resistance and Reluctance

- Understanding my own resistance to growth and not being surprised by client resistance.
- Accepting client reluctance and resistance and working with it rather than against it.
- Seeing reluctance and resistance and other difficulties in the helping process as problems in their own right and using the problem-solving approach to address them.

Evaluation

- Keeping an evaluative eye on the entire process with the goal of making each session better.

Chapter Eight

Step I-B: Challenging— New Perspectives at the Service of Action

We have noted that effective helpers not only are committed to understanding clients, including the ways in which they experience themselves and the world, but also are reality testers. Contrary to one version of the client-centered credo, empathic understanding, even permeated by respect and genuineness, may not be enough. Often enough clients need to be invited to challenge themselves to change. Indeed, writers who emphasize helping as a social influence process see some form of challenge as central to helping (Dorn, 1984, 1986; Ellis, 1987a, 1987b; Ellis & Dryden, 1987; Strong & Claiborn, 1982). The challenge-related hypotheses outlined by Farrelly and Brandsma (1974, p. 37) fit well with my own experience:

- Clients can change if they choose.
- Clients have more resources for managing problems in living and developing opportunities than they or most helpers assume.
- The psychological fragility of clients is overrated both by themselves and others.
- Maladaptive and antisocial attitudes and behaviors of clients can be significantly altered no matter what the degree of severity or chronicity.

If, like most of us, clients use only a fraction of their potential in managing their problem situations and developing unused resources, then challenge has a place in helping.

Note that the word "challenge" is used here rather than the more biting term "confrontation." Many see both confronting and being confronted as unpleasant experiences, ones to be avoided. Indeed, the history of psychology has seen periods when irresponsible confrontation was justified as "honesty" (Egan, 1970). Put most simply, challenge is an invitation to examine internal or external behavior that seems to be self-defeating, harmful to others, or both and to change the behavior if it is found to be so. For example, Alicia, a woman who experiences herself as unattractive, is a member of a counseling group.

Group Counselor: You say that you're unattractive, and yet I know that you get asked out a lot. I don't find you unattractive myself. And, if I'm not mistaken, I see people here react to you in ways that say they like you. I can't put all of this together with your being unattractive.

Alicia: Okay. What you say is true, and it helps me clarify what I mean. First of all, I'm no raving beauty, and when others find me attractive, I think that means that they find me intellectually interesting, a caring person, and things like that. At times I wish I were more physically attractive, though I feel ashamed when I say things like that. The fact is that much of the time I feel unattractive. And sometimes I feel most unattractive at the very moment people are telling me directly or indirectly that they find me attractive.

Group Member: So you've gotten into the habit of telling yourself in various ways that you're unattractive. I wonder where that came from.

Alicia: Yeah. It's a lousy habit. If I look at my early home life and my experiences in grammar school and high school, I could probably give you the long, sad story of how it happened. But the past is the past.

I. Present scenario   II. Preferred scenario   III. Strategy: Getting there

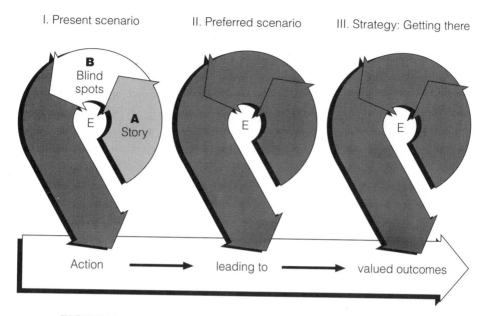

FIGURE 8-1   Step I-B: Identifying and Challenging Blind Spots

Since the counselor's experience of Alicia is so different from her experience of herself, he invites her to explore the difference in the group. Her self-exploration clarifies the issue greatly. Now that she wants to stop feeling unattractive and stop telling herself in a variety of ways that she is unattractive, she may not know how. The counselor and group members can help her discover how.

Figure 8-1 adds this second step to Stage I. However, while challenge is discussed here as a separate step, in reality it belongs in all stages and steps of the helping process. Clients can be challenged to

- talk about their problems when they are reluctant to do so;
- clarify problem situations in terms of specific experiences, behaviors, and feelings when they are being evasive;
- develop new perspectives on themselves, others, and the world when they prefer to cling to distortions;
- review new scenarios, critique them, develop goals, and commit themselves to reasonable agendas instead of wallowing in the past;
- search for ways of achieving goals in the face of obstacles;
- spell out specific plans instead of taking a scattered, hit-or-miss approach to action;
- persevere in the implementation of these plans when they are tempted to give up.

In a word, helpers can challenge clients to engage more effectively in the *process* of problem management.

In this chapter the *nature* of challenging is discussed. Chapter 9 focuses on the *communication skills and strategies* involved in challenging.

THE GOALS OF CHALLENGING

There are two general goals of this step—one cognitive, the other behavioral.

New Perspectives

First, if challenge is successful, clients are helped to replace blind spots with *new perspectives*. As Levy (1968) noted, if counselors see the world only as their clients see it, they will have little to offer them. The client's implicit interpretation of the world is in some ways distorted and unproductive, at least in the areas of life in which he or she is having problems. Helpers assume, however, that clients have the resources to see the world, especially the world of their own behavior, in an undistorted or less distorted way and to act on what they see. Since blind spots and distortions are so common in human experience, Strong and Claiborn (1982) see challenge, especially in terms of promoting attitude change and cognitive restructuring, as central to counseling and therapy.

There are many names for the process of helping clients develop the kinds of awareness and understanding that help them act to manage problems and develop opportunities: seeing things more clearly, getting the picture, getting insights, developing new perspectives, spelling out implications, transforming perceptions, developing new frames of reference, looking for meaning, shifting perceptions, seeing the bigger picture. Writers refer to framebreaking, framebending, reframing, or personalizing (Carkhuff, 1987); to developing different angles, seeing things in context, context-breaking, rethinking, getting a more objective view, interpreting, overcoming blind spots, and analyzing; to second-level learning, double-loop learning (Argyris, 1982), thinking creatively, reconceptualizing, discovery, having an "aha" experience, developing a new outlook, questioning assumptions, getting rid of distortions, relabeling, making connections, and others. You get the idea. All of these imply some kind of understanding or awareness that did not exist previously and that is needed or useful for engaging in situation-improving action.

Research shows that the development of new perspectives is highly prized by clients (Elliott, 1985). Ned discovered that even though he saw himself in a "contemporary" marriage, he covertly espoused a few rules related to household chores and the care of children that favored men. This was a new perspective. But just as creativity (a cognitive attribute) is useful insofar as it leads to innovation (behavior), so, too, new perspectives are useful insofar as they lead to changed patterns of behavior toward self, others, and the environment.

New Perspectives Linked to Action

Second, challenge is successful to the degree that clients engage in problem-managing and opportunity-developing action directly or indirectly because of the challenge. The route is indirect if it is mediated by a new perspective. For instance, Sally, a battered woman who has finally left her spouse, finds out through being challenged that she continues to play the "victim" game in her relationships with other men. Once she realizes this, she changes to more adult-adult interactions. The route is direct if the challenge deals with action itself. Kent, a 23-year-old who is HIV-positive, knows that he must change his sexual practices but finally does so only when challenged by a caring internist. Returning to the example of Ned, once he gets over the shock of hearing within himself an oink or two of the male chauvinist pig, he must translate his discovery into action. This means a more equitable sharing of household and child-rearing chores.

A caution is in order. Overstressing insight and self-understanding can actually stand in the way of action. The search for insight can become a goal in itself. Unfortunately, in psychology—especially the pop version—much more attention has been devoted to developing insight than to linking insight to action. The former is often presented as "sexy," while the latter is work. I do not mean to imply that achieving useful insights into oneself and one's world is not hard work and often painful. Ned's discovery was painful. But if the pain is to be turned into gain, behavioral change is required—whether the behavior is internal, external, or both. Ned had to work at changing his attitudes, keeping them changed, and delivering on the home front.

WHAT NEEDS TO BE CHALLENGED?

You will soon learn from experience areas in which clients might need to be challenged—or invited to challenge themselves. Here are some common areas, each of which will be illustrated with examples in this section:

• Failure to own problems.
• Failure to define problems in solvable terms.
• Faulty interpretations of critical experiences, behaviors, and feelings.
• Evasions, distortions, and game playing.
• Failure to identify or understand the consequences of behavior.
• Hesitancy or unwillingness to act on new perspectives.

Of course, this list is not exhaustive; we human beings are highly inventive when it comes to self-deception and avoidance.

Challenging Clients to Own Their Problems and Opportunities

It is all too common for clients to refuse to take responsibility for their problems and lost opportunities. Instead, there is a whole list of outside forces and other people who are to blame. Therefore, one of the first things many clients need to be challenged to do is to *own* the problem situation. Here is the experience of one counselor who had responsibility for about 150 young men in a youth prison within the confines of a larger central prison.

> I believe I interviewed each of the inmates. And I did learn from them. What I learned had little resemblance to what I had found when I read their files containing personal histories, including the description of their crimes. What I learned when I talked with them was that they didn't belong there. With almost universal consistency they reported a "reason" for their incarceration that had little to do with their own behavior. An inmate explained with perfect sincerity that he was there because the judge who sentenced him had also previously sentenced his brother, who looked very similar; the moment this inmate walked into the courtroom he knew he would be sentenced. Another explained with equal sincerity that he was in prison because his court-appointed lawyer wasn't really interested in helping him.
>
> Many of them reported the stories of their crimes, which usually involved the heavy influence of "the other guys." . . . I used to wonder what would happen to the crime rate if only we could have caught those mythological "other guys" who were responsible for all those young people being behind bars. (Miller, 1984, pp. 67–68)

This is not to deny that we can be victimized by others at times. However, all of us, to a greater or lesser extent, are affected by this "other guys" syndrome. It simply is not easy for people to accept responsibility for their acts and the consequences of their acts.

Not only problems but also opportunities need to be owned by clients.

> Challenges come from opportunities as well as from danger signals. Opportunities usually do not knock very loudly, and missing a golden opportunity can be just as unfortunate as missing a red-alert warning. (Wheeler & Janis, 1980, p. 18)

A social worker who had been out of work for over six months once told me that he had heard that the city was hiring social workers for a new "help the neighborhoods help themselves" program. When I asked him what his response had been, he said he had decided that it was probably only a rumor. Eventually, he discovered that the rumor was fact and set up an interview for the next day. But note that his first impulse was not to own—let alone seize—the opportunity, but to remain passive.

Robert Carkhuff (1987) talks about helping clients "personalize" meaning, problems, goals, and feelings: "Personalizing is the most critical dimension for human change or gain. It is so critical because it empha-sizes internalizing the helpees' responsibilities for their own problems" (p. 129). To illustrate, suppose a client feels that her business partner has been pulling a fast one. Consider the difference between the following helper statements:

Statement A: You feel angry because he unilaterally made the decision to close the deal on his terms.

Statement B: You're angry because *your* interests were ignored.

Statement C: You're furious because *you* were ignored, *your* interests were not taken into consideration, maybe *you* were even financially victimized, and *you* let him get away with it.

Personalizing means factoring the client's *self* and responsibilities into the problem situation and into its resolution, even though the client does not do this directly. Statement C does precisely that. If clients are to man-age problem situations, they must own their part of them. As Carkhuff notes, personalizing means going beyond empathy and sharing with cli-ents the ways in which you experience them. I often experience clients as failing to take responsibility for what happens to them.

Challenging Clients to State Problems as Solvable

It is not uncommon for clients to state problems so that they seem unsolv-able. This justifies a "poor me" attitude and a failure to act. It may also elicit the pity and the sympathy of the counselor.

Unsolvable problem: In sum, my life is miserable now because of my past. My parents were indifferent to me and at times even unjustly hostile. If only they had been more loving, I wouldn't be in this mess. I am the unhappy product of an unhappy environment.

Of course, clients will not use this rather stilted language, but the message is common enough. The point is that the past cannot be changed. There-fore, when a client defines the problem in terms of the past, the problem cannot be solved. "You certainly had it rough in the past and are still suf-fering from the consequences now" might be the kind of response that such a statement is designed to elicit. The client needs to move beyond such a point of view.

Solvable problem: Over the years I've been blaming my parents for my misery. I still spend a great deal of time feeling sorry for myself. As a result, I sit around and do nothing. I don't make friends, I don't involve myself in the community, I don't take any constructive steps to get a better job.

This message is quite different from that of the previous client. Stated in this way, the problem can be managed; the client can stop blaming her parents, since she cannot change them; she can increase her self-esteem and therefore stop feeling sorry for herself; and she can develop the interpersonal skills and courage she needs to enter more effectively into relationships with others.

Effective helpers invite clients to state problems as solvable.

Client: I can't get her out of my mind. And I can't start thinking of going out with other women.

Helper A: It's devastating. It's almost too much to cope with.
Client: I just can't cope with it (he begins crying).

Helper B: The misery of losing her just won't go away. . . . You've used the phrase "I can't" a couple of times. Could you tell me how this "I can't" feels for you?
Client: Well, I wake up every morning and that's the first thing I think about. And I lie awake at night in agony thinking about it, too. And I . . .

The first helper responds with empathy alone, and the client sinks deeper into his misery. The second helper is empathic, but then gently gets at the "I can't." The client begins to describe experiences, behaviors, and feelings that can be appreciated but that he can be invited to challenge.

Of course, helpers must distinguish carefully between "I can't" and "I won't" clients. Anscombe (1986) cited an example:

> Patients who can't are helped over what they cannot do in the hope that this will bring them into areas where their remaining capacities enable them to get along on their own. A demented man, for example, skulking alone and paranoid in his room because he cannot find his way around, may need help getting to the day room, but once there can carry on a lively conversation about baseball with other patients. (p. 27)

Anscombe also cites an example where someone who can't is treated like someone who won't, with negative consequences. It is the case of a

> young man recovering from a schizophrenic episode who was pushed to return to work too early. Although he was no longer delusional . . . he lacked energy and initiative, and had difficulty focusing his thoughts. When he was fired because he could not maintain his previous rate of work, this was attributed to laziness, an interpretation with which he agreed. (p. 27)

In the end, the young man thought that he was bad rather than sick. This could have started a whole new problem cycle.

Allowing for the genuine cases of "can't," helpers must assist clients to cast problems in solvable terms. Otherwise, problems will become *plights*. Problems are managed; plights are endured.

Challenging Faulty Interpretations

Often enough clients fail to manage problem situations and develop opportunities because of the ways in which they interpret, understand, or label their experiences, behaviors, and feelings. For instance, Lesley, a competent person, may be (1) unaware of her competence, (2) see herself as incompetent, or (3) label her competence as "pushiness" when it is, in fact, assertiveness. Or Duane, an aggressive and sometimes even violent person, may (1) be unaware that he is aggressive, (2) see himself as merely asserting his rights, or (3) label the assertive actions of others as forms of aggression. Here are a number of examples of helpers' challenging clients' interpretations.

The first client is a single, middle-aged man who is involved in an affair with a married woman. The helper is getting the feeling that the client is being used but does not realize it.

Helper: How often does she call you?
Client: She doesn't. I always contact her. That's the way we've arranged it.
Helper: I'm curious why you've arranged it that way.
Client: What do you mean?
Helper: Well, in mutual relationships, people are eager to get in touch with each other. I don't sense that in your relationship, but I could be wrong.
Client: Well, it's true that in some ways I'm more eager—maybe more dependent. But . . .

The helper is inviting the client to explore the relationship more fully. The danger, of course, is arousing suspicions without justification. That is why it is critical to base challenge on the client's experience.

In the preceding example a faulty interpretation of the client's *experience* is being challenged. Counselors can also help clients develop new perspectives on their *behavior*. Helping clients find messages and meaning, especially in patterns of behavior, can be the first step in behavioral change. Recall that behavior can be either internal or external. In the following example, the client, an 83-year-old woman, is a resident of a nursing home. She is talking to one of the nurses.

Client: I've become so lazy and self-centered. I can sit around for hours and just reminisce . . . letting myself think of all the good things of the past—you know, the old country and all that. Sometimes a whole morning can go by.

Nurse: I'm not sure what's so self-indulgent about that.
Client: Well, it's in the past. . . . I don't know if it's right.
Nurse: Sounds to me like reminiscing could be a form of meditation for you.
Client: You mean like a prayer?
Nurse: Yes . . . like a prayer.

The client is interpreting her internal behavior in a self-defeating way. The nurse offers an alternative perspective that might help her interpret her internal behavior more constructively.

In the next example, the client is a divorced woman who has been talking about her ex-husband and his failure to meet child payments.

Client: Oh, he's going to pay for all this. I'm planning ways to make sure he does. I've got lots of plans.
Helper: He's gone, but he's still getting to you.
Client: And I'm going to get to him.
Helper: The planning you talk about—I wonder if it's possibly another way he's getting to you.
Client: What do you mean?
Helper: If I hear what you're saying, your planning keeps the bitter feelings you have, no matter how justified, very much alive. And you're the one that stays miserable.
Client: You mean I'm still letting him get to me . . . in a kind of backhanded way?
Helper: "Letting him" . . .(She smiles.) Maybe even helping him?

At this point the helper does not directly challenge the client to stop engaging in what may well be a self-defeating pattern of internal behavior, but rather invites her to see her "planning" behavior from a different angle.

In the next example, a middle-aged man who has just been fired from his job is talking with a counselor.

Client: I knew I was going to get fired. I've been expecting it for about a year now. There was hardly a day that I didn't think about it. I even dreamed about it.
Helper: It sounds like actually getting fired was just the period at the end of the paragraph.
Client: Exactly!
Helper: Sometimes when I let negative thoughts flood in on me and get the better of me, I end up in self-fulfilling prophecies.
Client: You're not telling me I got myself fired, are you?
Helper: I don't mean to accuse you of anything. I'm more interested in what can be learned from all this.
Client: Well . . . maybe I did set myself up a bit. . . . My boss might have seen me as a sitting duck.
Helper: Almost as if he had said to himself, "I can easily let this guy go. He's already fired himself."
Client: Ouch! . . . Well, what do I do now?

As this example suggests, many clients defeat themselves by the way they talk to themselves (Ellis, 1987b; Ellis & Dryden, 1987; Firestone, 1988; Rusk & Rusk, 1988). The area of self-talk is so important that it will be discussed more fully later in this section.

In the following set of examples, the focus is on *external* behavior. The first deals with a client who is having trouble in interpersonal relationships. He is a man with a somewhat abrasive style.

Client: I have a right to be myself. I have a right to my own style. Why can't people let me be myself?
Helper: You feel that they have a right to their style and you have a right to yours.
Client: Exactly.
Helper: How would you describe your style?
Client: Well, it's humorous. I speak with a fair deal of irony at times. And sometimes a bit cynical. I'm not sure that everyone picks it up for what it is.
Helper: Could be. It's not uncommon for people to mistake irony and cynicism for sarcasm, and then take it personally. I wonder whether some people are experiencing you as sarcastic.
Client: Well, maybe . . . It certainly would explain a lot of the turmoil.

The helper invites the client to stand outside himself for a moment and get a look at his external behavior from other people's perspective.

In the next example a man is talking about his visits to his elderly father, who is living on his own.

Client: He gets so cantankerous. He puts me down constantly. I wonder why I keep going. Maybe it's just dumb.
Helper: Could it be anything else besides dumb?
Client: Well, he *is* my father . . . but he doesn't let you care for him much.
Helper: So visiting him could also be a way of caring. . . . It sounds like caring for him might take a bit of pluck at times.
Client: How often I have to screw up my courage just to go!

It is obvious that visiting his father is frustrating for this man, but a complementary perspective is that it may be a form of caring that involves courage.

Counselors can also help clients develop new perspectives on their *emotions*. The next client is a woman in her late fifties who is going to have an operation for cancer. The helper is a woman, about the same age, who is a minister from the patient's church.

Patient: I'm just so scared. I've never been so scared in all my life. (The minister holds her hand tightly.) I never thought I could be so desperate, so desperately scared.
Minister: You sound desperate for life.
Patient (crying): I love life so much. So much.

The minister suggests that the patient isn't just being consumed by fear. Her emotions are also a very human grasping for life.

The next example deals with a woman who was extremely sensitive to whatever she perceived as criticism.

> I asked the client if it would be all right to videotape one or two of our sessions, so that she could get a better feeling for her style. A bit to my surprise, she said yes. After one taped session we played about ten minutes of the tape. She asked me to stop the tape, turned to me, and said: "How do you put up with me? I'm so bitchy! I would never have believed it. Where is all this anger coming from?" One picture was worth a thousand words of challenge from me on her "bitchy" style.

There has been some speculation (see Beck & Strong, 1982; Claiborn, 1982) about what makes interpretation effective. One possibility is that interpretation is effective only when it "hits the mark," that is, when it is "correct." The client is moved by the truth of the challenge. Indeed, McNeill and Stoltenberg's (1988) research suggests that clients are influenced by high-quality messages—messages that hit the mark (see Heesacker, 1986). A second possibility is that, within reason, the content of the interpretation is not that important. What is important is that the helper is using interpretation as an instrument to express concern, care, and involvement. Clients are moved to reconsider their experiences, behavior, and emotions because the helper cares. A third possibility is that the content of the interpretation is not as important as the fact that the very act of interpreting stimulates a self-challenging process, opening up a new avenue to the client. A fourth possibility is that interpretations provide frameworks that enable clients to better understand their experiences, behaviors, and emotions. Of course, none of these possibilities excludes the others. It may be that they all contribute to the effectiveness of helpers' challenging clients to develop new perspectives.

Challenging Evasions and Distortions

The focus here is on the discrepancies, distortions, evasions, games, tricks, excuse making and smoke screens that keep clients mired in their problem situations. All of us have ways of defending ourselves from ourselves, others, and the world. But our defenses are two-edged swords. Daydreaming may help me cope with the dreariness of my everyday life, but it may also keep me from doing something to better myself. Blaming others for my misfortunes helps me save face, but it disrupts interpersonal relationships and prevents me from developing a healthy sense of self-responsibility.

The purpose of challenging clients is not to strip clients of their defenses, which in some cases could be dangerous, but to help them overcome blind spots and develop new perspectives. There is a fair degree of overlap among the categories discussed below.

Challenging Discrepancies

It can be helpful to zero in on discrepancies between what clients think or feel and what they say, between what they say and what they do, between their views of themselves and the views that others have of them, between what they are and what they wish to be, between their expressed values and their actual behavior. For instance, a helper might challenge the following discrepancies that take place outside the counseling sessions:

- Tom sees himself as witty; his friends see him as biting.
- Minerva says that physical fitness is important, but she overeats and underexercises.
- George says he loves his wife and family, but he is seeing another woman and stays away from home a lot.
- Clarissa, unemployed for several months, wants a job, but she doesn't want to participate in a retraining program.

Let's use the example of Clarissa to illustrate how this kind of discrepancy can be challenged.

Counselor: I thought that the retraining program would be just the kind of thing you've been looking for.

Clarissa: Well . . . I don't know if it's the kind of thing I'd like to do. . . . The work would be so different from my last job. . . . And it's a long program.

Counselor: So you feel the fit isn't good.

Clarissa: Yeah.

Counselor (smiling): What's going on, Clarissa?

Clarissa: What do you mean?

Counselor (pleasantly): Where's the old fire to get a job? I'm not even sure you believe what you're saying about the retraining program.

Clarissa: I guess I've gotten lazy. . . . I don't like being out of work, but I've gotten used to it.

The counselor suspects that Clarissa is slipping into what might be called the "culture of unemployment" (see Galbraith, 1979) and challenges her to take a look at what she's doing.

A counselor might challenge the following kinds of discrepancies that take place *inside* the counseling sessions:

- Mary is obviously confused and hurt, but she says she feels fine.
- Bernard says yes with his words, but his body language says no.
- Evita says she wants help, but she refuses to disclose herself enough to properly clarify the problem situation.

Again, we'll use the last example to illustrate how the helper might challenge the client.

Counselor: Evita, when we arranged this meeting you talked vaguely about "serious family problems," but it seems that neither you nor I think that what we've talked about so far is that serious. I'm not sure whether there's more and, if there is, what might be keeping you from talking about it.

Evita: There's a lot more, but I'm embarrassed to talk about it.

The counselor is properly tentative in pointing out the discrepancy, and the client moves forward. The client needs support and help to overcome her embarrassment.

Challenging Distortions

Some clients cannot face the world as it is and therefore distort it in various ways. For instance:

- Arnie is afraid of his supervisor and therefore sees her as aloof, whereas in reality she is a caring person.
- Edna sees her counselor in some kind of divine role and therefore makes unwarranted demands on him.
- Nancy sees her stubbornness as commitment.
- Eric, a young gay male, is very fearful about contracting AIDS. He blames his problems on an older brother who seduced him during the early years of high school.

How might a counselor challenge Eric?

Counselor: Eric, every time we begin to talk about your sexual behavior, you bring up your brother.

Eric: That's where it all began!

Counselor: Your brother's not around any more. . . . Don't talk about him. Tell me what Eric wants. Tell me straight.

Eric: I want people to leave me alone.

Counselor: I don't believe it, because I don't think you believe it. . . . Say what you want.

Eric: I want some one person to care about me. But that's deep down inside me. . . . And I'm never going to get it. And so, damn it, I'm bitter. I'm bitter.

The counselor bluntly but caringly invites Eric to let go of the past and to let himself think more clearly about the present.

Challenging Self-Defeating Internal Behavior

Many clients have ways of thinking that keep them locked into their problem situations. Ellis (1985a, 1987a, 1987b; Ellis & Dryden, 1987), in his "rational-emotive" therapy, and Meichenbaum (1974, 1977; Meichenbaum & Genest, 1980), in his "cognitive-behavior modification," both point out the need to challenge the inner or covert experiences and behavior that sustain self-defeating patterns of overt behavior. They have both developed methodologies for helping clients come to grips with what can be called self-limiting or self-defeating internal dialogue, or self-talk (also see Firestone, 1988; Rusk & Rusk, 1988).

Client: I've decided not to apply for that job.
Counselor: How come?
Client: Well, it's not exactly what I want.
Counselor: That's quite a change from last week. It sounded then as if it was just what you wanted.
Client: Well, I've thought it over. (Pauses)
Counselor: I've got a hunch based on what we've learned about your style. I think you've been saying something like this to yourself: "I like the job, but I don't think I'm good enough for it. If I try it, I might fall flat on my face, and that would be awful. So I'll stick to what I've got, even though I don't like it very much." Any truth in any of that?
Client: Maybe more than I'd like to admit.

Challenging clients' self-limiting ways of thinking can be one of the most powerful methodologies for behavioral change at your disposal. And, just as negative mind-sets stand in the way of problem solving, so positive mind-sets can contribute greatly to managing problems and developing opportunities (see Cypert, 1987; Fordyce, 1977, 1983).

Some of the common beliefs that Ellis believes get in the way of effective living are these:

- *Being liked and loved:* I must always be loved and approved by the significant people in my life.
- *Being competent:* I must always, in all situations, demonstrate competence, and I must be both talented and competent in some important area of life.
- *Having one's own way:* I must have my way, and my plans must always work out.
- *Being hurt:* People who do anything wrong, especially those who harm me, are evil and should be blamed and punished.
- *Being in danger:* If anything or any situation is dangerous in any way, I must be anxious and upset about it.
- *Being problemless:* Things should not go wrong in life, and if by chance they do, there should be quick and easy solutions.
- *Being a victim:* Other people and outside forces are responsible for any misery I experience.
- *Avoiding:* It is easier to avoid facing life's difficulties than to develop self-discipline; making demands of myself should not be necessary.
- *Tyranny of the past:* What I did in the past—and especially what happened to me in the past—determines how I act and feel today.
- *Passivity.* I can be happy by avoiding, by being passive, by being uncommitted, and by just enjoying myself.

Ellis suggests that if any of these beliefs are violated in a person's life, he or she tends to see the experience as terrible, awful, catastrophic. And, as everyone knows, catastrophes are out of our control.

Recently Ellis (1987c) has made a distinction between blatant and obvious irrational beliefs and those that are subtle and tricky. An example of a blatantly irrational belief is this: "Because I strongly desire to be approved by people I find significant, I absolutely must have their approval (and am an unlovable and worthless person if I do not)" (p. 372). A more subtle or tricky irrational belief in the same area goes like this: "Because I strongly desire to be approved by people I find significant, and because the lack of their approval makes me behave so badly, my dysfunctional behavior proves that I absolutely must have their approval" (p. 372).

Seligman (see Trotter, 1987) has pointed out that the way people explain unfortunate events can affect both achievements and health. Let's say that Lester's girlfriend gives him the gate. He says to himself: "I'll *never* have anyone who really loves me. Leading a loveless life will make *everything* I do miserable. It's *my fault*; no one could love the kind of person I am." Seligman would suggest that Lester is in trouble because he has given a negative event a negative explanation that implies that the situation is stable ("It's going to last forever"), global ("It's going to affect everything I do"), and internal ("It's all my fault"). Such explanations need to be ferreted out and challenged.

Daly and Burton (1983), in reviewing the literature on irrational beliefs, found that such beliefs are correlated with a variety of psychological problems, including depression, social anxiety, coronary-prone behavior, and lack of assertion. In their own research they found four specific irrational beliefs correlated with low self-esteem and its consequences: demand for approval, overly high self-expectations, anxious overconcern, and problem avoidance. Both research and clinical experience demonstrate vividly that clients can be infected to varying degrees with what Alcoholics Anonymous groups have called "stinkin' thinkin'."

The works of Ellis and Meichenbaum are too important to be given summary treatment here. I find them most useful, although Ellis is not without his critics (see Driscoll, 1984; Ellis, 1982; Eschenroeder, 1982; Rorer, 1983). I do find it difficult to base my entire approach to helping on a theory of irrational beliefs. I also object to the way in which Ellis seems to push his own set of values with clients. Driscoll (1984) objects to Ellis's approach on other grounds. As we have seen, he takes pains to point out to clients, not that they are irrational, but that they make sense. By pointing out to clients that there is some logic to their behavior—even though the behavior is ultimately self-defeating—he challenges their view of themselves as irrational. Instead of forcing clients to see how irrationally they are thinking and acting, he challenges them to find the logic embedded even in seemingly stupid ideas and behaviors. Then he challenges them to use this logic to manage problem situations instead of perpetuating them.

This is not the place to settle disputes between Ellis and his critics. To me it seems clear that all of us often get into trouble because of one form or another of "stinkin' thinkin'"—whether of the types described by Driscoll, Ellis, or Seligman, or other types they do not explore. Challenging clients' self-defeating explanations of the world can be most beneficial. The importance of empathy in this process is clear. The trouble with theories such as Ellis's is the tendency to suppose that clients are thinking what the theory says they are thinking without checking it out. To challenge the way clients think demands that I first understand what and how they think.

Challenging Games, Tricks, and Smoke Screens

If clients are comfortable with their delusions and profit by them, they will obviously try to keep them. If they are rewarded for playing games, inside the counseling sessions or outside, they will continue a game approach to life (Berne, 1964; Harris, 1969; James & Jongeward, 1971). For instance, Clarence plays the "Yes, but . . ." game: he presents himself as one in need of help and then proceeds to show his helper how ineffective she is. Dora makes herself appear helpless and needy when she is with her friends, but when they come to her aid, she is angry with them for treating her like a child. Kevin seduces others in one way or another and then becomes indignant when they accept his implied invitations. The number of games people can play in order to avoid the work involved in squarely facing the tasks of life is endless. Clients who are fearful of changing will attempt to lay down smoke screens in order to hide from the helper the ways in which they fail to face up to life. Such clients use communication in order not to communicate (Beier & Young, 1984).

One function of Step I-B is to set up an atmosphere that discourages clients from playing games. An attitude of "Nonsense is challenged here" should gently pervade the helping sessions. For instance, since effective helpers don't start out by giving advice, they prevent clients from playing "Yes, but . . ." games. If a client does attempt to play some game or to lay down diversionary smoke screens during the helping interviews, the counselor challenges this behavior.

Games are key ways of manifesting reluctance and resistance. Beier and Young (1984) suggested that some clients play one kind of game or another to attempt to restrict the helper's response in some way. The helper who becomes "engaged" in the game is easy to sidetrack.

The following client, Zach, has just begun to explore a sensitive area— how he manipulates an older brother into coming to his aid financially. Zach takes financial risks because he knows he can talk his brother into bailing him out.

Zach: I really like what you've been doing in these sessions. It feels good to be with such a strong person.

Counselor A (in an angry voice): See, that's exactly what I've been getting at. Now you're manipulating me and not even trying to be subtle!

Counselor B: Thanks. I think that it's important that we respect each other here. And perhaps that's the issue with your brother—respect.

Counselor A gets angry and lets himself be sidetracked, while Counselor B uses the client's game to refocus the issue at hand.

Helpers can also challenge the games that clients play outside the counseling sessions. In the following example, Sophie, a 55-year-old woman, has been exploring her relationships with her married children. She has her own game. She "confides" in one of them some kind of negative information about herself—for instance, that she can't seem to manage things at the house as well as she used to—and then counts on that one to tell the others. The payoff is that she remains the center of attention much of the time without seeming to do much to demand it. Lately, however, her children seem to be on to her game. She tries to see their behavior as "indifference." She is talking to her pastor about her "loneliness." The pastor has spent a good deal of time exploring the whole problem situation with her.

Pastor: I'd like to make a bet with you.
Sophie (a bit surprised): About what?
Pastor: If I've listened carefully to what you've been saying, you've gotten a lot of attention from the kids by playing one off against the other. Nothing evil, mind you, just a bit clever. Maybe just a bit too clever. My bet is that you could relate to them straight and get all the human contact you need. And I think my bet is safe, because I see you as a resourceful woman.
Sophie (cautiously): Tell me more about this bet.

The helper calls Sophie's game, but he does so in a way that challenges her strengths rather than her weaknesses. Casting his challenge in the form of a "bet" adds tentativeness. By exploring the "bet" together, they can come up with a goal that will have something to do with restructuring Sophie's relationships with her children.

Dreikurs (1967) suggests that clients at times use their symptoms to cover up their real intentions. He sees this as a game that needs challenging: "As Adler pointed out, one of the most effective therapeutic means [of challenging clients' games] is spitting in the patient's soup. He can continue what he's doing, but it no longer tastes so good" (p. 230).

Confronting the Victim Game

Some clients present themselves as victims of circumstances, of other people, of life itself. What do those who play the victim game get out of it? Driscoll (1984, see pp. 117–122) suggests several possibilities. There is a kind of nobility in being a victim; victims often gain attention and support; victims are not responsible; a victim's oppressors are by definition evil. Driscoll's approach, as we have seen earlier, is to recognize the logic, the sensibleness of the victim's approach. Since victims set up the game, they are in many ways doers. And that's the point: doers are not really victims. Playing the victim game is one way of exercising control. The helper can challenge the client to invest his or her resources more fruitfully. If the investment is wiser, the returns can be greater.

In the following example, Roberto has assumed the victim role in his marriage. His wife, Maria, has broken through a number of cultural taboos. She has put herself through college, gotten a job, developed it into a career, and assumed the role of mother-breadwinner. She makes more money than Roberto. His victimhood includes losing face in the community, feeling belittled by his wife's success, being forced into a "democratic" marriage, and so forth. He has created a series of minor crises at home in hopes that his wife will rethink what she is doing. She is not present for this session.

Helper: Roberto, you sound as if you are ready to give up.

Roberto: Do I sound that bad? You know what makes it all worse is the fact that we've got, at least financially, what most of our friends would sell their souls for.

Helper: Let's talk off the record—just between you and me.

Roberto: About what? You sound like this is going to hurt.

Helper: Maybe about sabotage. Not planned, but still quite effective. . . . You've described a number of crises at home, like your son's failure to get into the preschool you wanted. Off the record, what really happened there?

Roberto: If Maria had been around more . . .

Helper (leaning forward and in a gentle voice): Come on.

Roberto: Well, so I didn't do everything I could, so what?

Helper: Roberto, you're not on trial.

They go on to talk about the ways in which Roberto has been using benign forms of sabotage to get what he wants. It takes a number of sessions before he begins to accept the fact that his marriage is not going to be structured the way he wants it to be.

Challenging Excuses

Snyder, Higgins, and Stucky (1983; see also Snyder, 1984; Snyder & Higgins, 1988) examine excuse-making behavior in depth. Though we all know what it is, here is a more technical definition:

> Excuse making . . . is the process of shifting causal attributions for negative personal outcomes from sources that are relatively more central to the person's sense of self to sources that are relatively less central, thereby resulting in perceived benefits to the person's image and sense of control. (Snyder & Higgins, 1988, p. 23)

Excuse making, of course, is universal, part of the fabric of everyday life. Like games and distortions, it has its positive uses in life. Snyder and Higgins (1988) talk about "adaptive illusions." Even if it were possible, there is no real reason for setting up a world without myths. On the other hand, excuse making, together with avoidance behavior, probably contributes a great deal to the "psychopathology of the average" (Maslow, 1968). And it should be no surprise that Snyder and his colleagues (1983) found that excuse making contributes its share to severe problems in living (see Chapter 8, "Excuses Gone Awry").

Wheeler and Janis (1980) point out four categories of excuses that need to be challenged:

• *Complacency.* Clients fail to realize the seriousness of a situation. When Jeff and Jane were warned by a teacher that their son was in trouble, their excuse for not acting was "He's just going through a teenage phase." When he committed suicide, they said, "We did not know it was that serious."

• *Rationalization.* Clients cling to unwarranted assumptions or distort information: "He's just sowing a few wild oats." Rationalizations enable clients to avoid what they don't want to do. A member of a counselor training group, when confronted for her lack of participation, once told me that she was learning in the group by observing and that she was putting what she had learned to work in settings outside the group. She never even noticed the hostility her non-participation was causing.

• *Procrastination.* "It doesn't have to be done right away." Often enough clients seek the help of counselors only after procrastination has led to some crisis. A husband and wife notice all sorts of hints that their marriage is in trouble, but they ignore them ("We'll have to do something about that one of these days"). In the helping process itself, clients, often with the complicity of their helpers, explore problems endlessly and put off setting goals, developing strategies, and acting.

• *Passing the buck.* "I'm not the one who needs to act." Clients pass the buck both outside and inside the counseling sessions. A surprising number of clients will come to you with the expectation that you are going to do something to fix them. Not only do you have to enter a contract with them right from the start, but you also have to challenge them to live up to its provisions.

We have only skimmed the surface of the games, evasions, tricks, distortions, excuses, rationalizations, and subterfuges resorted to by clients (together with the rest of the population). Effective helpers are caring and empathic, but they do not let themselves be conned. That helps no one.

Challenging Clients to Explore the Consequences of Their Behavior

One way of helping clients get new and more creative perspectives on themselves and their behavior is to help them explore the consequences of patterns of behavior currently in place. In the following example, a counselor from a local human-services clinic is talking to Allister, a man of 58 who has been mugged twice. After the second mugging, he settled into the role of victim. He is involved in a vicious circle. The more he plays the role, the more he alienates those around him. Taking their alienation as aggression, he feels further victimized. And so begins the next turn of the screw. Sometimes he comes to sessions with his wife, but this time he's alone.

Allister: I'm glad she's not here. I can get my frustrations out. You know she has little patience. She doesn't seem to know how much this has upset me.
Helper: She's certainly a woman without sensitivity or gratitude.
Allister: What!
Helper (smiles): Come on, Allister, name two or three ways in which your behavior has changed since the second mugging.
Allister: Well . . . I'm much more security-conscious. You'd find a range of good locks on the doors, and I don't go out much any more. Let's see . . . I've been speaking out about the safety of our streets to anyone who'll listen. I've just been more careful about myself all the way round.
Helper (forcefully): You're not going to be a victim again.
Allister: You're damn right!
Helper: And you're not going to let the world forget that you've been a victim.
Allister: That's stupid. . . . Oh, geez . . . Is that how I come across?
Helper: Allister, I have no intention of discounting what's happened to you, but let's take a look at how you've been coming across.

Since the helper knows he has a solid relationship with the client, he uses what Beier and Young (1984) call an "asocial" response (see next chapter)—"She's certainly a woman without sensitivity or gratitude"—to reset the dialogue. He then focuses on the vicious circle that Allister has got himself into. He pushes Allister to spell out his post-mugging behaviors and the impact they have had on others.

The consequences of a client's behavior can be positive but unappreciated. Consider the case of a client in a rehabilitation unit after a serious accident. She has been sticking to the program, but progress is slow.

Client: Sometimes I think that the courageous thing to do is just to chuck all this stuff, admit that I'm a cripple, and get on with life. I don't want to delude myself that I'm going to be a whole human being again. I'm not. And I'm not a hero.
Counselor: So the depression's at you again.
Client: It's not at me—it's got me by the throat.
Counselor: I wish I had a videotape.
Client: Of what?
Counselor: Of the way you could, or rather *couldn't*, move that left arm of yours six weeks ago. . . . Move it now.
Client: (She moves her arm a bit.) You mean people can notice a difference? It's so damn hard seeing that the exercises make a difference.
Counselor: Sure. You know the exercises are making a difference, but you hate the snail's pace.
Client: By now you know me enough to know that patience has never been one of my strong points.

Helping the client look at the positive consequences of her behavior, in this case the exercises, is a supportive gesture on the part of the helper. His challenge is rooted in his empathic understanding of her frustration.

Challenging Clients to Act

The ultimate goal of challenging can be stated in one word: action. New perspectives and heightened awareness need to serve action. Action includes

- starting activities related to managing problems and developing opportunities;
- continuing and increasing activities that contribute to problem management and opportunity development; and
- stopping activities that either cause problems and limit opportunities or stand in the way of problem management and opportunity development.

These activities can be internal, external, or a combination of both. If Roberto, in our earlier example above, is going to manage the conflict between himself and his wife better, he might need to be challenged to

- start thinking of his wife as an equal in the relationship, start understanding her point of view, and start imagining what an improved relationship with her might look like;
- continue exploring with her the ways he contributes to their difficulties and increase the number of times he tells himself to let her live her life as fully as he wants to live his own;
- stop telling himself that she is the one with the problem, stop seeing her as the offending party when conflicts arise, and stop telling himself there is no hope for the relationship.

That is, he has to put his internal life in order and begin to mobilize internal resources.

Similarly, if problems are to be managed and opportunities developed, then some external behaviors need to be started, some continued or increased, and some stopped. For instance, if Roberto is going to do his part in developing a better relationship with his wife, he might need to be challenged to

- start spending more time looking at his own career, start sharing his feelings with her, start engaging in mutual decision making, and start taking more initiative in household chores and child care;
- continue visiting her parents with her and increase the number of times he goes to business-related functions with her;
- stop criticizing her in front of others, stop creating crises at home and assigning the blame for them to her, and stop making fun of her business friends.

With the counselor's help, Roberto can challenge himself to do all of these things.

Sometimes helping means challenging clients *not* to do something. In the following example, the client, a 50-year-old man, wants to check himself into a mental hospital. The therapist sees this as just one more step in a pattern of running away from problems instead of coping with them. Checking into the hospital is a program with no goal.

Helper: Tom, I have to assume that you are feeling awful right now. But what will checking into the hospital accomplish? I thought that it was clear to both of us that you're not sick.

Tom: I'll be safe there . . . Won't harm myself or others.

Helper: I could see that if harming yourself or others has been an issue. It hasn't.

Tom: Well . . . I'll be better off there. I'll feel better.

Helper: Tom, will you feel better because you'll be able to block out the world in there? I know you're extremely uncomfortable.

Tom: OK! . . . I'm looking for a safe place, a refuge. I just want to get away.

Helper: Let's see if we can find ways of staying out and still getting the sense of peace you're looking for.

The helper has seen too many clients use a trip to the hospital as the beginning of the end. She has a solid relationship with the client and feels that she can push hard.

THE RESPONSE OF THE CLIENT WHO IS CHALLENGED

Even when challenge is a response to a client's plea to be helped to live more effectively, it can precipitate some degree of disorganization in the client. Different writers refer to this experience under different names: "crisis," "disorganization," "a sense of inadequacy," "disequilibrium," and "beneficial uncertainty" (Beier & Young, 1984). As the last of these terms implies, counseling-precipitated crises can be beneficial for the client. Whether they are or not depends, to a great extent, on the skill of the helper.

Since challenge usually does induce some sense of inadequacy in clients, it can render them more open to influence. However, some clients can resist being influenced and respond defensively even to responsible challenge, that is, challenge that is not some form of coercion. One way of looking at the way in which clients sometimes resist challenge is from the point of view of cognitive-dissonance theory (Festinger, 1957). Since dissonance (discomfort, crisis, disequilibrium) is an uncomfortable state, the client will try to get rid of it. According to dissonance theory, there are five typical ways in which people experiencing dissonance attempt to rid themselves of this discomfort. Let's examine them briefly as they apply to being challenged.

1. Discredit challengers. The challenger is confronted and discredited. Some attempt is made to point out that he or she is no better than anyone else. In the following example, the client has been discussing her marital problems and has been challenged by the helper.

Client: It's easy for you to sit there and suggest that I be more responsible in my marriage. You've never had to experience the misery in which I live. You've never experienced his brutality. You probably have one of those nice middle-class marriages.

Counterattack is a common strategy for coping with challenge. Counselors who elicit this kind of response from their clients may merely be the victims of their clients' attempts to reduce dissonance. However, it is best not to jump to that conclusion immediately. The client might be airing a legitimate gripe. It may be that the counselor has been inaccurate or heavy-handed in his or her challenge.

2. Persuade challengers to change their views. In this approach challengers are reasoned with. They are urged to see what they have said as misinterpretations and to revise their views. In the following example, the client pursues this strategy by using rationalization.

Client: I'm not so sure that my anger at home isn't called for. I think that it's a way in which I'm asserting my own identity. If I were to lie down and let others do what they want, I would become a doormat at home. I think you see me as a fairly reasonable person. I don't get angry here with you because there is no reason to.

Sometimes a client like this will lead an unwary counselor into an argument about the issue in question. A client who uses rationalization a great deal is difficult to deal with, but arguing with him or her is not the answer.

3. Devalue the issue. This is another form of rationalization. For instance, a client who is being challenged about his sarcasm points out that he is rarely sarcastic, that "poking fun at others" is a minor part of his life and not worth spending time on. The client has a right to devalue a topic if it really isn't important. The counselor has to be sensitive enough to discover which issues are important and which are not.

4. Seek support elsewhere for the views being challenged. Some clients leave one counselor and go to another because they feel they aren't being understood. They try to find helpers who will agree with them. This is an extreme way of seeking support of one's own views elsewhere. But a client can remain with a counselor and still use this strategy by offering evidence that others contest the helper's point of view.

Client: I asked my wife about my sarcasm. She said she doesn't mind it at all. And she said she thinks that my friends see it as humor and as a part of my style.

This is an indirect way of telling the counselor she is wrong. The counselor might well be wrong, but if the client's sarcasm is really dysfunctional in his interpersonal life, the counselor should find some way of pressing the issue.

If the counseling takes place in a group, it is much more difficult for clients to use this approach to reducing dissonance.

Juan: Does anyone else here see me as biting and sarcastic?
Susan: I think you do get sarcastic from time to time. The reason I've said nothing about it so far is that you haven't been sarcastic with me. And I'm a bit afraid of you.

Direct feedback from the members of the group makes it harder for Juan to play games.

5. Agree with the challenger but don't act on the challenge. The client can agree with the counselor as a way of dismissing an issue. However, the purpose of challenging is not to get the client's agreement. Rather, it is to help the client reexamine his or her behavior in order to develop the kinds of perspectives needed to clarify the problem situation and establish goals.

Client: I think you're right. I'm much too blunt and forward when I speak; I should try to think what impact I'm going to have before I open my mouth.
Helper: I wonder how you're going to work on that.
Client: I knew you were going to say something like that!

Since the client's response may have been mere capitulation, the helper pursues the issue, and the client knows that he isn't off the hook. Clients can agree with challenges in order to get helpers off their backs. It needs to be made clear to them that constructive change is always the bottom line.

LINKING CHALLENGE TO ACTION

A counselor friend of mine makes an audiotape of each session, gives it to the client at the end of the session, and makes some suggestions on what to listen for. This makes the client *do* something about the process. But it can also influence the client to act in other ways. Once he gave a client the tape and said, "Listen to how you responded when I asked you about what you might do about patching up your relationship with your father. Up to that point your voice was strong. But when you talk about what you might do, your voice gets much softer and more tentative. Your words indicated what you were going to do. But your voice seemed to say, 'I'm not sure what I'm going to do.'"

Here is a helper who tries to forge links between insight and action. We helpers are beguiled by our clients' insights and "aha" experiences. They feel good. Too often we are lulled into believing that the clarity or the impact of the new perspective will sweep the client into action. This is simply not the case. Therefore, each challenge to gain some insight should contain within itself or be followed up by an exploration of the action implications of the insight.

Sometimes new perspectives lead to action. At other times action generates new perspectives.

> Woody, a sophomore in college, came to the student counseling services with a variety of interpersonal and somatic complaints. He felt attracted to a number of women on campus but did very little to become involved with them. After exploring this issue briefly, he said to the counselor: "Well, I just have to go out and do it." Two months later he returned and said that his experiment had been a disaster. He had gone out with a few women, but none of them really interested him. Then he did meet someone he liked quite a bit. They went out a couple of times, but the third time he called, she said that she didn't want to see him any more. When he asked why, she muttered vaguely about his being too preoccupied with himself and ended the conversation. He felt so miserable he returned to the counseling center. He and the counselor took another look at his social life. This time, however, he had some experiences to probe. He wanted to explore his being "too preoccupied with himself."

This student put into practice Weick's (1979) dictum that chaotic action is sometimes preferable to orderly inactivity. Some of his learnings were painful, but now there is a chance of examining his interpersonal style much more concretely. One of the assumptions of Alcoholics Anonymous is that people sometimes need to act themselves into new ways of thinking rather than think themselves into new ways of acting. For instance, heavy drinkers do not realize the degree to which alcohol has been controlling their lives until they stop drinking.

RELUCTANCE TO CHALLENGE: THE "MUM" EFFECT

Initially some counselor trainees are quite reluctant to place demands on others or, preferably, help others place demands on themselves. They become victims of what has been called the "MUM effect," the tendency to withhold bad news even when it is in the other's interest to hear it (Rosen & Tesser, 1970, 1971; Tesser & Rosen, 1972; Tesser, Rosen, & Batchelor, 1972; Tesser, Rosen, & Tesser, 1971). In ancient times the person who bore bad news to the king was sometimes killed. This obviously led to a certain reluctance on the part of messengers to bring such news. Bad news—and, by extension, the kind of "bad news" that is involved in any kind of challenging—arouses negative feelings in the challenger, no matter how he or she thinks the receiver will react. If you are comfortable with the supportive dimensions of the helping process but uncomfortable with helping as a social-influence process, you could fall victim of the MUM effect and become less effective than you might be.

Reluctance to challenge is not a bad starting position. In my estimation, this is far better than being too eager to challenge. However, as we have seen, all helping, even the most client-centered, involves social influence. It is important for you to understand your reluctance (or eagerness) to challenge, that is, to challenge yourself on the issue of challenging and on the very notion of helping as a social-influence process. When trainees examine how they feel about challenging others, these are some of the things they discover:

- "I am just not used to challenging others. My interpersonal style has had a lot of the be-and-let-be in it. I have misgivings about intruding into other people's lives."
- "If I challenge others, then I open myself to being challenged. I may be hurt, or I may find out things about myself that I would rather not know."
- "I might find out that I like challenging others and that the floodgates will open and my negative feelings about others will flow out. I have some fears that deep down I am a very angry person."
- "I am afraid that I will hurt others, damage them in some way or other. I have been hurt or I have seen others hurt by heavy-handed confrontations."
- "I am afraid that I will delve too deeply into others and find that they have problems that I cannot help them handle. The helping process will get out of hand."
- "If I challenge others, they will no longer like me. I want my clients to like me."

Some of these may or may not apply to you. The point is that it is useful to examine where you stand in terms of helping process, helping values, and personal feelings with respect to challenging others.

Some helpers are reluctant to challenge because they lack the communication skills and overall know-how of challenging. These are addressed in Chapter 9.

Chapter Nine

Communication Skills III: Skills and Guidelines for Effective Challenging

Helpers use a variety of communication skills to challenge clients to understand themselves, others, and the world more fully and act more constructively. This chapter first discusses and illustrates these skills. They are (1) information sharing, (2) advanced empathy, (3) helper self-disclosure, (4) immediacy, and (5) paradoxical and asocial responses. Second, since the *way* in which helpers go about challenging clients or inviting them to challenge themselves can make or break the challenging process, the chapter offers principles of effective challenging.

The following case will be used to provide focus throughout this chapter.

> Tim was a bright, personable young man. During college he was hospitalized after taking a drug overdose during a bout of depression. He spent six months as an inpatient. He was assigned to "milieu therapy," an amorphous mixture of work and recreation designed more to keep patients busy than to help them grapple with their problems and engage in constructive change. He was given drugs for his depression, seen occasionally by a psychiatrist, and assigned to a therapy group that proved to be quite aimless. After leaving the hospital, his confidence shattered, he left college and got involved with a variety of low-paying part-time jobs. He finally finished college by going to night school, but he avoided full-time jobs for fear of being asked about his past. Buried inside him was the thought "I have this terrible secret which I have to keep from everyone." A friend talked him into taking a college-sponsored communication skills course one summer. Rick, the psychologist running the program, noting Tim's rather substantial natural talents together with his self-effacing ways, remarked to him one day, "I wonder what kind of ambitions you have." In an instant Tim realized that he had buried all thoughts of ambition. After all, he didn't "deserve" to be ambitious. Instinctively trusting Rick, Tim divulged his "terrible secret" for the first time.

Tim and Rick had a number of meetings over the next few years. Challenge became an important part of the helping process.

NEW PERSPECTIVES THROUGH INFORMATION

Sometimes clients are unable to explore their problems fully and proceed to action because they lack information of one kind or another.

> Conveying information about the psychological and social changes accompanying a particular problem situation (e.g., divorce) may be a highly effective addition to any therapeutic strategy. This psychodidactic component has been neglected as an explicit part of treatment in spite of evidence indicating the therapeutic value of information about the client's problem situation. (Selby & Calhoun, 1980, p. 236)

It helps many clients to know that they are not the first to try to cope with a particular problem. In addition, there is much to be learned from other people's experience. Driscoll (1984) put it this way: "Information about others' experiences in similar situations may invite the client to alter unrealistically high standards and expectations, and to accept otherwise unacceptable aspects of himself" (p. 109).

The skill or strategy of information sharing is included under challenging skills because it helps clients develop new perspectives on their problems. It includes both giving information and correcting misinformation. In some cases the information can prove to be quite confirming and supportive. For instance, a parent who feels responsible following the death of a newborn baby may experience some relief through an understanding of the features of the Sudden Infant Death Syndrome. The parent's new perspective can help him or her handle self-blame.

The new perspectives clients gain from information sharing can also be quite challenging. Consider the following example.

> Troy was a college student of modest intellectual means. He made it through school because he worked very hard. In his senior year he learned that a number of his friends were going on to graduate school. He, too, applied to a number of graduate programs, in psychology. He came to see a counselor in the student services center after being rejected by all the schools to which he applied. In the interview it soon became clear to the counselor that Troy thought that many, perhaps even most, college students went on to graduate school. After all, most of his closest friends had been accepted in one graduate school or another. The counselor shared with him the statistics of what could be called the educational pyramid— the decreasing percentage of students attending school at higher levels. Troy did not realize that just finishing college made him part of an elite group. Nor was he completely aware of the extremely competitive nature of the graduate programs in psychology to which he had applied. He found much of this relieving, but then found himself suddenly faced with what to do now that he was finishing school. Up to this point he had not thought much about it. He felt disconcerted by the sudden need to look at the world of work.

Giving information is especially useful when ignorance either is one of the principal causes of a problem situation or is making an existing problem worse.

In some medical settings, doctors team up with counselors to give clients messages that are hard to hear and to provide them with information needed to make difficult decisions. For instance, Lester, a 54-year-old accountant, has been given a series of diagnostic tests for a heart condition. The doctor and counselor sit down and talk with him about the findings. Bypass surgery is one option, but it has risks and there is no absolute assurance that the surgery will take care of all the patient's heart problems. The counselor helps Lester cope with the news, process the information, and come to a decision.

There are some cautions to be observed in giving information. When information is challenging, or even shocking, the helper needs to be tactful and know how to help the client handle the disequilibrium that comes with the news. Also, do not overwhelm the client with information. Make sure that the information you provide is clear and relevant to the client's problem situation. Don't let the client go away with a misunderstanding of the information. Be sure not to confuse information giving with advice giving; the latter is seldom useful. Finally, be supportive; help the client process the information.

All of these cautions come into play for counselors of those who test positive for the AIDS virus.

> Angie, an unmarried woman who has just given birth to a baby boy, needs to be told that both she and her son are HIV-positive. The implications are enormous. She needs information about the virus, what she needs to do for herself and her son medically, and the implications for her sex life. Obviously the way in which this information is given to her can determine to a great extent how she will handle the immediate crisis and the ensuing lifestyle demands.

It is obvious that Angie's case is not one for an amateur. Experts, particularly those with special training in dealing with AIDS cases, know the range of ways in which clients receive the news that they have tested positive, how to provide support in each case, and how to challenge clients to rally resources and manage the crisis.

In some of their early sessions, Rick provided Tim with information that in a number of areas proved to be challenging:

- that Tim is probably more intelligent and talented than he realizes;
- that he is underemployed;
- that employers do not necessarily dig deeply into the background of prospective employees;
- that privacy laws protect him from damaging disclosures;
- that many employers look benignly on the peccadillos and developmental crises of a prospective employee's adolescent years;
- that the job market is strong and growing stronger, so that people with Tim's skills and potential are in high demand.

Of course, Rick did not dump all of this information on Tim in the first session. In fact, he encouraged Tim to dig out some of the information—for instance, the strength of the job market—on his own. All of the information, however, challenged Tim's views of himself, his assumptions about his past, and his ambitionless lifestyle.

At times of major decisions, information giving is not to be used by helpers as a subtle (or not too subtle) way of pushing their own values. For instance, helpers should not immediately give clients with unwanted pregnancies information about abortion clinics. Conversely, if abortion is contrary to the helper's values, then the helper needs to let the client looking for abortion counseling know that he or she cannot help her in this area. In Tim's case, Rick caught himself pushing career decisions that Tim may or may not have wanted. He backed off when he realized that it was stupid to try to remake Tim in his own image and likeness.

ADVANCED EMPATHY

Helpers, in the intensity of their listening and being with, and without going beyond the experience of their clients, sometimes see clearly what clients only half see and hint at. This deeper kind of empathy involves "sensing meanings of which the client is scarcely aware" (Rogers, 1980, p. 142). For instance, a client talks about his anger with his wife, but as he talks, the helper hears not just anger but also hurt. It may be that the client can talk with relative ease about his anger but not as easily about his feelings of hurt. In a basic empathic response, clients recognize themselves almost immediately: "Yes, that's what I said (meant, experienced, felt, and so forth)." The questions helpers ask themselves to probe a bit deeper as they listen to clients suggest that clients might not immediately recognize themselves and their experiences:

- What is this person only half saying?
- What is this person hinting at?
- What is this person saying in a confused way?
- What messages do I hear behind the explicit messages?

Here the response "You feel not only angry, but also hurt" can make the client stop and think. That's what makes advanced empathy challenging.

Note that advanced empathic listening deals with what the client is actually saying or expressing, however confusedly, and not with the helper's interpretations of what the client is saying. Advanced empathy is not an attempt to "psych the client out." Indeed, capturing what is only implied is only the first step. Bennis and Nanus (1985) suggested this in a book on leadership: "Leaders articulate and define what has previously remained implicit or unsaid; *then* they invent images, metaphors, and models that provide a focus for new attention" (p. 39). That is, the hidden meanings clients discover are the first step in a much more creative process. In Stage II, clients will be challenged to ask themselves, "Now that I have a much fuller understanding of just how things are, what do I want them to look like?"

Advanced empathy focuses not just on problems, but also on resources. Effective helpers listen for the resources that are buried deeply in clients and often have been forgotten by them. Cummings (1979) gave an example of this kind of listening in his work with addicts.

> During the first half of the first session the therapist must listen very intently. Then, somewhere in midsession, using all the rigorous training, therapeutic acumen, and the third, fourth, fifth, and sixth ears, the therapist discerns some unresolved wish, some long-gone dream that is still residing deep in that human being, and then the therapist pulls it out and ignites the client with a desire to somehow look at that dream again. This is not easy, because if the right nerve is not touched, the therapist loses the client. (p. 1123)

Rick listened to Tim in the same way and saw counseling not so much as a way of helping him manage problems as a way of helping him develop or reignite opportunities. Advanced empathy deals with both the overlooked positive side and the overlooked shadow side of the client's experience and behavior.

In the following example the client, a soldier doing a five-year hitch in the army, has been talking to a chaplain about his failing to be promoted. As he talks, it becomes fairly evident that part of the problem is that he is so quiet and unassuming that it is easy for his superiors to ignore him. He is the kind of person who keeps to himself and keeps everything inside.

Client: I don't know what's going on. I work hard, but I keep getting passed over when promotion time comes along. I think I work as hard as anyone else, and I work efficiently, but all of my efforts seem to go down the drain. I'm not as flashy as some others, but I'm just as substantial.

Chaplain A: You feel it's quite unfair to do the kind of work that merits a promotion and still not get it.

Chaplain B: It's depressing to put as much effort as those who get promoted and still get passed by. . . . Tell me more about the "not as flashy" bit. What in your style might make it easy for others not to notice you, even when you're doing a good job?

Chaplain A tries to understand the client from the client's frame of reference. He deals with the client's feelings and the experience underlying these feelings. This is basic empathy. Chaplain B, however, goes a bit further. From the context, from past interchanges, from the client's manner and tone of voice, he picks up a theme that the client states in passing in the phrase "not as flashy," that is, that the client is so unassuming that his best efforts go unnoticed. Advanced empathy, then, goes beyond the expressed to the partially expressed and the implied. If helpers are accurate and if their timing is good, they will assist the client to develop a new and useful perspective. Let's take a look at the client's response to each chaplain.

Client (in response to Chaplain A): Yeah . . . I suppose there's nothing I can do but wait it out. (A long silence ensues.)

Client (in response to Chaplain B): You mean I'm so quiet I could get lost in the shuffle? Or maybe it's the guys who make more noise, the "squeaky wheels," my dad called them, who get noticed.

In his response to Chaplain A the client merely retreats more into himself. However, in his response to Chaplain B the client begins to see that his unassuming, nonassertive style may contribute to the problem situation. Once he becomes aware of the self-limiting dimensions of his style, he is in a better position to do something about it.

Advanced empathy can take a number of forms. Let's consider some of them.

Making the Implied Explicit

The most basic form of advanced empathy is to give expression to what the client only implies. "The therapist's capacity to respond to the implicit is a kind of empathy, different from . . . an accurate grasp of [either] content or emotion" (Hendricks, 1986, p. 141). In the following example, the client has been discussing ways of getting back in touch with his wife after a recent divorce, but when he speaks about doing so, he expresses very little enthusiasm.

Client: I could wait to hear from her. But I suppose there's nothing wrong with calling her up and asking her how she's getting along.

Counselor A: As far as you can see, it's OK to take the initiative to find out if everything is well with her.
Client (somewhat drearily): Yeah, I suppose I could.

Counselor B: You've been talking about getting in touch with her, but, unless I'm mistaken, I don't hear a great deal of enthusiasm in your voice.
Client: To be honest, I don't really want to talk to her. But I feel guilty, guilty about the divorce, guilty about seeing her out on her own. I'm taking care of her all over again. And that's one of the reasons we got divorced—I mean my constant taking care of her when she was more interested in independence.

Counselor A's response might have been fine at an earlier stage of the helping process, but it misses the mark here, and the client grinds to a halt. In Step I-B the counselor needs to help the client dig deeper. Counselor B bases her response not only on the client's immediately preceding remark but on the entire context of the story-telling process. Her response hits the mark, and the client moves forward. As with basic empathy, there is no such thing as a good advanced empathic response in itself. The question is: Does the response help the client clarify the issue more fully so that he or she might begin to see the need to act differently?

In the following example, Tim is talking about his lack of any strong ambition.

Tim: I've never seen much reason for pushing myself forward. Then, of course, came the hospitalization, and that confirmed me in my non-ambition approach. I'm sure I can be happy with my own niche in life.

Rick: As I listen to you, Tim, I'm not sure whether I'm listening to someone who has taken a reasoned value stance on ambition—or to someone who has not even given "ambition" a chance. . . . Have you dismissed any kind of your own brand of reaching for the stars?

Tim: Hmm . . . reaching for the stars. You know, when you first used the word "ambition" with me, something like a shudder went through me. Not unpleasant. Not like I was being accused of something.

Rick: Maybe a shudder of recognition?

Tim: Yeah, that's more like it! Like a word I'd lost . . . but a word that somehow fit me.

Tim engages in a bit of rationalization about his lack of ambition. Rick's hunch is that Tim does not mean a *lack* of ambition but a *suppression* of ambition.

Advanced accurate empathy is part of the social-influence process; it places demands on clients to take a deeper look at themselves. Helpers' genuineness, respect, understanding, and rapport create a power base. In Step I-B helpers use this power to influence clients to see their problems from a more objective frame of reference. Challenges are still based on an empathic understanding of the client and are made with genuine care and respect, but they are demands nevertheless. Nonassertive helpers can find it difficult to place demands on their clients.

Identifying Themes

Advanced empathy also includes helping clients identify and explore behavioral and emotional themes in problems and opportunities, especially self-defeating patterns of behavior and emotion. Part of Tim's "lack of ambition" problem is a pattern of dependency. He still lives at home. His part-time jobs have come from the recommendations of relatives or friends. He is overly compliant in the helping sessions.

Rick: You have not said this in so many words, but it seems that you find it easy at times to let other people make decisions for you.

Tim: But once they do, then I'm usually dissatisfied, though I don't let them know.

Rick: I wonder if being dissatisfied has been a bad thing.

Tim (pauses and thinks): Like I don't want to be dependent in the first place?

Rick: What do you think?

Tim has given a number of hints indicating that he was vaguely aware that he has been too dependent and—an even more positive sign—that he does not particularly like it. Now the whole thing is out in the open. Tim eventually did get better at decision making. He moved into a full-time job and then got a better one in the same company within a year. After that he was chosen from among over 100 candidates for a very good job.

Recall the case of Roberto and Maria from the previous chapter. The counselor spends time with them together but also on occasion sees each of them alone. It is Maria's turn.

Counselor: I'd like to pull a few things together. If I have heard you correctly, you currently take care of the household finances. You are usually the one who accepts or rejects social invitations, because your schedule is tighter than Roberto's. And now you're about to ask him to move because you can get a better job in Boston. You reason that all of this makes life easier and better for him.

Maria: When you put it all together like that, it sounds as if I'm running his life.

Counselor: I'm not saying that. . . . One way of testing it out is to ask yourself, "What if the roles were reversed?"

Maria: Hmmm . . . Well, I'd . . . hmm . . . (laughs). I'm giving myself away!

Thematic material might refer to feelings (such as themes of hurt, of depression, of anxiety), to behavior (such as themes of controlling others, of avoiding intimacy, of blaming others, of overwork), to experiences (such as themes of being a victim, of being seduced, of being feared, of failing), or some combination of these. Once you recognize a self-defeating theme or pattern, your task is to communicate your perception to the client in a way that enables the client to check it out. This task often requires a high degree of assertiveness, empathy, and tact. Make sure that the themes you discover are based on the client's experience and are not just the artifacts of some psychological theory. Advanced empathy works because clients recognize themselves in what you say.

Connecting Islands

This metaphor suggests another approach to advanced empathy. The helper attempts to build "bridges" between the "islands" (Ivey, 1971; Ivey & Authier, 1978) of feelings, experiences, and behaviors revealed by the client in the self-exploration stage. The following client, who has a full-time job, is finishing his final two courses for his college degree and is going to get married right after graduation. He talks about being progressively more anxious and tired in recent weeks. Later he talks about getting ready for his marriage in a few months and about deadlines for turning in papers for current courses. Still later, he talks about his need to succeed, to compete, and to meet the expectations of his parents and grandparents.

He has begun to wonder whether all of this is telling him that it is a mistake to get married or that he is an inadequate person. The fact that a recent physical examination showed him to be in good health has actually made things worse.

Counselor: John, there might be a simpler explanation for your growing anxiety and tiredness. One, you are really working very hard at school and at work. Two, competing as hard as you do is bound to take its physical and emotional toll. And three, the emotional drain of getting ready for a marriage is enormous for anyone, including you. You're a solid guy, but not Superman.

John: Now that you say it, it makes sense. The point is that I'm not managing it well.

John had been talking about these three "islands" as if they were unrelated to one another. When the counselor connects them, his response indicates a need to act.

Advanced empathy means helping the client fill in the missing links in the data produced in the self-exploration process. In the course of his discussions with Rick, Tim presents two separate "islands" of behavior: (1) his "secret" and his reaction to it, that is, leaving school, part-time jobs, and generally settling for less, and (2) ambiguity about his sexuality. After several false starts, he begins to talk about his sexual ambiguity as "another" problem. Rick is empathic, but eventually he says something like this:

Rick: You describe the college "incident" as a kind of watershed in your life. Or a mule kick to your ego. While you were not the hottest property on campus, you were not a loner either. You became more of a loner once you got out of the hospital. As you described it, you ended up having "acquaintances" instead of friends. I hear you saying something like this: "No part of my being escaped the mule kick." I'm curious why you're intimating that your sexual being escaped.

Tim: I'm not. I'm saying just the opposite. It messed me up sexually.

Rick: Messed you up—or set you back a bit?

Tim: Oh.

Tim senses that something is not quite right sexually, but he jumps to a conclusion. Tim fears that he might not be "fully a man," as he puts it. Rick sees another possibility. At the time of the hospitalization everything developmental, including sexuality, took a beating.

Of course, counselors need to be accurate in the connections, relationships, and interpretations they propose. Counselors who are controlling rather than collaborative might well be able to force clients to accept interpretations of their behavior that do not help. Therefore, it is extremely important to check advanced empathic statements with the client.

Tim: Let's see if I can get it clear in my own head. When I say "messed up" sexually, I mean I think mostly about me. I masturbate just to get relief. Most of my acquaintances are guys. Well, you know. I was kind of shy before I went to the hospital. I, well, I'm not sure where to start.

Rick: Well, let's see if we can work on that.

And Tim did "work it out." At root he was fearful of human contact, not just contact with women. Within three years he was married; within four, a proud father.

From the Less to the More

The function of advanced empathy is to help clients move from the less to the more. If clients are not clear about some issue or if they speak guardedly, then the helper speaks directly, clearly, and openly. One client rambled, alluding lightly to "past indiscretions" as he moved along. It finally came out that these "indiscretions" led to a prison term. The counselor helps him face these issues more squarely.

Counselor: George, you sound like you'd like to say, "How does an ex-jailbird gather up his self-respect and get on with life again?" Is that too blunt?

George: Why can't I say that to myself?

Counselor: I have some ideas, but why, George? Answer it yourself.

George: (with tears in his eyes): Because I spend most of my time trying to justify to myself what I did.

The purpose of advanced empathy is not to help clients achieve the kinds of dramatic breakthroughs we see portrayed on TV. Rather, through advanced accurate empathy, what is said confusedly by the client is stated clearly by the helper; what is said half-heartedly is stated cogently; what is said vaguely is stated concretely; and what the client presents at a superficial level is re-presented by the helper at a deeper level.

The categories described here are neither exhaustive nor completely distinct. What they have in common is that they are all different kinds of *hunches* that, when shared with clients, can help them see a problem situation, a goal, a way out, a possible strategy, more clearly.

HELPER SELF-DISCLOSURE

A third skill of challenging involves the helper's sharing some of his or her own experiences with clients (Donley, Horan, & DeShong, 1989; Hendrick, 1988; Klein & Friedlander, 1987; Neimeyer & Fong, 1983; Peca-Baker & Friedlander, 1987, 1989; VandeCreek & Angstadt, 1985; Weiner, 1979). In one sense counselors cannot help but disclose themselves:

> The counselor communicates his or her characteristics to the client in every look, movement, emotional response, and sound, as well as with every word. Clients actively construe the personal characteristics, meanings, and causes behind the counselor's behaviors in order to evaluate the personal significance of the counselor's remarks. (Strong & Claiborn, 1982, p. 173)

This is indirect disclosure. As indicated earlier, effective helpers are aware of and know how to use indirect disclosure at the service of the helping process.

Direct helper self-disclosure can, as a form of modeling (Thase & Page, 1977), help clients with their own self-disclosure. Self-help groups (Gartner & Riessman, 1977, 1984) such as Alcoholics Anonymous use modeling extensively as a way of showing new members what to talk about and of encouraging them to talk freely about themselves and their problems. This approach is very useful in group settings with clients who don't know what to do or who are reluctant to talk about themselves in an intimate or personal way. It is the group's way of saying "You can talk here without being judged and getting hurt."

In one-to-one counseling dealing with alcohol and drug addiction, extensive helper self-disclosure may be the norm.

> Beth is a counselor in a drug rehabilitation program. She herself was an addict for a number of years, but "kicked the habit" with the help of the agency where she is now a counselor. It is clear to all addicts in the program that the counselors there were once addicts themselves and are not only rehabilitated but intensely interested in helping others both rid themselves of drugs and develop a kind of lifestyle that helps them stay drug free. Beth freely shares her experience, both of being a drug user and of her rather agonizing journey to freedom, whenever she thinks that doing so can help a client.

Ex-addicts can make excellent helpers in programs like this. They know from the inside the games addicts play. Sharing their experience is central to their style of counseling and is accepted by their clients. New perspectives are developed, and new possibilities for action are discovered.

Some writers make a distinction between positive and negative self-disclosure, that is, the revelation of successes or failures. Ex-addicts make no bones about their failures, but this is complemented, of course, by stories about how they eventually pulled themselves together. The end result is a balanced package that many clients find quite helpful. They appreciate the fact that the counselor or group leader is, like them, a human being prone to make mistakes; they also appreciate the fact that there is a way out. Indeed, the self-help movement, being generally more democratic in nature than other forms of helping, generally encourages this kind of helper self-disclosure. Helpers usually are people who have had or still have the problem in question. For instance, women who have had mastectomies and have come to terms with both the physical and psychological problems involved work as paraprofessional helpers who talk freely about their failures and successes.

Helper self-disclosure in other forms of one-to-one counseling and therapy is another story. Research has produced mixed and even contradictory results (DeForest & Stone, 1980; Donley, Horan, & DeShong, 1989; McCarthy, 1979; Nilsson, Strassberg, & Bannon, 1979; Simonson, 1976). Weigel and his associates (1972) found evidence suggesting that helper self-disclosure can frighten clients or make them see helpers as less well adjusted (see Derlega, Lovell, & Chaikin, 1976). Other studies (Klein & Friedlander, 1987; Peca-Baker & Friedlander, 1989) suggest that helper self-disclosure is appreciated by clients—self-disclosing helpers are seen as "down to earth" and "honest"—but the reasons are unclear. Is it the mere fact that helpers make themselves vulnerable for the sake of their clients? Or is it the actual content of the disclosure?

Helper self-disclosure is challenging for at least two reasons. First, it is a form of intimacy and, for some clients, intimacy is not easy to handle. Second, the message to the client is, indirectly, a challenging "You can do it, too," because helper revelations, even when they are negative, usually deal with conditions that have been overcome.

Rick: In my junior year in high school I was expelled for stealing. I thought that it was the end of the world. My Catholic family took it as the ultimate disgrace. We even moved to a different neighborhood in the city.
Tim: What did it do to you?

Rick briefly tells his story, a story that includes setbacks—not unlike Tim's—but one that eventually has a successful outcome. Rick does not overdramatize his story. He makes the point that developmental crises are normative. How they are managed is the critical issue.

The confused results of research studies tells us that, currently, helper self-disclosure is not a science, but an art. Here are some guidelines for using it.

Make helper self-disclosure part of the contract. In self-help groups and in the counseling of addicts by ex-addicts, helper self-disclosure is an explicit part of the contract. It is clear from the start that "high self-disclosure by the therapist is part of the professional role and is appropriate for effective treatment" (Doster & Nesbitt, 1979, p. 204). In short, if you don't want your disclosures to surprise your clients, let them know that you may self-disclose.

Make sure that your disclosures are appropriate. Sharing yourself is appropriate (Egan, 1976) if it helps clients achieve the treatment goals outlined in this helping process—that is, if it helps them talk about problem situations more concretely, if it helps them develop new perspectives and frames of reference, if it helps them set realistic goals for themselves, and if it moves them to act. Don't disclose more than you have to. Helper self-disclosure that is exhibitionistic or engaged in for effect is obviously inappropriate.

Keep your disclosure selective and focused. Don't distract clients with rambling stories about yourself.

Counselor (talking to a graduate student in psychology): Listening to you brings me right back to my own days in graduate school. I don't think that I was ever busier in my life. I also believe that the most depressing moments of my life took place then. On any number of occasions I wanted to throw in the towel. For instance, I remember once toward the end of my third year when . . .

It may be that selective bits of this counselor's experience in graduate school might be useful in helping the student get a better conceptual and emotional grasp of her problems, but he has wandered off into the kind of reminiscing that meets his needs rather than the client's.

Do not burden the client. Do not burden an already overburdened client. One counselor thought that he would help make a client who was sharing some sexual problems more comfortable by sharing some of his own experiences. After all, he saw his sexual development as not too different from the client's. However, the client reacted by saying: "Hey, don't tell me your problems. I'm having a hard enough time dealing with my own." This novice counselor shared too much of himself too soon. He was caught up in his own willingness to disclose rather than its potential usefulness to the client.

Do not overdo it. Helper self-disclosure is inappropriate if it is too frequent. This, too, distracts the client and shifts attention to the counselor. Research (Murphy & Strong, 1972) suggests that if helpers disclose themselves too frequently, clients tend to see them as phony and suspect that they have ulterior motives. Make sure that the pragmatism, respect, and genuineness discussed in Chapter 3 permeate your disclosures.

Remain flexible. Take each client separately. Adapt your disclosures to differences in clients and situations (Chelune, 1977; Neimeyer & Banikiotes, 1981; Neimeyer & Fong, 1983). For example, Rick shared his high school experience with Tim relatively early on in their talks as a way of challenging Tim to stop seeing himself as unique. When asked directly, clients say that they want helpers to disclose themselves (Hendrick, 1988), but this does not mean that every client in every situation wants it or would always benefit from it. Keep the client's interests and the goals of counseling in mind. Self-disclosure on the part of helpers should be a natural part of the helping process, not a gambit.

In summary, then, although the research on helper self-disclosure is ambiguous, self-disclosure can be useful under the appropriate circumstances even when clients do not expect or even prefer it (VandeCreek & Angstadt, 1985). Therefore, it is a skill that should be part of any helper's repertory—but it is only one skill among many, just as challenge itself is only one response among many. Helpers should be willing and able to disclose themselves, even deeply, in reasonable ways, but should actually do so only if it is clear that it will contribute to the client's progress.

IMMEDIACY: DIRECT, MUTUAL TALK

It has been suggested that many, if not most, clients who seek help have trouble with interpersonal relationships. This is either their central concern or part of a wider problem situation. Some of the difficulties clients have in their day-to-day relationships are also reflected in their relationships to helpers. For instance, if they are compliant outside, they are often compliant in the helping process. If they become aggressive and angry with authority figures outside, they often do the same with helpers. Therefore, the client's interpersonal style can be examined, at least in part, through an examination of his or her relationship with the helper. If counseling takes place in a group, then the opportunity is even greater.

The package of skills enabling helpers to explore their relationship with their clients has been called "immediacy" (Carkhuff 1969a, 1969b; Carkhuff & Anthony, 1979), "direct, mutual communication" (Higgins, Ivey, & Uhlemann, 1970; Ivey, 1971; Ivey & Authier, 1978), and "you-me" talk (Egan, 1976, 1977). All these terms refer to the ability to explore with another person what is happening in the relationship with that person.

Types of Immediacy in Helping

Immediacy in counseling serves a purpose. There are three types: self-involving statements, general relationship immediacy, and here-and-now immediacy. All have in common a move on the part of the helper to use some dimension of the client-helper relationship itself as the focus of challenge.

Self-Involving Statements

Self-involving statements are present-tense, personal responses to the client (Andersen & Anderson, 1985; Watkins & Schneider, 1989). They can be positive in tone:

Rick: Tim, I like the way you've begun to show initiative both in discussion and outside. I thought that telling your boss a bit about your past showed guts.

Here Rick expresses direct support for Tim. His self-involving remark is also a challenging statement, because the implication is "Keep it up." Positive self-involving statements tend to be appreciated by clients: "During the initial interview, the support and encouragement offered through the counselor's positive self-involving statements may be especially important because they put clients at ease and allay their anxiety about beginning counseling" (Watkins & Schneider, 1989, p. 345).

Negative self-involving statements are much more directly challenging in tone.

Rick: Tim, I'm surprised that you didn't send in your résumé for the job you talked about last week. What happened?

Tim: It's worse than that. I also skipped one of the interviews. . . . It all came crashing in on me. Maybe we're just building castles in the sky here.

Rick's negative self-involving statement is his way of not beating around the bush. Carl Rogers, when asked late in life about his thoughts on the place of challenging in counseling (Landreth, 1984), made the following remarks:

> I am quite certain even before I stopped carrying individual counseling cases, I was doing more and more of what I would call confrontation. That is, confrontation of the other person with my feelings . . . . For example, I recall a client with whom I began to realize I felt bored every time he came in. I had a hard time staying awake during the hour, and that was not like me at all. Because it was a persisting feeling, I realized I would have to share it with him. I had to confront him with my feeling and that really caused a conflict in his role as a client . . . . So with a good deal of difficulty and some embarrassment, I said to him, "I don't understand it myself, but when you start talking on and on about your problems in what seems to me a flat tone of voice, I find myself getting very bored." This was quite a jolt to him and he looked very unhappy. Then he began to talk about the way he talked and gradually he came to understand one of the reasons for the way he presented himself verbally. He said, "You know, I think the reason I talk in such an uninteresting way is because I don't think I have ever expected anyone to really hear me." . . . We got along much better after that because I could remind him that I heard the same flatness in his voice I used to hear. (p. 323)

Rogers's self-involving statement, genuine but quite challenging, helped the client move forward.

Relationship Immediacy

Relationship immediacy refers to your ability to discuss with a client where you stand in your overall relationship with him or her. The focus is not on the transaction at hand but on the way the relationship itself has developed. In the following example, the helper is a 44-year-old woman working as a counselor for a large company. She is talking to a 36-year-old man she has been seeing once every other week for about two months. One of his principal problems is his relationship to his supervisor, who is also a woman.

Counselor: We seem to have developed a good relationship here. I feel we respect each other. I have been able to make demands on you, and you have made demands on me. There has been a great deal of give-and-take in our relationship. You've gotten angry with me, and I've gotten impatient with you at times, but we've worked it out. I'm wondering what our relationship has that is missing in your relationship to your supervisor.

Client: Well, for one thing, you listen to me, and I don't think she does. On the other hand, I listen pretty carefully to you, but I don't think I listen to her at all, and she probably knows it. I think she's dumb, and I guess I'm not hiding it from her.

Notice how the review of the relationship helps the client focus more specifically on his relationship to his supervisor.

Here is another example. Lee, a 38-year-old trainer in a counselor training program, is talking to Carlos, 25, one of the trainees.

Trainer: Carlos, I'm a bit bothered about some of the things that are going on between you and me. When you talk to me, I get the feeling that you are being very careful. You talk slowly—you seem to be choosing your words, sometimes to the point that what you are saying sounds almost prepared. You have never challenged me on anything in the group. When you talk most intimately about yourself, you seem to avoid looking at me. I find myself giving you less feedback than I give others. I've even found myself putting off talking to you about all this. Perhaps some of this is my own imagining, but I want to check it out with you.

Carlos: I've been putting it off, too. I'm embarrassed about some of the things I think I have to say.

Carlos goes on to talk to Lee about his misgivings. He thinks that Lee is domineering in the training group and plays favorites. He has not wanted to bring it up because he feels that his position will be jeopardized. But now that Lee has made the overture, he accepts the challenge.

Here-and-Now Immediacy

Here-and-now immediacy refers to your ability to discuss with clients what is happening between you in the here and now of any given transaction. It is not the entire relationship that is being considered, but only this specific interaction. In the following example, the helper, a 43-year-old woman, is a counselor in a church-related human services center. Agnes, a 49-year-old woman who was recently widowed, has been talking about her loneliness. Agnes seems to have withdrawn quite a bit, and the interaction has bogged down.

Counselor: I'd like to stop a moment and take a look at what's happening right now between you and me.

Agnes: I'm not sure what you mean.

Counselor: Well, our conversation today started out quite lively, and now it seems rather subdued to me. I've noticed that the muscles in my shoulders have become tense and that I feel a little flush. I sometimes tense up that way when I feel that I might have said something wrong.

Agnes: What could that have been?

Counselor: Agnes, is it just me, or do you also feel that things are a bit strained between us right now?

Agnes: Well, a little.

Counselor: Last month you discussed how you control your friends with your emotions. This gets you what you want, but the price you pay can be too high. For instance, you describe some of your friends as becoming more and more wary of you. Now, all of a sudden you've gone a bit quiet, and I've been asking myself what I might have done wrong. To be truthful, I'm feeling a bit controlled, too. What's your perspective on all this?

The counselor uses self-disclosure and here-and-now immediacy to focus on a key issue in the client's interpersonal life. She begins to explore the possibility that what the client is doing here and now is an example of her self-defeating approach to interpersonal relationships in her day-to-day life.

People often fail to be immediate with one another in their interactions. For instance, a husband feels slighted by something his wife says. He says nothing and swallows his feelings. But he becomes a bit distant from her for the next couple of days, a bit more quiet. She notices this, wonders what is happening, but says nothing. Soon little things in their relationship that would ordinarily be ignored become irritating. Things become more and more tense, but still they do not engage in "direct, mutual talk" about what is happening. The whole thing ends in a game of "uproar" (see Berne, 1964), that is, a huge argument over something quite small. Once they've vented their emotions, they feel both relieved because they've dealt with their emotions and guilty because they've done so in a somewhat childish way.

Immediacy: A Complex Skill

Immediacy—both in counseling and in everyday life—is a difficult, demanding skill. It is not a skill that is readily learned. It is difficult, first of all, because the helper, without becoming self-preoccupied and without "psyching out" the client, needs to be *aware* of what is happening in the relationship and have enough psychological distance to catch difficult moments as they happen and react to them without trivializing the helping process. Second, immediacy often demands competence in all the communication skills discussed to this point—attending, listening, empathy, advanced empathy, self-disclosure, self-involving statements, and other forms of challenge. Third, the helper must move beyond the MUM effect and challenge the client even though he or she is reluctant to do so. The helper needs guts.

Consider the interaction between Rick and Tim at a time when things seemed to get bogged down.

Rick: Time out for a while, Tim. We've been thrashing around a bit here. A few blind alleys. Seems like we're stale.

Tim: I can buy that, I guess. But do we always have to be going at top speed?

Rick: No, but it's almost like we're in reverse. . . . I think that it's fair to say that we hit it off right from the beginning. But I felt uneasy when you came in today—maybe a leftover from last week. So I've been asking myself what I've been doing here to bog things down. . . . At times I've been pretty demanding with you, pretty challenging. Maybe even parental?

Tim: One father was enough for me. I didn't like him very much. He was a drunk, even violent at times. But that's past. I don't want to talk about him.

Rick: Okay, but you don't want me to be a substitute father either.

Tim: No. . . . Sometimes you talk to me, I don't know, like a friend or something. I mean someone with my interests at heart and things like that. But sometimes you do talk to me like a parent. And I suppose I've been resenting it. I don't know.

Rick: So it's not the fact that I push you every now and then that gets to you.

Tim: No, not at all. If you hadn't pushed, well, I don't think we'd have gotten anywhere. It's the *way* you push at times. I don't even know if I can explain the difference.

Rick: Let me hash this over between now and the next time we meet.

This conversation helped clear the air during that session, and Tim "went back to work." Afterward, as Rick reflected on this exchange, he realized that he *was* becoming possessive. As corny as it sounded, Tim *was* the son he would never have. His manner with Tim had taken on a certain tone: "Do it for me, Tim." And when Tim didn't "do it" to his satisfaction, he would let him know about it, under the guise of challenging him to do his best. So his challenging had become personal rather than professional. Rick knew that he had to change his attitude and his manner. When they got back together, Rick did not go into all of this with Tim, not because he was reluctant to, but because it would have been part of the problem instead of part of the solution. His relationship with Tim had become *too* personal. So, at the beginning of the next session he told Tim that he had thought the whole thing over:

Rick: I think that at times I've been pushing you because I want you to do well for me, as you said, like a father. I think I should back off that.

Tim: Back off that, okay, but that doesn't mean backing off entirely. You do tap into the best in me.

And then they got back to the work of the session.

Situations Calling for Direct, Mutual Communication

A good part of any of the communication skills is knowing when to use it. The skill of immediacy can be most useful in the following situations:

- When a session is directionless and it seems that no progress is being made: "I feel that we're bogged down right now. Perhaps we could stop a moment and see what we're doing right and what's going wrong."
- When there is tension between helper and client: "We seem to be getting on each other's nerves. It might be helpful to stop a moment and clear the air."
- When trust seems to be an issue: "I see your hesitancy to talk, and I'm not sure whether it's related to me or not. It might still be hard for you to trust me."
- When there is "social distance" between helper and client in terms of social class or widely differing interpersonal styles: "There are some hints that the fact that I'm black and you're white is making both of us a bit hesitant."
- When dependency seems to be interfering with the helping process: "You don't seem willing to explore an issue until I give you permission to do so. And I seem to have let myself slip into the role of permission giver."
- When counterdependency seems to be blocking the helping relationship: "It seems that we're letting this session turn into a struggle between you and me. And, if I'm not mistaken, both of us seem to be bent on winning."
- When attraction is sidetracking either helper or client: "I think we've liked each other from the start. Now I'm wondering whether that might be getting in the way of the work we're doing here."

Immediacy, of course, is a means, not an end. The primary goal of the helping process is not to establish and enjoy relationships but to explore and work through problem situations. Immediacy, used effectively, can accomplish two things. First, it can provide new perspectives on the counseling relationship and help client and counselor work together more effectively. Second, what clients learn about themselves in their interactions with helpers can provide new perspectives on how they relate to people outside.

ASOCIAL AND PARADOXICAL CHALLENGES

There is a growing literature dealing with forms of challenge that are somewhat off the beaten path. While these interventions seem more suited to advanced rather than beginning therapists, even the beginner can benefit from the basic concepts. A few words, then, on the "asocial" response and on paradoxical interventions.

The Asocial Response

Beier and Young (1984) discussed a benign and often humorous challenge dubbed the "asocial" response, a response the client does not expect in the therapeutic setting. They use the asocial response to cut through nonsense. Suppose that a married man has been describing his wife's faults at great length. After a while, the counselor responds, tongue-in-cheek:

Counselor: It was a mistake to marry such a woman, and maybe it's time to let her go.

This is not at all what the client has in mind, but since it is a logical conclusion to the case the client has been constructing against his wife, it pulls him up short. He realizes that he has gone too far, that he is making things sound worse than they are.

Client: Well, I don't think things are that bad. She does have her good points.

Beier and Young claim that such asocial responses make the client stop and think, providing what they call "beneficial uncertainty" for the client. Asocial responses, obviously, can be overused, too facetious, and—in the hands of an inept counselor—actually sarcastic. The counselor who is uncomfortable with this kind of communication can get the same result by using a social rather than an asocial response. The counselor in the last example might have said:

Counselor: I'm not sure whether you are trying to say that your wife has almost no redeeming qualities.
Client: Oh! Well, I didn't mean to be that hard on her.

Some clients, in a relationship that is not working out, have to make the other person the scapegoat in order to reduce their own culpability, at least initially. In this example the counselor realizes that the client is engaging in hyperbole, and he gently helps the client understand what he is doing.

Paradoxical Interventions

Paradoxical interventions are attracting a great deal of attention, both positive and negative (Brown & Slee, 1986; Cavell, Frentz, & Kelley, 1986; DeBord, 1989; Driscoll, 1985; Hill, 1987; Hunsley, 1988; Kraft & others, 1985; Perrin & Dowd, 1986; Seltzer, 1986; Shoham-Salomon & Rosenthal, 1987; Westerman & others, 1987). There are several problems complicating the picture: different authors have different classifications, the classifications overlap, research studies do not make clear the precise kind of intervention used, the motivations for using these interventions are not clear, paradoxical interventions are not placed in an overall helping context, there is a bit of the "latest thing" flavor to some of the writings, and ethical issues surrounding the use of these interventions are up in the air. In a word, the current literature is confusing. Despite all this, while I would certainly not counsel beginners to choose to become paradoxical therapists, as some call themselves, still I think that there are lessons to be gleaned and then integrated into an overall approach to helping. We will take a look at three somewhat overlapping forms of paradoxical interventions: paradoxical intention, symptom prescription, and paradoxical reframing. I will spare you a discussion of paradox itself. Most of the articles listed above provide that.

Paradoxical Intention

Some clients, in their very efforts to manage a problem, increase their anxiety over the problem and make it worse. For example, as anxiety-ridden clients fight their anxiety, they become even more anxious. Paradoxical interventions help clients to give up such problem-maintaining solutions.

> One who has insomnia might be instructed to see how long he or she can stay up at night, and try to enjoy it, until late nights are no longer dreaded and the turmoil subsides. One who is terrified about saying the wrong thing might be told to say intentionally the wrong thing, to introduce the idea that an occasional gaffe is not so terribly awful after all. Such interventions work when they aid the clients to smile at their catastrophic expectations and to see the symptoms as less important. . . . These involve "paradoxical intention" in that the *intention* is to bring on the feared condition and the outcome is that it [*paradoxically*] diminishes. (Driscoll, 1985, p. 775, emphasis added)

Rick found occasion to use paradoxical intention once with Tim. When Tim began to develop his social life more fully, he began having attacks of blushing, especially when he was with women. Rick urged him to try to blush—even more often and more intensely. Within four weeks, Tim was no longer bothered by blushing.

Some authors contend that, when using paradoxical intention, helpers can explain the entire rationale for its use to the client (DeBord, 1989). The client sees that the helper's suggestions make sense and finds no reason not to comply. But, as Driscoll (1985) has noted, "Were the way it works too obvious, then it would appear straightforward and commonsensical rather than paradoxical" (p. 774) Therefore, the question remains: How much should we tell the client?

Symptom Prescription

In symptom prescription, clients are directed to continue with their symptomatic behavior. For instance, in one study (Wright & Strong, 1982) procrastinators were divided into three groups. The first group was told just to continue in precisely the same procrastinating pattern; the second group was told to select procrastinating behaviors they wanted to continue; the third was a control group. Procrastinating behavior was reduced in both experimental groups. Symptom prescription has been used successfully with tantrum-prone children, disruptive students, stress-prone clients, clients with stubborn sexual problems, spouses who argue excessively, and difficult prisoners. Some say that we have just begun to tap its potential.

"Redirection" is an altered form of symptom prescription. In redirection, clients are urged to persist in their behavior, but to confine the behavior to a specific time and place. Spouses are asked to fight at a certain time in a certain room. Disruptive students are asked to practice their disruptive behavior for ten minutes a day with the teacher. The theory is that mandating the time and place for the unwanted behavior puts it into a new context that allows clients to see their behavior in a new light. Indeed, paradoxical interventions are often used in systems of one kind or another, such as family systems and marriages, to disrupt self-defeating patterns of behavior.

In symptom prescription a distinction may be made between resistant and cooperative clients. In the study on procrastination, the participants were probably cooperative. Yet, some say, in order to provide motivation the helper should offer even cooperative clients some rationale for trying to increase unwanted behaviors. The rationale offered need not be one the helper would accept.

> A client may be told that he or she is not in control of his or her anxiety when being anxious at night before going to sleep. In order to develop more control, practice at starting to be anxious is required. Therefore, to increase the element of client control, the client should practice being anxious several times during the day as well as in the evening. (Brown & Slee, 1986, p. 488)

While this explanation need not be a cock-and-bull story, it may not express the helper's view of things. It needs to have face validity for the client. The theory of paradoxical intervention itself is not shared with the client.

The dynamics with resistant clients are somewhat different. In this case, symptom prescription taps people's innate "orneriness," or what Driscoll (1985) called "oppositionality." If I tell you to do it, you'll stop doing it; if I tell you it's okay, you'll see it as not okay. Some helpers use symptom prescription with resistant clients because it taps into their oppositionality. Some see this as an unwarranted manipulation of the client; others do not. Underlying most forms of paradoxical intervention is this principle: Doing things intentionally brings unwanted behavior under control.

Paradoxical Reframing

Reframing in the context of paradoxical intervention means a verbal explanation that alters the meaning of a particular situation (for instance, a bout of depression) and is compatible with the client's current frame of reference. For instance, depression is described to a client, not as something bad and to be avoided, a kind of failure, but a normal reaction to distressing events and part of the human condition. This is a paradoxically positive interpretation of depression. Similarly, aggression may be described, not as attack against others, but as a way of preventing people from getting too close. Brown and Slee (1986) said that one way of strengthening the reframing is to ask the client to identify all the disadvantages of changing his or her behavior. The theory is that reframing gives clients distance from their problems and takes them out of a pressure-cooker atmosphere. Note, however, how different this is from both basic empathy and advanced empathy.

The Ethics of Paradoxical Interventions

Are paradoxical interventions ethical? As you might imagine, helpers line up on both sides of this question. On the one hand, these interventions seem to be based, at least in some cases, on deceit and manipulation, however benign. Does this not run counter to freedom of choice, disclosure of information about treatment, and protection of human dignity? When asked, teachers turned thumbs down to the use of paradoxical interventions with younger students (Cavell, Frentz, & Kelley, 1986). On the other hand, DeBord (1989) suggested that all therapies manipulate; that helping is about effectiveness, outcomes, and symptom reduction, not about client approval; that, when helpers explain what they are doing, they are seen more favorably by clients, but their interventions are less effective. I would rather say that all therapies involve social influence, which is not the same as manipulation. Nor should we forget that history is filled with atrocities committed by well-intentioned people driven by the principle that the end justifies the means.

I do not mean to overstate the case. Many ethical and highly respected practitioners find no problems using paradoxical interventions. Some clients see paradoxical directives as "tricky, manipulative, and confusing" (Perrin & Dowd, 1986, p. 207), but this does not necessarily destroy trust or break the social influence bond. Philosophers have devised the principle of "mental reservation." This states, in essence, that, while lying is wrong, allowing people to deceive themselves is not the same as lying. Many paradoxical interventions seem to follow this principle. I am sure that many would see "mental reservation" as a form of casuistry, though I personally think it has merit. Others find no problem with the "deceit" involved in paradoxical interventions, provided that the client is debriefed after the experience.

In short, there is a healthy debate about the ethics of some forms of paradoxical intervention. There has not been enough professional discussion to clear up the ethical issues or enough research on the efficacy of the various brands of paradoxical intervention to warrant teaching them to beginners. At this stage, these interventions are still part of helping as art. Used sparingly, nonmanipulatively, caringly, and without cynicism, paradoxical interventions have a place in the helper's kit bag.

PRINCIPLES UNDERLYING EFFECTIVE CHALLENGING

All challenges should be permeated by the spirit of the client-helper relationship values discussed in Chapter 3; that is, they should be caring (not power games or put-downs), genuine (not tricks or games), designed to increase rather than decrease the self-responsibility of the client (not expressions of helper control), and pragmatic (not endless interpretations and the search for the ultimate insight).

Clearly, challenging well is not a skill that comes automatically. It needs to be learned and practiced (McKee, Moore, & Presbury, 1982; Tamminen & Smaby, 1981). The following principles constitute some basic guidelines.

Keep the goals of challenging in mind. Challenge must be integrated into the entire helping process. Keep in mind that the goal is to help clients develop the kinds of alternative perspectives needed to clarify problem situations and to get on with the other steps of the helping process. Are the insights relevant rather than dramatic? To what degree do the new perspectives developed sit on the verge of action? Your challenges should have substance to them. If you become a confrontation specialist, you will end up being petty and ineffectual.

Encourage self-challenge. Invite clients to challenge themselves, and give them ample opportunity to do so. You can provide clients with probes and structures that help them engage in self-challenge. In the following excerpt, the counselor is talking to a man who has discussed at length his son's ingratitude. There has been something cathartic about his complaints, but it is time to move on.

Counselor: People often have blind spots in their relationships to others, especially in close relationships. I wonder whether you are beginning to see any blind spots in your relationship with your son.

Client: Well, I don't know. . . . I guess I don't think about that very much. . . . Hmm. A thought just struck me. Let's say that, like me, he was sitting someplace with a counselor. What would he be saying about me? . . . I think I know what some of the things would be.

Alternatively, the counselor might have asked this client to list three things he thinks he does right and three things that need to be reconsidered in his relationship with his son. The point is to be inventive with the probes and structures you provide to help clients challenge themselves. Remember, though, that clients with a history of being down on themselves might revel in giving you chapter and verse on their faults. This is not self-challenge. If such a client responded to the "blind spot" probe used above with something like "I think I spend too much time putting myself down and not enough doing something constructive with my life," then you would be getting somewhere.

Earn the right to challenge. Berenson and Mitchell (1974) maintained that some helpers don't have the right to challenge others, since they do not fulfill certain essential conditions. Here are some of the factors that earn you the right to challenge:

• *Develop a working relationship.* Challenge only if you have spent time and effort building a relationship with your client. If your rapport is poor or you have allowed your relationship with the client to stagnate, then deal with the relationship.

• *Make sure you understand the client.* Effective challenge flows from accurate understanding. Only when you see the world through the client's eyes can you begin to see what he or she is failing to see.

• *Be open to challenge yourself.* Don't challenge unless you are open to being challenged. If you are defensive in the counseling relationship, do not expect your clients to set aside their defensiveness.

• *Work on your own life.* Berenson and Mitchell claimed that only people who are striving to live fully according to their value system have the right to challenge others, for only such persons are potential sources of human nourishment for others. In other words, helpers should be striving to develop physically, intellectually, socially, and emotionally.

In summary, ask yourself: What is there about me that will make clients willing to be challenged by me? In a book on leadership, Bennis and Nanus (1985) quote a Taoist story of ancient China:

> When Yen Ho was about to take up his duties as tutor to the heir of Ling, Duke of Wei, he went to Ch'u Po Yu for advice. "I have to deal," he said, "with a man of depraved and murderous disposition. . . . How is one to deal with a man of this sort?" "I am glad," said Ch'u Po Yu, "that you asked me this question. . . . The first thing you must do is not to improve him, but to improve yourself." (p. 55)

While clients are not, in the main, people of "depraved and murderous dispositions," they are people who often resist change. To deal with clients, therefore, we helpers must first change ourselves.

Be tentative in the way you challenge clients. Jones and Gelso (1988) found that tentative interpretations are generally viewed more positively than absolute interpretations. The same challenging message can be delivered in such a way as to invite the cooperation or arouse the resistance of the client (Wachtel, 1980). Deliver challenges tentatively, as hunches that are open to discussion (see Strohmer & Newman, 1983) rather than as accusations. Challenging is not an opportunity to browbeat clients or put them in their place.

In the following example, a teacher has been talking to a counselor about problems he's having with fellow faculty and members of the administration. He has been describing himself as a victim, but in the examples he gives he hints that his interpersonal style might be part of the problem.

Client: And time after time I find myself having to swallow my anger.
Counselor A: You don't really swallow your anger, as you claim to. From what you say, it comes dribbling out unproductively all the time.

Counselor B: From what you say, it sounds like the anger you swallow at faculty meetings might not always stay down. I wonder whether others might say that it seems to leak out at times, perhaps in cynical remarks, in some aloofness, and occasionally in uncooperative behavior. Or am I reading too much into the picture you've painted?

Counselor A's challenge is simply an accusation. The way Counselor B qualifies her statement allows the client to explore it without getting into an argument. Effective challenging is not meant to pin clients down; it leaves them room to move.

On the other hand, challenges that are delivered with too many qualifications—either verbally or through the helper's tone of voice—sound apologetic and can be easily dismissed by clients. I was once working in a career-development center. As I listened to one of the clients, it soon became evident that one reason he was getting nowhere was that he engaged in so much self-pity. When I shared this observation with him, I overqualified it. It came out something like this:

Helper: Has it ever, at least in some small way, struck you that one possible reason for not getting ahead, at least as much as you would like, could be that at times you tend to engage in a little bit of self-pity?

I think it was almost that bad. I still remember his response. He paused, looked at me for a moment with surprise on his face, and said:

Client: A little bit of self-pity? . . . I wallow in self-pity.

We moved on to explore what he might do to decrease his self-pity.

Being tentative is not the same as being reluctant. You don't want to overburden the client, but, if a challenge is called for, other things being equal, don't put it off. Timing can be very important, but putting off a challenge can be a sign that you have given into the MUM effect.

Build on successes. High-level helpers do not urge clients to place too many demands on themselves all at once. Rather, they help clients place reasonable demands on themselves and in the process help them appreciate and celebrate their successes. In the following example, the client is a boy in a detention center who is rather passive and allows the others to push him around or ignore him. Recently, however, he has made a few minor attempts to stick up for his rights in the counseling group. The counselor is talking to him alone after a group meeting.

Counselor A: You're still not standing up for your own rights the way you need to. You said a couple of things in there, but you still let them push you around.

Counselor B: I notice two things. In the group meetings you have begun to speak up. You say what you want to say, even though you don't say it really forcefully. And I get the feeling that you feel good about that. But you still seem to let a couple of the guys push you around a bit. How do you see it?

The first counselor does not reinforce the client for his accomplishment; the second does.

Be specific. Specific challenges hit the mark. Vague challenges get lost. Clients don't know what to do about them. In the following example, Sandra, a young woman who has been "rescued" from a cult and who now has trouble making decisions on her own, has been talking with a counselor and an ex-cult member, Jason, together. While Sandra is glad that she is "free," she has not done much with her freedom. Her social life is limited to a counseling group and a few meetings with the counselor and Jason outside the meetings.

Jason: You're too passive, Sandra. You have to get off your butt and do something or you'll be a set-up for the next set of weirdos that come along.

The concept "passive" is too general, and the solution offered is too vague to help.

Counselor: Sandra, you said you've tried to develop more friends. Tell me more about it.

Sandra outlines a few rather anemic attempts to make new acquaintances.

Counselor: Let's see if we can draw a picture of what "trying to develop a better social life" would look like under the best of conditions. Let me throw something into the pot. I know you're a churchgoer. What kinds of clubs and things like that are at the parish? And, if you don't know, how could you find out?

Note that this is a challenge related to Stage III of the helping model. The preferred scenario for Sandra is "a fuller social life." That, too, needs to become more specific. But the counselor gets at it by challenging her to brainstorm possibilities.

Challenge strengths rather than weaknesses. Berenson and Mitchell (1974) discovered that successful helpers tend to challenge clients' strengths rather than their weaknesses. Individuals who focus on their failures find it difficult to change their behavior. As Bandura (1986) has pointed out, clients who regularly review their shortcomings tend to belittle their achievements, to withhold rewards from themselves when they do achieve, and to live with anxiety. All of this tends to undermine performance (see Bandura, 1986, p. 339). Challenging strengths means pointing out to clients the assets and resources they have but fail to use. In the following example, the helper is talking to a woman in a rape crisis center who is very good at helping others but who is always down on herself.

Counselor: Ann, in the group sessions, you provide a great deal of support for the other women. You have an amazing ability to spot a person in trouble and provide an encouraging word. And when one of the women wants to give up, you are the first to challenge her, gently and forcibly at the same time. Yet, when you get down on yourself, you don't accept what you provide so freely to others. You are not nearly as kind to yourself as you are to others.

The helper places a demand on Ann to use her resources on her own behalf.

In contrast, weakness confrontation, as the name implies, dwells on the deficits of the person being confronted. The helper in the next example is talking to woman living on welfare who has been accused of child neglect.

Counselor: You nagged at your husband and kept a sloppy house until he left. And now it's the kid's turn. You seem to think only of yourself. Life is a rat race and you're its principal victim.

Yelling at clients and putting them down are not creative interventions. Sometimes, when the relationship between client and helper is strong and there is a history of respect, strong words might do some good. But often they are dead ends. Ineffective helpers do not know how to help clients mobilize their resources, and so in their frustration they resort to punishment.

Realistically, most challenges have something negative about them. Even when you confront clients' strengths, you are doing so because clients are not using their strengths effectively. However, the unintended punitive effects of challenge are mitigated greatly by emphasizing strengths and potential.

Respect clients' values. Challenge clients to clarify their values and to make reasonable choices based on them. Be wary of using challenging, even indirectly, to force clients to accept your values.

Client (a 21-year-old woman who is a junior in college): I have done practically no experimentation with sex. I'm not sure whether it's because I think it's wrong or whether I'm just plain scared.

Counselor A: A certain amount of exploration is certainly normal. Perhaps some basic information on contraception would help allay your fears a bit.

Counselor B: Perhaps you're saying that it's time to find out which it is.

Counselor A edges toward making some choices for the client, while Counselor B challenges her gently to find out what she really wants. Effective helpers have a clear sense of their own values, without any need to force them on others. "What values am I implicitly pushing here?" is a question that counselors can profitably ask themselves throughout the helping process.

Helpers can assist clients to explore the consequences of the values they hold, but this is not the same as attacking the client's values. In the following example, Bill is a man who spends a great deal of time at work He has had a number of vague physical complaints, but his doctor has found nothing wrong with him physically.

Doctor: Bill, it seems obvious that you invest too much of yourself in work. Work doesn't really enhance your life any more; it imprisons you. You don't own your work; it owns you.

Bill: It's my life, and it's what I like to do. Do I have to be like everyone else?

Work is a legitimate value; and if the physician attacks it directly, he can expect the client to react defensively. A more effective tactic is to challenge

Bill to probe his own values in the area of work, see how he translates them into behavior, and work out the relationship of his work values to the other values in his life. Value conflicts rather than values themselves are the proper object of challenge

Deal with the client's defensiveness. Do not be surprised when clients react strongly to being challenged. Help them share and work through their emotions. If they seem not to react externally to what you have said, elicit their reactions.

Helper: I'm not sure how all this sounds to you.
Client: I thought you were on my side. Now you sound like all the others. And I'm paying you to talk like this to me!

Try to get into a dialogue with the disappointed or angered client. Remember, though, that an argument is not a dialogue. It may be that the client needs time to think about what you have said. Don't run from the interaction, but, on the other hand, don't insist on prolonging a conversation that is going nowhere.

In the long run, use your common sense. These are guidelines, not absolute prescriptions. As suggested in Chapter 1, take a no-formula approach. The more flexible and versatile you are, the more likely you are to be of benefit to your clients.

SOME CARICATURES OF CHALLENGING

Gordon (1970), in teaching parents ways of being effective in their relationships with their children, speaks of ineffective parental behaviors. These behaviors are caricatures of challenging as described in these pages. They are also ways in which helpers become ineffectually "parental" with their clients. The following is a checklist of these behaviors. Some of the categories overlap.

- *Commanding, ordering, directing:* "Go back to your wife and tell her what we've talked about."
- *Warning, admonishing, threatening:* "If you keep on being dependent, you're going to end up a very lonely woman. I've seen it happen before."
- *Exhorting, moralizing, preaching:* "Try to be more sensitive to her needs. Sensitivity is very important in intimate relationships."
- *Advising, giving suggestions, offering solutions:* "If I were you, I'd quit teaching as soon as possible and take a job in the business world."
- *Lecturing, giving logical arguments:* "She's not going to give in, and neither are you. The conclusion seems to be, end the relationship."

- *Judging, criticizing, disagreeing, blaming:* "If you can admit that getting fired was your own fault, then you'll be in a position to start thinking of new jobs."
- *Approving, praising, agreeing with:* "Telling your mother-in-law off was the best thing you could have done. It was your way of regaining your manhood."
- *Name-calling, ridiculing, shaming:* "I can't believe that you'd just drop him without letting him know why. What an awful way to treat someone."
- *Reassuring, consoling, sympathizing:* "Don't let this get you down. He probably didn't know he was hurting you this much."
- *Humoring, distracting:* "I bet you can see the humor in all this mess. You're the kind that doesn't let her sense of humor die."

I am sure you can add to the list.

Even though clients should not be badgered, and even though tact in challenging clients is often critical, this does not mean that challenge or invitations to self-challenge cannot be forceful. They can be as forceful as the relationship can tolerate. Some suggest that, once the relationship is established, a certain "impertinence" on the part of the helper is not only allowed but called for (Beier & Young, 1984; Farrelly & Brandsma, 1974). Effective helpers ask impertinent questions, share impertinent observations, and make impertinent demands. They see helping as a caring, but also a robust, activity.

LINKING CHALLENGE TO ACTION

In my experience a few well-placed challenges are all that some clients need. It is as if they were looking for someone to challenge them. Once challenged, they do whatever they need to manage their problems. Some of them are on the brink of challenging themselves and need only a nudge. Others, once they develop a few new perspectives, are off to the races. Still others have the resources to manage their lives better, but not the will. They know what they need to do but are not doing it. A few nudges in the right direction help them overcome their inertia. I have had many one-session encounters that included a bit of listening, some empathy, and some new perspective that sent the client off on some useful course of action. It was not my genius; rather, the client was ready.

In the following example, a counselor has been talking to a "high user" of mental health services. She has suggested that there are other ways for the client to satisfy his social needs.

Client: You mean what I'm looking for here is just attention.
Helper: Not at all. What you're looking for is what we all look for—human contact, consideration, someone to talk to. . . . My God, some kind of social life! And I think you should reach out and get what you need.

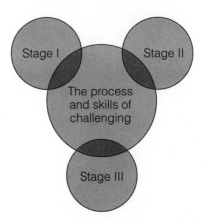

FIGURE 9-1   Challenge in the Helping Model

This proved to be a turning point. The counselor helped this client identify other social settings where his human needs might be better met. With a little help, the client did find some settings. This is not to suggest that "high users" are deadbeats (Goldman & Taube, 1988; Taube and others, 1988). Studies have shown that one-third of high users of mental health services were highly disabled clients with multiple medical disorders. But this particular client was doing himself in by trying to get something from the mental health clinic that, ultimately, it was not designed to provide.

For most clients, challenge is just one dimension of the whole helping process. Minor or major challenges are woven into all the stages and steps as needed. Action is still the key word, whether in terms of changing attitudes that change behaviors, getting new perspectives that are translated into action, or being nudged directly to act.

A FINAL NOTE

As indicated in the first two chapters, social influence and challenging are not limited to Step I-B. Figure 9-1 indicates graphically that challenging or invitations to self-challenge can be part of any stage and any step. Effective challenge blends in with the rest of the model instead of standing out, as Block (1981) notes, like a courtroom drama in which the helper is judge or jury or prosecutor or even apologetic defendant. Effective challenge, in Block's terms, is not "judgmental, global, stereotyped, lengthy, or complicated," but rather "descriptive, focused, brief, and simple" (p. 172). The checklist on the following pages summarizes the principles and skills of challenging as they have been presented in the last two chapters.

EVALUATION QUESTIONS FOR STEP I-B

How well am I doing the following as I try to help this client?

A. General

- Becoming comfortable with the social-influence dimension of the helping role
- Incorporating challenge into my counseling style without becoming a confrontation specialist
- Using challenge wherever it is needed in the helping process
- Developing enough assertiveness to overcome the "MUM effect"

B. The Goals of Challenging

- Challenging clients to participate fully in the helping process
- Helping clients become aware of their blind spots in thinking and acting and helping them develop new perspectives
- Challenging clients to own their problems and unused potential
- Helping clients state problems in solvable terms
- Challenging clients' games, distortions, and excuses
- Inviting clients to explore the short- and long-term consequences of their behavior
- Helping clients move beyond discussion and inertia to action

C. The Skills of Challenging

How effectively have I developed the communication skills that serve the process of challenging?

1. **Summarizing.** Summarizing, or inviting clients to summarize (to be discussed in Chapter 10) challenges them to see central issues more clearly and to move toward action.
2. **Information sharing.** Giving clients needed information or helping them search for it helps them see problem situations in a new light and provides a basis for action.
3. **Advanced empathy.** This skill involves sharing hunches with clients about their experiences, behaviors, and feelings. These hunches can help clients move beyond blind spots and develop needed new perspectives. Some of the forms your hunches can take include

- helping clients express clearly what they are implying.
- identifying themes in clients' stories.
- connecting islands of experiences, behaviors, and feelings.

4. **Helper self-sharing.** This skill enables you to share your own experience with clients as a way of modeling nondefensive self-disclosure, helping them move beyond blind spots and see possibilities for problem-managing action.

5. **Immediacy.** This skill enables you to discuss your relationship with your clients in three ways with a view to improving the working alliance:
   - *self-statements*—present-tense, self-involving responses to clients.
   - *relationship immediacy*—your ability to discuss your overall relationship with a client, with a view to managing whatever problems exist and maintaining strengths.
   - *here-and-now immediacy*—your ability to discuss with a client whatever is standing in the way of working together right now.

   Immediacy can involve a whole range of communication skills, including the basic communication skills of attending, listening, and empathy, plus the other challenging skills.

6. **Asocial and paradoxical interventions.** These specialized skills enable you, on occasion, to use "outlandish" responses and paradox to help clients take problem-managing action. Included here are asocial responses, paradoxical intention, symptom prescription, and paradoxical reframing. In using this set of skills, take care to preserve basic client-helper values and to check ethical implications.

D. The Principles of Effective Challenging

Finally, there are certain principles to be followed in all modes of challenging. When you do challenge, how effectively do you incorporate the following principles into your style?

- Keeping the goals of challenging in mind.
- Inviting clients to challenge themselves.
- Earning the right to challenge by
  - developing an effective working alliance with the client.
  - working at seeing his or her point of view.
  - being open to challenge yourself.
  - managing problems and developing opportunities in your own life.
- Being tactful and tentative in challenging without being insipid or apologetic.
- Being specific, developing challenges that hit the mark.
- Challenging clients' strengths rather than their weaknesses.
- Not asking clients to do too much too quickly.
- Inviting clients to clarify and act on their own values, not yours.

Chapter Ten

Step I-C: Leverage— Helping Clients Get the Most out of Helping

As indicated in Figure 10-1, Step I-C is called, generically, leverage, but includes four processes: screening, the search for leverage, focused exploration, and effective decision making. There are goals or outcomes associated with each of these elements.

THE GOALS OF STEP I-C

Although the following goals can be distinguished conceptually, in practice they often overlap. Furthermore, Step I-C itself overlaps and intermingles with all the stages and steps of the helping model. That is, there is no point where counselors are not trying to help clients become effective decision makers and get the most out of their investment.

1. Screening. A judgment needs to be made whether the problems or opportunities revealed in the telling of the story merit serious consideration. The first goal, then, is to decide whether or not to continue. If the story being told has little substance, then a decision may be made to terminate the relationship or probe for a more substantive story.

2. Leverage. Since all the concerns in a complex problem/opportunity situation cannot be dealt with at once, a second goal is to help clients establish some priorities. This is especially true when a client comes with a number of concerns. Even problems that are told as single-issue stories—"I'd like to get rid of these headaches"—often become, when examined, multiple-issue problem situations. For instance, the headaches are a symptom of overwork, poor interpersonal relationships, and financial concerns. Effective counselors help clients work on problems and opportunities that will make a difference. This is the search for leverage. The helper asks, "What can I do to help this client get the most out of his or her investment?"

3. Focus: Exploration that makes a difference. Once an issue is chosen for attention, it needs to be explored and clarified in terms of relevant experiences, behaviors, and emotions. The third goal of this step is to help clients explore issues in a focused way, to look at things that count, to consider actions that can make a difference.

4. Effective decision making. To do all this, clients will have to make good decisions. To help clients achieve this goal, helpers need to have a working knowledge of the decision-making process in both its rational and "arational" dimensions.

SCREENING

Counseling and psychotherapy are expensive in terms of both financial and psychological costs. They should not be undertaken lightly. Relatively little is said in the literature about screening—that is, about making a

I. Present scenario   II. Preferred scenario   III. Strategy: Getting there

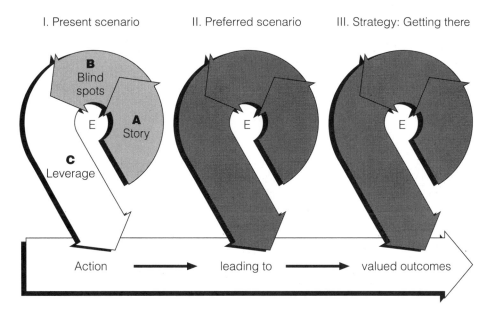

FIGURE 10-1 Step I-C: Leverage

decision whether any given problem situation or opportunity deserves attention. The reasons are obvious. Helpers are urged to take their clients and their clients' concerns seriously. They are also urged to adopt an optimistic attitude, an attitude of hope, about their clients. Finally, they are schooled to take their profession seriously and are convinced that their services can make a difference in the lives of clients. For these and other reasons, the first impulse of the average counselor is to try to help clients no matter what the problem situation might be.

There is something very laudable about this. It is rewarding to see helpers prize people and express interest in their concerns. It is rewarding to see helpers put aside the almost instinctive tendency to evaluate and judge others and to offer their services to clients just because they are human beings. However, like other professions, helping can suffer from the "law of the instrument." A child, given a hammer, soon discovers that almost everything needs hammering. Helpers, once equipped with the models, methods, and skills of the helping process, can see all human problems as needing their attention. In fact, in many cases counseling may be a useful intervention and yet be a luxury whose expense cannot be justified. The problem-severity formula discussed in Chapter 7 is a useful tool for screening.

Under the rubric "differential therapeutics," Frances, Clarkin, and Perry (1984) discuss ways of fitting different kinds of treatment to different kinds of patients. They also discuss the conditions under which no treatment is the best option. In this category they include clients who have a history of treatment failure or who seem to get worse from treatment, criminals trying to avoid or diminish punishment by claiming to be suffering from psychiatric conditions ("We may do a disservice to society, the legal system, the offenders, and ourselves if we are too willing to treat problems for which no effective treatment is available" [p. 227]), patients with malingering or fictitious illness, chronic nonresponders to treatment, clients likely to improve on their own, healthy clients with minor chronic problems, and reluctant and resistant clients who refuse treatment. While a decision needs to be taken in each case, and while some might dispute some of the categories proposed, the possibility of no treatment deserves serious attention.

The no-treatment option, according to Frances, Clarkin, and Perry, can do a number of beneficial things: interrupt helping sessions that are going nowhere or that are actually destructive; keep both client and helper from wasting time, effort, and money; delay help until the client is ready; consolidate gains from previous treatments; provide the client with an opportunity to discover that he or she can do without treatment; keep helpers and clients from playing games with themselves and one another; and provide motivation for the client to find help in his or her own daily life. However, a no-treatment decision on the part of helping professionals is countercultural and therefore difficult to make.

It goes without saying that screening, or helping clients screen their stories, can be done in a heavy-handed way. Statements such as the following are not useful:

• "Your concerns are actually not that serious."
• "You should be able to work that through without help."
• "I don't have time for problems as simple as that."

Whether such sentiments are expressed or implied, they obviously indicate a lack of respect and constitute a caricature of the screening process. Helpers are not alone in grappling with this problem. Doctors, too, face clients day in and day out with problems that run from the life-threatening to the inconsequential. Statistics suggest that more than half of the people who come to doctors have nothing physically wrong with them. Doctors consequently have to find ways to screen patients' complaints. I am sure that the best find ways to do so that preserve the dignity of their patients.

Poorly executed, screening can lead to premature judgments about the seriousness of a client's problems. As mentioned in an earlier chapter, some clients discuss relatively inconsequential problems as a way of putting a toe in the water or testing the humanity of the helper. For instance, a student talks about study habits when his real concern is about his sexual identity; a woman talks about boredom when her real concern is about aging. At one end of the continuum is a willingness on the part of helpers to work with clients no matter how petty their concerns. At the other end is the demand that clients come with serious problems and that they prove that they are in need of help and will benefit from it. Virtue lies somewhere in the middle.

A second screening issue relates to the commitment of clients to do something about their problem situations. This means that there should be some reasonable hope that a client will be willing to do more than merely talk about his or her concerns, that he or she will become productively involved in the helping process. Again, at one end of the continuum is a willingness on the part of helpers to work with clients who give little or no evidence of a commitment to working for change. At the other end of the continuum is a tendency to ignore the understandable hesitancies of clients to commit themselves to change and to throw down the gauntlet: "Come back when you want to do something about it." Such an approach is meaningless in settings in which reluctant clients are the norm.

Experienced helpers do not opt for the end points of either of these continuums. Because they are empathic, they stay close to the experience of clients and develop hypotheses about both the substance of a client's problems and the client's commitment and then test these hypotheses in a humane way. If clients' problems seem inconsequential, they probe for more substantive issues. If clients seem reluctant, resistant, and unwilling to work, they challenge clients' attitudes and help them work through their resistance. In both cases they realize that there may come a time, and it may come fairly quickly, to judge that further effort is uncalled for because of lack of results. It is better, however, to help clients make such a decision themselves or challenge them to do so. In the end, the helper might have to call a halt, but his or her way of doing so should reflect basic counseling values.

THE SEARCH FOR LEVERAGE

Clients often need help to get a handle on complex problem situations. A 41-year-old depressed man with a failing marriage, a boring job, deteriorating interpersonal relationships, health concerns, and a drinking problem cannot work on everything at once. Priorities need to be set. Put bluntly, the question is: Where is the biggest payoff? Where should the resources of both client and helper be invested? If the problem situation has many dimensions, the helper and client are faced with the problem of where to start.

> Andrea, a woman in her mid-thirties, is referred to a neighborhood mental health clinic by a social worker. During her first visit she pours out a story of woe both historical and current—brutal parents, teenage drug abuse, a poor marriage, unemployment, poverty, and the like. Andrea is so taken up with getting it all out that the helper can do little more than sit and listen.

Where is Andrea to start? How can the time, effort, and money invested in helping provide a reasonable return to her? In the broadest sense, what are the economics of helping?

The following principles of leverage—a reasonable return on the investment of the client's and helper's resources—serve as guidelines for choosing issues to be worked on. These principles overlap; more than one might apply at the same time.

- If there is a crisis, first help the client manage the crisis.
- Begin with issues the client sees as important.
- Begin with the problem that seems to be causing pain for the client.
- Focus on an issue, regardless of importance, that the client is willing to work on.
- Begin with some manageable sub-problem of a larger problem situation.
- Begin with a problem that can be managed relatively easily, one that shows promise of being successfully handled by the client.
- Begin with a problem that, if handled, will lead to some kind of general improvement in the client's condition.
- When possible, move from less severe to more severe problems.
- Focus on a problem for which the benefits will outweigh the costs.

Counselors use these principles to help clients discover points of leverage in the management of problem situations and in the development of opportunities. Underlying all these principles is an attempt to make clients' initial experiencing of the helping process rewarding so that they will have the incentives they need to continue to work. Examples of the use and abuse of these principles follow.

If there is a crisis, first help the client manage the crisis. While crisis intervention is usually seen as a special form of counseling (Baldwin, 1980; Janosik, 1984), it can also be seen as a rapid application of the three stages of the helping process to the most distressing aspects of a crisis situation.

> *Principle violated:* A resident-hall assistant (RA), a graduate student, meets an obviously agitated undergraduate student, Zachary, in the hall. Zachary says that he has to talk to him. They go to the RA's office to talk. As Zachary sits down, he is literally shaking. He finds it extremely difficult to talk. The problem is a case of attempted homosexual rape. Once Zachary blurts it out, the RA begins asking questions such as "Has this ever happened before?" "Do you think you did anything to make him think you were interested?" "How do you feel about your own sexual orientation?" "Do you think you should press charges?" and the like.
>
> *Principle used:* Zachary talks with the RA for a few minutes and then explodes: "Why are you asking me all these silly questions?" He

stalks out and goes to a friend's house. Seeing his agitation, his friend says, "Good grief, Zach, you look terrible. Come in. What's going on?" He listens to Zachary's account of what has just happened, interrupting very little, merely putting in a word here and there to let his friend know he is with him. He sits with Zachary when he falls silent or cries a bit, and then slowly and reassuringly "talks Zach down," engaging in an easy dialogue that gives his friend an opportunity gradually to find his composure again.

The friend's instincts are much better than those of the RA. He does what he can to defuse the immediate crisis.

Begin with issues the client sees as important. The frame of reference of the client is a point of leverage. Given the client's story, you may think that he or she has not chosen the most important issues for initial consideration. However, helping clients work on issues that are important to them sends an important message: "Your interests are important to me."

> *Principle violated:* A woman comes to a counselor complaining about her relationship to her boss. She believes that he is sexist, and there are hints of sexual overtures. After listening to her story, the counselor believes that she probably has some leftover developmental issues with her father that affect her attitude toward older men. He pursues this line of thinking with her. The client is confused and feels put down. When she does not return for a second interview, the counselor says to himself that she is not motivated to do something about her problem.
>
> *Principle used:* A dying patient talks to a pastoral counselor about his concerns for his wife. As the counselor listens to the patient, she picks up indications that the patient has strong feelings and unresolved issues about his own dying that he is not admitting to. However, for the present she does not address these issues. She helps him deal with his concerns about his wife's pain. She will look for an opportunity to help him come to grips with his concerns about himself later on.

It may well be that a client's immediate frame of reference needs broadening. But helping at its best starts with the frame of reference of the client.

Begin with the problem that seems to be causing pain. Clients usually come for help because they are hurting. Their hurt, then, becomes an incentive, a source of leverage. Their pain also makes them vulnerable. This means they are open to influence from helpers. If it is evident that they are open to influence because of their pain, seize the opportunity, but move cautiously. Their pain may also make them demanding. They can't understand why you cannot help them get rid of it immediately. This kind of impatience may put you off, but it, too, needs to be understood. Such clients are like patients in the emergency room, each one seeing himself or herself as needing immediate attention. Their demands for immediate relief may well signal a self-centeredness that is part of their character and therefore part of the broader problem situation. It may be that their pain is, in your eyes, self-inflicted, and ultimately you may have to challenge them on this. But pain, whether self-inflicted or not, is still pain. Part of your respect for clients is your respect for them as vulnerable.

> *Principle violated:* Rob, a man in his mid-twenties, comes to a counselor in great distress because his wife has just left him. The counselor sees quickly that Rob is an impulsive, self-centered person with whom it would be difficult to live. The counselor immediately challenges him to take a look at his interpersonal style and the ways in which he alienates others. Rob seems to listen, but he does not return.
>
> *Principle used:* Rob goes to a second counselor who also sees a number of clues indicating self-centeredness and a lack of maturity and discipline. However, she listens carefully to his story, even though it is one-sided. Instead of adding to his pain by making him come to grips with his selfishness, she focuses on the future, Rob's preferred scenario. Of course, his wife's return is the principal element in this scenario. But she helps him describe in some detail what life would be like once they got back together. His hurting provides the incentive for working with the counselor on the future scenario. Once the preferred scenario is outlined, she helps him explore what he needs to do, ways in which he might need to change, to get the preferred scenario on line. He is now in a better position to see how he has contributed to his wife's leaving him.

The helper's focusing on a better future responds to Rob's need. This future, then, becomes the stepping-stone to challenge. What is Rob willing to do to create the future he says he wants?

Focus on an issue, regardless of importance, that the client is willing to work on. The client's willingness to work on an issue can be a point of leverage. It is important to elicit the client's cooperation early in the helping process. Making premature demands on clients to explore and clarify highly sensitive issues may only alienate them.

> *Principle violated:* In the initial presentation of his concerns, a college student talks about a variety of issues: doing poorly in his courses, inconsistent relationships with his friends, fights with his parents, misgivings about his sexuality. The counselor believes that sexual conflicts may be central and begins by probing the young man's sexual concerns. The client shows a fair amount of reluctance to talk about sex so quickly, but the counselor persists.

Principle used: A woman describes the disastrous interactions that characterize her relationship with her husband. She talks about his faults readily but is much more reluctant to talk about the ways in which her behavior contributes to their difficulties. The counselor notices this reluctance immediately and, without taking sides, helps her focus on her husband's behavior, and, perhaps more importantly, her reactions to his behavior. He knows that this frame of reference needs to be transcended, but he does not immediately challenge the client to do so.

Although pushing clients to work on more painful and more important issues too quickly can backfire, clients should not be allowed to squander time and energy on trivial issues. This is the dilemma helpers sometimes face.

Begin with some manageable sub-problem of a larger problem situation. Large, complicated problem situations remain vague and unmanageable. Dividing a problem into manageable bits can provide a point of leverage. Most larger problems can be broken down into smaller, more manageable sub-problems.

Principle violated: Carl and Carla arrive for marriage counseling. The history of their marriage is a stormy one. Both of them have been saving up their grievances and now want to pour them out to the counselor and, if possible, force her into the role of judge. They both have been married before, they both work, they each have good friends they do not share with the other. There are problems with sex, child care, communication, and finances. The counselor takes a somewhat passive, understanding role, so that for all practical purposes Carl and Carla are in charge of the sessions. They argue, jump from issue to issue, and generally involve themselves in the same kind of chaos they generate at home. The counselor continues to use basic empathy as her principal approach.

Principle used: Lisa, a single woman in her mid-thirties, has not held a job for more than a year or two. Though intelligent and talented, she has been laid off several times. Two of the companies, when laying her off, talked about "general cutbacks," but a third said that she did not fit in with the other personnel. Lisa is seen by most people as "difficult." Her abrasive ways tend to alienate people who come in close contact with her. The counselor, too, finds her an abrasive person who has little insight into how demanding she is. Lisa is presently between jobs and is seeking career counseling. The counselor does not immediately deal with her abrasiveness. Rather, he suggests that one practical step is to help her see how she comes across in job interviews. He videotapes a couple of role-playing sessions and helps her critique what she sees.

In the second case the counselor starts with a felt need of the client—getting a job—and focuses on one dimension of the job-seeking process, the interview, in which she expresses some dimensions of her style. Having Lisa critique her own performance in an interview is more manageable than dealing with the entire area of interpersonal style.

Begin with a problem that can be managed relatively easily. Starting with a simple problem can be a point of leverage. If clients are helped to manage some relatively easy part of a problem situation, the reinforcement they experience may well empower them to attack more difficult areas.

> *Principle violated:* Elmer has been through bankruptcy twice because of mismanagement of two small businesses he has started. Now, on the verge of his third bankruptcy, he has been told by the court that he must see a counselor. The counselor has Elmer explore his entire history of financial mismanagement. He wants him to spot what goes wrong so that he can avoid the same mistakes in the future. They soon get lost in long discussions about accounting procedures and about Elmer's managerial techniques and style.
>
> *Principle used:* Since they seem to be getting nowhere, the counselor refers Elmer to a self-help group made up of individuals with similar financial problems. In this group Elmer is first helped to explore how he manages his personal rather than his business finances. He learns what he is doing well and what he is doing poorly and makes some changes. Then he is helped to transfer his learnings to business situations.

In some cases an initial experience of success with a simple problem can release a great deal of unused resources.

Begin with a problem that, if handled, will lead to some kind of general improvement. Some problems, when addressed, yield results beyond what might be expected. This is the "spread effect."

> *Principle violated:* Jeff, a middle-aged carpenter, comes to a community mental health center with a variety of complaints, including insomnia, excessive drinking, and temptations toward exhibitionism. He also has an intense fear of dogs, something that occasionally affects his work. The counselor sees this problem as one that can be managed through the application of behavior modification methodologies. He and Jeff spend a fair amount of time in the desensitization of the phobia. However, most of the client's other complaints still remain. His phobia is not related closely enough to his other concerns.
>
> *Principle used:* Cassie, a high school senior, is having a number of developmental problems—poor relationships with her parents, failure in school, conflicted peer relationships, low self-esteem,

and bouts of both anxiety and depression. The counselor notes that a lack of self-discipline is a thread running through many of Cassie's problems. Although she is not an athlete, she is interested in physical fitness. The counselor helps her get involved in a simple physical fitness program as a way of putting some discipline into her life. She enjoys seeing herself making steady, measurable progress. Other areas of her life begin to improve. Then, with the counselor's help, she begins to put some discipline into her school work and interpersonal relationships in more direct ways.

Effective counselors help clients find these "leverage" themes and capitalize on the resources they already have.

When possible, move from less severe to more severe problems. This is especially the case when the more serious problems are chronic and do not currently constitute a crisis. Moving gradually can be a point of leverage.

> *Principle violated:* Ted has been a resident of a state mental hospital since being diagnosed as schizophrenic several years ago. He has been leading a rather colorless life on an open ward. He practically never interacts with his fellow patients unless he absolutely has to. Recently he has been having some problems with his work assignments. He asks to see the therapist because he thinks she can do something about his work situation. The therapist, who is new to the hospital, decides to use this opportunity to deal with Ted's refusal to socialize. Ted returns for a second session but then refuses to see the helper anymore.

> *Principle used:* Mildred, a patient discharged from a state mental hospital to a halfway house, has spent a good deal of time in group sessions learning simple social skills, including grooming, interacting with other patients, doing chores around the house itself, and using the city bus system. Now that she has achieved a certain degree of success in these tasks, the therapist thinks of other possibilities, for instance, some kind of work with a company that has a track record of working with people with disabilities.

The helper in the first case misuses the principle of leverage. He tries to force an issue rather than look for a point of leverage in the client. As we have seen, helping clients place demands on themselves is a very important strategy, but helpers need to understand clients enough to know when to use it.

Focus on a problem for which the benefits will outweigh the costs. This is not an excuse for not tackling difficult problems. If you demand a great deal of work from both yourself and the client, then basic laws of behavior suggest that there be some kind of reasonable payoff for both of you.

Principle used: Angie, a middle-aged homemaker, feels locked into the house. As she tells her story, it soon becomes clear that she is the victim of her own lack of assertiveness. She grew up as a "nice," compliant girl; womanhood and marriage have not changed the picture very much. Angie spends some time in a consciousness-raising, assertiveness-training group for women. The benefits far outweigh the costs. She begins to develop a rewarding life outside the home that includes a part-time job. This complements her life as a homemaker.

We live in an age of cost cutting and a search for efficiency. Mental-health programs have not been spared (see the Special Issue of *Psychotherapy*, 25 [1988], No. 3). Greater efficiency can be brought to helping without dehumanizing it. In fact, we owe our clients and society efficient approaches to helping.

The principles of leverage, used judiciously and in combination, can help counselors shape the helping process to suit the needs and resources of individual clients. However, helpers must avoid using these very same principles to water down or retard the helping process. Ineffective helpers

- begin with the framework of the client, but never get beyond it.
- fail to challenge clients to consider significant issues they are avoiding.
- allow the client's pain and discomfort to mask the roots of his or her problems.
- fail to build on clients' successes.
- continue to deal with small, manageable problems and fail to help clients face more demanding problems in living.
- fail to help clients generalize learning in one area of life (for instance, self-discipline in a fitness program) to other, more difficult areas of living (for instance, self-control in close interpersonal relationships).

In a word, ineffective helpers are afraid of making reasonable demands of clients or of influencing clients to make reasonable demands of themselves.

HELPING CLIENTS FOCUS ON WHAT COUNTS

Lazarus (Rogers, Shostrom, & Lazarus, 1977), in a film on his multimodal approach to therapy (Lazarus, 1976, 1981), uses a focusing technique I find useful. He asks the client to use just one word to describe her problem. She searches around a bit and then offers a word. Then he asks the client to put the word in a simple sentence that would describe her problem. It is a simple way to begin, but it provides a lesson in helping clients focus on what is important. As has already been seen in the discussions of the communication skills of attending, listening, empathy, probing, and challenging, helping clients choose the right issues to work on needs to be complemented by the clarification of these issues in terms of specific and relevant experiences, behaviors, and feelings.

In the following example, a young man talks to a counselor because he is shy. The counselor knows that helping the client deal with his shyness has leverage for a number of reasons: it is important to the client, it is causing him pain, the client is willing to talk about it, it is a sub-problem that can act as a gateway to other, more serious considerations, such as sense of identity and self-esteem, and managing his shyness will help the client manage other concerns he has about his interpersonal style.

Client: My problem is that I'm shy. I'm just too shy for my own good.
Helper: And you'd like to do something about it.
Client: Yeah . . . but I don't know what.
Helper: Shyness is different with different people. Could you tell me a little bit more about yours?
Client: Well, some of it has to do with girls. I'm very shy around girls. That's one of the worst.
Helper: So. Though your shyness is not limited to girls, that causes you a lot of difficulty. Any examples of when this hits you really hard?
Client: Yeah, like when I'm at a dance. I tend to stand around and talk with the guys. I want to be noticed by girls, and I don't want to be noticed. I get butterflies if I think some girl is going to walk up and talk with me.
Helper: Because of the butterflies, you do things that send signals that you're not available. And yet you want to be available.
Client: Yeah, I'm my own worst enemy. You know, I think that I'm not really a bad guy. . . . People can . . . well . . . sort of like me when they're with me.
Helper: But girls don't get that chance. . . . Hmmm. What lousy things will happen if you make yourself a little more available to girls? I mean, besides your feeling butterflies, what goes on in your head when you see a girl headed toward you?
Client: Oh, that she won't see me as important enough. You know, one of the big guys. . . . And I'm not that good-looking. Or that she'll think I'm a drip, you know, not with it.
Helper: You have quite a conversation with yourself before she even gets there!

The helper uses attending, listening, empathy, and probes—all directed to helping the client get a clearer picture of the problem situation so that he can eventually say, though not in so many words, "Now that I understand what I'm experiencing, doing, and feeling, I'm beginning to get some idea of what I have to change or what I'd like to change."

Summarizing as a Way of Providing Focus

Summarizing can be used by counselors to help clients explore problem situations in a more focused and concrete way. Brammer (1973) lists a number of goals that can be achieved by judicious use of summarizing: "warming up" the client, focusing scattered thoughts and feelings, bringing the discussion of a particular theme to a close, and prompting the client to explore a theme more thoroughly. Notice how these contribute to both helping clients clarify the problem situation from their own perspective and helping them develop new perspectives. Often, when scattered elements are brought together, the client sees the "bigger picture" more clearly. Thus, summarizing can lead to new perspectives or alternate frames of reference. In the following example, the client is a 52-year-old man who has revealed and explored a number of problems in living and is concerned about being depressed.

Helper: Let's take a look at what we've seen so far. You're down—not just a normal slump; this time it's hanging on. You worry about your health, but you check out all right physically, so this seems to be more a symptom than a cause of your depression. There are some unresolved issues in your life. One that you seem to be stressing is the fact that your recent change in jobs has meant that you don't see much of your old friends anymore. Since you're single, you don't find this easy. Another issue—one you find painful and embarrassing—is your struggle to stay young. You don't like facing the fact that you're getting older. A third issue is the way you—to use your own word—"overinvest" yourself in work, so much so that when you finish a long-term project, suddenly your life is empty. That is, a number of factors in your lifestyle seem to contribute to your depression.

Client: (Pauses) It's painful to hear it all that baldly, but that about sums it up. I've suspected I've got some screwed-up values, but I haven't wanted to stop long enough to take a look at it. Maybe the time has come. I'm hurting enough.

Helper: One way of doing this is by taking a look at what all this would look like if it looked better.

Client: That sounds interesting—and hopeful. How would we do that?

This client, in the self-exploratory phase, produces data that point to certain painful conclusions: he is immature in some areas of life (for example, in his overvaluing youth), he is "out of community" (his interpersonal life is at a low ebb), and he is trying ineffective solutions to his problems (dealing with loneliness by fleeing into work). The counselor's summary hits home—somewhat painfully—and the client draws his own conclusion. Perhaps this summary would have been more effective if the helper had also summarized some of the client's strengths. This would have provided a more positive context. However, the helper instinctively realizes that the client needs hope and offers a way of providing it. Instead of going more deeply into the client's problem areas (Stage I), he suggests that they move into Stage II.

There are certain times when summaries prove particularly useful: at the beginning of a new session, when the session seems to be going nowhere, and when the client gets stuck.

At the beginning of a new session. When summaries are used at the beginning of a new session, especially when clients seem uncertain about how to begin, they prevent clients from merely repeating what has already been said before. They put clients under pressure to move on. In the following example, the client is a 65-year-old widower who has just retired.

Counselor: Last week you talked about your loneliness and your fears of dying. You mentioned how these feelings are particularly intense in the evening and on weekends. You also talked quite a bit about how much you depended on your wife and how much you defined yourself through your job. At the end of the session you were discussing your feelings about being too old to do anything about all of this. I'm wondering if this is how you see our last session and whether you want to add anything to it.

The counselor's summary serves several purposes. It shows the client that she listened carefully to what he had to say and that she reflected on it after the session. It gives the client a jumping-off point for the new session. It gives him an opportunity to add to or modify what was said. It prevents him from merely repeating what he has already said. It places the responsibility for moving on with the client. The client might well need help to move on, but the summary gives him the opportunity to exercise initiative.

Sessions that are going nowhere. A summary can be used to give focus to a session that seems to be going nowhere. In the following example, a young white ghetto resident who has had several run-ins with the police is talking to a black counselor associated with the probation office. The client is jumping from one topic to another, and the counselor is having a hard time pulling it all together.

Counselor: I'm not sure where we're headed here. Here's what I think I do understand. You're angry because your probation officer made you come see me. You feel it's a waste of time talking to me because I'm black. And you feel that we can't do much for you here. Talking about your problems doesn't make any sense when the whole system's got you boxed in.
Client: You got it. Where do we go from here?

The counselor presents the central issues as he thinks the client sees them. Doing so doesn't produce any magical change, but it does stop the rambling process and gives both of them a chance to ask, "Now what do we do?"

When a client gets stuck. Summaries can be used when clients seem to have exhausted everything they have to say about a particular issue and seem to be stuck. However, the helper does not always have to provide the summary. Often it is better to ask the client to pull together the major points. This helps the client own the process, pull together the salient points, and move on.

In the following example, a young woman has been talking about her difficult relationship with her father. She has revealed a great deal about the history of that relationship and now stops dead and seems frustrated and confused.

Counselor A: It's hard to pull all this together. You feel you don't really have much more to say about your relationship with your father.
Client: Yeah, that's about where it stands. (She remains silent.)

Counselor B: Why don't you try to pull together the major points of what you have been saying in a kind of summary.
Client: Well, I'll try. My father never had a good word for me when I was a kid, just criticism when I did something wrong. When I went to college, he seemed to resent it—perhaps because I was a woman and was getting ahead, getting more education than he had. He ridiculed the idea. Then his abuse of my mother and the divorce was the last straw. Since I saw him as pretty much in the wrong, I was very angry and hurt, so I cut off all communication with him. That was over three years ago. Now he's gotten in contact with me once more. He seems to want to reestablish a relationship, almost as if nothing happened. He's taking a "let bygones be bygones" approach, but that doesn't play well with me at all.
Counselor B: Is it that you simply don't want to even think about reestablishing a relationship, or are you just put off by his heavy-handed way of trying to reestablish contact?
Client: I'm not sure. . . . My mother's remarried, but she doesn't seem to hold a grudge. Maybe it's just his cocky way of doing things.

Counselor A's basic empathy does not help. Counselor B's request for a summary, however, opens up a new avenue. The client's summary pulls together the salient facts in her experience with her father. Later in the counseling session (this is an actual case), the counselor role-played the client's father and had the client say directly what she wanted to say. This "rehearsal" was part of an action program that culminated in the client's speaking directly to her father.

THE INS AND OUTS OF DECISION MAKING

There are many decision points in therapy. Clients must decide to come to a counseling interview, to talk about themselves, to return for a second session, to respond to the helper's empathy, probes, and challenges, to choose issues to work on, to set goals, to develop strategies, and to make plans. These helping-related decisions are complemented by a host of decisions in their everyday life as they choose to adopt certain patterns of behavior and abandon others. More importantly, deciding—or letting the world decide for you—is at the heart of living. A few words about client decision making, then, are in order.

Counselors can help clients not only in making individual decisions, but, as Heppner (1989) has suggested, in identifying and managing their decision-making styles. For example, clients who let others make significant decisions for them can be helped to see the cost of such a style and what they need to do to change it.

Decision making in the broad sense is the same as problem solving. Indeed, this book could be called a decision-making approach to helping. In this section, however, the focus is on decision making in the narrower sense of the internal (mental) action of choosing from among alternatives or options. It is a commitment to do or to refrain from doing something: "I have decided to ask the courts to remove artificial life support from my comatose wife"; "I have decided not to undergo chemotherapy." The commitment can be to an internal action ("I'm not going to let myself become preoccupied by him") or to an external one ("I'm going to confront my son about his drinking"). Decision making in the fullest sense includes the implementation of the decision: "I made a resolution to give up smoking, and I haven't smoked for three years"; "I decided that I was being too hard on myself, and I haven't given in to negative thoughts about myself for months."

Rational Decision Making

Traditionally, decision making has been presented as a rational, linear process. Gelatt (1989) talks about the three parts of decision making: information gathering, analysis, and choice. A word about each.

Information gathering. The first part is getting information that relates to the particular issue or concern. A patient who must decide whether to have a series of chemotherapy treatments needs some essential information. What are the treatments like? What will they accomplish? What are the side effects? What are the consequences of not having them? What would another doctor say? And so forth. There is a whole range of ways in which she might gather this information: reading, talking to doctors, and talking to patients.

Analysis. The next step is processing the information, or, in Gelatt's terms, "arranging and rearranging." This includes analyzing, thinking about, working with, discussing, meditating on, and immersing oneself in the information. Just as there are many different ways of gathering information, so there are many different ways of processing it. Effective information processing leads to a clarification and understanding of the range of possible choices and an understanding of the consequences of each choice. "I can decide not to return to the counselor for a third visit; I can look for another counselor; I can remain with this counselor and continue as I did in the first two sessions; I can continue with this counselor but change my mode of participation. Now, let's see, what are the advantages and disadvantages of each of these choices?" This assumes that decision makers have criteria, whether objective or subjective, for comparing alternatives.

Making a choice. Finally, the decision maker needs to make a choice, that is, commit himself or herself to some internal or external action that is based on his or her analysis ("After thinking about it, I have decided to sue for custody of the children"). As indicated above, the fullness of the choice includes an action: "I had my lawyer file the custody papers this morning." March (1982) talked about "decision rules": "Decision makers have rules by which to select a single alternative of action on the basis of its consequences for the preferences" (p. 29). In rational decision making, the choice point is often described in terms of a scale or balance: If the evidence points toward a particular option, that is the option to be chosen.

According to Gelatt, the "process part of arranging and rearranging, which takes place in the decision maker's mind, is . . . the crucial part for counselors" (p. 253). That is, counselors can help their clients process the information as effectively as possible. However, counselors can also help clients get the right information, make a choice based on the analysis, and actually move into action. As usual, there is no formula; help the client where he or she needs help.

Janis and Mann (1977) give the name "vigilance" to the full execution of this logical process: there is a search for relevant information; it is carefully analyzed; a choice based on the analysis is made; the decision is carried out into action. At first glance, then, decision making is a rational, straightforward process (Gelatt, 1962; Gelatt, Varenhorst, & Carey, 1972). But we all know that this is not the case.

The Shadow Side of Decision Making: Choices in Everyday Life

In actuality, decision making is a highly complicated process that is not easy to articulate. It has a "shadow side." As Heppner and Krauskopf (1987) learned in their research, "people are often quite unsystematic and irrational" in their decision making (p. 376). To help clients make decisions about the helping process itself and about the management of their problems and opportunities, you should understand something about the "shadow side" of decision making (see Gelatt, 1989; Heppner, 1989). In order to discover some of the ways that decision making as it is actually practiced is a "tricky business," let's return to Gelatt's three parts.

Information Gathering

Information gathering should lead to a clear definition of the matter to be decided. A client trying to decide whether to pursue a divorce needs information about that entire process. However, information gathering is practically never straightforward. Decision makers can, for whatever reason, be complacent and engage in an inadequate search; they can get too much, too little, inaccurate, or misleading information; information can be clouded with emotion. The client trying to decide whether to proceed with therapy may have already made up his or her mind and therefore not be open to information. Since full, unambiguous information is never available, all decisions are more or less well informed. In fact, there is no such thing as completely objective information. All information, especially in decision making, is received by the decision maker and takes on a subjective cast. In view of all this, Ackoff (1974) called human problem solving "mess management" (p. 21).

On the other hand, the model in this book, as indicated earlier, is a model counselors can use to help clients gather the kind of information they need. Probing and challenging help clients stay objective as they tell their stories and look for the kind of information that will help them manage their lives better. Granted, stories are never complete, and information will always be partial. Nevertheless, though counselors cannot help clients make information gathering perfect, they can help them make it adequate.

Processing the Information

Since it is impossible to separate the decision from the decision maker, the processing of information is as complex as the person making the decision. Factors affecting the "arranging and rearranging" of information include the clients' feelings and emotions, their working values, their assumptions about "the way things work," and their level of motivation. There is no such thing as full, objective processing of gathered information.

In everyday decision making, poorly gathered information is often subjected to further mistreatment in the analysis stage. For instance, because of their biases, clients focus on bits and pieces of the information they have gathered rather than the full range. Furthermore, few decision makers have the time or patience to spell out all possible choices related to the issue at hand, together with the pros and cons of each. Therefore, some say, most decisions are based, not on evidence, but on taste: "I like it."

Up to a point, counselors can help clients overcome inertia and biases and tackle the work of analysis. If a client says his values have changed, but he still automatically makes decisions based on his former values, then he can be challenged to get his new values into his decision making. One client of mine, trying to make a decision about a career change, kept moving toward options in the helping professions even though he had become quite interested in business. There was something in him that kept saying, "You have to choose a helping profession. Otherwise you will be a traitor." I helped him see his bias. He first became a consultant, then a manager, then a senior manager. He came to realize that one important form of social helping was running a healthy business. Counselors can also help clients get out of ruts and add a bit of creativity to decision making. As Gelatt (1989) has noted, "The process of arranging and rear-ranging, in the mind's eye, is where reflection, imagination, and creativity take place. These are the new decision-making skills of the future" (p. 255). Clients can be challenged to factor "what-ifs" into the analysis phase. More will be said about creativity in decision making in the next chapter.

Choice and Execution

A host of things can happen at the point of decision—the point of commitment—and at the implementation stage to make decision making an unpredictable process. Decision makers sometimes

- skip the analysis stage and move quickly to choice.
- ignore the analysis and base the decision on something else entirely; the analysis was nothing but a sham, because the decision criteria, however covert, were already in place. Or, as Pascal wrote, "The heart has reasons the mind knows not of."
- engage in what Janis and Mann (1977) called "defensive avoidance." That is, they procrastinate, attempt to shift responsibility, or rationalize delaying a choice.
- panic and seize upon a hastily contrived solution that gives promise of immediate relief. The choice may work in the short term but have negative long-term consequences.
- are swayed by "what seems right," by a course of action that is most salient, or by one that comes most highly recommended.
- translate the decision into action only half-heartedly.
- announce a choice, whether to themselves or others, but then do nothing about it.
- decide one thing but do another.

It is clear that counselors cannot help clients avoid all these pitfalls, but they can help clients minimize them.

Decision Making: Messy, Exciting, Human

Gelatt makes the point that the world has changed: rational, linear decision making is not what it used to be. We live in a world of great uncertainty, a world that has come to appreciate and accept intuition and risk taking. He proposes "positive uncertainty" as a new approach to decision making: "What is appropriate now is a decision and counseling framework that helps clients deal with change and ambiguity, accept uncertainty and inconsistency, and utilize the nonrational and intuitive side of thinking and choosing" (1989, p. 252). Positive uncertainty means, paradoxically, being positive (comfortable and confident) in the face of uncertainty (ambiguity and doubt)—feeling both uncertain about the future and positive about the uncertainty.

I am not so sure that the fact that the world has changed and that the tempo of change seems to be constantly picking up—something I do not deny—is the issue. Rather, in my view decision-making theory is now beginning to catch up with age-old human practice. Gelatt says that rational strategy is not obsolete but is not enough. It never was. Helpers need to understand the problem-solving and decision-making process for what it is: "a highly complex, intermittent, rational, irrational, logical, and intuitive process" (Heppner, 1989, p. 258). Pascal's observation about the reasons of the heart is a song of the richness of the human person.

A FINAL NOTE ON STAGE I

Stage I is both a stage and a process. As a *stage*, it deals with clients' telling their stories, choosing issues to focus on, and clarifying these issues in terms of specific experiences, behaviors, and emotions. As we have seen, counselors can use a variety of skills and methods to help clients achieve these objectives. Ideally, helpers both support and challenge clients in this pursuit. As *process*, story telling, challenging, and the search for leverage belong in all the stages of the helping encounter. There is no time when further relevant elements of a story or a new part of the overall story cannot emerge. Both self-challenge and the challenges meted out by helpers need to permeate the entire process. These kinds of challenge are what make the helping interviews different from day-to-day life—and the helping sessions have to be different if they are to make a difference. Finally, the search for leverage is also a process that must permeate every stage. As we have seen, counseling is a heavy investment of resources. The search for themes and changes that will make a difference is critical. A principle adapted from the work of the economist Vilfredo Pareto—and therefore sometimes called the Pareto Principle—states that you can get a great deal of payoff from relatively little effort if you know where to concentrate your effort. This principle has been applied to management: Managers get 80% of their results from 20% of the things they do. The principle applies to the entire helping process. Effective helpers don't choose models and then use them mindlessly. They keep looking for ways in which they can *add value* to clients' efforts to manage their lives more effectively. Counselors can also help clients apply the Pareto Principle to their own lives.

I had an unexpected encounter with a client just an hour before writing this paragraph. He is going through a rough patch. He has multiple sclerosis, but has been able to handle it quite well. He has derived a great deal of satisfaction from helping others cope with the disease and all that it entails. But a series of reversals—legal and financial—have knocked him out of kilter. He's not himself. He is obsessed with self-defeating ideas, his anxiety is unusually high, he fears for his wife and child, he feels alienated, he can't do his job the way he wants to. Still he smiled through the tears, at least occasionally. Since he lives in another city, I knew I would see him only this one time. I used just about every stage, step, and skill in this book in our encounter, trying to squeeze in the help he has not been getting. At the end, I asked, "What do you need?"

"What I'm getting here," he answered. "Common sense and tough love."

We agreed to make a joint effort to find the same in his neck of the woods. My best bet is that all the logical talk in the world is not going to "solve" anything. He's going to have to tough it out, with some support and challenge. He knows what to do. He's helped dozens do it. Now it's his turn.

EVALUATION QUESTIONS FOR STEP I-C

How well am I doing the following?

- Helping clients focus on issues that have payoff potential for them.
- Helping clients make critical decisions.
- Maintaining a sense of movement and direction in the helping process.
- Using summaries or getting clients to summarize as a way of remaining concrete and avoiding rambling.
- Avoiding unnecessarily extending the problem identification and exploration stage.
- Moving to other stages of the helping process as clients' needs dictate.
- Encouraging clients to act on what they are learning.
- Helping clients make their actions prudent and directional.

STAGE II: DEVELOPING PREFERRED SCENARIOS

Stage II asks: What would this problem situation look like if it were being managed successfully? What would the opportunity look like if developed? It has three steps.

Step II-A: Helping clients **construct the future** by helping them decide what they want to be different in their lives.

Step II-B: Helping clients **craft productive agendas** with goals that are both realistic and substantive.

Step II-C: Helping clients work out **the dynamics of commitment** to preferred scenarios and goals.

The Bias toward Stage I

Too many helpers are biased toward Stage I. That is, they spend what I would consider an inordinate amount of time helping clients identify, explore, and clarify problem situations; they also spend an inordinate amount of time using a variety of theories to help clients develop insights into themselves and their problems in living. In many cases, this is self-defeating. The real challenge of helping is not to identify and clarify problem situations, however essential this might be, but to help clients manage them. Too many helper training programs begin and end with basic communications skills and the steps of Stage I. A friend of mine in Australia who teaches the model offered here once said to me: "If I have two years, I teach the entire model; if I have two months, I teach the entire model; if I have two days, I teach the entire model; if I have two hours, I teach the entire model." Helpers who spend most of their time with clients in Stage I may be doing both their clients and themselves a disservice. Their clients are ill served because they are not helped to move to problem-managing action. Helpers themselves are ill served because failure to move beyond Stage I can lead to burnout.

The Power of Possibilities

Stage II is an essential bridge between the exploration in Stage I and the development of action strategies in Stage III.

When coupled with an assessment of the present stage [Stage I], this "picture" of the future condition [Stage II] provides the information necessary for [clients] to develop realistic action plans and timetables for managing the change [Stage III]. (Beckhard & Harris, 1987, p. 20)

In most helping and problem-solving models Stage II is, unfortunately, overlooked. The power of preferred-scenario possibilities is lost. Too often, exploration and clarification of problem situations are followed, almost immediately, by the search for "solutions." As I noted earlier, "solutions" is an ambiguous word. It can refer to the series of actions that will lead to the resolution of the problem situation. But it can also refer to what will be in place once these actions are completed. There is great power in visualizing solutions in this sense of outcomes, just as there is a danger in formulating action strategies before visualizing the accomplishments or outcomes these strategies are to produce. As Albert Einstein put it, "Perfection of means [strategies] and confusion of goals [outcomes] seem, in my opinion, to characterize our age." Stage II is about outcomes; Stage III is about strategies and plans for delivering these outcomes.

A Sense of Direction

Clients come to helpers because they are stuck. Counseling is a process of helping clients get "unstuck" and develop a sense of direction.

A client comes to an interview stuck—having either no alternatives for solving a problem or a limited range of possibilities. The task of the interviewer is to eliminate stuckness. . . . Stuckness is an inelegant, but highly descriptive, term to describe the opposite of [a sense of direction]. Other words that represent the same condition include immobility, blocks, repetition compulsion, inability to achieve goals, lack of understanding, limited behavioral repertoire, limited life script, impasse, lack of motivation, and many other terms. (Ivey, 1983, p. 213)

Consider the case of Ernesto. He was very young, but very stuck for a variety of sociocultural-emotional reasons.

I first met Ernesto in the emergency room of a large urban hospital. He was throwing up blood into a pan. He was a street gang member, and this was the third time he had been beaten up in the last year. He had been so severely beaten this time that it was likely that he would suffer permanent physical damage. Ernesto's style of life was doing him in, but it was the only one he knew. He was in need of a new way of living, a new scenario, a new way of participating in city life. This time he was hurting enough to consider the possibility of some kind of change.

Markus and Nurius (1986) have used the term "possible selves" to represent "individuals' ideas of what they might become, what they would like to become, and what they are afraid of becoming" (p. 954). I worked with Ernesto, not by helping him explore the complex sociocultural-emotional reasons why he was in this fix, but principally by helping him explore his "possible selves" in order to discover a different purpose in life, a different direction, a different lifestyle.

Wheeler and Janis (1980) suggest that it is sometimes useful to have clients work through some "gloomy scenarios" (p. 12) such as the dissolution of a marriage, the loss of a job, failing health, and the like. This is not an exercise in pessimism. Working through such scenarios provides useful, often overlooked, information. Also, by putting clients in touch with the "worst case," it helps them mobilize their resources to see to it that the worst case does not happen.

Exploring possible scenarios is a step toward developing a sense of direction. People with a sense of direction

- have a sense of purpose.
- live lives that are going somewhere.
- have self-enhancing and other-enhancing patterns of behavior in place.
- focus on outcomes and accomplishments.
- don't mistake aimless action for accomplishments.
- set long-term and short-term goals and objectives.
- have a defined rather than an aimless lifestyle.

The inevitable crises and problem situations of life are seen and managed against this background of purpose and direction. People with a sense of direction don't waste time in wishful thinking. Rather, they "translate abstract wishes and expectations into clearly defined outcomes against which [they] can measure progress" (Center for Constructive Change, 1984, p. 16).

Picture a continuum. At one end is the aimless person; at the other, a person with a sense of direction. Your clients might come from any point on the continuum. They may be at different points at different times or with respect to different issues—mature in seizing opportunities for education, for instance, but aimless in developing sexual maturity. All of us are "marginal" at one time or another. Helping clients establish and commit themselves to problem-managing goals is the principal task of Stage II.

Chapter Eleven

Step II-A: Helping Clients Construct the Future

Problems can make clients feel hemmed in and closed off. To a greater or lesser extent they have no future, or the future they have looks troubled. With the counselor's help, the client needs to address the future. As Gelatt (1989) has noted, "The future does not exist and cannot be predicted. It must be imagined and invented. . . . One must invent the future or let someone else invent it. . . . The counselor of the future must help clients imagine and invent their own future" (p. 255). Through this step, indicated in Figure 11-1, clients are helped to open up the world that has closed in on them.

THE GOAL OF STEP II-A

The goal of Step II-A is to help clients develop a range of *possibilities* for the future that can then be turned into realistic *goals*. This chapter deals principally with possibilities. The next chapter, on Step II-B, deals with goals.

The term *preferred scenarios*, which I use to describe Stage II, implies pictures of a better future. There are usually more possibilities for the future than clients imagine. In Step II-A clients are helped to picture themselves in the future, managing a problem situation or some part of it. They are helped to see themselves engaging in patterns of behavior with outcomes that are more constructive than the outcomes of the self-defeating patterns of behavior currently in place. They are helped to see themselves accomplishing things that enable them to manage their lives more effectively.

This is not a promise of pie in the sky. Possibilities also imply limitations: "Probably everyone over 30 has experienced the anguish of realizing that a cherished possible self is not to be realized, even though this possible self remains as vivid and compelling as the day it was constructed" (Markus & Nurius, 1986, p. 966). Unfortunately, many of us are more ready to think of limitations than to invent possibilities. Helping clients construct the future is a critical helper mandate. Consider the case of the Washington family.

> Lane, the 15-year-old son of Troy and Rhonda Washington, was hospitalized with what was diagnosed as an "acute schizophrenic attack." He had two older brothers, both teenagers, and two younger sisters, one 10 and one 12, all living at home. The Washingtons lived in a large city. Although both parents worked, their combined income still left them pinching pennies. They also ran into a host of problems associated with their son's hospitalization—the need to arrange ongoing help and care for Lane, financial burdens, behavioral problems among the other siblings, marital conflict, and stigma in the community ("They're a funny family with a crazy son"; "What kind of parents are they?"). To make things worse, they did not think the psychiatrist and psychologist they met at the

I. Present scenario   II. Preferred scenario   III. Strategy: Getting there

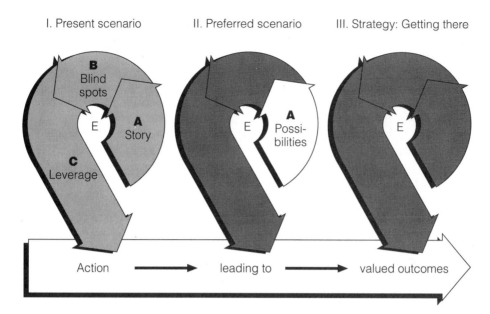

FIGURE 11-1   Step II-A: Developing Preferred-Scenario Possibilities

hospital took the time to understand their concerns. They felt that the helpers were trying to push Lane back out into the community; in their eyes, the hospital was "trying to get rid of him." "They give him some pills and then give him back to you" was their complaint. No one explained to them that short-term hospitalization was meant to guard the civil rights of patients and avoid the negative effects of long-term institutionalization.

When Lane was discharged, his parents were told that he might have a relapse, but they were not told what to do about it. They faced the prospect of caring for Lane in a climate of stigma without adequate information, services, or relief. Feeling abandoned, they were very angry with the mental-health establishment. They had no idea what they should do to respond to Lane's illness or to the range of family problems that had been precipitated by the episode.

By chance the Washingtons met someone who had worked for the National Alliance for the Mentally Ill (NAMI), "an advocacy and education organization that now has more than 850 local affiliates throughout the United States and represents more than 70,000 families" (Backer & Richardson, 1989, p. 547). This person referred them to an agency that provided support and help.

What does the future hold for such a family? With help, what kind of future can be fashioned? Bernheim (1989) suggested seven sets of tasks for families of the severely mentally ill. They have been translated here into seven sets of possible outcomes that could be realized if everything were to go well.

• *The home environment.* The Washingtons will have in place an environment in which the needs of all the family members are balanced. The home will not be an extension of the hospital. Lane will be taken care of, but the needs of the other children and of Rhonda and Troy themselves will be attended to as well.

• *Care outside the home.* A service program for Lane will be in place. That is, possible services will be reviewed, relevant services identified, and access to these services arranged, together with the means of payment. The logistics of getting Lane to and from hospital appointments will be seen to.

• *Care inside the home.* Family members will have learned how to cope with Lane's residual symptoms. He might be withdrawn or aggressive, but they will know how to relate to him and help him handle behavioral problems. They will know how to care for him without turning the home into a hospital.

• *Prevention.* Family members will have been taught to spot early warning symptoms of impending relapse. They will have a program to follow when they see such signs. The program will include such things as contacting the clinic or, in the case of more severe problems, arranging for an ambulance or getting help from the police.

• *Family stress.* They will have learned how to cope with the increased stress all of this will entail. They will have forums for working out their problems. Blow-ups with one another will decrease, and those that happen will be managed without damage to the fabric of the family.

• *Stigma.* Special attention will be paid to managing whatever stigma might be attached to Lane's illness. Family members will know whom to tell, what to say, how to respond to inquiries, and how to deal with blame and insults.

• *Limitation of grief.* The normal guilt, anger, frustration, fear, and grief that go with problem situations like this will be resolved or managed.

Bernheim's (1989) schema helps counselors and caseworkers identify a range of possible outcomes that can help families such as the Washingtons manage the crisis of severe mental illness more effectively. For our purposes the point to note is that the Washingtons first needed to be helped to develop possibilities for a better future. The next step would be to translate those possibilities into specific goals.

Here is a case that involves a single individual struggling with her current lifestyle.

> Anita is experiencing stress because she is simply trying to do too many things—being a wife and mother, holding down a part-time job, serving on church committees, and volunteering at a local nursing home. She needs to establish priorities and cut back to a reasonable schedule. If she is to do this, she must also manage others' expectations. One of the associate ministers helps her develop a range of different, more livable scenarios. Anita, after listing all the things she really likes to do and feels

committed to, puts together different scenarios or lifestyle "packages." Then, using the priorities derived from her values, she sets about the work of determining which scenario appeals to her most. Each scenario contains a different mix of activities.

The counselor helps Anita start with possibilities and then put these possibilities into different packages. The outcome will be a different lifestyle for Anita.

A new scenario can be quite complex and require clients to generate a wide range of possibilities. Tom, an AIDS victim who found himself abandoned by many of his friends and shunned by society, was helped to come up with the following possibilities. In the new scenario:

- He would have someone such as a minister with whom he could occasionally talk about the "ultimate" issues of life and death.
- He would have found a context for creating some kind of meaning out of suffering.
- He would have some sort of counselor to whom he could go when things got rocky.
- He would have some kind of community, maybe a self-help group of fellow AIDS victims, people who did not fear him.
- He would have fewer financial worries.
- He would have one or two intimates with whom he could share the ups and downs of daily life.
- He would be engaged in some kind of productive work, whether paid or not.
- He would have a decent place to live, maybe with others.
- He would have access to decent medical attention from medical staff who would not treat him like a new-age leper.
- He would be managing bouts of anxiety and depression better than he is now.
- He would be taking care of unfinished business with relatives.
- He would have made peace with one or two of his closest friends who abandoned him when they learned of the diagnosis.

These are the kinds of behaviors and outcomes that could, in very down-to-earth ways, constitute Tom's "possible selves." Possible selves are "the cognitive components of hopes, fears, goals, and threats . . . and they give specific . . . form, meaning, organization, and direction to these dynamics" (Markus & Nurius, 1986, p. 954). Ultimately, the "package" of possibilities Tom chooses constitutes the new and preferred scenario.

HELPING CLIENTS DEVELOP NEW SCENARIOS

The main complaint I hear from helpers about Stage II sounds something like this: "All this is well and good. It's easy to say, 'Help clients develop new-scenario possibilities,' and this works if the client is intelligent, verbal, and motivated. But many of my clients are not. This part of the model is lost on them." My best bet is that these helpers are expecting both too much and too little from their clients. They are expecting too much if they believe that most clients, on their own, can come up with a broad range of preferred-scenario possibilities and then compose these into a neatly painted picture of a better future. However, even if clients are helped to paint a relatively sketchy picture of the future, this is better than none at all. On the other hand, helpers are expecting too little of most clients if they see them as totally unimaginative, uncreative, and uninnovative. Research in creativity suggests that most people can be more creative than they are. We helpers need to use our imaginations to create ways of helping clients stimulate imaginations that seem moribund.

I once was sitting at the counter of a late-night diner when a young man sat next to me. The conversation drifted to the problems he was having with a friend of his. I listened for a while and then asked, "Well, if your relationship was just what you wanted it to be, what would it look like?" It took him a bit to get started, but eventually he drew a picture of the kind of relationship he could live with. Then he stopped, looked at me, and said, "You must be a professional." I believe he thought that because this was the first time in his life that anyone had ever asked him to describe a better future.

As Gelatt (1989) noted, part of the counselor's task is to find ways of helping clients invent better futures. There are various ways of doing so. A few possibilities follow.

Ask the Right Future-Oriented Questions

One way of helping clients invent the future is to ask them, or get them to ask themselves, future-oriented questions that are relevant to their current unmanaged problems or undeveloped opportunities. Here are the kinds of questions that clients can be helped to ask themselves.

• *What would this problem situation look like if I were managing it better?* Ken, a college student who has been a "loner," has been talking about his general dissatisfaction with his life. His answer: "I'd be having fewer anxiety attacks. And I'd be spending more time with people rather than by myself."

• *What changes in my present lifestyle would make sense?* Cindy, who describes herself as a "bored homemaker," replies: "I would not be drinking as much. I'd be getting more exercise. I would not sit around and watch the soaps all day."

• *What would I be doing differently with the people in my life?* Lon, a graduate student at a university near his parents' home, realizes that he has not yet developed the kind of autonomy suited to his age. He mentions these possibilities: "I would not be letting my mother make my decisions for me. I'd be sharing an apartment with one or two friends."

• *What patterns of behavior would be in place that are not currently in place?* Bridget, a depressed resident in a nursing home, has this suggestion: "I'd be engaging in more of the activities offered here in the nursing home."

• *What current patterns of behavior would be eliminated?* Bridget adds: "I would not be putting myself down for incontinence I cannot control. I would not be complaining all the time. It gets *me* down!"

• *What would exist that doesn't exist now?* Angie, a single parent in counseling because of child abuse, replies: "I would have my temper under control; I would no longer be hitting Jimmy. I would have a better job. I'd have some interests outside, so I wouldn't see the house as a prison."

• *What would be happening that is not happening now?* Sam, a widower with arthritis, puts these outcomes on his list: "I would not be experiencing as much chronic pain as I am now. My welfare checks would be arriving on time. My sons would visit me more."

• *What would I have that I don't have now?* Sissy, a single woman who has lived in a housing project for eleven years, says: "I'd have a place to live that's not rat-infested. I'd have some friends. I wouldn't be so miserable all the time."

• *What decisions would I have made and executed?* Lynn, 60, a woman in a lifeless marriage, answers: "I would be retired, and I would be separated from my husband. I wouldn't be living in this awful city."

• *What accomplishments would be in place that are not in place now?* Ryan, a divorced man in his mid-thirties, says: "I'd have my degree in practical nursing. I'd be doing some part-time teaching. I'd have someone to marry."

• *What would this opportunity look like if I developed it?* Enid, a woman who feels like a second-class citizen in the company in which she works, has this to say: "In two years I'll be an officer of this company or have a very good job in another firm."

My dialogues with clients are peppered with questions and probes like these. Of course, these are not the only questions that can prompt scenario-building. Effective helpers learn how to formulate questions and probes that respond to each client's needs.

It is a mistake to suppose that clients will automatically gush with answers. Ask the kinds of questions just listed, or encourage them to ask themselves the questions, but then help them answer them. I once was talking to a client with AIDS. He had come to the city from a smaller town because he wanted to avoid all the guilt and stigma attached to his disease. He wanted to die in peace anonymously, or so he said. "What would your death look like?" I asked. "Well, I'd have all the medical help I needed, but I would not want them to prolong my life artificially." A dialogue about his death ensued. At one point I asked him whether it bothered him to think about his death so specifically. "No," he said, "better now than when it's impossible to do so. In fact, strangely enough it's kind of comforting."

At one point I asked, "What else?" He paused and looked at the ground. "Well, a couple of my friends would be around." "Here?" I asked. He paused again. He finally said, "No. I don't want to die alone. I think I've come to Chicago to get my mind straight, to prepare for dying. To prepare for going home to die. Not to die." And he did go home to die.

Help Clients Find Models

Some clients can see future possibilities better when they see them embodied in others. You can help the brainstorming by helping them to identify models. By models I don't mean superstars. Their example could prove self-defeating. In the next example, a marriage counselor is talking with a middle-aged, childless couple. When he asked them "What would your marriage look like if it looked a little better?" he could see that they were stuck.

Counselor: Maybe the question would be easier to answer if you reviewed some of your married relatives, friends, or acquaintances.

Wife: None of them have super marriages. (Husband nods in agreement.)

Counselor: No, I don't mean super marriages. I'm looking for things you could put in your marriage that would make it a little better.

Wife: Well, Fred and Lisa are not like us. They don't always have to be doing everything together.

Husband: Who says we have to be doing everything together? I thought that was your idea.

Wife: If we weren't always together, we wouldn't be in each other's hair all the time.

Even though it was a somewhat torturous process, these people were able to come up with a range of possibilities. The counselor had the couple write them down so they wouldn't lose them. At this point the purpose was not to get the clients to commit themselves to these possibilities but to have them review the possibilities and relate them to the problem issues in their own marriage.

In the following case, the client finds herself making discoveries by observing people she had not identified as models at all.

Fran, a somewhat withdrawn college junior, realizes that when it comes to interpersonal competence, she is not ready for the business world she intends to enter when she graduates. She wants to do something about her interpersonal style and a few nagging personal problems. She sees a counselor in the Office of Student Services. After a couple of discussions with him, she joins a "lifestyle" group on campus that includes some training in interpersonal skills. Even though she expands her horizons a bit from what the members of the group say about their experiences, behaviors, and feelings, she tells her counselor that she learns even more by watching her fellow group members in action. She sees behaviors that she would like to incorporate in her own style. A number of times she says to herself in the group: "Ah, there's something I never thought of." Without becoming a slavish imitator, she begins to incorporate some of the patterns she sees in others into her own style.

Some counselors have clients read biographies to stimulate thinking about different lifestyle possibilities. A friend of mine has come up with an interesting variation of this technique. He collects short "biographies" of clients who have successfully managed some problem situation. His file deals with a whole range of problem situations. If he feels that a client might benefit from one of the "biographies," he makes reading it part of the client's homework.

Models can be found anywhere: among the client's relatives, friends, and associates, in books, on television, in history, in movies. Counselors can help clients identify models, choose those dimensions of others that are relevant, and translate what they see into realistic possibilities for themselves.

Review Better Times

For some, reviewing better times experienced in the past is a royal route to future possibilities. In the following example, a drug counselor is talking to a client.

Client: Those were easier times.
Counselor: What did you like about them? There's a glint in your eye. Tell me a little bit about life before drugs.
Client: I had this girlfriend. She may have been crazy, but she really liked me. And she could have had a lot of guys, but she liked me.
Counselor: So she liked even you. (Client smiles.) No girlfriend now?
Client: Some sex, but no girlfriend. Certainly not like her.
Counselor: Sounds like you wouldn't mind that happening again.
Client: I was so different then. She wouldn't look at me now.
Counselor: What would you have to be like for someone like her to give you a second look?

Bit by bit the counselor helped the client etch out possibilities for a different lifestyle.

The best in a client's past can be a mine for the future. The couple mentioned earlier was asked to describe what their marriage was like "when it was at its best." Their description produced a whole range of possibilities for their future.

Help Clients Discover Possibilities by Getting Involved in New Experiences

An action-oriented way of helping clients explore possibilities is to help them get involved in new experiences. Here are three examples:

• A college senior, unsure about a career in the helping professions, took a year off and worked in a mental hospital. He learned a great deal about himself, his interpersonal style, his aspirations, and the human condition. Ultimately he decided against a career as a professional helper.

• A couple with marital difficulties decided to live apart for six months. Neither was contemplating divorce. The separation was specifically desig- nated as a time for learning, not just a period of respite. Since this was the husband's first experience of shifting for himself, he learned a great deal about what he had taken for granted in the marriage. The wife learned more about her own dependence and began to formulate possibilities for doing things on her own.

• A single, middle-aged man who came to a counselor because he was becoming obsessed with fears about death became a hospital visitor in a program sponsored by his church. Coming in contact with pain and mor- tality helped desensitize his fears. He also learned about how "out of com- munity" and self-centered he had become. He began to formulate and im- plement possibilities for a different lifestyle.

There are no limits to the kinds of experiences that can help clients orient their thinking to future possibilities rather than to current problems.

Use Writing Approaches to Develop Possibilities

Clients can also be encouraged to explore new possibilities through writ- ing. Obviously, this will work best with people who can and like to write, but don't underestimate clients' ability to do so. Again, do not expect too much or too little. A poet taught elderly nursing-home residents how to expand their horizons and enjoy themselves by expressing themselves in poetry. They were, in the main, not Longfellows and St. Vincent Millays, but they did write credible verse, they did derive enjoyment out of ex- pressing themselves, and they did get to know one another much better through their poems.

Some helpers have their clients write their epitaphs. This is not an exercise in gloom but rather a search for possibilities and priorities. One client wrote the following:

> Yvonne Smith died after a full life. She was best known for her hobbies. In the middle of her life she learned how to sew and work with leather. She also took up drawing and pottery. She became well-known in arts-and- crafts circles. Her hobby became her life work. She never married, but she led a full life with all the friends she made as she pursued her art.

This woman had dabbled a bit with sewing, but this exercise proved a turning point in her life. She stopped bemoaning the fact that she had never been lucky in love and began trying to turn her imagined epitaph into reality.

Other helpers have their clients write their résumés—not as they exist now, but the kind of résumé they would like to be able to write two, three, or four years in the future. They are asked to assume that their future employer is not interested just in their work-related achievements but in all their achievements as human beings. One client wrote in part:

> He is very personable. Others seek him out as an informal counselor because he is both understanding and wise.

This was hardly an accurate portrayal of the writer at the time of the writing, but it was an indication of both possibilities and perhaps motivation.

Use Fantasy and Guided Imagery

Most of us underestimate and underuse the power of imagination. Stage II can be an exciting one for both client and helper because it involves stimulating clients' underused imaginations.

> In order to shape [a] preferred future, we need to hold in our minds an image of what it is that we really want. . . . Use of imagination is what propels persons into the future, whether it is by idle dreaming or conscious intention. In ages past, future thinking was generally accepted as the turf of the prophet; more recently, that of the science fiction writer; but now we are beginning to realize that it is within the domain of every thoughtful person. (Lindaman & Lippitt, 1979, p. 3)

Some helpers are wary of the use of imagination and imagery in counseling. And it is true that those of us who are highly logical will have difficulty using these as tools. However, it might be time to revisit this area, even though we have memories of the misuses of "creativity" from the days when the "human potential movement" was in full swing.

> In a darkened gymnasium, members of the United States women's Olympic volleyball team are mentally rehearsing their upcoming match. In the Minneapolis Children's Hospital, youngsters with cancer are learning relaxation imagery to assist in the treatment of their disease. In a counselor's office in a community mental health center, a client is completing a 10th imagery session, which has included imaginary encounters with parents and assertive confrontations with a co-worker and now focuses on career alternatives. These three examples illustrate the scope of settings in which imagery is now being employed to expand human possibilities. Imagery seems to be moving into the mainstream of counseling and human development after almost a 50-year period of disrepute. (Witmer & Young, 1985, p. 187)

Brief descriptions such as this do not, of course, provide the skills for helping people use imagination and imagery to create possibilities for themselves. But the potential is there. Witmer and Young point out that imagery is being used for increasing self-awareness, increasing sensitivity to others, planning the future, giving direction to lifestyle changes, developing self-discipline, reducing stress, improving learning, and managing a range of problems, including insomnia, obesity, sexual malfunctioning, phobias, anxieties, and psychosomatic disorders. Imagery, imagination, and fantasy can be used to open up the future and engender a sense of hope (see Zdenek, 1987).

A FUTURE-CENTERED APPROACH TO HELPING

The focus of this chapter is on a possibility-rich future rather than on a past that cannot be changed or a present that is problematic. What follows is a nonlinear, future-oriented version of the helping model. I often use this version of the model in both long-term and short-term counseling.

1. The story. Help clients tell their stories. It is not necessary for the client to reveal all the details of the problem situation all at once in the beginning of the helping encounter. Sometimes a relatively quick look at the highlights of the story is enough to begin with.

> Jay, a single man, aged 25, tells a story of driving while drinking and of an auto accident in which he was responsible for the death of a friend as well as his own severe back injuries. He has told the story over and over again to many different people, as if telling it enough will make what happened go away.

When Jay met the counselor he had already told his story a number of times to different people. Retelling the whole thing in great detail was not going to help. A summary was enough.

2. The preferred scenario. Help clients take an initial cut at formulating the elements of a preferred scenario. This can help clients develop a sense of hope. They identify a better future early in the helping process, and this future pervades the rest of the process.

> Jay is helped to spell out a scenario in which he is more responsible for his actions, in which he is not hounded by regret and guilt, in which he has made peace with the family of his friend, in which he is physically rehabilitated within the limits of his injuries, and in which he is coping with the physical and psychological consequences of the accident.

This is not the time to set clear-cut behavioral goals. The client is being helped to outline a picture, not draft a blueprint. The purpose of this quick move to the preferred scenario is to help clients focus on a better future rather than a problematic and unchangeable past.

3. Return to Stage I. In the light of a preferred scenario, help clients

- identify gaps between the present scenario and what they want;
- identify and manage blind spots and develop new perspectives;
- identify points of leverage—critical things to be worked on.

Even a brief visit to Stage II—what things would look like if the problem situation were managed—can act like a spotlight that illuminates the client's story and gives it a different cast. The client no longer focuses on the past but comes to see the difference between the current scenario and the preferred scenario as a gap or set of gaps. A gap is not the same as a problem. A gap implies action: bridging the gap. And it is easier for clients to see blind spots, develop new perspectives, and choose high-leverage issues after an even brief visit to the future.

> Jay is helped to explore some of the gaps between his current and preferred scenarios and to develop new perspectives. For instance, he comes to see his overpowering regret and guilt as partially self-inflicted (through his own internal self-dialogue) and as actually standing in the way of managing his crisis effectively. When he engages in self-recrimination, he is not in the right frame of mind either to make peace with the family of his friend or to get seriously involved in a physical rehabilitation program. Managing the current flood of self-defeating emotions is a point of leverage. One blind spot is that he does not see that continual self-chastisement is actually standing in the way of what he wants. He has unwittingly decided that self-chastisement is "good" and that more is even better.

The current scenario is now seen in the light of the preferred scenario, and the clarification of the problem situation is much more upbeat. Points of leverage and blind spots are easier to identify, because the client has a better idea of where he wants to go. A kind of dialogue takes place between Stage II and Stage I, with the vision of Stage II helping the client illuminate and complete the work of Stage I. More specific work in Stage I—analyzing gaps, identifying blind spots, developing new perspectives, and seeing possibilities for immediate action—can then lead to the formulation of meaningful goals.

4. Return to Stage II. Help clients use what they have learned in their return to Stage I to complete the formulation of a problem-managing agenda.

> Through a dialogue between what is and what could be, Jay begins to formulate an agenda for himself. He cannot change the past, but he can learn from it. The energy he has been putting into self-recrimination can be put into self-reformation. He begins to explore more specifically what a self-responsible Jay would look like: not a person hounded by guilt, but not the irresponsible free spirit that lives on the edge of disaster, either. He sees a person whose energy is not squashed, but channeled. These ideas begin to get translated into specific goals, for instance, the goals of the physical rehabilitation program he is involved in.

The exploration of the problem situation is no longer an end in itself. It actually becomes a tool to be used to fashion the future.

5. Transition state. Help clients formulate strategies and plans to accomplish goals and get the new scenario on line. Help them implement their plans.

> Jay is helped to develop and implement strategies for controlling the flood of emotions that are now victimizing him. He uses his guilt as a stimulus to develop a way of meeting and making peace with the family of his friend. He explores with the counselor the ways he has allowed emotions to dominate his behavior. As he develops new perspectives, he begins to formulate strategies for making his emotions his allies instead of his enemies.

The purpose of this brief example is to illustrate a different, more upbeat movement in the helping process, what might be called a Stage-II-centered approach to helping. It demonstrates that the helping process, at its best, is not a slavish, linear working through of the three stages. The best helpers keep finding different ways to use the stages, steps, and skills of the helping model to meet the needs of different clients.

Listen to a friend of mine, the marriage counselor we met earlier in this chapter, who has adopted this "back-and-forth" approach to his work with couples:

> When a couple comes, they don't need to spend a great deal of time talking about what is going wrong. They know what's going wrong because they're living it every day. If I let them tell their stories, they inevitably tell entirely different stories. It's as if they were not even married to each other. They begin to fight the way they fight at home. I don't find all of this very useful. And so, early on I make them focus on the future. I ask them questions like "What would your marriage look like if it were a little bit better, not perfect, but just a little bit better?" If they get stuck, I ask them to think about other couples they know, couples that seem to have decent, if not perfect, marriages. "What's their marriage like? What parts of it would you like to see incorporated into your own marriage?" What I try to do is to help them use their imaginations to create a vision of a marriage that is different from the one they are experiencing. It's not that I never let them talk about the present. Rather, I try to help them talk about the present by having them engage in a dialogue between a better future and the unacceptable present. For instance, if one of them says, "I'd like a marriage in which the household tasks were divided up more fairly," then I might let the person explore how those tasks are currently divided up. They use a better future as a tool to help them clarify a problematic present.

This is not a quick lesson in how to do marriage counseling, but it does give the flavor of a future-oriented approach.

STEP II-A: LINKS TO ACTION

The work of Step II-A is just what some clients need. It frees them from thinking solely about problem situations and unused resources and enables them to begin fashioning a better future. Here is the case of a school principal who asked to talk to me because she was depressed and thinking of getting out of the "education business."

> Monica looked depressed when she arrived. We spent about two hours together. Her story included the whole range of problems that principals in urban schools faced. I thought that across the country there must be hundreds like her with similar stories. After a while I said, "I've got an idea. Pretend that you were asked to build a new high school from scratch. There would be the usual financial constraints, but otherwise you could make it the best high school in the country. What would it look like?"
>
> "Why not?" she responded, and she plunged into the task. We spend about an hour and a half in dialogue. She used a flip chart to spell out her ideas, sometimes actually making rough sketches of what a room would look like to make a point. I was startled by her enthusiasm. No more depression—instead, total dedication to the task. At the end of the session she said, "That's the best time I've had in two years. But even better, I bet that I can implement a lot of these ideas over the next year. Boy, have I been letting this job get me down!"

That was the only session I had with Monica. About a year later I saw her at a conference. She did not look depressed. She had indeed tried to implement her ideas. Some had worked, some hadn't. But she was at the conference as a member of the new mayor's task force on the reformation of the city's beleaguered education system.

EVALUATION QUESTIONS FOR STEP II-A

- How at home am I in working with my own imagination?
- In what ways can I apply the concept of "possible selves" to myself?
- What problems do I experience as I try to help clients use their imaginations?
- How effectively do I use empathy, probes, and future-oriented questions to help clients develop preferred-scenario possibilities?
- Besides direct questions, what kinds of strategies do I use to help clients develop problem-managing possibilities?
  - Do I help them find models?
  - Do I help them review "better times"?
  - Do I help them learn from others?
  - Do I help them get involved in experiences that will suggest preferred-scenario possibilities to them?
  - Are there any writing approaches I find helpful?
  - To what degree am I comfortable helping clients use fantasy or imagery in developing a more promising future?
- How easily do I move back and forth in the helping model, especially in establishing a "dialogue" between Stage I and Stage II?
- How well do I help clients act on what they are learning?

Chapter Twelve

Step II-B: Helping Clients Craft Productive Agendas

Once a range of preferred-scenario possibilities has been developed, clients need to turn possibilities into agendas. Step II-A is, in many ways, about creativity. Step II-B is about innovation—that is, creativity made practical. In this step, added in Figure 12-1, clients are helped to create innovative agendas that contribute to the management of problem situations and the development of unexploited opportunities. In traditional terms, this step is about *aims, goals,* and *objectives.*

THE ADVANTAGES OF GOAL SETTING

According to Locke and Latham (1984), helping clients develop new, preferred scenarios and set problem-managing goals can help them in four ways:

• *Setting goals focuses clients' attention and action.* New scenarios give clients a vision toward which they can direct their energies. Clients with goals are less likely to engage in aimless behavior.

• *Setting goals mobilizes energy and effort.* Clients who seem lethargic during the problem exploration phase can come to life when it is a question of spelling out alternate scenarios. Goal setting is not just a cognitive exercise. Clients begin moving toward goals in a variety of ways once they set them.

• *Setting goals increases persistence.* Not only are clients with goals energized to do something, but they tend to work harder and longer. Clients with clear and realistic goals don't give up as easily as clients with vague goals or with no goals at all.

• *Setting goals motivates clients to search for strategies to accomplish them.* Setting goals, a Stage-II task, leads naturally into a search for means to accomplish them, a Stage-III task. Meaningful goals push clients toward action.

Sometimes clients want to skip the step of goal setting. Once they see a problem, they want to do something about it immediately. While the desire to act is laudable, action needs to be both directional and wise. In the following case it is neither.

> Harry was a sophomore in college who was admitted to a state mental hospital because of some bizarre behavior at the university. He was one of the disc jockeys for the university radio station. He came to the notice of college officials one day when he put on an attention-getting performance that included rather lengthy dramatizations of grandiose religious themes. In the hospital it was soon discovered that this quite pleasant, likable young man was actually a loner. Everyone who knew him at the university thought that he had a lot of friends, but in fact he did not. The campus was large, and his lack of friends went unnoticed.

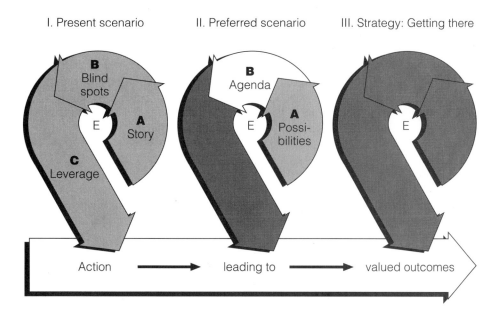

I. Present scenario   II. Preferred scenario   III. Strategy: Getting there

FIGURE 12-1   Step II-B: Crafting Productive Agendas

Harry was soon released from the hospital but returned weekly for therapy. At one point he talked about his relationships with women. Once it became clear to him that his meetings with women were perfunctory and almost always took place in groups—he had actually thought he had a rather full social life with women—Harry launched a full program of getting involved with the opposite sex. His efforts ended in disaster, because Harry had some basic sexual and communication problems. He also had serious doubts about his own worth and therefore found it difficult to make a gift of himself to others. With the therapist's help he returned to the problem-clarification and new-perspectives part of the helping process and then established more realistic short-term goals.

Harry's leaping from problem clarification to action without taking time to set a direction and establish reasonable goals was part of the problem rather than part of the solution. His lack of success with women actually helped him see his problem with women more clearly.

THE LANGUAGE OF GOAL SETTING

When it comes to goal setting, different people use different terms in different ways. Therefore, it is helpful to say what is meant by the terms used in this chapter. Three terms are central to our discussion: (1) a declaration of intent, (2) an aim, and (3) goals.

A Declaration of Intent

A declaration of intent is an indication on the part of the client that he or she intends to do something about a problem situation or opportunity. In the following example, the client, Jon, has been discussing his relationship with his wife and children. The counselor has been helping him see how some of his behavior is perceived negatively by his family. Jon is open to challenge and is a fast learner. He says this:

Jon: Boy, this session has been an eye-opener for me. I've really been blind. My wife and kids don't see my investment—rather, my overinvestment—in work as something I'm doing for them. I've been fooling myself, telling myself that I'm working hard to get them the good things in life. In fact, I'm spending most of my time at work because I like it. My work is mainly for me. *It's time for me to realign some of my priorities.*

The last statement is a declaration of intent, an indication on Jon's part that he wants to do something about a problem now that he sees it more clearly.

In the next example, a 48-year-old woman, Laureen, has discovered that she has breast cancer and will need a mastectomy. She has had a couple of sessions with a self-help group composed of women who have had to face the same problem. She says to the group:

Laureen: As I listen to all of you tell your stories, I'm beginning to see how passive I've become since I found out the diagnosis. I feel that I'm surrendering myself to doctors and to the whole medical establishment. No wonder I feel so depressed. I'm ordinarily an active woman. I usually take charge of my life. *Well, I want to take charge of it again.*

Laureen does not say what she is going to do to handle her passivity— what pattern of behavior will replace the current one—but she is determined to do something. This is a declaration of intent.

An Aim

An aim is more than a declaration of intent. It is a declaration of intent that identifies the area in which the client wants to work and makes some general statement about that area. Let's return to the example of Jon and his overinvestment in work.

Jon: I don't think I've got so taken up with work deliberately. That is, I don't think I'm running away from family life. But family life is deteriorating because I'm just not around enough. I must spend more time with my wife and kids. Actually, it's not just a case of "must." I want to.

This is more than a declaration of intent because it says in a general way what Jon wants to do: "spend more time with my wife and kids." However, while Jon's statement is an aim, it is not yet a goal, because it does not specify precisely what he wants to do, precisely what the new pattern of behavior will look like.

If a problem is defined fairly clearly, then aims begin to emerge. For instance, Laureen, the woman about to undergo a mastectomy, realizes that she has become passive in various ways. "I used to be careful about my personal appearance, but I notice that I've been letting myself go." One aim, then, is to reinvest herself in her personal appearance. "I'm going to force myself to take care of how I look."

Goals

Goals move beyond aims in being clear and specific statements of what a person wants to put in place in order to manage a problem situation or develop an opportunity. The problem with aims is that their very vagueness makes it too easy to put them off. All of us are familiar with the "New Year's resolutions" phenomenon. Lots of people indicate in vague ways what they are going to do better or differently in the coming year. "I'm really going to get into shape this year." Few people carry out such resolutions. To move Jon toward greater specificity, the counselor asks him such questions as "What will your life with your family look like when you make the change?" Jon says:

Jon: I'm going to consistently spend three out of four weekends a month at home. During the week I'll work no more than two evenings.

Notice how much more specific this statement is than "I'm going to spend more time with my family." Here Jon talks about a pattern of behavior he wants to put in place. He will reach his goal when he is habitually spending the indicated time with his family.

Helping clients move from a declaration of intent to an aim and on to goals that translate their aim into accomplishments is a shaping process, one that can, for many clients, be quite useful. Some authors use a fourth term, *objectives*. In this parlance, goals are, in terms of specificity, somewhere between aims and objectives. For our purposes three levels are enough.

Consider the example of a father who has been involved in child abuse.

- *Declaration of intent:* "I've got to change. If I don't, I'll just ruin the family."
- *Aim:* "I've got to get my temper under control and not take things out on Tommy."

• *Goal:* "Every time I feel myself getting angry, I'm going to call the Save the Children hotline and get some help in talking myself down. I'm going to do this until I feel I have myself under control. I hate feeling dependent like this, but hurting Tommy is worse."

This parent is talking about a pattern of behavior he wants to put in place. He can see himself consistently calling the hotline whenever he experiences cues indicating that he's headed out of control.

In the next example, a marriage has degenerated into constant bickering, especially about finances.

• *Statement of intent:* "We want to straighten out our marriage."
• *Aim:* "We want to handle our decisions about finances in a much more constructive way."
• *Goal:* "We try to solve our problems about family finances by fighting and arguing. We'd like to reduce the number of fights we have and increase the number of times we make decisions about money by talking them out. We're going to set up a month-by-month budget. We will have next month's budget ready the next time we meet with you."

These two people want to change their style of dealing with finances, an aim that includes changing their style of dealing with each other. More specifically, they want to replace one pattern of behavior with a more constructive pattern. The goal is accomplished when the new pattern is in place.

CRAFTING USEFUL AGENDAS

The root meaning of *agenda* is a series of things *to be done*. Here it means a goal or group of goals that needs to be accomplished. The achievement of the goals constitutes the management of the problem situation or the development of the opportunity. In the case just presented, the married couple's agenda includes reducing fighting behavior and putting in place a mutually agreed-upon budgetary system. The accomplishment of the goals in their agenda constitutes the management or partial management of their problem situation.

A No-Formula Approach to Goal Setting

As I have noted, the model presented in this book focuses on a range of things helpers and clients can do so that clients manage their lives better. It is not a set of things you absolutely must do but a set of guidelines for providing whatever a client needs to manage his or her life more effectively. The package delivered to one client will look different from the package delivered to another.

This no-formula approach applies to goal setting. What follows is a series of guidelines you can use to help clients set direction for themselves and then actively pursue that direction.

After reviewing my own experience and that of other helpers, I have "softened" my approach to goal setting.

> The means-end model of thinking has for so long dominated our thinking that we have come to believe that not to have clearly defined purposes for our activities is to court irrationality or, at the least, to be professionally irresponsible. Yet life . . . is seldom neat and linear. . . . Many of our most productive activities take the form of exploration or play. In such activities, the task is not one of arriving at a preformed objective but rather to act, often with a sense of abandon, wonder, curiosity. (Eisner, 1979, p. 100)

Perhaps Langer (1989) put it well in suggesting that we should be goal-guided rather than goal-governed. Picture a continuum. At one end, counselors help clients set direction but let goals emerge along the route. At the other end, clients are helped to set explicit goals early on in the helping process. Taussig (1987) showed that clients respond positively to goal setting even when problems are discussed and goals set very early in the counseling process. Help clients choose the point on the continuum that makes sense for them.

A word on the "emergence" of goals: Some, seeing an overemphasis on specific goal setting as overly "technological," suggest that the client's goals should be allowed to "emerge" in a natural way. "Emerge" can mean a couple of things in this context. First of all, it might mean that clients, once helped to clarify a problem through a combination of probing, empathy, and challenge, begin to see more clearly what they want to do to manage the problem. Second, it could also mean that some clients must first act in some way before they find out just what they want to do. Such forms of "emergence" and others can indeed be productive.

However, if emergence means that clients should wait around until "something comes up," or if it means that clients should try a lot of different solutions in the hope that one of them will work, then emergence can be a self-defeating process. Setting specific goals may not be part of a client's ordinary style, but this does not make it either unnatural or overly technological. Trying one "solution" after another is a way of spinning one's wheels. In my experience, helping clients set clear and realistic goals has been one of the most useful and human parts of the helping process.

Helping Clients Shape Their Agendas

Once clients begin to specify goals, counselors can help them craft their agendas. Agendas are rationally shaped if they include goals that are (1) stated as accomplishments, (2) clear and specific, (3) measurable or verifiable, (4) realistic, (5) substantive, (6) in keeping with the client's values, and (7) set in a reasonable time frame. These characteristics can be seen as tools for shaping a workable agenda.

1. Stating Goals as Accomplishments

Help clients state goals or preferred scenarios in terms of outcomes or accomplishments rather than activities leading up to these accomplishments.

It helps if clients can visualize each accomplishment. "I want to start doing some exercise" is not as clear as "Within six months I will be running three miles in less than 30 minutes at least four times a week." The former is an aim stated as an activity—"doing some exercise"—whereas the latter is a goal stated as an accomplishment, a specific outcome *in place*. The client can actually see herself engaged on a regular basis in this self-enhancing pattern of behavior.

An agenda is a group of goals stated as accomplishments or outcomes, not the activities that lead up to these accomplishments. If a client says, "My goal is to get some training in interpersonal communication skills," then she is stating her goal as a program or set of activities rather than as an accomplishment. Her goal is achieved only when the skills are acquired, practiced, and actually used in interpersonal situations. Similarly, the goal of a person who is drinking too much is not to join Alcoholics Anonymous or attend meetings regularly. Joining AA is a program. This person has reached his goal when the drinking has stopped.

You can help clients develop this "past-participle" approach (drinking *stopped*, skills *acquired, practiced*, and *used*, number of marital fights *decreased*, anger habitually *controlled*) to agenda setting. Stating agendas in terms of accomplishments (or at least developing accomplishment-oriented ways of thinking about the future) is not just a question of language. Clients often leap into action (activities, programs) without knowing where they are going (goals, outcomes, accomplishments, preferred scenarios). In this sense, helping can focus *too much* on action—action that is without direction or that may not be prudent. If a client with AIDS says that he thinks he should join a self-help group of fellow AIDS victims, he should be helped to see what he wants to get out of such a group.

Knowing where they are going in terms of outcomes helps clients work, not just hard, but smart. However, if some clients persist in using activity language rather than accomplishment language in talking about goals, there is no need to make them talk your language. In such cases I gently probe for outcomes every once in a while.

Consider the case of Dan, a former Marine diagnosed as suffering from post-traumatic shock syndrome.

> Dan was stationed in Beirut for a while and saw many of his buddies killed. Since that was his last tour of duty, he came home and was discharged. Ever since he has lived a rather aimless life. He went to college

but dropped out during the first semester. He became rather reclusive but, as a friend who referred him to the helper said, "never really showed odd behavior." He has moved in and out of a number of low-paying jobs. He also has become less careful about his person. "You know, he used to be very careful about the way he dressed. Kind of proud of himself. Don't get me wrong; he's not a bum and doesn't smell or anything, but he's not himself." Dan has been drinking more than he used to, though he is far from being an alcoholic. But the whole direction of Dan's life is wrong, and serious trouble could lie down the road. He's bothered by dreams about Beirut and has taken to sleeping whenever he feels like it, day or night.

Ed, Dan's counselor, has a good relationship with Dan. He has helped Dan tell his story and has challenged some of his self-defeating thinking. He has been moving back and forth between Stage I and Stage II. Now Dan has begun talking about some of the ways he might change his lifestyle.

Dan: I'm going to stop hiding in my hole. I'm going to get out and see people more. I'm going to stop feeling so damn sorry for myself. Who wants to be with a mope!

Counselor: What will Dan's life look like a year or two from now?

Dan: One thing for sure. He will be seeing women again. He will probably have a special girlfriend. And she will see him as an ordinary guy. Not so damn hyper.

Dan talks about lifestyle changes in terms of activities. A simple question from Ed helps him start to translate these activities into outcomes.

2. Making Goals Clear and Specific

Help clients set goals that are clear and specific enough to drive action.

Goals stated, not only as outcomes, but as *specific* outcomes, tend to motivate or drive behavior. "I need to do something about this" is a statement of intent that could have a low probability of driving client behavior. This is not always the case. When some clients say that they are going to do something about their lives, they go out and do it, and what they accomplish has direction and is prudent. But if statements of intent remain just words, helping clients move to aims and goals stated in terms of clear accomplishments might be just what they need.

Specific goals will, of course, be different for each client. An organization that provides services for autistic citizens has stated its "goals" for its clients in the following terms:

1. Increased behavioral control.
2. Appropriate social interactions.
3. Improved communication skills.
4. Independent daily living skills.
5. Employable vocational skills.
6. Higher academic functioning.

In our language, these are aims rather than goals (some would say that they are goals rather than objectives). The aims of this agency must be stated this way, because they need to be tailored to clients in different ways. Since one client's problems are not the same as another's, one client's agenda will be different from another's.

Agenda shaping includes helping clients develop the level of clarity and specificity they need in order to act. Use probes and challenges to help them say what they really want to accomplish. Dan said that he wanted to become "more disciplined." This struck his counselor as a good statement of intent, but one that needs more meat on it.

Counselor: Any particular areas you want to focus on?

Dan: Well, yeah. If I'm going to put more order in my life, I need to look at the times I sleep. I've been going to bed whenever I feel like it and getting up whenever I feel like it. That was my way of coping with the dreams. But I'm not nearly as anxious about the dreams any more.

Counselor: So "more disciplined" means a more regular sleep schedule because there's no particular reason now for not having one.

Dan: Right. Actually I can live quite well on about seven hours.

Dan goes on to formulate a sleep-awake package that makes sense for some of the other things he wants to do in terms of school and work.

3. Establishing Measurable or Verifiable Outcomes

Help clients establish outcomes that can be measured or verified.

This is a corollary of (2): If the goal is clear enough, the client should be able to determine progress toward the goal. For many clients, being able to measure progress is an important incentive. Therefore, it helps if the criteria for the accomplishment of goals are clear. "I want to have a better relationship with my wife" is an aim, not a goal because, stated in this way, it cannot be verified. "I want to spend more time with her" comes closer, but it is still not clear what "more time" means. Clients can be helped to ask themselves: "How will I know whether I'm moving closer to my goal? How will I know that I have achieved my goal? How will I know when the preferred scenario is in place?"

Clients can't know whether they are making progress if they don't know where they started. One of Dan's goals was to reduce the number and severity of his bouts of free-floating anxiety. If he knows how frequent and how severe these bouts are in the first place, then he can judge whether he is making progress. Helping clients collect what behavioral scientists call "baseline data" can be part of the process of problem clarification.

Dan: I had been having about four attacks of anxiety a week. Two of them were usually very intense. And usually one of them would last for hours no matter what I'd do. It was driving me crazy. Now I have an attack about once a week or even once every two weeks. It usually doesn't last very long, and it's never as intense as it used to be.

Dan knows he is making progress because he has stated his goal in verifiable terms *and* has a clear-cut idea of his starting point.

It is not always necessary to count things in order to determine whether a goal has been reached, though sometimes counting is quite helpful. At a minimum, however, goals or outcomes need to be capable of being verified in some way. For instance, a couple might say something like "Our relationship is better, not because we've found ways of spending more time together, but because the quality of our time together has improved. By that we mean that we listen better, we talk about more personal concerns, we are more relaxed, and we make more mutual decisions about issues that affect us both, such as finances." The couple's accomplishment is one they can verify because they have spelled out what they mean by quality in their relationship.

4. Making Agendas Realistic

Help clients fashion realistic agendas.

A goal is realistic if (a) the resources necessary for its accomplishment are available to the client, (b) external circumstances do not prevent its accomplishment, (c) the goal is under the client's control, and (d) the cost of accomplishing it is not too high. Let's take a brief look at each of these.

Make sure that necessary resources are available. It does little good to help clients develop clear and verifiable goals if the resources are not available for their accomplishment.

> *Unrealistic:* John decides to go to graduate school without having either the financial or academic resources needed to do so.
>
> *Realistic:* John decides to work and to take one graduate course at night in rehabilitation counseling to see whether he is really interested in this field and to determine whether he is capable of the work. His goal is to gather the data he needs to make a good decision.

Clients sabotage their own efforts if they choose goals beyond their reach. Sometimes it is impossible to determine beforehand whether the personal or environmental resources needed are available. If this is the case, it might be best to start with goals for which the resources are certainly available and then move on to those that are more questionable in terms of resources.

Human resources are, for many, a critical part of the picture. Many clients come to counselors "out of community," that is, with troubled, slim, or even nonexistent relationships with others. If early on in the counseling process I feel that I am the sole or principal human resource for a client, I see that as part of the problem situation, whether the client describes it as such or not. Part of the new scenario must then be the development of human resources. If the person is "out of community," then getting "into community" is an aim.

Some scenarios or goals are unrealistic because their execution assumes, often indirectly, human resources that are not in place in the lives of clients. To accomplish certain goals, clients will need support from people other than the counselor, that is, support in "real" time rather than counseling time.

> Nick was confronted with his addiction to gambling the hard way. Like other heavy gamblers, he gambled away his liquid assets, gambled away loaned money, gambled away money borrowed on nonliquid assets such as his house, and finally gambled away funds he did not have, so that he ended up in debt to bookies who began to pressure him for their money. He borrowed money from relatives and friends, using some of it to stave off the bookies and some of it to try to recoup his losses through further bets. The whole situation collapsed when a friend from whom he had borrowed money threatened to tell Nick's wife, his employer, his banks, and his other creditors the whole story unless he immediately sought help.
>
> Under pressure, Nick sought help from Gamblers Anonymous. Part of the program was to put in place a network of people from whom Nick could receive both help and support. For instance, he was put in touch with a couple of people who had gotten in debt as deeply as he had, and they shared with him the ways they had been managing their financial lives. Nick also attended weekly group meetings where he heard horror stories like his own. Meeting people like himself, some of whom were still hurting badly, helped him to begin to demythologize for himself the unreal world of gambling. It hit him how gambling had become his life. For instance, at social gatherings he wasn't really with people; his preoccupation with baseball or basketball scores kept him distracted or on the phone. Through GA he made friends, spending time with two members who lived near him. They provided camaraderie, and they also helped him set financial goals and begin working his way out of his financial mess. In a word, GA helped him find a support group, role models, and mentors.
>
> One of Nick's aims was to straighten things out with his family. His wife suspected that he was gambling, but she had no idea of the extent of it. What he learned from other GA members helped him a great deal. He met with his wife and teenage children, told them the entire story, and asked for both their forgiveness and their help. There was some resentment and anger to work through, but basically his wife and children became allies instead of adversaries.

Clients will each have their own human resource deficits and needs. These should be diagnosed early on in the helping process and the development of human resources "out there" made one of the aims in almost every counseling case.

Make sure that environmental obstacles can be managed. A goal is not really a goal if there are environmental obstacles that prevent its accomplishment—obstacles, that is, that cannot be overcome by the use of available resources.

> Jessie feels like a second-class citizen at work. He feels that his supervisor gives him most of the dirty work and that there is an undercurrent of prejudice against Hispanics in the plant. He wants to quit and get another

job, one that would pay the same relatively good wages he is now earning. However, the country is deep into a recession, and there are practically no jobs available in the area where he works. For the time being, his goal is not workable. He needs another, interim goal that relates to coping with his present situation.

Sometimes an interim goal can be to find a way around an environmental obstacle. For instance, it may be that there are openings in other departments of the factory in which Jessie works but not in his specialty. An interim goal might be to get training at work that makes him more flexible. Once he is qualified, he can get a job in a different department.

Make sure that the goal is under the client's control. Sometimes clients defeat their own purposes by setting goals that are not under their control. For instance, it is common for people to believe that their problems would be solved if only other people would not act the way they do. In most cases, however, we do not have any direct control over the ways others act.

> Cybelene wanted a better relationship with her parents. She said that the relationship would be better if only her parents would make fewer demands on her now that she is married and has her own career and home to attend to. It was under her control to let her parents know some of her needs, but there was relatively little she could do to make her parents respect these needs. For instance, she wanted her parents to come to her new home for either Thanksgiving or Christmas. Her parents, however, insisted that she and her husband come to their house, since both of these celebrations were "traditional" and therefore best spent "back home." She refused to go home for both, and her parents kept telling her how much they were hurt.

Usually, clients have much more freedom in changing their own behavior than the behavior of others. Consider the following example.

> Tony, a 16-year-old boy, felt that he was the victim of his parents' inability to relate to each other. Each tried to use him in the struggle, and at times he felt like a ping-pong ball. A counselor helped him see that he could probably do little to control his parents' behavior, but that he might be able to do quite a bit to control his reactions to his parents' attempts to use him. For instance, when his parents started to fight, he could simply leave instead of trying to "help." If either tried to enlist him as an ally, he could say that he had no way of knowing who was right. Tony also worked at creating a good social life outside the home. This helped him weather the tension he experienced there.

Tony's goal is a new pattern of behavior, that is, a new way of managing his parents' attempts to use him.

Help client set goals that don't cost too much. Some goals that can be accomplished carry too high a cost in relation to the payoff. It may sound overly technical to ask whether any given goal is "cost effective," but the principle remains important. Skilled counselors help clients budget rather than squander their resources.

> Enid discovered that she had a terminal illness. In talking with several doctors, she found out that she would be able to prolong her life a bit through a combination of surgery, radiation treatment, and chemotherapy. However, no one suggested that these would lead to a cure. She also found out what each of these three forms of treatment and each combination would cost, not so much in terms of money, but in terms of added anxiety and pain. Ultimately she decided against all three, since no combination of them promised much in terms of the quality of the life that was being prolonged. Instead, with the help of a doctor she developed a scenario that would ease both her anxiety and her physical pain as much as possible.

It goes without saying that another patient might have made a different decision. Costs and payoffs are relative. Some clients might value an extra month of life no matter what the cost.

Goals should be set neither too high nor too low. If they are set too high, counseling can do more harm than good.

> Nothing breeds success like success. Conversely, nothing causes feelings of despair like perpetual failure. A primary purpose of goal setting is to increase the motivation level of the individual. But goal setting can have precisely the opposite effect if it produces a yardstick that constantly makes the individual feel inadequate. (Locke & Latham, 1984, p. 39)

The counselor must help clients challenge goals that are set too high.

5. Making Goals Substantive

Help clients develop substantive goals.

Goals are unrealistic if they are too high, but they are inadequate if they are set too low. A goal is adequate only if its accomplishment is relevant to the original problem situation and contributes in a substantial way to managing the situation or some part of it. I knew a man whose "solution" to his marital problems was to go off to an island in the Indian Ocean and become a beach bum for a few months. Needless to say, his solution was relevant to the problem situation only in the sense that it was a further expression of it. To take another example, if a client drinks two fifths of gin and one can of beer per week, her drinking problem will not be effectively handled if she eliminates the beer. If the quality of the time spent by a man at home is not good, then merely increasing the time spent at home will do little to help him develop a better relationship with his family.

If the problem is not clearly defined, then it may be impossible to determine whether a given goal is a substantive response to it.

Doug was extremely anxious and depressed when he learned that he would have to undergo major surgery for the removal of a brain tumor. There was no way of telling whether the tumor was malignant or benign until the surgery had been performed. A minister talked to him in rather general terms about "the love of God" and suggested that he pray more. Doug became more and more agitated.

In crisis situations such as this, it might be terribly difficult to help a client identify a goal or scenario that will contribute in a substantial way to handling his or her emotions. In Doug's case, just "holding on" might have been a reasonable agenda if given expression in some meaningful goals. Suggesting stylized goals or activities that have little meaning for the client ("just pray harder") might only make things worse. An effective counselor might have been able to help Doug develop some images of hope and find ways of hanging on until the operation.

Substantial goals stretch clients—but not to the breaking point. Helping clients get a realistic idea of what success looks like in their problem areas can benefit them a great deal. The best quarterbacks in football complete only six out of every ten passes; the best basketball players make only about half their shots; successful TV actors may be turned down in 95% of their auditions. Of course, what counts as stretching might be quite different from one client to another. And all clients run the risk of setting goals that are so substantive that they become unrealistic. No formulas. Help each client.

6. Making Goals Consistent with the Client's Values

Help clients develop goals in keeping with their values.

As we have seen, although helping is a process of social influence, it remains ethical only if it respects, within reason, the values of the client. Values are criteria we use to make decisions. While helpers may challenge clients to reexamine their values, they should in no way encourage clients to perform actions that are not in keeping with their values. For instance, the son of Antonio and Consuela Garza is in a coma in the hospital after an automobile accident. He needs a life-support system to remain alive. His parents are experiencing a great deal of uncertainty, pain, and anxiety. They have been told that there is practically no chance that their son will ever come out of the coma. The counselor should not urge them to terminate the life-support system if that action is counter to their values. However, the counselor can help them explore and clarify the values involved. In this case the counselor suggests that they discuss their decision with a clergyman. In doing so, they find out that the termination of the life-support system would not be against the tenets of their religion. Now they are free to explore other values that relate to their decision.

It is impossible to help clients make good choices without helping them clarify the values and principles on which they are basing these choices. Tom, the client with AIDS discussed in the last chapter, does not have the time and the resources to choose and accomplish all the elements in his scenario. He needs to be helped to review his values and use them as criteria in setting priorities.

Some clients show dissatisfaction because their behavior is guided by conflicting or contradictory goals or because they experience an inconsistency or clash in values. These clients often complain that their behavior in one life sector or at one time is incompatible with their beliefs in another sector or at another time. Such clients can be aided by a reordering of the importance of various goals and values or by a compromise in setting different goals for different life sectors. Dan, the ex-Marine, wants to get an education, but he also wants to make a decent living. The former goal will put him in debt, but failing to get a college education will lessen his chances of securing the kind of job he wants. In this case the counselor helps him identify and use his values to sort out tradeoffs in the decision-making process. Dan chooses to work part-time and go to school part-time. He chooses a job in an office over a construction job. Even though the latter pays better, it is much more exhausting and would leave him with little energy for school.

7. Establishing Realistic Time Frames

Help clients set realistic time frames for the accomplishment of goals.

Goals that are to be accomplished "sometime" probably won't be accomplished at all. If Jon says: "I'm going to spend three out of every four weekends and three out of every five weekday evenings at home with my family whenever business conditions stabilize again," then he violates this condition, because the time frame is not clear. If his business is bad and needs a great deal of attention, then the deteriorating relationship with his family will have to be managed in some way other than spending more time at home. For instance, another aim might be to increase the quality of the time he does spend at home. This, of course, is merely an aim and would have to be translated into more specific goals.

Here, too, flexibility is called for. Greenberg (1986) talked about "immediate outcomes," that is, changes evident in the helping sessions themselves; "intermediate changes," that is, changes in attitudes and behaviors that lead to further change; and "final outcomes," that is, the completion of the overall agenda through which problems are managed and opportunities developed. For Jensen, a 22-year-old on probation for shoplifting, an immediate outcome was the lessening of his resistance to his court-appointed counselor; he quickly came to see her as "on his side." An intermediate change was attitudinal. Besotted by commercial television, he thought that America owed him some of its affluence and that personal effort had little to do with it. The counselor helped him see that everyone was not a Lotto winner by right, that hard work played a key role in most payoffs. The final outcome in Jensen's case was a probation period free of any further shoplifting attempts and a job that helped him pay his debt to a retailer.

Taussig (1987) talks about mini-goals set and executed early in the helping process. Such mini-goals not only are important in themselves, but have the potential for kicking off a process of goal-relatedness in the client's life.

> Terry, 16, was arrested for arson. Though he lived in the inner city and came from a single-parent household, it was difficult to discover just why he had turned to arson. He had torched a few structures that seemed safe to burn. No one was injured. Was his behavior a cry for help? Social rage expressed in vandalism? A way of getting kicks? The social worker assigned to the case found these questions quite speculative and tried to help Terry set some simple goals that appealed to him and that could be accomplished relatively quickly. One week she asked him to come back the next time with the story of the Great Chicago Fire. He did, and he liked his first foray into history. She included him in the search for other mini-goals that appealed to him. Terry profited from these small successes. Goal setting began to become important to him.

Goal setting is not a facile answer to intractable social problems. Sometimes, however, if goal setting can become a challenge followed by mini-successes rather than a chore followed by failure, then a process of goal-relatedness can be kicked off for clients. At any rate, this did work for Terry.

There is no such thing as a set time frame for every client. Some goals need to be accomplished now, some soon; others are mid-term goals; still others are long-term. Consider Dan, our ex-Marine.

- *A "now" goal:* Some immediate relief from debilitating anxiety attacks, followed by a gradual decrease in the number and severity of the attacks.
- *A "soon" goal:* Better care of his personal appearance consistently in place.
- *A mid-term goal:* Decisions made with respect to the mix of school and work.
- *A long-term goal:* The fashioning of a career and prospects for marriage and a family.

There is no particular formula for helping all clients choose the right mix of goals at the right time and in the right sequence. Helping is based on scientific principles, but it remains an art.

Flexibility in Helping Clients Set Goals

In general, a goal, to be workable, must meet all seven of the requirements described in this chapter. The goal of the alcoholic mentioned above—to eliminate beer from her life—fulfilled all the criteria but one: It had little substance. Failure to meet one of the seven criteria may prove to be the fatal flaw in a client's movement toward problem-managing action.

There is another way of saying this that opens the door for some flexibility in helping clients set goals and craft agendas. When clients finally act in their own interests and these actions actually accomplish problem-managing or opportunity-developing outcomes, the seven characteristics outlined above are in place whether they have been dealt with explicitly in the helping process or not.

> A young man from the People's Republic of China, studying in the United States, was horrified by the massacre of students in Beijing, the subsequent crackdown on student dissent, and the spate of executions. He tried to figure out what he could do to publicize his opposition to what was happening in his homeland. After talking through with a counselor the emotions that were flooding through him, he decided that he wanted to do something that would put his opposition on public record. He explored with the counselor the possible consequences of doing so. This is as far as he got with the counselor. Afterward, however, he organized an open forum in Washington in which a dozen excellent students from different universities openly discussed their reactions to the events in China. Since the forum received both TV and press coverage, it came to the attention of Chinese officials, and the students knew that they were now in jeopardy.

The Chinese student had discussed only an overall aim with the counselor—to do something public to express his opposition to events at home. But the final event had all seven characteristics outlined in this chapter. It was a clear, verifiable, realistic, and substantial accomplishment in keeping with his values and carried out within a reasonable time frame.

It is not always necessary, then, to make sure that each goal in a client's agenda has all of the seven characteristics. For some clients, like the Chinese student, aims are enough. For others, some help with goals is called for. The principle is clear: Help clients develop goals and agendas that have some probability of success. In one case, this may mean helping a client deal with clarity; in another, with substance; in still another, with realism, values, or time frame. The helping model, including the "tools" for crafting workable agendas outlined in this chapter, provides a menu of interventions. Which interventions a helper chooses in any given case depends on what the client needs, wants, and will tolerate.

HELPING CLIENTS UNDERSTAND THE CONSEQUENCES OF THEIR CHOICE OF GOALS

To make reasonable decisions about goals, clients often need help exploring the consequences of their choice of scenarios or goals. Consider the case of Tom, the man with AIDS. One part of his agenda was to make peace with one or two of his closest friends who abandoned him when they found out that he had AIDS. While he can work for reconciliation, reconciliation itself demands the good will of all the parties involved. Since he has not been contacted by his friends, he would have to initiate contact even though he feels that he is the offended party. His effort might, in the long run, prove futile, in which case he would have to face the pain of rejection once more and perhaps even more intensely. Tom can ask himself how much reconcilation would contribute to the quality of his life now that he knows that his life is quite limited. It could be that a partial reconciliation would only cause him more anxiety. Tom can ask himself:

- *What would life be like if this goal were to be accomplished?* What satisfactions would accomplishing this goal involve for me? To what degree would it take care of the concerns I am feeling right now? To what degree would it be an implementation of values I hold dear?
- *What would life be like if this goal were not to be accomplished?* Would it mean that my present concerns would not be substantially managed?

Answering these questions will help Tom establish some priorities among his goals. In the end, he might decide to put off reconciliation attempts for the time being because his goal of establishing a community of human resources on which he can depend has higher priority for him.

A final example: Janice, a woman with an unwanted pregnancy, can be helped to sort out the consequences of different options. She can have an abortion, she can have the child and keep it without getting married, she can marry the father and have and keep the child, she can have the child and put him or her up for adoption immediately. To assess the consequences adequately, Janice needs to review her own values and become aware of the probable or usual consequences associated with each possibility. For instance, it would help her to know how many women in her situation choose to have and keep the child without getting married and how this decision works out. In this case, the counselor would need to be informed about the sociology of unwanted pregnancies or know how to help Janice get this information.

STEP II-B: LINKS TO ACTION

Helping clients set goals that are both realistic and challenging, so the research tells us (Locke & Latham, 1984), is one of the best ways to help them get moving in the right direction.

First, setting goals *focuses* clients' attention and action. Agendas give clients a vision toward which they can direct their energies. Clients with clear goals are less likely to engage in aimless behavior both within the helping sessions and in everyday life.

Second, setting goals *mobilizes* energy and effort. Clients who seem lethargic while exploring problem situations often come to life when it comes to exploring problem-managing goals. Goal setting, although in itself a cognitive exercise, arouses in clients a need to act.

Third, setting goals tends to *increase persistence*. Clients with goals not only are energized to do something, but tend to work longer and harder than clients who have some direction but no specific goals. Clients with clear and realistic goals don't give up as easily as clients with vague goals or no goals at all.

Fourth, setting goals motivates clients to *search for strategies* to accomplish them. Setting goals, a Stage II task, leads naturally into a search for strategies, a Stage III task. The focus moves from the *what* to the *how*.

EVALUATION QUESTIONS FOR STEP II-B

- Am I helping clients craft agendas from among a reasonable number of preferred-scenario possibilities?
- To what extent are the goals set by each client
  - stated as accomplishments?
  - clear and specific?
  - measurable or verifiable?
  - realistic?
  - substantive?
  - in keeping with the client's values?
  - set in a reasonable time frame?
- How well do I challenge clients to translate declarations of intent into aims and aims into goals?
- To what degree am I helping clients own the process of goal setting?
- How effectively do I help clients explore the consequences of the goals they are setting?
- How well do I use principles but avoid formulas in helping each client approach goal setting in a way that makes sense to him or her?

Chapter Thirteen

Step II-C: Helping Clients Commit to Agendas

In an earlier chapter we explored some of the sources of resistance. Resistance, of course, can appear at any time in the helping process. It can be expected especially (1) at times when clients need to make decisions and (2) at times when clients need to move from discussion to action. When effort is required of us, there is something in each of us that asks, "Why should I?" The poet Goethe suggested an answer:

> The moment one definitely commits oneself, then providence moves too. All sorts of things occur to help one that would never otherwise have occurred. A whole stream of events issues from the decision, raising in one's favor all manner of unforeseen incidents and meetings and material assistance which no one could have dreamed would have come his way. Whatever you can do or dream you can, *begin it.* . . . Begin it now.

It seems that Goethe knew something about self-efficacy (Bandura, 1986) before the term was invented. However, committing ourselves to preferred scenarios means dealing not just with "possible selves" (Markus & Nurius, 1986) that we *want* to become, but possible selves we are *afraid* of becoming. How can counselors help clients move beyond their hesitations to commit themselves?

THE PERSONAL POLITICS OF COMMITMENT

Making decisions and moving to action involve the commitment of the client's resources, both physical and psychological. These resources are not in endless supply. The drama is set. It is as if the client's "old self" or old lifestyle is vying for resources with the client's "new self" or new lifestyle. Politics is about, among other things, vying for scarce resources. In a sense, therefore, commitment on the part of clients involves the personal politics of behavior change. "Why should I pursue this agenda? Is it worth it? Where do I want to invest my limited resources of time, energy, money, and effort? What competes for my attention? What other goals compete against the goals I have chosen? How strong are these competing goals? Who are my allies and my adversaries in this struggle?"

It can be a tough job to help clients realign their priorities, tap into their scarce resources, and place them at the service of a problem-managing or opportunity-developing agenda. Figure 13-1 adds this final step to Stage II. Again, there is no formula. Some clients, once they establish goals, race to accomplish them. At the other end of the spectrum are clients who, once they decide on goals, stop dead in the water. Further, the same client might speed toward the accomplishment of one goal and drag her feet on another. In Step II-C the job of the counselor is to help clients face up to the personal politics of commitment. Of course, if the client's goals involve relationships with other people, then the political picture is even more complicated. What happens to one spouse when the other stops

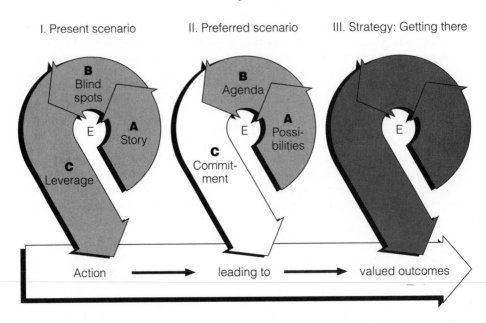

I. Present scenario   II. Preferred scenario   III. Strategy: Getting there

B Blind spots   **B** Agenda

E   **A** Story   E   **A** Possi-bilities   E

C Commit-ment

C Leverage

Action ——→ leading to ——→ valued outcomes

FIGURE 13-1   Step II-C: Helping Clients Commit to Agendas

drinking? What if a great deal of a spouse's identity has come to center on "caring for an invalid"? To some spouses the reformation would come as a great relief; to others it would mean loss of identity and a challenge to reorient their lives.

HELPING CLIENTS MAKE AN INITIAL COMMITMENT TO GOALS

To help us explore the personal politics of commitment, let's consider a new twist to Dan's story.

> Ed, Dan's counselor, did not find out until they were well into the helping process that Dan was a heavy user of tranquilizers such as Valium and a variety of painkillers. Dan found it relatively easy to get the drugs he thought he needed. Since helping is often a back-and-forth process, Ed returned to Stage I and helped Dan explore this newly discovered problem area. He challenged Dan to use his common sense in exploring his dependency.
>
> One day Dan came in and said, "I ran across a saying that probably relates to me: 'He who has himself as a doctor has a fool for a patient.'" His first mini-goal was to see a doctor to talk about his drug problem. The politics of commitment soon emerged. Dan kept coming back to the sessions with an array of excuses as to why it had been "impossible" to see the doctor. When he finally did make and keep an appointment, it was decided

that he could drop the painkillers immediately but that he should withdraw more gradually from the Valium, which he used heavily. He and the doctor worked out the withdrawal schedule. Ed helped Dan monitor it. When Dan became evasive about the withdrawal program, Ed knew that the politics of commitment was front and center once more.

Dan is what we might call a "good" client: he is hurting, and his motivation is relatively high. However, this does not mean that he will not manifest resistance. Never be surprised at resistance from any client.

There is a difference between initial commitment to a goal and an ongoing commitment to a strategy or plan to accomplish the goal. The proof of initial commitment is some movement to action. Ongoing commitment takes the form not only of steady progress toward goals but also of getting up and moving forward after failures. This chapter deals with initial commitment. Chapter 17 deals with ongoing commitment.

There are a range of things you can do to help clients in their initial commitment to goals and the actions that lead to their implementation. Many of these are logical extensions of the criteria established in Step I-C for choosing problems for attention. Leverage here deals with commitment. Help clients set goals that involve the following characteristics.

- *Ownership.* Make sure that the goals chosen are the client's goals.
- *Appeal.* Help clients set appealing agendas and goals and find ways of increasing their appeal.
- *Options.* To the degree possible, help clients choose goals from among options.
- *Reduction of crisis and pain.* Focus on goals that will reduce the client's pain.
- *Detailed scenarios.* Help clients add useful detail to their preferred scenarios.
- *Challenge.* Help clients set not just substantive goals but challenging ones.
- *Management of disincentives.* Help clients see ways of managing current disincentives that stand in the way of goal attainment.
- *Contracts.* Use contracts to help clients commit themselves to their choices.
- *Action strategies.* Help clients identify strategies for accomplishing their goals

In this section we examine each of these points.

1. Ownership

Make sure that the goals clients set are their own.

It is essential that the goals chosen be the client's rather than the helper's goals or someone else's. Various kinds of probes can be used to help clients discover what they want to do in order to manage some dimension of a problem situation more effectively. For instance, Carl Rogers, in a film of a counseling session (Rogers, Perls, & Ellis, 1965), is asked by a woman what she should do about her relationship with her daughter. He says to her: "I think you've been telling me all along what you want to do." She knew what she wanted the relationship to look like; what she was asking for was his approval. If he had given it, the goal would, to some degree, have become his goal instead of hers. At another time he asks: "What is it that you want me to tell you to do?" This question puts the responsibility for goal setting where it belongs—on the shoulders of the client.

> Cynthia was dealing with a lawyer because of an impending divorce. They had talked about what was to be done with the children, but no decision had been reached. One day she came in and said that she had decided on mutual custody. She wanted to work out such details as which residence, hers or her husband's, would be the children's principal one and so forth. The lawyer asked her how she had reached a decision. She said that she had been talking to her husband's parents—she was still on very good terms with them—and that they had suggested this arrangement. The lawyer challenged Cynthia to take a closer look at her decision. "Let's start from zero," he said, "and you tell me what arrangements you want." He did not want to help her carry out a decision that was not her own.

Clients tend to work harder for goals that are their own. Moreover, choosing goals they do not own enables them to blame others if they fail to reach the goals or if they find out that reaching them does little to help them manage a problem situation.

2. Appeal

Help the client set an appealing agenda.

This is common sense, but sometimes it is difficult to help clients choose goals that really appeal to them, especially if they are reluctant to act in the first place or if the goal demands that they give up something they like. For many if not most addicts, a drug-free life is not immediately appealing, to say the least.

> Ed tries to help Dan work through his resistance to giving up drugs. He listens and is empathic; he also challenges the way Dan has come to think about drugs and his dependency on them. Creating an image of a pre-ferred scenario is difficult because it is a question of giving something up. One day Ed says something about "giving up the crutch and walking straight." In a flash Dan sees himself as a cripple. Many of his buddies had become cripples in Beirut and could not wait for the day when they could throw their crutches away. Using drugs was like walking with a crutch. The image of "throwing away the crutch" and "walking straight" proved to be very appealing to Dan

Negative goals—giving something up—need to be translated into pos-itive goals, into getting something. It was much easier for Dan to commit himself to returning to school than to giving up drugs, because school represented a positive goal. Images of himself with a degree and of holding some kind of professional job appealed to him very much. In helping clients set goals, put yourself in their place and keep asking yourself, "Why should I?"

3. Options

Help clients choose goals from among options whenever possible.

Clients are more likely to commit themselves to goals if they choose from among options than if a goal seems forced. This is one reason why the work done in Step II-A to generate possibilities is very important. Counseling, at its best, has both a freeing and an enabling effect on clients.

> George, a heavy drinker, reviewed the options open to him and chose the option of cutting down on drink rather than eliminating it from his life. While his problems with drink decreased somewhat, he was still a problem drinker. He finally chose to eliminate drink altogether. He said that he felt free to do so because no one had forced him into such a "radical" decision from the beginning.

In this case, the counselor might know that alcoholics choosing to restrict rather than eliminate alcoholic intake are courting trouble, but—no formula. It may be better for a client to make a choice, even though it is not the "best" one, than to be talked into one. Perhaps if George had considered the option of eliminating drink entirely for a limited period of time, say two months or even two weeks, he could have experienced the benefits of an alcohol-free life without feeling constrained by a lack of choice in his goal setting.

4. Reduction of Crisis and Pain

Help clients choose goals that will manage a crisis or alleviate pain.

Clients are more likely to commit themselves to goals if they are hurting and if they see hope in new scenarios. Goals are instruments to help them reduce their emotional pain. However, since people who are hurting are more open to social influence, helpers must be careful not to influence vulnerable clients to adopt the helper's goals rather than their own.

> Ernesto, the gang member who had been severely beaten three times within a year, was wounded both physically and psychologically. Since he was hurting, he longed for a better future. At first his images of the future included establishing a rival gang and performing acts of revenge. When challenged to see that it was precisely this kind of behavior that put him in the hospital—that caused his crisis and pain—Ernesto slowly began to picture details of a social life outside the gangs. He needed a great deal of support and challenge to create these images, since practically all his social rewards had come from his membership in a gang.

Despite the caution about vulnerable clients, if a client is hesitant about creating new scenarios and setting goals, it may be that his or her current lifestyle is not experienced as all that uncomfortable. Some counselors see challenge as a way of making clients feel uncomfortable enough to want to change. A depressed person in a dead-end job who is reluctant to think of other possibilities can be challenged to spell out in detail the consequences of remaining in the job. It could be that the dismal images that evolve will make the client hurt enough to want to work toward a better future.

5. Detailed Scenarios

Help clients add useful detail to their preferred scenarios.
Detailed scenarios are more likely to drive behavior than vague ones. The details give the client a feeling for the usefulness of the change.

Robert, a computer specialist who had recently been operated on for testicular cancer, was still suffering from postoperative anxiety and depression a year after the operation. One testicle had been removed, but there was no physical reason why this should have interfered with a normal sexual life. His physical recovery had been excellent, and so his bouts of impotence were seen as psychological in origin. The counselor had Robert imagine a future in which the problems he was experiencing had disappeared. Robert, relying on his past experience, described in great detail what it was like feeling at peace rather than anxious, enthusiastic rather than depressed. He pictured himself having normal sexual relations that were as satisfying as any he had had in the past. He pictured himself feeling good about himself and carrying on a positive internal dialogue instead of putting himself down. He developed these detailed "images of a better future" not only during the counseling sessions but also outside. These positive images gradually drove out the cognitive load with which he had become burdened.

In this case, images of a better future constituted the centerpiece of the helping process. The details Robert created appealed to him so much that he was much more open to committing himself to do something.

6. Challenge

Help clients set not just substantive but challenging goals.
There is a good deal of research (Locke & Latham, 1984; Locke, Shaw, Saari, & Latham, 1981) suggesting that, other things being equal, harder goals can be more motivating than easier goals.

Extensive research . . . has established that, within reasonable limits, the . . . more challenging the goal, the better the resulting performance. . . .

[P]eople try harder to attain the hard goal. They exert more effort. . . . In short, people become motivated in proportion to the level of challenge with which they are faced. . . . Even goals that cannot be fully reached will lead to high effort levels, provided that partial success can be achieved and is rewarded. (Locke & Latham, 1984, p. 21, 26)

I met an AIDS patient who was, in the beginning, full of self-loathing and despair. Eventually, however, he painted a new scenario in which he saw himself, not as a victim of his own lifestyle, but rather as a helper to other AIDS patients. Until close to the time of his death, he worked hard, within the limits of his physical disabilities, seeking out other AIDS sufferers, getting them to join self-help groups, and generally helping them to manage an impossible situation in a more humane way. When he was near death, he said that the last two years of his life, though at times they were very bitter, were among the best years of his life. He had set his goals high, but they proved to be quite realistic.

7. Managing Disincentives

Help clients get rid of obstacles to goal commitment.

Clients are more likely to commit themselves to goals if they can get rid of a few roadblocks.

Joyce, a flight attendant nearing middle age, centered most of her non-flying life around her aging mother. By Joyce's admission, her mother had been pampered and given her way by her now-deceased husband and her three children all her life. Her mother now played the role of the tyrannical old woman who constantly feels neglected and who can never be satisfied, and she played it very well. Though Joyce was able to elaborate a number of scenarios in which she lived her own life without abandoning her mother, she found it very difficult to commit herself to any of them. Guilt stood in the way of any change in her relationship with her mother. She even said that being a virtual slave to her mother's whims was not as bad as the guilt she experienced when she stood up to her mother or "neglected" her.

The counselor helped Joyce experiment with a few new ways of dealing with her mother. For instance, Joyce went on a two-week trip with friends even though her mother objected, saying that it was ill-timed. Although the experiments were successful in that no harm was done to Joyce's mother and Joyce did not experience excessive guilt, counseling did not help her restructure her relationship with her mother in any radical way. The experiments did give her a sense of greater freedom. For instance, she felt freer to say no to this or that demand on the part of her mother. This provided enough slack, it seems, to make Joyce's life more livable.

In this case, counseling helped the client fashion a life that was "a little bit better," though not as good as the counselor thought it could be.

This example brings up the issue of what the decision-making litera-ture (Janis & Mann, 1977; Wheeler & Janis, 1980) calls "satisficing."

> [S]ometimes it is more reasonable to choose a satisfactory alternative than to continue searching for the absolute best. The time, energy, and ex-pense of finding the best possible choice may outweigh the improvement in the choice. (Wheeler & Janis, 1980, p. 98)

The problem with satisficing, of course, is that the client finds out later on that his or her choice is doing little to make life more acceptable. With Joyce, the counselor thought that little purpose would be served by con-tinuing to challenge her choice. Joyce's "new" scenario did not differ dramatically from the old. But perhaps it was enough for her. Only time would tell.

8. Contracts

Use contracts to help clients commit themselves to their choices.

The use of contracts for the helping process itself was discussed in Chapter 3. Specific contracts can also help clients commit themselves to new courses of action (Katz & Torres, 1982). While contracts are promises clients make to themselves to behave in certain ways and to attain certain goals, they are also ways of making new scenarios more focused, more salient. It is not only the expressed or implied promise that helps, but the explicitness of the commitment.

> About a month after one of Dora's two young sons disappeared, she began to grow listless and depressed. She was separated from her husband at the time the boy disappeared. By the time she saw a counselor a few months later, a pattern of depressed behavior was quite pronounced. While her conversations with the counselor helped ease her feelings of guilt—she stopped engaging in self-blaming rituals—she remained list-less. She shunned relatives and friends, kept to herself at work, and even distanced herself emotionally from her other son. She resisted developing images of a better future, because the only better future she would allow herself to imagine was one in which her son had returned.
>
> Some strong confrontation from both Dora's counselor and her sister-in-law, who still visited her from time to time, helped jar her loose from her preoccupation with her own misery. "You're trying to solve one hurt, the loss of Bobby, by hurting Timmy and hurting yourself. I can't imagine in a thousand years that that's what Bobby would want!" her sister-in-law screamed at her one night. Afterward Dora and the counselor discussed a "recommitment" to Timmy, to herself, and to their home. Through a se-ries of contracts she began to reintroduce patterns of behavior that had been characteristic of her before the tragedy. For instance, she contracted to opening her life up to relatives and friends once more, to creating a

much more positive atmosphere at home, to encouraging Timmy to have his friends over, and so forth. Contracts worked for Dora because, as she said to the counselor, "I'm a person of my word."

Contracts helped Dora in both her initial commitment to a goal and her movement to action. In counseling, contracts are not legal documents but human instruments to be used if they are helpful. They often provide both the structure and the incentives clients need in order to act.

9. Action Strategies

Help clients find action strategies to pursue and accomplish their goals.
Finally, clients are more likely to commit themselves to goals if they are helped to see precisely what they need to do to get where they want to go. This is the work of Stage III and is covered in the next three chapters.

Are there other ways of helping clients commit themselves to goals and to initial action toward these goals? Of course. One of your jobs as a helper is the continual search for methods for helping clients move through each stage and step that relates to their situation.

HELPING CLIENTS TRANSLATE COMMITMENT INTO ACTION

"The proof of the pudding," so the saying goes, "lies in the eating thereof." The proof of commitment lies in the kind of problem-managing action that flows from it.

> A woman with two sons in their twenties was dying of cancer. The doctors thought she could go at any time. However, one day she told the doctor that she wanted to live to see her older son get married in six months' time. The doctor talked vaguely about "trusting in God" and "playing the cards she had been dealt."
>
> Against all odds the woman lived to see her son get married. Her doctor was at the wedding. During the reception he went up to her and said, "Well, you got what you wanted. Despite the way things are going, you must be deeply satisfied." She looked at him wryly and said, "But, Doctor, my second son will get married some day."

We all know stories of how the will to do something has been so strong in a person that he or she has been able to accomplish seemingly impossible things. The *ability* of clients to commit themselves to accomplish problem-managing and opportunity-developing goals usually surpasses the degree to which they actually commit themselves. Gilbert (1978), I am sure, would see this from an optimistic perspective, more as a cause for hope than as a reason for despair. He would see a client's unused *ability*

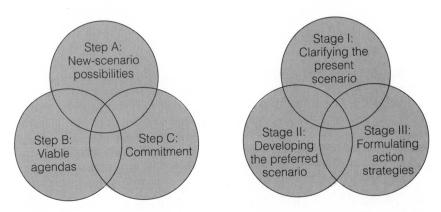

FIGURE 13-2 Overlays in the Steps and Stages of the Helping Process

to commit himself or herself as a rather large PIP, that is, "potential for improving performance." The psychopathology of the average that afflicts us all cuts two ways. If I am using 20% of my ability, I have 80% in reserve. The trick is to translate potential into action.

In practice the three steps of Stage II will overlap, just as Stage II itself will overlap with the other two stages. This is illustrated in Figure 13-2. Clients will commit themselves to new scenarios, redo them, act on them, redo them again, go back and redefine the problem situation, and engage in other permutations of the helping process. In principle there is nothing wrong with this. However, counselors should help clients find some overall direction in the helping process itself and avoid merely random approaches to working out their problems in living.

EVALUATION QUESTIONS FOR STEP II-C

- What do I do to make sure that the goals the client is setting are really his or her goals and not mine or those of a third party?
- In what ways do I help clients focus on the appealing dimensions of the goals being set?
- How effectively do I perceive and deal with the misgivings clients have about the goals they are formulating?
- How do I help a client who feels that he or she has too few options?
- How effectively do I help clients focus on the pain-reduction potential of the goals they are setting?
- What do I do if I perceive that the client does not find the goals being developed very challenging?
- How effectively do I help clients handle the disincentives that stand in the way of full commitment to goals?
- To what degree do I help clients enter into contracts with respect to the accomplishment of goals?
- What do I do to help clients move to initial goal-accomplishing action?
- What do I do when clients fail to act, even initially, on goals they set?

STAGE III: LINKING PREFERRED
SCENARIOS TO ACTION
The Tasks of Stage III

The next three chapters outline and illustrate the steps and tasks of Stage III, moving to action. These include:

Step III-A: Helping clients **develop strategies** for bringing preferred scenarios on line.

Step III-B: Helping clients choose **best-fit strategies** tailored to their preferences, capabilities, and resources.

Step III-C: Helping clients **formulate plans**, or ordered "packages" of strategies.

All of this has been put much more poetically by Henry David Thoreau:

If you have built castles in the air, your work need not be lost; there is where they should be. Now put foundations under them.

Setting substantial goals is not a problem if the strategies for implementing them are identified and carried out. Stage II deals with *what* needs to be in place. Stage III deals with *how* to get there. The theory is that knowing what needs to be accomplished (preferred-scenario goals) makes the process of finding and implementing action strategies more focused and efficient.

As indicated earlier, some problems are coped with and managed, not solved. Consider the following case.

Some 20 years ago, Vickey was diagnosed as manic-depressive. She admits that she has never fully "conquered" her illness. The current picture looks something like this: "I have six weeks on a high, then the crash comes and for about six weeks I'm in the pits, and then for about eight weeks I'm normal." About 12 years ago, five years into her "illness," during a period in which she was in and out of the hospital, she made a decision. "I'm not going back into the hospital again."

In terms of Step II-B, Vickey's agenda consisted of the following aims:

- highs managed, energy channeled;
- lows managed or at least endured;
- disruptive behavior minimized, silly decisions avoided.

Vickey learned as much as she could about her illness, including cues about crisis times and how to deal with both highs and lows. To manage her highs, she learned to channel her excess energy into useful—or at least not destructive—activity. Some of her strategies for controlling her highs centered on the telephone. She set up her own phone-answering business and worked very hard to make it work. During her free time she would spend long hours on the phone with a host of friends, being careful not to overburden any one person. Phone marathons became part of her lifestyle. She made the point that a big phone bill was infinitely better than a stay in the hospital. She called the telephone her "safety valve." At the time of her highs, she would do whatever she had to do to tire herself out and get some sleep, for she had learned that sleep was essential if she was to stay out of the hospital. This included working longer shifts at the business. She developed a cadre of supportive people, including her husband. She took special care not to overburden him. She made occasional use of a drop-in crisis center, but preferred avoiding any course of action that reminded her of the hospital.

Here is a woman who took charge of her life. She set some simple goals and devised a set of simple strategies for accomplishing them. She had a plan for managing her highs and lows and implemented it consistently. To this day, she has not gone back to the hospital. Some would say that her approach lacks elegance. Who cares!

Chapter Fourteen

Step III-A: Helping Clients Develop Strategies for Action

Some clients, once they have a clear idea of what they want to do to manage some problem situation, mobilize their own and whatever environmental resources are necessary to achieve their goals. Other clients, however, even though they have a fairly clear understanding of the problem situation and know where they want to go, still lack a clear idea of how to get there. Consider the following examples.

> Jeff had been in the army for about ten months. He found himself both overworked and, perhaps not paradoxically, bored. He had a couple of sessions with one of the educational counselors on the base. During these sessions Jeff began to see quite clearly that not having a high school diploma was working against him. The counselor mentioned that he could finish high school while in the army. Jeff realized that this possibility had been pointed out to him during the orientation talks, but he hadn't paid any attention to it. He had joined the army because he wasn't interested in school and couldn't find a job. Now he decided that he would get a high school diploma as soon as possible.
>
> Jeff obtained the authorization needed from his company commander to go to school. He found out what courses he needed and enrolled in time for the next school session. It didn't take him long to finish. Once he received his high school degree, he felt better about himself and found that opportunities for more interesting jobs opened up for him in the army. Achieving his goal of getting a high school degree helped him manage the problem situation.

Jeff was one of those fortunate ones who, with a little help, quickly set a goal (the "what") and identify and implement the strategies (the "how") to accomplish it. Note, too, that his goal of getting a diploma was also a means to other goals—feeling good about himself and getting better jobs in the army.

Jeff's experience is quite different from Grace's. She needed much more help.

> As long as she could remember, Grace had been a fearful person. She was especially afraid of being rejected and of being a failure. As a result, she had a rather impoverished social life and had held a series of jobs that were safe but boring. She became so depressed that she made a half-hearted attempt at suicide, probably more a cry of anguish and for help than a serious attempt to get rid of her problems by getting rid of herself.
>
> During the resulting stay in the hospital Grace had a few therapy sessions with one of the staff psychiatrists. The psychiatrist was supportive and helped her handle both the guilt she felt because of the suicide attempt and the depression that had led to the attempt. Just talking to someone about things she usually kept to herself seemed to help. She began to see her depression as a case of "learned helplessness." She saw quite clearly how she had let her choices be dictated by her fears. She also began to realize that she had a number of underused resources. For instance, she was intelligent and, though not good-looking, attractive in other ways. She had a fairly good sense of humor, though she seldom gave

herself the opportunity to use it. She was also sensitive to others and basically caring.

After Grace was discharged from the hospital, she returned for a few outpatient sessions. She got to the point where she wanted to do something about her general fearfulness and her passivity, especially the passivity in her social life. A psychiatric social worker taught her relaxation and thought-control techniques that helped her reduce her anxiety. Once she felt less anxious, she was in a better position to do something about establishing some social relationships. With the social worker's help, she set goals of acquiring a couple of friends and becoming a member of some social group. However, she was at a loss as to how to proceed, since she thought that friendship and a fuller social life were things that should happen "naturally." She soon came to realize that many people had to work at acquiring a more satisfying social life, that for some people there was nothing automatic about it at all.

The social worker helped Grace identify various kinds of social groups that she might join. She was then helped to see which of these would best meet her needs without placing too much stress on her. She finally chose to join an arts and crafts group at a local YMCA. The group gave her an opportunity to begin developing some of her talents and to meet people without having to face demands for intimate social contact. It also gave her an opportunity to take a look at other, more socially oriented programs sponsored by the Y. In the arts and crafts program she met a couple of people she liked and who seemed to like her. She began having coffee with them once in a while and then an occasional dinner.

Grace still needed support and encouragement from her helper, but she was gradually becoming less anxious and feeling less isolated. Once in a while she would let her anxiety get the better of her. She would skip a meeting at the Y and then lie about having attended. However, as she began to let herself trust her helper more, she revealed this self-defeating game. The social worker helped her develop coping stategies for those times when anxiety seemed to be higher.

Grace's problems were more severe than Jeff's, and she did not have as many immediate resources. Therefore, she needed both more time and more attention to develop goals and strategies

Helping clients develop strategies to achieve goals can be a most thoughtful, humane, and fruitful way of being with them. This step in the counseling process is another that helpers sometimes avoid because it is too "technological." However, in my experience, many clients get stuck at the strategy stage. They have in common some idea of what they want without knowing how to get it.

THE DEVELOPMENT OF ACTION STRATEGIES

Strategy is the art of identifying and choosing realistic courses of action for achieving goals and doing so under adverse (war) conditions. The problem situations in which clients are immersed constitute adverse conditions; they often are at war with themselves and the world around them.

For many clients, the problem is not that they refuse to act. Rather, they act without direction or they act imprudently. Rushing off to try the first "strategy" that comes to mind is not prudent action.

> Elmer injured his back and underwent a couple of operations. After the second operation he felt a little better, but then his back began troubling him again. When the doctor told him that further operations would not help, Elmer was faced with the problem of handling chronic pain. It soon became clear that his psychological state affected the level of pain. When he was anxious or depressed, the pain always seemed much worse.
>
> Elmer was talking to a counselor about all of this when he read about a pain clinic located in a western state. Without consulting anyone, he signed up for a six-week program. Within ten days he was back, feeling more depressed than ever. He had gone to the program with extremely high expectations because his needs were great. The program was a holistic one that helped the participants develop a more realistic lifestyle. It included programs dealing with nutrition and quality of interpersonal life. Group counseling was part of the whole picture, and the groups included a training-as-treatment approach. For instance, the participants were trained in behavioral approaches to the management of pain. The trouble was that Elmer had arrived at the clinic, which was located on a converted farm, with unrealistic expectations. He had expected to find marvels of modern medicine that would magically help him. He was extremely disappointed when he found that the program focused on reducing and managing rather than eliminating pain.

Elmer's aim was to be free of pain, and he refused to see that this might not be possible. A more realistic aim would have been to reduce and manage pain. He did not spend enough time setting up a realistic goal and, in his desperation, seized the first "strategy" that came along.

Brainstorming of possible strategies to accomplish goals, Step III-A of the helping process illustrated in Figure 14-1, is usually a very fruitful exercise. The research on problem solving (D'Zurilla & Goldfried, 1971; Heppner, 1978) suggests that the quality and efficacy of an action program tend to be better if the program is chosen from among a number of possibilities. Consider the case of Karen, who has come to realize that heavy drinking is ruining her life. Her goal is to stop drinking. She feels that it simply would not be enough to cut down; she has to stop. To her the program seems simple enough: whereas before she drank, now she won't. Because of the novelty of not drinking, she is successful for a few days; then she falls off the wagon. This happens a number of times until she finally realizes that she could use some help. Stopping drinking, at least for her, is not as simple as it seemed.

A counselor at a city alcohol and drug treatment center helps her explore a number of techniques that could be used in an alcohol management program. Together they come up with the following possibilities.

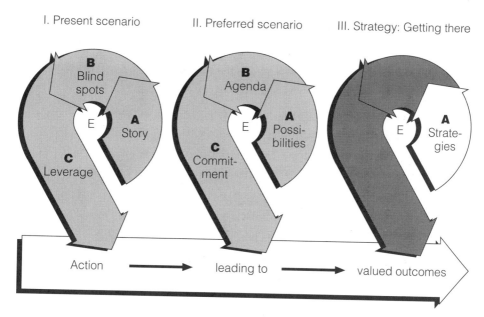

FIGURE 14-1   Step III-A: Developing Action Strategies

- Join Alcoholics Anonymous.
- Move someplace declared "dry" by local government.
- Take Antabuse, a drug that causes nausea if followed by alcohol.
- Replace drinking with other rewarding behaviors.
- Join some self-help group other than Alcoholics Anonymous.
- Get rid of all liquor in the house.
- Take the "pledge" not to drink; to make it more binding, take it in front of a minister.
- Join a residential hospital detoxification program.
- Avoid friends who drink heavily.
- Change other social patterns; for instance, find places other than bars and cocktail lounges to socialize.
- Try hypnosis to reduce the drive to drink.
- Use behavior modification techniques to develop an aversion for alcohol; for instance, pair painful but safe electric shocks with drinking or even thoughts about drinking.
- Change self-defeating patterns of self-talk, such as "I have to have a drink" or "One drink won't hurt me."
- Become a volunteer to help others stop drinking.
- Read books and view films on the dangers of alcohol.
- Stay in counseling as a way of getting support and challenge for stopping.
- Share intentions of stopping drinking with family and close friends.
- Stop without help from anyone else.

- Spend a week with an acquaintance who does a great deal of work in the city with alcoholics, and go on his rounds with him.
- Walk around skid row meditatively.
- Have a discussion with members of the family about the impact drinking has on them.
- Discover things to eat that might help reduce the craving for alcohol.
- Get a hobby or avocation that captures the imagination.
- Substitute a range of self-enhancing activities for drinking.

While this is not an exhaustive list, it contains many more items than Karen would have thought of had she not been stimulated by the counselor to take a census of possible strategies. One of the reasons that clients are clients is that they are not very creative in looking for ways of getting what they want. Once goals are established, getting them accomplished is not just a matter of hard work. It is also a matter of imagination.

Rook (1985) reviews strategies for helping the lonely and socially isolated. Since strategies are ways of achieving goals, she first discusses three general goals: (1) helping lonely people establish satisfying interpersonal ties; (2) helping prevent loneliness from evolving into or contributing to more serious problems such as depression, drug abuse, or suicide; and (3) helping people prevent rather than remedy loneliness. In each category she considers individual, group, and environmental strategies.

> One project took place in inner-city, single-room occupancy hotels that housed many elderly persons. Physical disability, poverty, and fear of crime prevented most of these inner-city residents from venturing beyond their hotel rooms, and as a result their social contacts were extremely limited. Public health nurses set up stations in the lobbies of these hotels and offered free blood pressure checkups as an initial means of contact. Over the course of several months they were able to identify shared interests among the residents, which provided a basis for linking dyads or large groupings. After a year of such informal interaction, residents formed their own Senior Activities Club, which came to function as an independent, active support group. (Rook, p. 1395)

These strategies helped residents not only alleviate but prevent loneliness.

DIVERGENT THINKING AND CREATIVITY

Creativity and divergent thinking are resources needed to identify both preferred-scenario possibilities (Stage II) and strategies and plans for turning agendas into reality.

Divergent Thinking

Many people habitually take a convergent-thinking approach to problem solving; that is, they look for the "one right answer." Such thinking has its uses, of course. However, many of the problem situations of life are too complex to be handled by convergent thinking. Such thinking limits the ways in which people use their own and environmental resources.

Divergent thinking, on the other hand, assumes that there is always more than one answer—in the terms that concern us here, more than one way to manage a problem or develop an opportunity. Unfortunately, divergent thinking often is not rewarded in our culture and sometimes is actually punished. For instance, students who think divergently can be thorns in the sides of teachers. Some teachers feel comfortable only when they ask questions in such a way as to elicit the "one right answer." When students who think divergently give answers that are different from the ones expected, even though these responses might be quite useful (perhaps more useful than the expected responses), they may be ignored, "corrected," or even punished. Students learn that divergent thinking is not rewarded, at least not in school, and they may generalize their experience and end up thinking that it is simply not a useful form of behavior.

> Quentin wanted to be a doctor, so he enrolled in the pre-med program at school. He did well, but not well enough to get into medical school. When he received the last notice of refusal, he said to himself: "Well, that's it for me and the world of medicine. Now what will I do?" When he graduated, he took a job in his brother-in-law's business. He became a manager and did fairly well financially, but he never experienced much career satisfaction. He was glad that his marriage was good and his home life rewarding, because he derived little satisfaction from his work.

Not much divergent thinking went into handling this problem situation. For Quentin, becoming a doctor was the "one right career." He didn't give serious thought to any other career related to the field of medicine, even though there are dozens of interesting and challenging jobs in the allied health sciences.

Creativity and Helping

A review of the requirements for creativity (Cole & Sarnoff, 1980; Robertshaw, Mecca, & Rerick, 1978, pp. 118–120) shows, by implication, that people in trouble often fail to use whatever creative resources they might have. The creative person is characterized by

- optimism and confidence, whereas clients are often depressed and feel powerless;
- acceptance of ambiguity and uncertainty, whereas clients may feel tortured by ambiguity and uncertainty and want to escape from them as quickly as possible;
- a wide range of interests, whereas clients may be people with a narrow range of interests or whose normal interests have been severely narrowed by anxiety and pain;

- flexibility, whereas clients may have become rigid in their approach to themselves, others, and the social settings of life;
- tolerance of complexity, whereas clients are often confused and looking for simplicity and simple solutions;
- verbal fluency, whereas clients are often unable to articulate their problems, much less their goals and ways of accomplishing them;
- curiosity, whereas clients may not have developed a searching approach to life or may have been hurt by being too venturesome;
- drive and persistence, whereas clients may be all too ready to give up;
- independence, whereas clients may be quite dependent or counter-dependent;
- nonconformity or reasonable risk taking, whereas clients may have a history of being very conservative and conformist, or may be people who get into trouble with others and with society precisely because of their particular brand of nonconformity.

A review of some of the principal *obstacles* to creativity surfaces further problems. Innovation is hindered by

- fear, and clients are often quite fearful and anxious;
- fixed habits, and clients may have self-defeating habits or patterns of behavior that may be deeply ingrained;
- dependence on authority, and clients may come to helpers looking for the "right answers" or be quite counterdependent (the other side of the dependence coin) and fight efforts to be helped with "Yes, but" and other games;
- perfectionism, and clients may come to helpers precisely because they are hounded by this problem and can accept only ideal or perfect solutions.

It is easy to say that imagination and creativity are most useful in Stages II and III, but it is another thing to help clients stimulate their own perhaps dormant creative potential. However, once you know the conditions that favor creativity, you can use responding and challenging skills to help clients awaken whatever creative resources they might have. As we shall see later, training clients to use their imaginations and become more innovative may be part of the solution.

The case of Miguel, who also wanted to become a doctor but failed to get into medical school, is quite different from that of Quentin.

> Miguel thought to himself: "Medicine still interests me; I'd like to do something in the health field." With the help of a medical career counselor, he reviewed the possibilities. Even though he was in pre-med, he had never realized that there were so many careers in the field of medicine. He decided to take whatever courses and practicum experiences he needed to become a nurse. Then, while working in a clinic in the hills of Appalachia, where he found the experience invaluable, he managed to get an M.A. in

family-practice nursing by attending a nearby state university part-time. He chose this specialty because he thought that it would enable him to be closely associated with delivery of a broad range of services to patients and would also enable him to have more responsibility for the delivery of these services.

When Miguel graduated, he entered private practice with a doctor as a nurse practitioner in a small midwestern town. Since the doctor divided his time among three small clinics, Miguel had a great deal of responsibility in the clinic where he practiced. He also taught a course in family-practice nursing at a nearby state school and conducted workshops in holistic approaches to preventive medical self-care. Still not satisfied, he began and finished a doctoral program in practical nursing. He taught at a state university and continued his practice. Needless to say, his persistence paid off with an extremely high degree of career satisfaction

A successful professional career in health care remained Miguel's aim throughout. A great deal of divergent thinking and creativity went into the elaboration of this aim into specific goals and into coming up with the courses of action to accomplish them. But for every success story like this, there are many failures. Even Miguel's life was not all roses. His marriage fell apart, in part because of his tenacious pursuit of his career.

BRAINSTORMING

One excellent way of helping clients surface possible strategies and tactics for accomplishing goals is brainstorming (Maier, 1970; Osborn, 1963). Brainstorming is a technique for generating ideas, possibilities, or alternate courses of action. The brainstormer tries, through divergent thinking, to identify as many ways of achieving a goal as possible. There are certain rules that help make this technique work (see D'Zurilla & Goldfried, 1971; Osborn, 1963): suspend judgment, produce as many ideas as possible, use one idea as a takeoff for others, get rid of normal constraints to thinking, and produce even more ideas by clarifying items on the list. Let's apply these points to the helping task in Step III-A.

Suspend your own judgment, and help clients suspend theirs. In the brainstorming phase, do not let clients criticize the strategies they are generating and do not criticize these possibilities yourself (Bayless, 1967; Davis & Manske, 1966; Parloff & Handlon, 1964). There is some evidence that this rule is especially effective when the problem situation has been clarified and defined and goals have been set. This is the case in a problem-solving approach to helping. In the following example, a man who is in pain because he has been rejected by a woman he loves is exploring ways of getting her out of his mind.

Client: One possibility is that I could move to a different city, but that would mean that I would have to get a new job.
Helper: Add it to the list. Remember, we'll criticize them later.

Having clients suspend judgment is one way of handling the tendency on the part of some to play a "Yes, but" game. By the same token, don't let yourself say such things as "Explain what you mean," "I like that idea," "This one is useful," "I'm not sure about that idea," or "How would that work?"

Encourage clients to come up with as many strategies as possible. The principle is that quantity ultimately breeds quality. Studies also show that some of the best ideas come along later in the brainstorming process (Maier & Hoffman, 1964; Parnes, 1967).

Client: Maybe that's enough. We can start putting it all together.
Helper: It didn't sound like you were running out of ideas.
Client: I'm not. It's actually fun.
Helper: Well, let's keep on having fun for a while.

Some say that the quantity principle is the most important of all (D'Zurilla & Nezu, 1980).

Help clients use one idea as a takeoff point for another. Without criticizing the client's productivity, encourage him or her both to develop strategies already generated and to combine different ideas to form new possibilities. In the following example, the client is trying to come up with ways of increasing her self-esteem.

Client: One way I can get a better appreciation of myself is to make a list of my accomplishments every week, even if this means just getting through the ordinary tasks of everyday life.
Helper: Expand that a bit for me.
Client: (Pause) Well, I could star the ones that took some kind of special effort on my part and celebrate them with my husband.

Variations and new twists in strategies already identified are taken as new ideas.

Help clients let themselves go and develop some "wild" ideas. When clients seem to be "drying up" or when the strategies being generated are quite pedestrian, I often say, "Okay, now draw a line under the items on your list and write the word 'wild' under the line. Now let's see if we can develop some really wild ways of getting your goals accomplished." It is easier to cut suggested strategies down to size than to expand them (Maltzman, 1960). The wildest possibilities often have within them at least a kernel of an idea that will work.

Helper: So you need money for school. Well, what are some wild ways you could go about getting the money you need?
Client: Well, let me think. . . . I could rob a bank . . or print some of my own money . . . or put an ad in the paper and ask people to send me money.

This client ended up "printing money" by starting a modest desktop publishing business.

Clients often need "permission" to let themselves go even in such a harmless way.

Too often we repress "good" ideas because when they are first stated they sound foolish. The idea is to create an atmosphere where such apparently foolish ideas will not only be accepted but encouraged. (*PS News*, 1982, No. 20, p. 14)

Help clients think of conservative strategies, liberal strategies, radical strategies, and even outrageous strategies.

Help clients clarify items on the list. Without criticizing their proposals, help clients clarify them. When a proposal is clarified, it can be expanded. In the next example, a college student is talking about getting financial support now that he has moved out of the house and his parents have cut off funds.

Client: . . . And I suppose there might be the possibility of loans.
Counselor: What kind of loans? From whom?
Client: Well, my grandfather once talked about taking out a stake in my future, but at the time I didn't need it. (Pause.) And then there are the low-interest state loans. I never think of them because none of the people I know use them. I bet I'm eligible. I'm not even sure, but the school itself might have some loans.

Clarifying ideas should not be a way of stopping the process or justifying items already brainstormed. Done right, it is an avenue to new possibilities.

Brainstorming is not the same as free association. While clients are encouraged to think of even wild possibilities, still these possibilities must in some way be stimulated by and relate to the client's problem situation and the goals within his or her agenda.

Nor is brainstorming restricted to this step. It can be useful at a number of points in the helping process, for instance, in helping clients develop preferred-scenario possibilities. Finally, brainstorming is not an end in itself. If clients develop effective action strategies without it, well and good; there are no formulas. However, my bet is that even short brain-storming periods constitute time well spent. I once worked with a client who brainstormed a few ideas and then wanted to stop. I pushed him. He generated a few more. Then I used the "wild ideas" approach. In the end, he generated over 25 strategies. About seven of the strategies were used in his plan. But five out of the seven came from the last dozen strategies brainstormed. If we had stopped, he would still have formulated an action plan—but I'm not so sure that it would have been as good.

PROBES AND PROMPTS

Without taking over responsibility for the census of strategies, you can use certain probes and prompts to stimulate your clients' imaginations.

> Jason has terminal cancer. He has been in and out of the hospital several times over the past few months, and he knows that he probably will not live more than a year. He would like the year to be as full as possible, and yet he wants to be realistic. He hates being in the hospital, especially a large hospital, where it is so easy to be anonymous. One of his goals is to die outside the hospital. He would like to die as benignly as possible and retain possession of his faculties as long as possible. How is he to achieve the goals of this agenda?

Probes and prompts can be based on possible resources, including people, models, places, things, organizations, programs, and personal resources.

People. What people might help clients achieve their goals?

> Jason has heard of a doctor in Wisconsin who specializes in the treatment of chronic pain. The doctor teaches people how to use a variety of techniques to manage pain. Jason says that perhaps his wife and daughter can learn how to give simple injections to help him control the pain. Also, he thinks that talking every once in a while with a friend whose wife died of cancer, a man he respects and trusts, will help him find the courage he needs.

Models. Does the client know people who are presently doing what he or she wants to do?

> One of Jason's fellow workers died of cancer at home. Jason visited him there a couple of times. That's what gave him the idea of dying at home, or at least outside the hospital. He noticed that his friend never allowed himself "poor me" talk. He refused to see dying as anything but part of living. This touched Jason deeply at the time, and now reflecting on that experience may help him develop realistic attitudes, too.

Places. Are there particular places that might help?

Jason immediately thinks of Lourdes, the shrine to which believers flock with all sorts of human problems. He doesn't expect miracles, but he feels that he might experience life more deeply there. It's a bit wild, but why not a pilgrimage? He still has the time and also enough money to do it.

Things. What things exist that can help the client achieve the goal?

Jason has read about the use of combinations of drugs to help stave off pain and the side effects of chemotherapy. He notices that the use of marijuana by terminal cancer patients to help control nausea has just been legalized in his state. He has heard that certain kinds of electric stimulation can ward off chronic pain. He explores all these possibilities with his doctor and even arranges for second and third opinions.

Organizations. Are there any organizations that help people with this kind of problem?

Jason knows that there are mutual-help groups composed of cancer patients. He has heard of one at the hospital and believes that there are others in the community. He learns that there are such things as hospices for those terminally ill with cancer.

Programs. Are there any ready-made programs for people in the client's position?

A hospice for the terminally ill has just been established in the city. They have three programs. One helps people who are terminally ill stay in the community as long as they can. A second makes provision for part-time residents. The third provides a residential program for those who can spend little or no time in the community. The goals of these programs are practically the same as Jason's.

The inner resources of the client. What personal resources does the client have that can be used to achieve the goal?

Jason knows something about such principles of behavior as reinforcement, aversive conditioning, and shaping. He has read that these principles can be used in the management of anxiety and pain (Fordyce, 1976). He also has strong religious convictions that can help him face adversity. These resources relate to possible courses of action.

If a client is having a difficult time coming up with strategies, the helper can "prime the pump" by offering a few suggestions.

Alternatives are best sought cooperatively, by inviting our clients to puzzle through with us what is or is not a more practical way to do things. But we must be willing to introduce the more practical alternatives ourselves, for clients are often unable to do so on their own. Clients who could see for themselves the more effective alternatives would be well on their way to using them. That clients do not act more expediently already is in itself a good indication that they do not know how to do so. (Driscoll, 1984, p. 167)

While the helper may need to suggest alternatives, this can be done in such a way that the principal responsibility for evaluating and choosing possible strategies stays with the client.

TRAINING AS TREATMENT

D'Zurilla and Goldfried (1971) suggested a "deficiency" rather than a "pathology" view of client behavior.

> Much of what we view clinically as "abnormal behavior" or "emotional disturbance" may be viewed as ineffective behavior and its consequences, in which the individual is unable to resolve certain situational problems in his life and his inadequate attempts to do so are having undesirable effects, such as anxiety, depression, and the creation of additional problems. (p. 107)

It often happens that people get into trouble or fail to get out of it because they lack the needed life skills (Gazda, 1982, 1984) or coping skills (De-Nelsky & Boat, 1986) and do not know how to mobilize resources, both internal and environmental, to cope with problem situations. "According to the Coping Skills Model, symptoms such as depression, anxiety, and psychophysiological disturbances are viewed as predictable by-products of a mismatch between the demands of individuals' life situations and their abilities to cope with these situations" (DeNelsky & Boat, p. 323). If this is the case, then training clients in the life skills they need to cope more effectively will be an important part of the helping process. Indeed, the use of skills training as part of therapy—what Carkhuff early on (1971b) called "training as treatment"—seems to be growing in a wide variety of helping settings (for example, Foxx and others, 1985; Hawkins, Catalano, & Wells, 1986; Liberman, Mueser, & Wallace, 1986; Schneider & Byrne, 1987; Stravynski, Grey, & Elie, 1987; Van Dam-Baggen & Kraaimaat, 1986). One of the most important ways of helping clients accomplish their preferred-scenario goals is helping them acquire the life skills and coping skills associated with that new scenario. A constant question throughout the helping process should be: What kinds of skills does this client need to get where he or she wants to go?

I assume that skills training is an underused helping strategy. Let's consider an example.

Jerzy and Zelda fall in love. They marry and enjoy a relatively trouble-free "honeymoon" period of about two years or so. Eventually, however, the problems that inevitably arise from living together in such intimacy assert themselves. They find, for instance, that they counted too heavily on positive feelings for each other and now, in their absence, cannot "communicate" about finances, sex, and values. They lack certain critical interpersonal communication skills. Jerzy has little working knowledge of the developmental demands of a 20-year-old woman; Zelda has little working knowledge of the kinds of cultural blueprints that affect her 26-year-old husband. The relationship begins to deteriorate. Since they have few problem-solving skills, they don't know how to handle their situation. Things get worse until they settle down into living miserably, or separate, or divorce, or perhaps take their problems—for better or worse—to a helper.

In the case of this young couple, it seems reasonable to assume that helping will necessarily include both education and training as essential elements of an action plan. One marriage counselor I know does marriage counseling in groups, usually of four couples. Training in communication skills is part of the process. He separates men from women and trains them in attending, listening, and empathy. For practice he begins by pairing a woman with a woman and a man with a man. Next he has a man and a woman—but not spouses—practice the skills together. Finally spouses are paired and are expected to use the skills they have learned to engage in problem solving with each other. Since he uses the helping model outlined in this book, his form of marriage counseling also includes, both directly and indirectly, training in basic problem-solving skills. The helping model gives his clients a problem-management language they use to talk to and help one another.

LINKING STRATEGY FORMULATION TO ACTION

Step III-A has great potential for action. There are many clients who want to "get something done" but don't know how. Once they see some routes toward their destination, they embark. The very words "action strategies" suggest that this step and action are closely linked. However, we are not looking for action for the sake of action. We are looking for client action that has direction (toward preferred-scenario goals) and is prudent (an ethical and reasonable use of the client's resources).

At this point we can talk about the "action chain":

- Clearly defined problems (Stage I) drive either
  - problem-managing action directly or
  - the search for preferred outcomes (Stage II).

- Substantive and realistic goals (Stage II) drive either
  - problem-managing action or
  - the search for goal-accomplishing strategies (Stage III).
- Realistic, goal-linked strategies for accomplishing goals drive
  - problem-managing action.

In practice, this process may not look very elegant. For example, Vickey did not understand the root causes of her manic-depressive episodes, but she did come to see them as manageable. Once she decided that her overall goal was to stay out of the hospital, she began her search for the strategies that would help her do so. She stumbled on a package (her phone-answering business, the support of her husband and friends, her phone calls) that worked for her.

EVALUATION QUESTIONS FOR STEP III-A

How effectively do I do the following?

Generating Action Strategies

- Stimulate the clients' imaginations at the service of action.
- Help clients engage in divergent thinking.
- Help clients brainstorm as many ways as possible to get a preferred scenario or some part of it on line.
- Use probes and prompts to stimulate clients' thinking about strategies.

Training as Treatment

- Help clients to see which skills they need to accomplish preferred-scenario goals.
- Train clients in essential life and coping skills or help them find out where they can get this training.
- Use the helping model itself as a form of training.

Chapter Fifteen

Step III-B: Helping Clients Choose Best-Fit Strategies

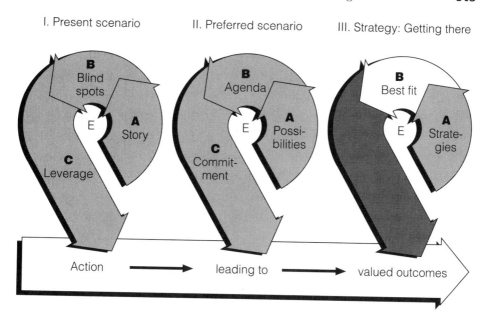

FIGURE 15-1 Step III-B: Choosing Best-Fit Strategies

Some clients, once they are helped to develop a range of goal-related strategies, move forward on their own; that is, they choose the best strategies, put together an action plan, and implement it. Others seem to make it without formally choosing the strategies that seem best for them. Still others, however, need help in choosing strategies that best fit their situation, and so we add Step III-B, illustrated in Figure 15-1, to the helping process. It is useless to have clients brainstorm if they don't know what to do with all the action strategies they generate.

Consider the case of a man who found his agenda for establishing stability in two key strategies.

One morning, Bud, then 18 years old, woke up unable to speak or move. He was taken to a hospital and diagnosed as a catatonic schizophrenic. After repeated admissions to hospitals, where he underwent both drug and electroconvulsive therapy (ECT), his diagnosis was changed to paranoid schizophrenia. He was considered incurable.

A quick overview of Bud's earlier years suggests that much of his emotional distress was caused by unmanaged life problems and the lack of human support. He was separated from his mother for four years while he was young. They were reunited in a strange city, and there he suffered a great deal of harassment at school because of his "ethnic" looks and accent. There was simply too much stress and change in his life. He protected himself by withdrawing. He was flooded with feelings of loss, fear, rage, and abandonment. Change became intolerable. He had his catatonic attack one autumn when the time change occurred. It was the last straw.

In the hospital Bud became convinced that there were reasons behind his own illness and that of his fellow patients. Reflecting on his hospital stays and the drug and ECT treatments, he later said he found his "help" so disempowering that it was no wonder that he got crazier. However, Bud was a person with inner resources. He managed to get out of the hospital and stay out for the most part. Eventually he got a job and married.

One day, after a series of problems with his family and at work, Bud felt himself becoming agitated and thought he was choking to death. His doctor sent him to the hospital "for more treatment." There Bud had the good fortune to meet Sandra, a psychiatric social worker who was convinced that many of the hospital's patients were there because of lack of support before, during, and after their bouts of illness.

There may well have been some physical problem that caused Bud's relapses, but the doctors never found anything wrong. His overall aim was stability, and he wanted to do whatever was necessary to achieve it. As he talked to Sandra, both during his stay in the hospital and afterward, he found two generic strategies that seemed to be the key to his stability— human support and helping others. These proved to be the best-fit strategies or package of strategies for him. Sandra provided a great deal of support in the hospital, a self-help group did the trick outside. Sandra also coached his wife on providing support. As to helping others, Bud founded a group of ex-patients from mental hospitals and ended up turning it into a self-help organization. He has found the stability he was looking for.

CRITERIA FOR CHOOSING STRATEGIES

The criteria for choosing goal-accomplishing strategies are somewhat like the criteria for crafting an agenda outlined in Step II-B. These criteria are reviewed briefly here through a number of examples. Strategies to achieve goals should be specific and clearly tied to the desired goal, realistic, effective, owned by the client, and in keeping with his or her values.

Help the client choose clear and specific strategies for accomplishing goals. Suppose Karen says, "My goal is to stop drinking. In order to achieve this goal, I'm going to lessen the amount of stress in my life. If I feel less stress, I won't be tempted to drink as much." This "strategy" statement violates the "clear and specific" criterion. While the principle Karen suggests may be sound, her application of it is much too vague to be of any use. On the other hand, if John's goal is to reduce and manage the pain from a chronic back condition, then learning to control his reaction to pain through a biofeedback program is a specific way of moving toward his goal.

Note that being specific is important throughout the helping process—in clarifying and defining the problem situation, in setting goals, and now in elaborating strategies. Bud took a generic strategy—helping others—and made it quite specific, starting a self-help group and then starting and running an organization of self-help groups.

Make sure that the strategy chosen is capable of delivering the goal or moving the client toward the goal. Sometimes it is important to explore the link between the strategy and the goal. The link is there in one of the two following cases, but not in the other.

> Susan intends to take some kind of communication course as a way of helping her be more assertive in class, in talking with her parents, and in her relationships with her peers. The course she takes, however, is a "sensitivity training" program that consists mainly of aimless talking in a group. She attends the meetings, but does not know exactly what she is learning, if anything. There is no way of telling whether this program is helping her be more assertive.

> Trish has the same goal as Susan, but she takes a course in interpersonal communication skills. She is given a clear idea of what each skill is and how it can be used. She learns and practices the skills in the training group and is given help in transferring them to other settings. She knows what she is learning and how it contributes to her goal.

The relationship between the strategy and the goal should be clear. "Maybe this will help me" is simply a roll of the dice. Bud noticed the difference immediately when he was treated like a human being instead of being treated like a diagnostic category. He experienced stability both in the hospital and at home during the weeks afterward because of the supportive relationships he experienced with Sandra and in the self-help group.

Help clients choose realistic strategies. Realistic strategies are within the resources of the client, under their control, and unencumbered by obstacles.

> Desmond is in a halfway house after leaving a state mental hospital. From time to time he still has bouts of depression that incapacitate him for a few days. He wants to get a job because he thinks that a job will help him feel better about himself, become more independent, and manage his depression better. He answers want ads in a rather random way and keeps getting turned down after being interviewed. He simply does not yet have the kinds of resources needed to put himself in a favorable light in job interviews. Moreover, he is not yet ready for a regular, full-time job.

Desmond's counselor helps him explore some companies that have specific programs to help the disabled. These companies have found that some of their best workers come from the ranks of those rejected by others. After a few interviews Desmond gets a job that is within his capabilities.

There is, of course, a difference between realism and selling a client short. Strategies that make clients "stretch" for a valued goal can be most rewarding. In the last chapter we saw that a successful career in medicine was one of Miguel's principal goals. He constantly stretched himself—even at the expense of his marriage—to achieve this goal. It goes without saying that Bud stretched himself by establishing a self-help group and then an organization.

Help clients choose strategies that are powerful enough to be effective. It is not enough for strategies to be linked to a goal. They must have the power to provide some substantial movement toward the goal.

Stacy was admitted to a mental hospital because she had been exhibiting bizarre behavior in her neighborhood. She dressed in a slovenly way and went around admonishing the residents of the community for their "sins." She was diagnosed as schizophrenic, simple type. She had been living alone for about five years, since the death of her husband. It seems that she had become more and more alienated from herself and others. In the hospital, medication helped control some of her symptoms. She stopped admonishing others and took reasonable care of herself, but she was still quite withdrawn. She was assigned to "milieu" therapy, a euphemism meaning that she followed the more or less benign routine of the hospital. She remained withdrawn and usually seemed moderately depressed. No therapeutic goals had been set, and the nonspecific program to which she was assigned was totally inadequate.

This "action" program lacked bite. Sometimes courses of action are inadequate because the resources needed are not available. In this example, "milieu" therapy meant that the hospital lacked adequate therapeutic resources. Bud's strategies, on the other hand, proved to be powerful. They not only helped him stabilize but gave him a new perspective on life.

Help clients develop action strategies they can own. Strategies, like goals, must be owned by the client. Advice giving ("Why don't you try . . . ?") does not help. However, helpers can be active without taking over the client's responsibility.

There is a "prompt and fade" technique that can be used with clients who are having a hard time coming up with possible strategies. The counselor can say, "Here are some possibilities. . . . Let's review them and see whether any of them make sense to you or suggest further possibilities." Or, "Here are some of the things that people with this kind of problem situation have tried. . . . How do they sound to you?" The "fade" part of this technique keeps it from being advice giving: prompts are stated in such a way that the client has to work with the suggestion.

The overall goal is clear. Make sure that clients are committing them-selves to *their* strategies, not yours. Bud, of course, owned his "helping others" strategies because he invented them. Also, when he experienced a truly supportive relationship in the hospital, perhaps for the first time, he had no trouble owning the concept, even though it had been suggested by and provided by Sandra.

Make sure that the strategies chosen are consistent with the client's values. Ownership includes helping clients choose strategies that are in keeping with their values. Clients don't always observe this principle on their own.

> In defining a problem, people dislike thinking about unpleasant eventu-alities, have difficulty in assigning . . . values to alternative courses of action, have a tendency toward premature closure, overlook or undervalue long-range consequences, and are unduly influenced by the first formula-tion of the problem. In evaluating the consequences of alternatives, they attach extra weight to those risks that can be known with certainty. They are more subject to manipulation . . . when their own values are poorly thought through. . . . A major problem . . . for . . . individuals is knowing when to search for additional information relevant to decisions. (Goslin, 1985, pp. 7–9)

Once more we see the irrationalities of decision making. As we saw in Stage II, clients have a difficult time thinking about the future. And future thinking is needed to examine the possible consequences of the choice of courses of action. Here is an example of a counselor who should have helped a client explore his values so that they could be used as decision-making criteria but did not.

> Glenn was cited for battering his 2-year-old child. Mandatory counseling was part of the suspended sentence he received. He had a violent temper; that is, he got angry easily, did little to control his anger, and vented it on others, including the child. The counselor discovered that Glenn and his wife were having sexual problems and that sexual frustration had a great deal to do with his anger. The counselor suggested that Glenn lower his frustration (and therefore control his anger) by engaging in sexual relations with other women. Glenn did this, but felt guilty and became depressed.

The counselor is wrong in suggesting a course of action without helping the client explore his values. He might be doing so because he thinks that Glenn's having sex with other women, if evil at all, is less evil than his abusing his child, but this is not the counselor's decision to make. Take

Bud's case. If Sandra had urged Bud to lower his expectations and adopt a safe lifestyle, she would have been suggesting strategies counter to his values.

THE BALANCE-SHEET METHOD FOR EVALUATING STRATEGIES

The balance sheet is a decision-making aid counselors can use to help clients choose best-fit strategies for achieving goals (Janis, 1983a; Janis & Mann, 1977; Wheeler & Janis, 1980). It is a way of helping clients examine the consequences of different courses of action in terms of both utility ("Will this course of action get me where I want to go?") and acceptability ("Can I live with this course of action?"). It helps clients consider not just themselves but also significant others and the social settings of their lives.

Here we will first look at the balance-sheet methodology, then at an example, and finally at practical and flexible ways of using the balance sheet.

The Balance-Sheet Methodology

The balance-sheet form is illustrated in Figure 15-2. In this step you are helping clients make the kinds of decisions they can live with. Note, too, that the balance sheet could be used to evaluate goals themselves (Step II-B) and not just the strategies for achieving them.

The issues considered in the balance sheet are possible gains, possible losses, and the acceptability or unacceptability of each.

Benefits or Gains

If I follow this course of action, what benefits or gains are in it

- for me?
- for significant others in my life?
- for the social settings of which I am a member?

Acceptability of benefits. In each case, these potential benefits or gains are acceptable to me because . . .

- My gains are acceptable because . . .
- The gains for significant others are acceptable because . . .
- The gains for relevant social settings are acceptable because . . .

Unacceptability of benefits. In each case, these potential benefits or gains are unacceptable to me because . . .

If I choose this course of action:		
The self		
Gains for self:	Acceptable to me because:	Not acceptable to me because:
Losses for self:	Acceptable to me because:	Not acceptable to me because:
Significant others		
Gains for significant others:	Acceptable to me because:	Not acceptable to me because:
Losses for significant others:	Acceptable to me because:	Not acceptable to me because:
Social setting		
Gains for social setting:	Acceptable to me because:	Not acceptable to me because:
Losses for social setting:	Acceptable to me because:	Not acceptable to me because:

FIGURE 15-2   The Decision Balance Sheet

- My gains would be unacceptable because . . .
- The gains for significant others would be unacceptable because . . .
- The gains for relevant social systems would be unacceptable because . . .

Losses or Costs

If I choose this program or follow this course of action, what losses or costs can I expect to incur

- for myself?
- for significant others?
- for relevant social systems?

Acceptability of losses. In each case, these potential losses or costs are acceptable to me because . . .

- My losses or costs are acceptable because . . .
- The losses or costs to significant others are acceptable because . . .
- The losses or costs to relevant social systems are acceptable because . . .

Unacceptability of losses or costs. In each case, these potential losses or costs are unacceptable to be because . . .

- My losses or costs are unacceptable because . . .
- The losses or costs to significant others are unacceptable because . . .
- The losses or costs to relevant social systems are unacceptable because . . .

An Example

An example will clarify the use of the balance sheet. Let's return to Karen, the woman who has admitted that she is an alcoholic and whose goal is to stop drinking. One possible strategy is to spend a month as an inpatient at an alcoholic treatment center. This possibility intrigues her. Since choosing this possibility would be a serious decision, the counselor, Joan, helps Karen use the balance sheet to weigh possible costs and benefits. After Joan explains the sheet, Karen fills it out at home. Joan has told her to mark the spots she feels she needs to discuss after filling out the sheet. She returns with the following.

Benefits of Choosing the Residential Program

• *For me:* It would help me because it would be a dramatic sign that I want to do something to change my life. It's a clean break, as it were. It would also give me time just for myself; I'd get away from all my commitments to family, relatives, friends, and work. I see it as an opportunity to do some planning. I'd have to figure out how I would act as a sober person.

• *For significant others:* I'm thinking mainly of my family here. It would give them a breather, a month without an alcoholic wife and mother around the house. I'm not saying that to put myself down. I think it would give them time to reassess family life and make some decisions about any changes they'd like to make. I think something dramatic like my going away would give them hope. They've had very little reason to hope for the last five years.

• *For relevant social settings:* I can't think of many benefits for social settings apart from the family. I'd probably be more "with it" in my part-time job, but they've never had any real complaints.

Acceptability of benefits.

• *For me:* I feel torn here. But looking at it just from the viewpoint of acceptability, I feel kind enough toward myself to give myself a month's time off. Also something in me longs for a new start in life.

• *For significant others:* I think that my family would have no problems in letting me take a month off. I'm sure that they'd see it as a positive step from which all of us would benefit.

• *For relevant social settings:* This does not seem to be an issue at work. They like me now. I might be more efficient, and most likely I'd be less moody.

Unacceptability of benefits.

• *For me:* Going away for a month seems such a luxury, so self-indulgent. Also, taking such a dramatic step would give me an opportunity to change my current lifestyle, but it would also place demands on me. My fear is that I would do fine while "inside," but that I would come out and fall on my face. I guess I'm saying it would give me another chance at life, but I have misgivings about having another chance. *I need some help here.*

• *For significant others:* The kids are young enough to readjust to a new me. But I'm not sure how my husband would take this "benefit." He has more or less worked out a lifestyle that copes with my being drunk a lot. Though I have never left him and he has never left me, still I wonder whether he wants me "back"—sober, I mean. Maybe this belongs under the "cost" part of this exercise. *I need some help here.* And, of course, I need to talk to my husband about all this. I also notice that some of my misgivings relate not to a residential program as such but to a return to a lifestyle free of alcohol. Doing this exercise helped me see that more clearly.

• *For relevant social settings:* As far as I can see, there's nothing unacceptable about my being more efficient or more personable at work!

Costs of Choosing a Residential Program

• *For me:* Well, there's the money. I don't mean the money just for the program, but I would be losing four weeks' wages. The major cost seems to be the commitment I have to make about a lifestyle change. And I know the residential program won't be all fun. I don't know exactly what they do there, but some of it must be demanding. Probably a lot of it.

• *For significant others:* It's a private program, and it's going to cost the family a lot of money. The services I have been providing will be missing for a month. It could be that I'll learn things about myself that will make it harder to live with me (though living with a drinking spouse and mother is no joke). What if I come back more demanding of them—I mean, in good ways? *I need to talk this through more thoroughly.*

• *For relevant social settings:* There may be one cost here. If I change my lifestyle, I may want a better job, or I may make the decision not to work at all. In that case, they would lose someone they see as a decent employee.

Acceptability of costs.

• *For me:* I have no problem at all with the money nor with whatever the residential program demands of me physically or psychologically. I'm willing to pay. The demand the program places on me for a new lifestyle? Well, in principle I'm willing to pay what that costs. *I need some help here.*

• *For significant others:* They will have to make financial sacrifices, but I have no reason to think that they would be unwilling. Still, I can't be making decisions for them. I see much more clearly the need to have a counseling session with my husband and children present. I think they're also willing to have a "new" person around the house, even if it means making adjustments and changing their lifestyle a bit. I want to check this out with them, but I think it would be helpful to do this with the counselor. I think they will be willing to come.

• *For relevant social settings:* If getting better means not working or getting a different job, let it be. I can hardly base my decisions on what they will think at work.

Unacceptability of costs.

• *For me:* While I'm ready to change my lifestyle, I hate to think that I will have to accept some dumb, dull life. I think I've been drinking, at least in part, to get away from dullness; I've been living in a fantasy world, a play world a lot of the time. A stupid way of doing it perhaps, but it's true. I have to do some life planning of some sort. *I need some help here.*

• *For significant others:* It strikes me that my family might have problems with a sober me if it means that I will strike out in new directions. I wonder if they want the traditional homebody wife and mother. I don't think I could stand that. All this should come out in the meeting with the counselor.

• *For relevant social settings:* They can get along without me for a month at work. And, if necessary, they can get along without me completely.

Karen concludes: "All in all, it seems like the residential program is a good idea. There is something much more 'total' about it than an outpatient program. But that's also what scares me."

Karen's use of the balance sheet helps her make an initial program choice, but it also enables her to discover issues that she has not yet worked out completely. By using the balance sheet, she returns to the counselor with work to do; she does not come merely wondering what will happen next. This highlights the usefulness of exercises and other forms of structure that help clients take more responsibility for what happens both in the helping sessions and outside.

Using the Balance Sheet

Now, a more practical and flexible approach to using the balance sheet. I am not suggesting that you use it with every client to work out the pros and cons of every course of action. The example of Karen has been presented to illustrate the process in its entirety. But you can also use parts of the balance sheet and tailor them to the kinds of action strategies the client is exploring.

In fact, one of the best uses of the balance sheet is not to use it directly at all. Keep it in the back of your mind whenever clients are making decisions. Use it as a filter to listen to clients. Then turn relevant parts of it into probes to help clients focus on issues they may be overlooking. "How will this decision affect the significant people in your life?" is a probe that originates in the balance sheet. "Is there any down side to that strategy?" might help a client who is being a bit too optimistic. No formula. Recall Gelatt's (1989) cautions about making decision making an overly rational process. You want to help clients head in the right direction, not get them to cross every *t* and dot every *i*. Logic has its limits.

STRATEGY SAMPLING

Some clients find it easier to choose strategies if they first sample some of the possibilities.

> Karen, surprised by the number of program possibilities there were to achieve the goal of getting liquor out of her life, decided to sample some of them. She went to an open meeting of Alcoholics Anonymous, she attended a meeting of a women's lifestyle-issues group, she visited the hospital that had the residential treatment program, she joined up for a two-week trial physical-fitness program at a YWCA, and she had a couple of strategy meetings with her husband and children. While none of this was done frantically, it did occupy her energies and strengthened her resolve to do something about her alcoholism.

Of course, some clients could use strategy sampling as a way of putting off action. With Bud it was quite the opposite. His attending the meeting of a self-help group after leaving the hospital was a kind of strategy sampling. He was impressed by the group, but he thought that he could start a group limited to ex-patients that would focus more directly on the kinds of issues ex-patients face.

MANAGING RISK IN SELECTING STRATEGIES

In choosing courses of action, clients can be helped to evaluate the risks involved and determine whether the risk is balanced by the probability of success. Gelatt, Varenhorst, and Carey (1972) suggested four ways in which clients may try to deal with the factors of risk and probability: wishful thinking, playing it safe, avoiding the worst, and achieving some kind of balance.

Wishful Thinking

In this case clients choose a course of action that might (they hope) lead to the accomplishment of a goal regardless of risk, cost, or probability. For instance, Jenny wants her ex-husband to increase the amount of support he is paying for the children. She tries to accomplish this by constantly nagging him and trying to make him feel guilty. She does not consider the risk (he might get angry and stop giving her anything), the cost (she spends a lot of time and emotional energy arguing with him), or the probability of success (he does not react favorably to nagging). The wishful-thinking client operates blindly, using some preferred course of action without taking into account its usefulness. At its worst, this is a reckless approach. Clients who "work hard" and still "get nowhere" may be engaged in wishful thinking, persevering in using means they prefer but that are of doubtful efficacy. On the other hand, some approaches that might initially seem reckless may not prove to be so in the end. To some, Bud's "helping others" approach to gaining stability must have seemed reckless. Bud intuitively knew that it was not.

Playing It Safe

In this case, the client chooses only safe courses of action, ones that have little risk and a high degree of probability of producing at least limited success. For instance, Liam, a man in his early forties, is very dissatisfied with his work but is afraid of losing the job he has if anyone finds out that he is thinking of changing. He chooses only job possibilities for which interviews are given in the evening, and he excludes possibilities he thinks might be too competitive or too challenging. He simply wants a job different from the one he has.

The trouble with this strategy is that it places limitations on the kinds of goals that can be pursued. Clients might well end up safe, but also sorry. Bud did not play it safe.

Avoiding the Worst

In this case, clients choose means that are likely to help them avoid the worst possible result. They try to minimize the maximum danger. Let's say that a client has had fits of violence. He commits himself to a mental hospital, for he feels that there he will be protected from his own violence. For him, the greatest danger is harming another person. By placing himself in custodial care, he minimizes this danger.

There is an obvious problem with this approach to managing risk: since it is based on avoidance, it can prevent any new learning from taking place. The worst for Bud was being hospitalized in an institution where little human support was provided. In the end he did avoid the worst, but not by directly trying to minimize the maximum danger. Avoidance was not in his repertory.

Striking a Balance

In this case, clients choose strategies for achieving goals that balance risks against the probability of success. This "combination" approach is the most difficult to apply, for it involves a great deal of analysis, including clarification of objectives, a solid knowledge of personal values, and the ability to rank a variety of action strategies according to one's values, plus the ability to predict results from a given course of action.

This is a very "rational" approach to decision making. But it involves a great deal of skill and a great deal of work. Sometimes clients have neither the time nor the will for this kind of detailed work. Bud did not go into all the detail suggested by the "balanced" approach—or perhaps he did, but intuitively and covertly. Again, rationality has its limits.

This brings up an interesting question. Is the job of the counselor to help the client achieve the "best" solution to his or her problem? The idealist within us says, "Of course." But this is not the reality of helping. In Chapter 3, one cluster of values was given the title "pragmatism." Of course we want to do the best job *we can* with our clients, but this does not mean that each stage and step of this helping model will be done perfectly. Helpers and clients both work with limited aspirations and limited resources. If clients engage in wishful thinking, play it safe, try to avoid the worst rather than seek the better, or spend a great deal of time and effort searching for the perfect course of action, counselors can challenge them to think through the consequences of their approach to decision making. In the end, however, helpers do not make decisions for clients.

LINKING STEP III-B TO ACTION

Some clients are filled with great ideas for getting things done but never seem to do anything. They lack the discipline to evaluate their ideas, choose the best, and turn them into action. This kind of work seems too tedious to them, even though it is precisely what they need. Help clients who balk at analytic work try things (strategy sampling), not in a random, but in a focused way.

> Clint came away from the doctor feeling depressed. He was told that he was in the high-risk category for heart disease and that he needed to change his lifestyle. He was cynical, a man very quick to anger, a man who did not readily trust others. Venting his suspicions and hostility did not make them go away; it only intensified them. Therefore, one critical life-style change was to change this pattern and develop what Williams (1989) has called a "trusting heart." A counselor gave him Williams' article, in which three aims were outlined: reducing mistrust of others' motives, reducing the frequency and intensity of such emotions as rage, anger, and irritation, and learning how to treat others with consideration. This meant changing thoughts, external actions, and emotions. Clint read through the strategies suggested to help people pursue these aims:
>
> • keeping a hostility log to discover the patterns of cynicism and irritation in one's life;
> • finding someone to talk to about the problem, someone to trust;
> • "thought stopping," catching oneself in the act of indulging in hostile thoughts or in thoughts that lead to hostile feelings;
> • talking sense to oneself when tempted to put others down;
> • developing empathic thought patterns, walking in the other's shoes;
> • learning to laugh at one's silliness;
> • using a variety of relaxation techniques, especially when negative thoughts come up;
> • finding ways of practicing trust;
> • developing active listening skills;
> • substituting assertive for aggressive behavior;
> • getting perspective, seeing each day as one's last;
> • practicing forgiving others without patronizing or condescending.
>
> Clint prided himself on his rationality (though his "rationality" was one of the things that got him in trouble). So, as he read down the list, he chose strategies that could form an "experiment," as he put it. He decided to talk to a counselor (for the sake of objectivity), keep a hostility log (data gathering), and use the tactics of thought stopping and talking sense to himself at times of "temptation." The counselor noted to himself that none of these necessarily involved changing Clint's attitudes toward others. However, he did not challenge Clint at this point. His best bet was that through "strategy sampling" Clint would learn more about his problem, that he would find that it went deeper than he thought. Clint set himself to his experiment with vigor.

Here it is a question of Clint choosing strategies that fit his values. The problem was that the values themselves needed reviewing. But Clint did act, and action gave him the opportunity to learn.

EVALUATION QUESTIONS FOR STEP III-B

How well am I doing the following as I try to help clients choose best-fit strategies?

- Helping clients choose strategies that are clear and specific, that best fit their capabilities, that are linked to goals, that have power, and that are suited to clients' styles and values.
- Helping clients use the balance sheet as a way of choosing strategies by outlining the principal benefits and costs for self, others, and relevant social settings.
- Using the balance sheet flexibly as a source of client-tailored probes.
- Helping clients manage risk in selecting courses of action without assuming that the same formula applies to all clients.
- Helping clients take an action approach to choosing strategies through strategy sampling.

Chapter Sixteen

Step III-C: Helping Clients Formulate Plans

Planning, in its broadest sense, would include Stages II and III—brainstorming possible goals, choosing specific goals, brainstorming implementation strategies, choosing implementation strategies, and then putting these strategies into a sequence with timelines for each activity—all at the service of managing the problems and developing the unused opportunities discovered and analyzed in Stage I. In Step III-C, however, the term *planning* is used in its narrow sense, that is, putting implementation strategies into a sequential order and assigning timelines for each activity. Carkhuff (1985) has noted the power of this kind of program development:

> Program development lets us minimize and ultimately rise above our human limitations. It enables us to achieve goals we once only imagined reaching. And just as program development has made it possible for human beings to walk in space, it allows us to walk proudly on earth: strong, healthy, skilled, and productive. (from the Preface)

Consider the case of Tammy.

> After consulting her doctor, Tammy undertook a physical fitness regimen as part of a weight-reduction program. Her counselor gave her a book that outlined a variety of exercises and a running schedule. The book described three kinds of programs—slow, medium, and fast—and scaled each of these according to age groups. Tammy decided that she needed a taste of success, so she chose the slow program for her age group. The book indicated each objective and the time allotted to it. Each day Tammy had a clear idea of exactly what to do. Three things began to happen: she began to lose some weight, she began to tone her muscles and get her cardiovascular system in shape, and she began to feel good about herself.

This client benefited from having a clear map of what needed to be done and a timetable for doing it. The detailed plan helped her to get started and to stick to the program. Other clients balk at a map that is too detailed. It makes them feel constrained. In planning, too, there is no one formula for every client.

The lack of a plan, that is, a clear step-by-step process in which strategies are used to achieve goals, does keep some people mired in the "psychopathology of the average," in unmanaged problem situations and undeveloped opportunities. Consider the case of Frank, a vice-president of a large West Coast corporation.

> Frank was a go-getter. He was very astute about business and had risen quickly through the ranks. Vince, the president of the company, was in the process of working out his retirement. From a business point of view, Frank was the heir apparent. But there was a glitch. The president was far more than a good manager; he was a leader. He had a vision of what the company should look like five to ten years down the line. Though tough, he related well to people. Frank was quite different. He was a "hands on" manager, meaning, in his case, that he was slow to delegate tasks to

others, however competent they might be. He kept second-guessing others when he did delegate, he reversed their decisions in a way that made them feel put down, he was a poor listener, and he took a fairly short-term view of the business ("What were last week's figures like?"). He was not a leader, but an "operations" man.

One day Vince sat down with Frank and told him that he was the heir apparent, but that his promotion would not be automatic. "Frank, if it were just a question of business acumen, you could take over today. But my job, at least in my mind, demands a leader." Vince went on to explain what he meant by a leader and to give Frank feedback on some of the things in his style that had to change.

Afterward Frank saw a consultant, someone he trusted who had given him similar feedback. They worked together for over a year, often over lunch and in hurried meetings early in the morning or late in the evening. Frank's aim was to become, within reason, the kind of leader Vince had described. Being very bright, he came up with some inventive strategies for moving in this direction. But he could never be pinned down to an overall program with specific milestones by which he could evaluate his progress. The consultant pushed him, but Frank was always "too busy" or would say that a formal program was not his "style." This was odd, since formal planning was one of his fortes in the business world.

Frank remained as astute as ever in his business dealings, and the business prospered. But he merely dabbled in the strategies meant to help him achieve his goal. At the end of two years, Vince retired after appointing someone else president of the company.

Frank had two major blind spots that the consultant either could not or did not help him overcome. First, he thought the president's job was his, that business acumen alone would win out in the end. Second, he thought he could change his management style at the margins, when more substantial changes were called for. If the consultant had said, "Come on, Frank, I know you hate doing it, but let's map out a program and find ways to get you to stick to it," maybe things would have been different. It was not a question of changing Frank's entire personality, but of changing certain patterns of behavior. The changes even fell into the range of Frank's espoused values.

The trick is to discover how formal planning might help any given client. It is more likely that you will use bits and pieces of planning with your clients than a complete, formal planning process. Even bits and pieces would have helped Frank.

Some clients, once they have chosen action strategies, have no difficulty sequencing them properly and turning them into action. Others, though, need help at this stage. And so Figure 16-1 adds this last formal step to the helping process. However, since some clients (and some helpers!) fail to appreciate the power of planning, it is useful to start by reviewing the advantages of planning.

I. Present scenario   II. Preferred scenario   III. Strategy: Getting there

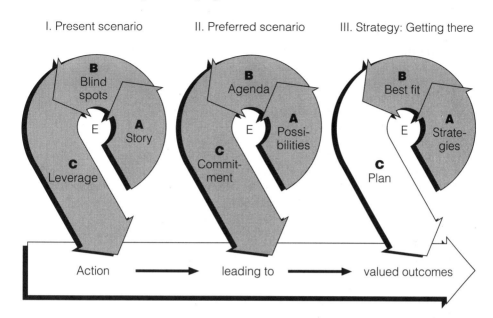

FIGURE 16-1   The Helping Model: Step III-C

SOME REASONS FOR HELPING CLIENTS PLAN

A plan, then, takes strategies for accomplishing goals, divides them into workable bits, puts the bits in order, and assigns a timetable for the accomplishment of each bit. These are reasons why plans help people attain goals in general, and the following discussion adapts these reasons for planning to the counseling process.

1. Formulating plans helps clients search for more useful ways of accomplishing goals, that is, even better strategies.

When Mr. Johnson's wife and children began to formulate a plan for coping with their reactions to his alcoholism, they realized they had not been very inventive in looking for workable strategies. With the help of an Al-Anon self-help group member, they went back to the drawing board. She helped them review ways other families cope with the same problem.

Sometimes it is only at the planning stage that a client might say, "Oh, oh, that won't work."

2. Plans provide an opportunity to evaluate the realism and adequacy of goals.

When Walter began tracing out a plan to cope with the loss of his job and a lawsuit filed against him by his former employer, he realized that his goals of getting a better job and of filing and winning a countersuit were unrealistic. He scaled back his expectations.

Effective plans give clients a realistic picture of what they must actually do to achieve a goal. Only in drawing up the plan did Walter realize that he had set his goals unrealistically high. On the other hand, in formulating plans, some clients discover that more substantive goals are called for. One client devised a set of preferred-scenario goals relating to becoming a more effective parent. When she saw how easily she could accomplish her goals, she cried, "Good grief! I've been too easy on myself. I guess that's part of my problem, being too easy on myself." Only at the formal planning stage did she realize that she had set her sights too low.

3. Plans tell clients something about the resources they will need to implement their strategies.

When Lynn was helped to get an overview of the rehabilitation program she was about to get involved in after an automobile accident, she saw clearly that the psychological costs were going to be quite high. She talked with the counselor about ways of keeping her spirits up.

Knowing costs in terms of time and stress can help clients fortify themselves for action.

When Nancy was helped by a counselor to formulate a plan to pull her life together after the disappearance of her younger son, she realized that she couldn't do it alone. She had retreated from friends and even relatives, but now she knew she had to get back into community.

Sometimes the human resources needed to implement a plan are not factored in when strategies are being formulated.

4. Formulating plans helps clients uncover unanticipated snags or obstacles to the accomplishment of goals.

Only when Ernesto, the badly beaten gang member, started putting together a plan for a different lifestyle did he realize what an obstacle his lack of a high school diploma would be. He came to realize that he needed the equivalent of a diploma if he was to develop the kind of lifestyle he wanted.

5. Planning can help clients manage post-decisional depression.
Sometimes people get depressed after making a relatively important decision like buying a house or a car or choosing a course of action to face up to some problem situation (see Janis & Mann, 1977). They keep asking themselves whether they could have made a better decision. They feel sad that their resources are now committed. In a sense they have given up

some of their freedom, and they mourn this loss. One way of helping clients deal with post-decisional sadness is to help them get back to work and develop the specifics of accomplishing the goal they have chosen. The best way to help clients manage such depression is to help them start implementing the courses of action they have chosen.

SHAPING THE PLAN

If a plan is to drive action, then it must be well-shaped. That is, it must first clearly specify subgoals leading up to the accomplishment of the overall preferred-scenario goal. It must then specify the sequence of activities through which each subgoal is to be accomplished.

Formulating Subgoals

If a problem situation is complex, a number of goals might be needed to manage it. Furthermore, any one goal a client chooses may have a number of subgoals. Once Bud decided to start an organization of self-help groups composed of ex-patients from mental hospitals, there were a number of subgoals that needed to be accomplished before the organization would be a reality. For instance, he had to set up some kind of charter for the organization. "Charter in place" was one of the subgoals leading to his overall goal.

In general, the simpler the plan or program, the better—provided that it helps clients achieve their goals. However, simplicity is not an end in itself. The question is not whether a plan or program is complicated but whether it is well-shaped. If complicated programs are broken down into subgoals and the strategies or activities needed to accomplish them, they are as capable of being achieved, if the time frame is realistic, as simpler ones.

In some cases you will be worth your salt if you help clients identify subgoals—that is, major steps on the way toward the achievement of a main goal—and help them organize these subgoals into a sequence leading to the main goal. This is a plan or program. In schematic form, shaping looks like this:

Subprogram 1 leads to subgoal 1.
Subprogram 2 leads to subgoal 2.
Subprogram n (the last in the sequence) leads to the accomplishment of the major goal.

Take the case of Wanda, a client who has set a number of goals in order to manage a complex problem situation. One of these goals is finding a job. The program leading to this goal can be divided into a number of steps, each of which leads to the accomplishment of a subgoal. The following subgoals are part of Wanda's job-finding program. Since they are goals, they are stated as accomplishments (the past-participle approach).

> *Subgoal 1:* Kind of job wanted determined and résumé written.
> *Subgoal 2:* Job possibilities canvassed.
> *Subgoal 3:* Best job prospects identified.
> *Subgoal 4:* Job interviews arranged.
> *Subgoal 5:* Job interviews completed.
> *Subgoal 6:* Offers evaluated.
> *Major goal in total program:* Job chosen and started.

If all of this is accomplished, then Wanda achieves one of the major goals in her agenda, satisfactory employment.

For each of these subgoals there is a step-by-step process, or set of strategies to accomplish the subgoal. The program for the subgoal "job possibilities canvassed" might include such things as reading the "help wanted" section of the local papers, contacting friends or acquaintances who might be able to offer jobs or provide leads, visiting employment agencies, reading the bulletin boards at school, and talking with someone in the job placement office. There is nothing against Wanda's doing all of these in a somewhat random order. In other programs, however, the sequence is important.

> Harriett, an undergraduate student at a small state college, wanted to become a helper. Although the college offered no formal program in applied psychology, she identified several undergraduate courses that would help her toward her goal. One was called "Problem-Solving Approaches to Caring for Self and Others," a second, "Effective Communication Skills," a third, "Developmental Psychology: The Developmental Stages and Tasks of Late Adolescence and Early Adulthood." Harriett took the courses as they came up. Unfortunately, the first course was the one in problem-solving approaches, and it included brief one-on-one practice in the skills being learned. The further into the course Harriett went, the more she realized that she would have gotten more out of the course if she had taken the communication skills program first.
>
> Harriett had also volunteered for the peer-helper program offered by the Office of Student Services. While those running the program were careful about whom they selected, they did not offer much training. Good will was supposed to bring the volunteers a long way. Harriett realized that the developmental psychology course would have helped her in this program. Seeing that her activities needed to be better organized, she dropped out of the volunteer program and sat down with an adviser who had some background in psychology to come up with a reasonable plan.

The next client, Leroy, was helped by a formal approach to planning.

One of Leroy's problems was that he was "out of community"; that is, he had no close friends and no group with which he interacted regularly. It became clear that many of his other problems were related to having such an impoverished social life. Therefore, one major goal of his total program was "getting into community," that is, participating in groups and establishing friendships. Although Leroy was somewhat fearful of making contact with others, he was lonely enough to want to do something about his social life. Through discussions with the counselor, he came up with the following subgoals related to becoming a member of some kind of social group:

Group possibilities identified within two weeks.
Best possibilities explored.
Social group chosen.
Social group joined.

Leroy had never thought of taking such direct action to improve his social life, and at first he was put off by the idea. He had been "waiting for something to happen." But, predictably, nothing had. It became clear to him that he had to make it happen.

Leroy was like many of us who balk at being regimented by plans. However, those who learn to spice their lives with a bit of planning can make significant inroads on the "psychopathology of the average."

One of the main reasons plans go awry is that planners bite off more than they can chew all at once. That is why establishing subgoals as part of the overall plan is important. The cardinal rule: No step should be too large. Any step that seems too large can be broken down into two or more smaller steps. Of course, what seems like a giant step to one client will be an ordinary step for another.

Arranging Activities

For some people, time hangs heavy on their hands: they don't know what to do to fill it. To them, time is an enemy. Others have too many things to do, so that time proves elusive. Once more time is an enemy. Planning will not solve all our problems and those of our clients, but it is one way of making time an ally instead of an enemy. Planning at its best is a very humane process. It helps our clients get where they want to go (effectiveness) through the optimal use of resources (efficiency).

Planning involves activities, order, and time frame and a question about each.

- *The strategy-based activities of the plan:* Identify the activities that make up the strategies for achieving goals. What are the concrete things that need to be done?

- *The sequencing of activities:* Put these activities into some kind of sequence or order. What should be done first, what second, what third?
- *The time frame for activities:* Determine when each activity is to be done. What should be done today, what tomorrow, what next month?

Let's see what part of a plan for Frank, the vice-president who needed leadership skills, could have looked like in terms of these three categories. In this fantasy, Frank, like Scrooge, gets a second chance.

The strategy-based activities of the plan. To become a leader, Frank decides to reset his style with his subordinates by involving them more in decision making. He wants to listen more, set work objectives through dialogue, ask subordinates for suggestions, and delegate more. He decides to visit subordinates to see what he can do to help them, coach them when they ask for advice, give them feedback, recognize their contributions, and reward them for achieving results beyond their objectives. Mischel and Patterson (1976) suggested that both subgoals and the action-strategy activities act as "commands" for the planner. What Frank is saying to himself through his list, then, is "listen more to those who report to you," "Coach those who need your advice," and so forth. He believes that he does not have to get more specific than this. The package of things he will do with each subordinate will have to be tailored to the needs of each.

The sequencing of activities. Frank decides that the first thing he will do is call in each subordinate and ask, "What do you need from me in order to get your job done? And what management style on my part would help you do it?" Their responses will help him decide which of the other activities will make sense with each subordinate. The second step is also clear. The planning cycle for the business is about to begin, and each manager needs to know what his or her objectives are. It is a perfect time to begin setting objectives collaboratively. Frank therefore sends a memo of his direct reports to each, asking them to review the company's business plan and the plan for each of their functions, and to write down what they think their key managerial objectives for the year should be.

The time frame for activities. Frank calls in each of his subordinates immediately to discuss what they need from him. He completes his objective-setting sessions with them within three weeks. He puts off further action on delegation until he gets a better reading on their objectives and what they need from him.

This gives you a rough idea of what a plan for Frank might have looked like and how it might have improved his abortive effort to change his managerial style. Notice that the plan does not spell out every last detail.

Kirschenbaum (1986) challenged the notion that planning should always provide an exact blueprint of the specific activities to be engaged in, their sequencing, and the time frame. There are three questions:

- How specific do the activities have to be?
- How rigid does the order have to be?
- How soon does each activity have to be carried out?

Kirschenbaum suggested that, at least in some cases, being less specific and rigid in terms of activities, sequencing, and deadlines can "encourage people to pursue their goals by continually and flexibly choosing their activities" (p. 492). That is, flexibility in planning can help clients become more self-reliant and proactive. This is another way of saying, "Principles, yes; formulas, no." For a much more detailed approach to planning, see the works of Robert Carkhuff (1985, 1987).

HELPING CLIENTS DEVELOP CONTINGENCY PLANS

One important reason for helping clients develop alternatives, or contingency plans, is the possibility that the chosen plan, or part of it, might not work.

> Jason, the man dying of cancer, decided to become a resident in the hospice he had visited. Of course, the hospice had an entire program in place for helping patients like Jason die with dignity. Along the way, Jason would have to make some decisions about the steps in the program, but he did not formulate it. He thought that this would be the best way both for him and for his family to handle his dying. However, although he had visited the hospice and had liked what he had seen, he could not be absolutely sure that being a resident there would work out. Therefore, with the help of the counselor, he settled on two other possibilities as back-up plans. One was living at home with some outreach services from the hospice. The other was spending his last days in a smaller hospital in a nearby town. This last alternative would not be as convenient for his family, but he would feel more comfortable there, since he hated large hospitals. If for any reason he had to move to his second or third choice, he would need to do further planning.

Contingency plans are needed especially when clients choose a high-risk program to achieve a critical goal. Having back-up plans also helps clients develop more responsibility. If they see that a plan is not working, then they have to decide whether to try the contingency plan. Back-up plans need not be complicated. A counselor might merely ask: "If that doesn't work, then what will you do?" As in the case of Jason, clients can be helped to specify a contingency plan further once it is seen that the first choice is not working out. Recognize, though, that some clients might have the patience to develop a plan, but not to consider back-up plans.

LINKING STEP III-C TO ACTION

Both as a counselor and a consultant, I have learned one thing about plans, both those formulated by individuals and those formulated by organizations: many of them end up in a drawer someplace. Plans have a way of putting us face to face with the work we will have to do to accomplish our goals and touching off our resistance to change. As a friend once said, only half in jest, "I want to be happy, so I don't make plans."

Some clients are filled with great ideas for getting things done, but never seem to do anything. They lack the discipline to evaluate their ideas, choose the best, and then cast them into a step-by-step plan. This kind of work seems too tedious, even though it is precisely what they need. What you must be with this kind of client is a planner—or rather, a consultant to their planning. Ask questions such as, What are you going to do today? Tomorrow? The next day? Such questions may sound very simple, but it is surprising how much leverage they can provide. Linking planning and the entire helping process to action is so important that it is revisited in the next chapter.

EVALUATION QUESTIONS FOR STEP III-C

Helpers can ask themselves the following questions as they help clients formulate the kinds of plans that actually drive action.

- What is the place of planning in my own life?
- To what degree do I believe in the advantages of planning?
- How quickly do I move to planning when I see that it is what the client needs in order to manage problems and develop opportunities better?
- What do I do to help clients overcome inertia and resistance to planning?
- How effectively do I help clients formulate subgoals that lead to the accomplishment of overall preferred-scenario goals?
- How practical am I in helping clients identify the activities needed to accomplish subgoals, sequence these activities, and establish realistic time frames for them?
- How well do I adapt the specificity and detail of planning to the needs of each client?
- How well do I help clients who need them develop contingency plans?
- Even at this planning step, how easily do I move back and forth among the different stages and steps of the helping model as the need arises?
- How readily do clients actually move to action because of my work with them in planning?
- What do I need to do to become more effective at planning?

Chapter Seventeen

Action II: Helping Clients Put Strategies to Work

Unless a capacity for thinking be accompanied by a capacity for action, a superior man exists in torture.

Benedetto Croce

Unless there be correct thought, there cannot be any action, and when there is correct thought, right action will follow.

Henry George

The two quotations above each underscore the need for both thought and action. However, they need to be adapted if they are to be applied to the helping process. First, the superior client, whether challenged by self or others, *finds* some way to move toward his or her goals. There is always some kind of capacity to act. Second, while meaningful analysis and planning (correct thought) provide direction for problem-managing and opportunity-developing action, they do not assure it. Counselors often need to help clients generalize what they learn in the helping sessions and transfer it to everyday-life conditions (Monroe, 1988). Indeed, helping clients generalize and transfer what they learn and then maintain what they gain is an ethical imperative. Unfortunately, some research (Llewelyn, 1988) shows that while many clients want to get on with managing their problems, some helpers are more interested in helping them explore the past and discover the causes of their problems. For such counselors, helping clients initiate and sustain problem-managing action takes a back seat. Indeed, there is evidence that helpers know little about their clients once they leave the helping relationship (Lewis & Magoon, 1987).

Some clients, once they have a clear idea of what to do to handle a problem situation—whether or not they have a formal plan—go ahead and do it. They need little or nothing in terms of further support and challenge from a helper. They either find the resources they need within themselves or get support and challenge from the significant others in the social settings of their lives. Other clients, however, still need a greater or lesser degree of support and challenge from a helper to implement their strategies and plans. For one reason or another, they feel uncertain about taking action: perhaps they distrust their own resources or come to see the action program as too demanding. Many clients fall somewhere between these two extremes. Although a client may be able to handle most of the implementation process on her own, she may find that some part of an action program seems so difficult for her to handle that she still needs help.

Luisa, an unmarried woman in her early fifties, was living in a halfway house after a five-year stay in a mental hospital located in a rural area of the state. At the halfway house she had been trained in various social skills to help her cope with her new urban environment. The aim of the program was to help her develop greater independence so that, ultimately,

I. Present scenario II. Preferred scenario III. Strategy: Getting there

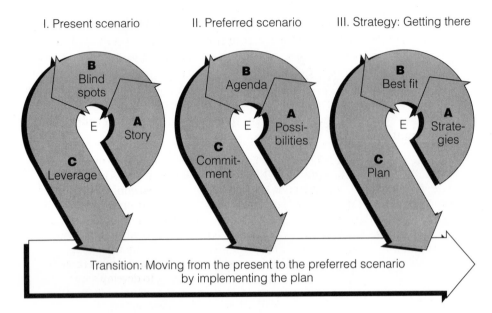

FIGURE 17-1 Transition: Moving from the Present to the Preferred Scenario

she could leave the halfway house and live on her own. One of the programs involved helping her and other residents learn how to use the transportation system of the city. As part of the program, Luisa had already ridden both buses and subways to various locations in the city, including the Social Security office, the state welfare office, and the park along the lake front. Up to this point, however, staff members had always accompanied residents on these journeys. Now Luisa was about to "solo," and she was frightened. The counselor helped her talk through her fears and encouraged her to take the short and simple trip that was the next part of the program. Luisa wanted to become more independent, but she had learned a great deal of dependence in the hospital and was finding it hard to overcome.

Luisa needed help at the implementation stage. The training program had given her some of the skills she needed to become more independent, but she needed further support and challenge to help her stick to the program. It is often critical not only to encourage clients to act but to support them when they do.

The action arrow of the helping model in Figure 17-1 constitutes the "transition state" (Beckhard & Harris, 1977) in which clients move from the current to the preferred scenario by implementing strategies and plans. However, as Ferguson (1980) noted, clients often feel at risk during transition times. They have the "trapeze" feeling of letting go of one trapeze bar, that is, familiar but dysfunctional patterns of behavior, and grabbing hold of the other bar, that is, new and more productive patterns of behavior. Some clients, anticipating the terror of being in midair without support, refuse to let go. Inertia wins. This is one reason why it is important to encourage clients to act, at least in small ways, from the first session on. If they start acting to change things right from the beginning, that is, if each stage and step of the helping model is used as a driver of action, then they are less likely to be stymied by the actions called for by a more formal plan.

> Enid, a 40-year-old single woman, is making a great deal of progress in controlling her drinking through her involvement with an AA program. In terms of managing her drinking, she is on the transition arrow of the helping model. But she is just deciding what she wants to do about a troubled relationship with a man. In fact, her drinking was, in part, an ineffective way of avoiding the problems in the relationship. She knows that she no longer wants to tolerate the psychological abuse she has been getting from her male friend, but she fears the vacuum she will create by cutting off the relationship. She is, therefore, trying to develop some preferred-scenario possibilities for a better relationship, while realizing that ending the relationship might turn out to be the best option.
>
> Because of counseling Enid has been much more assertive in the relationship. She now cuts off contact whenever her companion becomes abusive. That is, she is engaging in a series of "small acts" that help her manage her life better and discover further possibilities. Since this is not the first time she has experienced psychological abuse, she is beginning to wonder what it is about herself that in some way almost draws contempt. She has a sneaking feeling that the contempt of others might mirror the way she feels about herself. She has also begun to wonder why she has stayed in a safe, but low-paying, job so long. She realizes that at work she is simply taken for granted. In other words, there are some issues Enid has yet to explore.

Enid, with a number of interrelated problems, is at different stages of action with respect to different problems. In terms of her drinking, she is on the transition arrow. But her relationship problems still need to be addressed. The "little acts" constitute a short-term remedy while preparing her for whatever more substantive action might be called for. She has not yet done much about changing her internal self-belittling behavior.

IN PURSUIT OF VALUED OUTCOMES

The helping model does not emphasize action for the sake of action, but rather action that leads to valued outcomes in terms of problems managed and opportunities developed. In the end we need to ask: Did a change of "clinical significance" (Kazdin, 1977)—that is, a change that made a difference in the client's life—actually take place? Monroe (1988) talked about the need for "durable, clinically significant changes" (p. 452). For instance, in counseling a client like Enid with self-esteem problems, a helper should be more interested in hearing her say that she has switched to a more demanding, lucrative job than that she is "feeling better" (Leahey & Wallace, 1988).

Remember, however, that the value of any outcome lies, to a degree, in the eye of the beholder. A client's redefining of the original problem can be a sign of a successful outcome. Leahey and Wallace (1988, p. 216) offered the following example.

> "For the last five years, I've thought of myself as a person with low self-esteem and have read self-help books, gone to therapists, and put things off until I felt I had good self-esteem. I just need to get on with my life, and I can do that with excellent self-esteem or poor self-esteem. Treatment isn't really necessary. Being a person with enough self-esteem to handle situations is good enough for me." (Leahey & Wallace, 1988, p. 216)

It may be that, in the end, Enid will say something like this. The following client redefines the problem situation, seeing it now from a different angle.

> "I would say that I am completely cured. . . . I can still pinpoint these conditions which I had thought to be symptoms. . . . These worries and anxieties make me prepare thoroughly for the daily work I have to do. They prevent me from being careless. They are expressions of the desire to grow and to develop." (Kora, 1967, quoted in Weisz, Rothbaum, & Blackburn, 1984, p. 964)

Some helpers, reviewing these last two examples, would be disappointed. Others would see them as legitimate examples of adapting to rather than changing reality.

FOLLOW-THROUGH: SUSTAINED ACTION

We have discussed client action in general in Chapter 4. This chapter deals with translating explicit strategies and plans into action and sustaining problem-managing and opportunity-developing action once initiated. Kanfer and Schefft (1988, p. 58) differentiated between *decisional* self-control and *protracted* self-control. In the former, a single choice terminates a conflict, while in the latter, continued resistance to temptation is required. Most clients need both kinds of self-control to manage their lives better. Enid's choice to give up alcohol completely (decisional self-control) needs to be complemented by the ability to handle inevitable longer-term temptations. It is the latter type of self-control that demands that clients become effective tacticians. For example, it is easier for Enid to turn down an invitation to go to a bar in the first place than to sit in a bar all evening and refrain from drinking.

Many clients eagerly initiate action programs but give them up once they run into obstacles either within themselves (such as flagging motivation) or in the environment (such as unexpected obstacles). A married couple trying to reinvent their marriage might eventually say to themselves, "We had no idea that it would be so hard to change ingrained ways of interacting with each other. Is it worth the effort?" Their motivation is on the wane. Or Enid might find that her friends are not ready for a new Enid. They prefer the Enid that let others run roughshod over her, the Enid who drowned her pride and self-respect in drink. This environmental obstacle is unexpected, because Enid thought that everyone would like the new Enid.

Kirschenbaum (1987) investigated factors involved in "self-regulatory failure" and found that a number of factors can contribute to giving up, including low initial commitment to change, weak efficacy and outcome expectations, the use of self-punishment rather than self-reward, depressive thinking, failure to cope with emotional stressors, lack of consistent self-monitoring, failure to use effective habit-change techniques, giving in to social pressure, failure to cope with initial relapse, and paying attention to the wrong things (for instance, how the environment is doing me in rather than how I am failing to cope with the environment). And this is only a partial list. Sometimes I say something like this to clients: "Let's play a little game. Now that you have a plan, let's assume that the probability of your acting on it in a sustained way is zero. What do you need to do to raise the probability from nothing to something?" This is not a statement of despair, but a challenge to cope with the realities discovered by Kirschenbaum's investigations.

Entropy: The Enemy of Sustained Action

Inertia, as we saw in Chapter 4, is the human tendency to put off problem-managing action. With respect to inertia, I often say to clients: "The action program you've come up with seems to be a sound one. The main reason that sound action programs don't work, however, is that they are never tried. Don't be surprised if you feel reluctant to act or are tempted to put off the first steps. This is quite natural. Ask yourself what you can do to get by that initial barrier."

Entropy, on the other hand, is the tendency to give up action that has been initiated. We start diets or exercise programs, and they fall apart or trail off. Phillips (1987) identified what he calls the "ubiquitous decay curve": "Psychotherapy, medical delivery systems, and client behavior in addiction treatment all show the 'same' negatively accelerating, declining, decay curve that is based, respectively, on attrition, noncompliance, and relapse" (p. 650). He goes on to say that this is simply the way human beings tend to operate: "The decay curve is descriptive of how delivery systems operate and is not a deviation from normalcy" (p. 650). Wise helpers know that the decay curve is part of life and help clients deal with it. With respect to entropy, I might say: "Even sound action programs begun with the best of intentions tend to fall part over time, so don't be surprised when your initial enthusiasm seems to wane a bit. That's only natural. Rather, ask yourself what you need to do to keep yourself at the task." Brownell and her associates (1986) provide a useful caution: "A fine line must be drawn between preparing a person for mistakes and giving 'permission' for mistakes to occur by inferring that they are inevitable" (p. 773). They also make a distinction between "lapse" and "relapse." A slip or a mistake in an action program (a lapse) need not lead to a relapse, that is, giving up the program entirely.

> Graham has been trying to change what others see as his "angry interpersonal style." Using a variety of self-monitoring and self-control techniques, he has made great progress in changing his style. On occasion he might lose his temper, but never in any extreme way. An occasional lapse does not end up in relapse.

Stein (1980) suggested that action programs need to be buttressed by "rachets," that is, strategies and tactics designed to keep action programs from falling apart. Helping clients find the right set of rachets might be one of the best things a helper can do. Getting frequent feedback from two close friends has been one of Graham's rachets.

The decay curve is not restricted to clients and patients. All of us have experienced the problems involved in trying to implement programs. We make plans, and they seem realistic to us. We start the steps of a program with a good deal of enthusiasm. However, we soon run into tedium, obstacles, and complications. What seemed so easy in the planning stage now seems quite difficult. We become discouraged, flounder, recover, flounder again, and finally give up, offering ourselves rationalizations why we did not want to accomplish those goals anyway.

> Tina launched herself on a program that involved changing her eating habits. The novelty of the program carried her along for the first two weeks. However, during the third week the program lost its novelty, her ultimate goal seemed as distant as ever, and she kept reminding herself of how hungry she was. She became discouraged and depressed. During the middle of the fourth week, she quit the program. She talked about her probably incurable "glandular imbalance" and the stupid way our culture views "heavier" people.

Tina did not know the principles of effective implementation; nor did she have the skills of putting them into practice.

Wise helpers are neither cynical nor naive about inertia and entropy. They are part of the human condition and need to be factored into the helping process. If we don't deal with inertia and entropy, they will deal with us.

Helping Clients Become Effective Tacticians

Up to this point in the helping process the emphasis has been on strategy, that is, the overall action program or plan for achieving goals and objectives. In the implementation and follow-through phase the focus is switched from strategy to tactics and logistics. Tactics is the art of adapting a plan to the immediate situation. This includes being able to change the plan on the spot in order to handle unforeseen complications. Logistics is the art of being able to provide the resources needed for the implementation of a plan.

> During the summer Rebecca wanted to take an evening course in statistics so that the first semester of the following school year would be lighter. Having more time would enable her to act in one of the school plays, a high priority for her. Her goal and program were adequate, but she didn't have the money to pay for the course, and at the university she planned to attend prepayment for summer courses was the rule. Rebecca had counted on paying for the course from her summer earnings, but she would not have the money until later. Consequently, she did some quick shopping and found that the same course was being offered by a community college not too far from where she had intended to go. Her tuition there was minimal, since she was a resident of the area the college served. She switched schools.

In this example, Rebecca keeps to her overall plan (strategy). However, she adapts the plan to an unforeseen circumstance (tactics) by locating another resource (logistics). This chapter provides some guidelines for counselors in helping clients become effective tacticians in coping with external obstacles to action and all the faces of entropy within.

Using Behavioral Principles to Encourage Sustained Action

Brownell and her associates (1986) have noted that relatively little work has been done on methods of enhancing client motivation: "Many [clients] . . . are motivated, but many are not. A major challenge is to enhance motivation when it is low in order to maximize readiness for change. Little systematic work has been done in this area" (p. 773). Kanfer and Schefft (1988, see pp. 105–114, 123–166, and 215–294) have gone a long way toward filling this gap by developing a wide range of strategies for increasing motivation and commitment both to goals and to the action programs through which they are achieved. They suggest that counselors help clients do such things as the following:

- Modify the environment to make action easier.
- Simplify the action-strategy sequence needed to accomplish the goal.
- Disrupt automatic responses so that habit does not always win.
- Find substitutions for unwanted behavior.
- Engage in self-monitoring.

- Set their own behavioral standards.
- Build mini-successes into the program.
- Find mentors and models.
- Readjust the time frames of action programs.
- Learn to relax and to enjoy life.

The "technology" of helping clients move to and sustain action exists (Watson & Tharp, 1989). It needs to be appreciated by helpers and transferred to clients.

Motivation to keep at a difficult action program is, at root, a question of incentives and rewards, the ability of clients to use the principles of incentive/reward-based behavior change to pursue their goals. Counselors can help clients make the principles of behavior—using incentives and rewards, avoiding the extinction of goal-directed action, using self-punishment judiciously, managing temptations to avoid the work of change, and shaping action programs—work for instead of against them. Since action means behavior, every helper, as suggested earlier, should become grounded in the principles of behavior. Let's take a brief look at how some of these principles apply to client action.

Incentives and Rewards

Just as incentives are important in clients' committing themselves to preferred scenarios, so are they important in carrying out the action programs that get goals accomplished. Clients are more likely to embark on any given step of a program if they have clear and meaningful incentives for doing so. Since distant goals may not appear that rewarding in the heat of battle, it is often necessary to help clients identify both the intrinsic and the extrinsic reinforcements or rewards that are available at each step. Perhaps one of the best things a helper can do is to join with a client in celebrating the successful completion of a step or even in savoring the learnings that can come from unsuccessful or only partially successful attempts to implement a course of action.

> Dwight was about to give up an arduous physical rehabilitation program. The counselor asked him to visit the children's ward. Dwight was both shaken by the experience and amazed at the courage of many of the kids. He was especially struck by one teenager who was undergoing chemotherapy. "He seems so positive about everything," Dwight said. The counselor told him that the boy was tempted to give up, too. He suggested a pact: that Dwight not give up if the boy didn't; that the boy not give up if Dwight didn't.
>
> Dwight and the boy saw each other frequently. Dwight put up with the pain. The boy hung in there. Three months later the boy died. Dwight's response, besides grief, was, "I can't give up now; that would really be letting him down."

Don't immediately blame clients who do not participate in action programs they contract for or who falter along the way. It may well be that they do not see strong enough short-term or even long-term incentives for sticking to the implementation of strategies. Do work at helping clients find the kinds of intrinsic and extrinsic incentives that will help them stick to programs the way Dwight found his.

Extinction

Activities that are not rewarded tend over time to lose their vigor, decrease, and even disappear. This process is called *extinction*.

> Luigi, a middle-aged man, had been in and out of mental hospitals a number of times. He discovered that one of the best ways of staying out was to use some of his excess energy helping others. He had not returned to the hospital once during the three years he worked at a soup kitchen. However, finding himself becoming more and more manic over the past six months and fearing rehospitalization, he sought the help of a counselor.
>
> Luigi's discussions with the counselor led to some interesting findings. They discovered that, while in the beginning he had worked at the soup kitchen because he wanted to, he was now working there because he thought he should. He felt guilty about leaving and also thought that doing so would leave him exposed to a relapse. In sum, he had not lost his interest in helping others, but his current work was no longer interesting or challenging. As a result of his sessions with the counselor, Luigi began to work for a group that provided housing for the homeless and elderly. He poured his energy into his new work and no longer felt manic.

The lesson here is that incentives cannot be put in place and then be taken for granted. Like many other organic things, they need tending.

Punishment or Sanctions

The use of punishment, including self-punishment, is often a poor way of attempting to change behavior. Still there are exceptions. One form of punishment, withholding a reward, can be useful in many cases.

> Enid was avoiding a complete physical checkup even though certain physical symptoms were persisting. She planned taking a weekend trip to see a very good friend. After talking to the counselor, she contracted with herself to put off the trip until she had had the checkup. Two weeks later she finally made an appointment.

Enid terminated her procrastination behavior by withholding a reward. In some circumstances this kind of self-punishment can be an aid in getting action programs on line.

Dealing with Avoidance

Clients avoid engaging in action programs when the incentives and rewards for *not* engaging in the program are stronger than the rewards for doing so.

> Miguel kept saying that he wanted to leave his father's business and strike out on his own, especially since he and his father had heated arguments

over how the business should be run. He earned an MBA in night school and talked about becoming a consultant to small, family-run businesses. A medium-sized consulting firm offered him a job. He accepted on the condition that he could finish up some work in the family business. But he always found "one more" project in the family business that needed his attention. All of this came out as part of his "story" even though his main concern was the fact that his woman friend of five years had given him an ultimatum: get married or forget about the relationship.

If clients are not implementing some step of a program, if they are putting it off, or if they are implementing it in only a desultory way, help them ask themselves questions like the following:

- What punishing consequences are involved with this step of the program?
- What can I do to minimize them?
- What rewards do I experience for *not* implementing a strategy?
- What can I do to neutralize them?
- Do I have a reasonable but firm time line for completing the step?
- What payoff do I get for completing the step?
- Is the payoff clear to me and suited to my needs and wants?

In his discussions with the counselor, Miguel learned some painful truths about himself.

- He prized comfort, and moving to another job would be uncomfortable, at least in the beginning.
- He prized autonomy. His father let him do what he wanted. Almost any other job would mean less autonomy.
- Both of these characteristics were at the center of his problems with the woman in his life.

The counselor helped Miguel focus on the rewards of moving on to another job: the chance to test his mettle and to learn new skills, advancement, excellent salary prospects. But in this case Miguel lost both the job offer and his woman friend. Even though he was 28, he kept saying that he was too young and that there were too many things he wanted to do before tying himself down. It is always important to remember that what is an incentive for one person might seem a punishment to another.

Force-Field Analysis: Forewarned Is Forearmed

Force-field analysis (Lewin, 1969; Organization Design and Development, 1986; Spier, 1973) is a simple tool to help clients cope with obstacles and develop resources during the implementation of an action program.

> A force-field is the social-psychological field that immediately surrounds a decision or action. . . . An examination or analysis of a [client's] force field, especially one that focuses on the resources available and the obstacles to

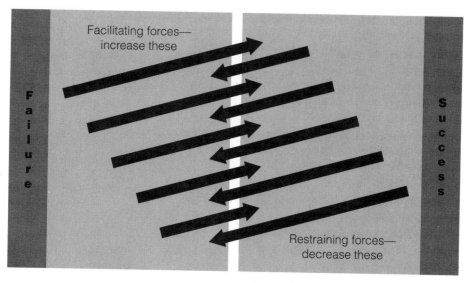

FIGURE 17-2   Force-Field Analysis

action, is frequently useful for four reasons: (a) by focusing on the [client's] perceptions of environmental influences, the nature of these perceptions becomes open to scrutiny, revision, . . . and test; (b) a complete account of obstacles and resources decreases the likelihood that pitfalls or potentials will be overlooked in the [execution of an action program]; (c) using knowledge of the influences in the [client's] environment helps to capitalize on opportunities . . . that go beyond the resources under a [client's] direct control; and (d) alternative strategies . . . to implement an [action plan] can be created and assessed in the context of the force field. (Gottfredson, 1984, p. 1105)

Force-field analysis, then, is simply an analysis by the client of the major obstacles to, and resources for, the implementation of strategies and plans. Once clients see what their goals are and draw up plans to achieve these goals, they can be helped to discover what forces will keep them from implementing their programs (restraining forces) and what forces will help them implement these programs (facilitating forces). This look into the future can save clients a great deal of grief down the line. "Forewarned is forearmed" is the philosophy underlying force-field analysis.

Restraining Forces

Restraining forces are the obstacles that might be encountered during the implementation process, while facilitating forces are the resources at hand for moving toward a goal. This process is illustrated in Figure 17-2. The identification of possible obstacles to the implementation of a program helps make clients forewarned.

Raul and Maria are a childless couple living in a large midwestern city. They have been married for about five years and have not been able to have children. They finally decide that they would like to adopt a child, and so they consult a counselor familiar with adoptions. The counselor helps them work out a plan of action that includes helping them examine their motivation and lifestyle, contacting an agency, and preparing themselves for an interview. After the plan has been worked out, Raul and Maria, with the help of the counselor, identify two restraining forces: the negative feelings that often arise on the part of prospective parents when they are being scrutinized by an adoption agency and the feelings of helplessness and frustration caused by the length of time and uncertainty involved in the process.

The assumption here is that if clients are aware of some of the "wrinkles" that can accompany any given course of action, they will be less disoriented when they encounter them. This part of the force-field analysis process is, at its best, a straightforward census of probable pitfalls rather than a self-defeating search for every possible thing that could go wrong.

Restraining forces can come from within the clients themselves, from others, from the social settings of their lives, and from larger environmental forces. Once a restraining force is identified, ways of coping with it can be identified. Sometimes simply being aware of a pitfall is enough to help clients mobilize their resources to handle it. At other times a more explicit coping strategy is needed. For instance, the counselor arranged a couple of role-playing sessions with Raul and Maria in which she played the role of the examiner at the adoption agency and took a "hard line" in her questioning. These rehearsals helped them stay calm during the actual interviews. The counselor also helped them locate a mutual-help group of parents working their way through the adoption process. The members of the group shared their hopes and frustrations and provided support for one another. In a word, Raul and Maria were trained to cope with the restraining forces they might encounter on the road toward their goal.

Facilitating Forces

In a more positive vein, force-field analysis can help clients identify important resources to be used in implementing programs. These are the facilitating forces. Facilitating forces can be persons, places, or things. One client identified and used another person as a facilitating force.

Shirley was going to stop smoking as part of a physical fitness program. Shirley listed her mother as a facilitating force because she, too, had decided to quit. Shirley knew that their friendly vying with each other and the mutual encouragement that they got from talking to each other would provide much of the challenge and support they both would need.

Another client found the Bible and meditation facilitating forces.

Nora found it extremely depressing to go to her weekly dialysis sessions. She knew that without them she would die—but she wondered whether it was worth living if she had to depend on a machine. The counselor helped her see how she was making life more difficult for herself by letting herself think such discouraging thoughts. He helped her learn how to think thoughts that would broaden her vision of the world instead of narrowing it down to herself, her pain and discomfort, and the machine.

Nora was a religious person and found in the Bible a rich source of positive thinking. She initiated a new routine: The day before she visited the clinic, she began to prepare herself psychologically by reading from the Bible. Then, as she traveled to the clinic and underwent treatment, she meditated slowly on what she had read.

In this last case the client substituted positive thinking, a facilitating force, for "stinking thinking," a restraining force.

The following steps may be used in helping clients use force-field analysis:

- Help clients list all the restraining forces that might make them discard an action program. Brainstorming is used in this step.
- Help clients list all the facilitating forces that can help them persevere in implementing strategies and plans. This step deals with resources. It helps clients look at what they have going for themselves.
- Have clients underline the forces in each list (facilitating and restraining) that seem most critical with respect to carrying out the action plan. Clients cannot deal with every facilitating and every restraining force. Some are more important than others.
- Help clients identify ways of reducing significant restraining forces and of strengthening significant facilitating forces.

Obviously this process need not be used formally as outlined here. Rather, effective helpers have the force-field paradigm in their minds and use it to both probe and challenge. For instance, after Enid tells the counselor that she has decided to terminate her relationship with her abusive friend, the following exchange takes place.

Counselor: When are you going to tell him?
Enid: When I see him tomorrow night.
Counselor: What's the one thing that might keep you from doing it?
Enid: I can immediately think of two. Strange as it might seem, I'll feel sorry for him. And also I'll be saying to myself, "Now I'll have no one."
Counselor: And what's the one thing that will make you go through with it?
Enid (emphatically): My self-respect!
Counselor: I think I know which is going to win.

STRATEGIES FOR INITIATING AND SUSTAINING ACTION

There is no want of strategies for helping clients initiate and sustain problem-managing action. It is a question of counselors' being aware of and helping clients use them. Only a few are reviewed here.

"Check" or "Think" Steps

A practical concept that helps clients bridge between planning and action is what Carkhuff (1985, Chapter 6) called "check" or "think" steps.

> Check steps are actually "question steps." That is, they indicate to clients what they should be asking themselves during the implementation stage. Check steps are used to guide clients' . . . performance. There are three types of check steps: "before" check steps; "during" check steps; and "after" check steps. As the names suggest, "before" check steps indicate what clients should think about before performing a certain behavior; "during" check steps indicate what clients should think about while performing the step; "after" check steps indicate what clients should think about after performing the step. (Anthony, Pierce, & Cohen, 1979, p. 53)

These authors suggested that the last step before implementation of a course of action is to draw up a list of practical check steps. This technique extends force-field thinking into the field of action itself.

Let us return to Luisa, a client we met earlier in this chapter.

> Luisa has spent almost a year in the halfway house. She has gotten a decent part-time job and is now considering moving out of the halfway house as the next step toward becoming more independent. She does not yet feel ready to live on her own, however, and would like to live with a family or a friend for a while. The staff of the halfway house acts as an intermediary between the residents and families or individuals who are open to having residents come live with them temporarily. Luisa has a couple of friends and knows one family she might ask.
>
> With the help of the counselor Luisa decides to talk with a couple of families and a few single people. It is made clear to everyone that these chats are exploratory. No final decision is being made by either party on the basis of this one talk. This makes Luisa feel free, but she still wants to put her best foot forward in these meetings. The counselor helps her deal with her misgivings by the use of check steps.

Here are some questions Luisa asks herself before she goes for the interview:

- Is it clear in my mind what I want to say about myself?
- How do I control the "You're going to reject me" feelings I have before I even get there?
- What do I do if people seem to be putting me down or making me feel like a "case"?

Here are the kinds of things she wants to ask herself during the interview:

- To what degree am I being myself instead of some person I think these people would like me to be?
- How well am I listening to these people, trying to understand their point of view?
- What do I need to do now that I sense a certain lack of enthusiasm on their part?

Finally, here are some questions she asks herself when she returns to the halfway house:

- What do I do to avoid letting myself get depressed because everything did not go perfectly?
- What would I like to add to what I said to them?
- What further questions do I have of them?

A caution is in order here: Cluttering up the program-development process with unneeded check steps can make clients overly self-conscious. A force-field analysis of the facilitating and restraining factors in the implementation of a program can help pinpoint the check steps that are needed.

In addition to providing a useful tool for clients, the think-step paradigm can be a source of helper probes and challenge. Back to Enid and her counselor:

Counselor: As you're talking to him tomorrow night, what's the most important thing you have to ask yourself?

Enid: I'd ask, "Enid, are you being true to yourself? Are you saying what you have to say without losing your self-respect?"

Most of the models and techniques in this book can be used as a basis for this kind of probing and challenge.

Kanfer and Schefft (1988, pp. 108–114) formulated their own six "think rules," basing them on a cognitive-behavioral approach to helping. These rules are action-oriented and should be woven into the helping process from the very beginning:

1. Think *behavior*, because helping is about action.
2. Think *solution*, because helping is about problem-managing outcomes.
3. Think *positive*, because action needs to be based on resources and strengths, not problems and weaknesses.
4. Think *small steps*, because the action needed to accomplish small steps tends to be clear and specific.
5. Think *flexible*, because clients must adapt their action programs to changing circumstances.
6. Think *future*, because helping at its best equips clients to transfer what they learn from dealing with current problems to future problems.

Action-Based Contracts

Earlier we discussed self-contracts as a way of helping clients commit themselves to their preferred scenarios. Since many clients find it rewarding to make contracts with themselves and keep them, self-contracts are also useful in helping them both initiate and sustain problem-managing action. Such contracts specify precisely what they are to do and indicate rewards for success and sanctions for failures (see Cormier & Cormier, 1979, pp. 506–512; Ferguson, 1987a; Rudestam, 1980, pp. 122–127). Self-contracts are especially helpful for more difficult aspects of action programs; they help focus clients' energies.

> Eunice and Edgar are involved in a deteriorating marriage. The assessment stage indicates that the problems are multiple. One aim agreed to by both of them is that the present chaos in the home needs to be reduced. For instance, neither spouse does much housework, and Edgar comes and goes as he pleases, missing meals (however poorly prepared) without notice. They seem to be deeply committed to punishing each other by this chaotic behavior. An initial contract to which both agree includes Eunice's keeping the house clean and orderly for a week and Edgar's sticking to a schedule that allows him to take care of work commitments but still leaves him time at home. Actually both are committing themselves to self-contracts, because they each agree to carry out their program despite what the other does.

In this case the contracts prove most useful in introducing a degree of order into the couple's home life. Neither the counselor nor the clients assume that fulfilling these contracts will solve all the problems of the relationship. What they are trying to do is to create the kind of climate that will enable them to begin to work together in sorting out issues that are critical to the marriage.

In the next example, several parties must commit themselves to the provisions of the contract.

> A boy in the seventh grade was causing a great deal of disturbance by his outbreaks in class. The usual kinds of punishment did not seem to work. After the teacher discussed the situation with the school counselor, the counselor called a meeting of all the stakeholders—the boy, his parents, the teacher, and the principal. The counselor offered a simple contract. When the boy disrupted the class, one and only one thing would happen: He would go home. Once the teacher indicated that his behavior was disruptive, he was to go to the principal's office and check out without receiving any kind of lecture. He was to go immediately home and check in with whichever parent was at home, again without receiving any further punishment. The next day he was to return to school. All agreed to the contract, though both principal and parents said they would find it difficult not to add to the punishment.
>
> The first month the boy spent a fair number of days or partial days at home. The second month, however, he missed only two partial days, and the third month only one. He really wanted to be in school with his classmates. That's where the action was. And so he paid the price of self-control in order to get what he wanted. The contract proved an effective tool of behavioral change.

Note: When a contract is drawn up, it should stipulate when it is to be reviewed.

Helping Clients Find Social Support and Challenge

Clients often find counseling goals attractive and threatening at the same time. Since adherence to stressful decisions is painful, both social support and challenge can help them move to action, persevere in action programs, and maintain gains (Breier & Strauss, 1984; Bruhn & Philips, 1984; Janis, 1983a; Lieberman, 1986; Marziali, 1987). Breier & Strauss (1984) discovered that supportive and challenging relationships can provide many benefits for clients, among them a forum for ventilation, reality testing, social support and approval, integration into a community, problem solving, and constancy. While their research focused on clients recovering from psychotic disorders, their findings have wide application. Even though, ideally, support and challenge are woven together in the social systems of people's lives, they will be touched on separately here.

Social Support

We have already discussed how necessary it is to help isolated clients develop social resources. These resources are critical when clients are "out there" acting on their own. Protracted contact with the helper is usually not feasible, yet support remains essential.

> Despite the enormous research literature on social influence . . . we still know relatively little about when, how, and why social support is effective in helping people change their actions. . . . In a recent review of pertinent research, Judith Rodin . . . concludes that social support can buffer the individual from potentially unfavorable effects of all sorts of crises and environmental changes by facilitating coping and adaptation. She cites numerous empirical studies indicating that men and women who have social support from significant others . . . tend to manifest higher morale, to have fewer somatic illnesses, and to live longer than those who do not. (Janis, 1983a, p. 144)

We know that social support is extremely important for most people, even though we do not know how it works. But in helping clients develop social-support systems we must remember both the positives and the negatives: Social relationships are not just comforting but stressful (Coyne & DeLongis, 1986). Too little social support can actually be alienating, while too much social support can be suffocating or may relieve clients of the burdens of self-responsibility.

Individual differences are important. Some have suggested that "it is not social activity per se that is health protective, but how that activity is perceived and interpreted" (Heller, Swindle, & Dusenbury, 1986, p. 466). Two women discussed in this chapter, Luisa and Enid, had quite different social-support requirements. Luisa was a much more introverted person. When she got offers for accommodations from both a couple and a single person, she chose the couple because she thought that they would have each other and would not make excessive social demands on her. On the other hand, Enid, once she made the decision to break with her abusive partner, needed an active social-support system.

Such support is neither an admission of defeat nor an abdication of the principles of self-responsibility advocated in Chapter 3. It is an exercise in common sense. Support groups and self-help groups (Gottlieb & Schroter, 1978; Pancoast, Parker, & Froland, 1983; Pearson, 1982, 1983) seem to be especially needed in socially fragmented and high-tech societies (Naisbitt, 1982). Effective helpers are aware of such resources in the community and are prepared to develop them if they do not exist.

One problem with social support is that the kinds of supportive communication skills discussed earlier are not widely distributed in the population. People confuse sympathy and empathy and do not readily communicate the latter. In the case of both Luisa and Enid, empathic relationships were established even though the individuals involved did not use the skills of active listening and empathy very well.

Challenging Relationships

It was suggested earlier that support without challenge can be hollow and that challenge without support can be abrasive. Ideally, the people in the lives of clients provide a judicious mixture of support and challenge. Or, put in a way that respects clients' self-responsibility, they help clients make reasonable demands on themselves. Friendship, like helping, is, in part, an exercise in social influence. This undermines neither my "unconditional positive regard" for my friend nor my commitment to his or her self-responsibility. Clients, like the rest of us, do not need social systems filled with yes-men and yes-women. The couple with whom Luisa lived did not make excessive social demands on her, but they did nudge her toward developing the kind of simple social life that made sense for her. Enid's more robust friends actively challenged the ways she kept putting herself down. This kind of challenge helped her deal with her lack of self-esteem.

Quentin, a man in his early 50s, was suddenly stricken with a disease that called for immediate and drastic surgery. He came through the operation quite well, even getting out of the hospital in record time. For the first few weeks he seemed, within reason, to be his old self. However, he had problems with the drugs he had to take following the operation. He became quite sick and took on many of the mannerisms of a chronic invalid. Even after the right mix of drugs was found, he persisted in invalid-like behavior. Whereas right after the operation he had "walked tall," he now began to shuffle. He also talked constantly about his symptoms and generally used his "state" to excuse himself from normal activities.

At first Quentin's friends were in quandary. They realized the seriousness of the operation and tried to put themselves in his place. They provided all sorts of support. But gradually they realized that he was adopting a style that would alienate others and keep him out of the mainstream of life. Support was essential, but it was not enough. They used a variety of ways to challenge his behavior: mocking his "invalid" movements, engaging in serious one-to-one talks, turning a deaf ear to his discussion of symptoms, and routinely including him in their plans.

Quentin was fortunate. As with active listening and empathy, the skills of effective challenge are not widely distributed in the population. The MUM effect takes over and friends "let their friends be." Or, when they do challenge, they are aggressive rather than assertive.

Helping Clients Get Feedback on Performance

Gilbert (1978), in his book on human competence, claims that "improved information has more potential than anything else I can think of for creating more competence in the day-to-day management of performance" (p. 175; see Kirschenbaum, 1985). Feedback is one way of providing both support and challenge. If clients are to be successful in implementing programs, they need adequate information about how well they are performing. The purpose of feedback is not to pass judgment on the performance of clients but rather to provide guidance, support, and challenge. Feedback can be

- *confirmatory* when it lets clients know when they are on course, that is, moving successfully through the steps of an action program toward a goal;
- *corrective* when it provides clients with information they need to get back on course if they have strayed;
- *motivating* when it points out the consequences of both adequate and inadequate program implementation and includes suggestions for improving performance.

According to Gilbert (1978), good feedback does not take away the responsibility of the client. He urges those who give feedback to "supply as much backup information as needed to help people *troubleshoot their own performance*" (p. 179, emphasis added). Furthermore, when feedback is corrective, it should be concrete, that is, it should "relate various aspects of poor performance to specific remedial actions" (p. 179).

Consider the differences in the following two feedback approaches to a person having trouble with keeping to his diet.

Client: I can't seem to control myself. I want to stay on the diet, but sometimes almost without knowing what I'm doing I find myself eating. I followed it fairly well earlier in the week. I thought I should congratulate myself!

Counselor A: You don't seem to be motivated enough to stop overeating. I think the diet plan we worked out together is a good one.

Client: I think it's a good one, too. I seem to be lying to myself when I say that I want to lose weight.

Counselor B takes a different tack.

Client: I can't seem to control myself. I want to stay on the diet, but sometimes almost without knowing what I'm doing I find myself eating. I followed it fairly well earlier in the week. I thought I should congratulate myself!

Counselor B: Tell me as concretely as possible what happened. (*The client describes what he did and didn't do the previous week with respect to dieting.*) Okay, that's pretty clear. Now tell me what *you* think went wrong.

Client: Well, I just blew it. I bought too much food, for one thing. And the wrong kinds of things.

Counselor B: The times you followed your diet were early in the week, when your enthusiasm was still high. It seems that you showed yourself you can do it when the incentives are there. As for the rest of the week, I see two things. First of all, you forgot to set up immediate rewards for keeping to your diet schedule and perhaps mild punishments, like putting off something you'd like to do, for not doing so. Second, you probably are right in thinking that you can do something about stimulus control. You couldn't have eaten what you did if it hadn't been in the refrigerator in the first place! But that seems fairly clear to you now. How can you put what you've learned into practice this coming week?

Counselor A's feedback is vague and at least mildly judgmental. Counselor B offers some confirmatory and some corrective feedback without adopting a judgmental tone.

Here are some hints for giving feedback that supports sustained, problem-managing action.

First, train clients *to give feedback to themselves*. When Quentin falls back into invalid-like behavior, he can stop and tell himself what he's doing.

Second, help clients *identify feedback resources* in their everyday lives. Enid has a number of friends, but she knows two she especially trusts because of the way they understand and care about people and their willingness to say what they think.

Third, show clients how they have to *ask* for feedback at times instead of waiting for others to give it to them. Luisa eventually asks the couple with whom she is living to suggest things that will prepare her to live on her own. When asked, they point out that when she does go out she always seems to return refreshed and more in charge of herself. Then this wanes until she almost has to force herself to go out again.

Fourth, helper feedback should incorporate the principles of effective feedback:

• It should be confirmatory, corrective, and motivating.
• It should be brief and to the point.
• It should deal with behaviors rather than more elusive personality characteristics.

- It should be given in moderate doses. Overwhelming the client defeats the purpose of the entire exercise.
- The client can be invited not only to comment on the feedback but to expand on it.
- When feedback is corrective, clients should be helped to discover alternative ways of doing things.

Of course, feedback will be meaningless unless the client is motivated to improve his or her performance. The issue of incentives and rewards is ubiquitous. However, feedback, even corrective feedback, given in the proper spirit and in conformity to the suggestions above, is often experienced as rewarding by clients.

Training: Helping Clients Acquire the Skills They Need to Act

Sometimes clients do not act because they lack the working knowledge and skills required by strategies and action programs. If this is the case, then education and training link planning to action. The principle is clear: Either help clients devise action programs within the limitations of their current knowledge and skills or help them acquire the working knowledge and skills needed for more ambitious programs. The helper may be the trainer or may know where training can be obtained.

> Ken, a gay man who was one of Sid's clients, was engaging in high-risk sexual activities. Luckily, he was still HIV-negative. A colleague of Sid ran a small-group education and training program for such clients based on a multifaceted prevention program devised by Kelly and his associates (1989). Ken enrolled in this four-part program. In the first few sessions he learned about AIDS, HIV infection, how the virus is transmitted, and safer sex practices. In part two, group members, using situations in which they had engaged in high-risk activities, learned how to analyze risky encounters in terms of such things as mood, emotional need, setting, and substance use, with a view to improving self-control and behavioral self-management. Part three involved assertiveness training, including how to get commitment from a partner to low-risk activities, how to resist demands for high-risk activities, and how to decline an immediate sexual proposition. In part four, group members learned the skills of establishing mutually supportive social relationships, social dating, and involvement in health-conscious gay-community activities. With the help of the program Ken practically eliminated high-risk sexual activities.

Training can also be done in self-help groups. Of course, it is important that the skills taught be related to the client's problems and opportunities. One advantage of training done in groups is social facilitation; group members provide both support and challenge for one another as they put their newly learned skills to use.

Since clients do most of their problem-managing work outside the helping sessions, training them in self-regulation skills (Watson & Tharp, 1989) can be most helpful. Indeed, if people were routinely trained in self-regulation skills early in life, fewer would be in need of helpers in the first place.

CHOOSING NOT TO CHANGE

There is a kind of inertia and passivity in the makeup of many people that makes change difficult and distressing for them. Therefore, some clients who seem to do well in analyzing problems, developing goals, and even identifying reasonable strategies and plans end up by saying—in effect, if not directly—something like this: "Even though I've explored my problems and understand why things are going wrong—that is, I understand myself and my behavior better, and I realize what I need to do to change—right now I don't want to pay the price called for by action. The price of more effective living is too high."

There are at least two kinds of client dropouts: the ones who are being helped by unskilled counselors and who realize they are going nowhere, and the ones with high-level counselors who think that the price for change is too high. Miguel was one of the latter. He would be the last to blame the helper for his predicament. Even though he sees it as a predicament, for him there are more incentives for cherishing his autonomy and freedom than for pursuing the demanding developmental tasks of his stage of life.

The question of human motivation seems almost as enigmatic now as it must have been at the dawning of the history of the human race. So often we seem to choose our own misery. Worse, we choose to stew in it rather than endure the relatively short-lived pain of behavioral change. Helpers can and should challenge clients to search for incentives and rewards for managing their lives more effectively. They should also help clients understand the consequences of not changing. Beyond that, clients must struggle with their own demons and deities.

IN SUMMARY

Not all the suggestions in this chapter will be used with all clients. Each client has to be seen in terms of both his or her needs and his or her capabilities. Adapt the process to the resources of the person while helping him or her stretch.

With this caution in mind, here is a summary of the principal ideas related to helping clients make the transition to action.

- Before clients implement a formal course of action, use techniques such as force-field analysis to help them identify the major obstacles they will encounter and the major resources that will be available to them.
- Help clients develop a clear picture of the incentives that will help them stick to action programs.
- As clients implement programs, provide the kinds of support and challenge they need to give themselves as fully as possible to the work of constructive behavioral change.
- Use the problem-management model itself to help clients cope with the kinds of problems that arise in any effort to translate plans into action.
- Help clients evaluate the quality of their participation in the action program, the degree to which the program is helping them move toward their goal, and the degree to which the achievement of the goal is helping them manage the original problem situation.
- Finally, help clients make a decision to recycle any or all of the problem-management process, to focus on some other problem, or to terminate the helping relationship.

A FINAL LOOK AT EVALUATION

Some clients who are having trouble acting might need to backtrack. That is, they are not acting because of flaws earlier in the helping process. It may be that they

- have failed to identify the problem clearly and accurately;
- are working on the wrong thing;
- are still being led astray by their blind spots;
- have no clear idea of what they really want;
- have set unrealistic goals;
- are not committed to the goals they have set;
- have chosen ineffective strategies; or
- have no real plan and are riding off in all directions at once.

Whether carried out by clients themselves or by clients in conjunction with helpers, the helping process is cumulative. Mistakes made at an earlier stage of the process come back to haunt clients at the time of action. Whenever a client comes to you, you need to discover what step he or she is in in the problem-management process and what kind of foundation has been laid for it. If the client is not prepared to do the work of any given step, then return to whatever step will provide leverage. The ultimate evaluation question is always: Is the client managing his or her life better through his or her interactions with you?

EVALUATION QUESTIONS FOR ACTION II

How well am I doing the following as I try to help this client make the transition to action?

- Understanding how widespread both inertia and entropy are and how they are affecting this client.
- Using force-field analysis to help the client discover and manage obstacles to action.
- Using force-field analysis to help the client discover resources that will enable him or her to act.
- Helping the client use before, during, and after "check" or "think" steps as he or she implements programs.
- Helping the client construct and live up to realistic self-contracts.
- Providing feedback on the results of the client's action programs and encouraging him or her to seek out other sources of feedback.

Using the Principles of Behavior

How well am I doing the following?

- Helping clients identify the kinds of incentives that move them toward action.
- Making sure that clients use self-punishment sparingly and intelligently as a stimulus for action.
- Helping clients manage the punitive side effects of the programs in which they are involved.
- Helping clients learn how to replenish incentives for action lest they become victims of the extinction process, whereby behaviors without incentives tend to wane and extinguish.
- Making clients aware of the incentives and rewards that exist for avoiding action; helping them find incentives to counteract avoidance.
- Helping clients shape their action programs, so that they do not try to do too much too soon, on the one hand, or too little, on the other.

Chapter Eighteen

Time and Termination

This book is about a model of helping and the skills and techniques that make it work. It is not directly a book on case management, that is, how the model is applied to a specific client in a specific set of circumstances. Questions concerning the length of the helping process and how and when to terminate the helping relationship are, in large part, case-management issues. While many of the principles of case management are found in the pages of this book, at least indirectly, much of case management is learned in experiential training sessions and in supervised practicum and internship experiences. However, since even shorter-term helping is beyond the scope of the problem-management model, it makes sense to discuss the factors involved in bringing the helping process to a close.

The question "How should a helping arrangement be brought to a conclusion?" supposes a previous one, "How long should helping take?" Helpers differ widely in answers to both questions. This chapter lays down views on the length of the helping process and the principles involved in terminating it that are in keeping with the spirit and values of the overall helping model.

TIME: HOW LONG SHOULD HELPING TAKE?

The most reasonable answer to the question of how long helping should take is "It depends." Because individual helpers take such different approaches and because the needs of clients are so different, there can be no formulas. There are, however, some principles and guidelines. Before discussing these, it is useful to place the entire discussion of time and termination in the context of what actually happens in helping encounters.

Time: What Actually Happens

How long does helping take? Research on this topic is incomplete, but the consensus suggests that in most cases helping is a relatively short-term process. Phillips (1988) discovered that "the national mean length of psychotherapy probably varies each year somewhat between five and six sessions" (p. 669). There are several reasons why helping, on the average, is relatively short-term. To begin with, someone has noted that the modal number of visits to a helper is minus one: that is, a client makes an appointment and then does not show up. Clients often have mixed feelings about helping. They are not sure whether they want to go in the first place and, once there, they are not sure whether they want to stay. Therefore, if we were to show what the time-spent-in-helping distribution actually looks like, we would see most clients bunched at the short-term end of the distribution (Reich & Neenan, 1986).

Of course, "short-term" is itself a rubber-band phrase. Howard and his associates (1986) noted that "by eight sessions approximately 50% of patients are measurably improved, and approximately 75% are improved after 26 sessions" (p. 159). This does not mean that eight sessions constitute short-term helping while 26 constitute long-term. For some, short-term means a few sessions; for others, 30 sessions would still be called short-term. To muddy the waters a bit more, many clients—some 30% to 60% of all outpatient psychotherapy patients, by some estimates (Pekarik, 1983)—drop out of helping "prematurely." Phillips (1988) pointed out that this "attritional curve" leaves us with an increasingly atypical client population. Perhaps we need two sets of guidelines for terminating the helping process, one for relatively short-term clients and another for relatively long-term clients. The literature on termination does not make the distinction. Most of what is written deals, by implication, with longer-term clients, even though these constitute only a fraction of the client population.

The Current Focus on Brief Psychotherapy

Short-term helping is any form of helping that limits the number of helping interviews and uses this limitation as an integral part of the helping process. So-called "brief" psychotherapy and counseling and the kind of helping skills and methodologies that make them work are currently getting a great deal of attention (Budman & Gurman, 1988; Fisch, Weakland, & Segal, 1985; Hill et al., 1988; Janis, 1983b; Johnson & Gelso, 1981; Reich & Neenan, 1986; Siddall, Haffey, & Feinman, 1988). It is difficult to determine the reasons behind the emerging popularity of so-called brief psychotherapy. It may be that practitioners are coming to grips with the fact that in most cases helping is a short-term proposition anyway, or it may be that third-party payers are demanding concrete results in a limited number of sessions. With health-care costs skyrocketing, counseling and psychotherapy are predictable cost-containment targets. In many cases, helping stops when the money runs out.

Of course, helping can also be brief by design. Peake, Borduin, and Archer (1988) have pointed out that brief approaches are especially useful at critical developmental crisis points over the lifespan, for instance, the age-30 transition, marriage, the birth of a first child, a career change, and so forth.

The principles underlying "brief" helping are not foreign to the spirit of the helping model discussed in this book. The following have been adapted from Reich & Neenan (1986):

- Make sure that the client is willing to work.
- Do not use brief therapy with clients who have severe psychiatric disorders.

- Use a contract to establish realistic expectations.
- Provide support to help the client renew hope and morale.
- Avoid "deep" probing into the client's problem situation and its history.
- Clarify problems to the point where preferred options and the strategies for achieving them can be explored.
- Limit the number of helping sessions as part of the contract.
- Keep the relationship between helper and client free of distortions.

In my view this kind of pragmatism should be built into all kinds of helping.

Differentiating Helping from Learning, Growth, and Development Methods

The answer to the question "How long should helping take" also depends on how we define "helping." Some people apply helping to everything. For instance, Wolberg (1954) claimed, "Theoretically, psychotherapy is never ending, since emotional growth can go on as long as one lives" (p. 551). Shectman (1986) suggested that psychotherapy is an ongoing process that is independent of treatment duration.

> According to this unfolding perspective, therapy is a process set in motion that aims toward helping patients learn a method, a different way of thinking and feeling about themselves and their distress and even future life issues, rather than only resolving a problem or providing a solution. In this way, therapy restarts a growth process and becomes a special form of education rather than a circumscribed treatment. (p. 526)

In the same vein, some studies (see Howard et al., 1986) indicate that the longer the therapy the better. Indeed, helping, as described in this book, can be useful throughout the life span. Since it deals, not just with problems, but with opportunities, there is no opportunity for growth and development that falls outside its sphere.

On the other hand, some social critics are worried about the over-professionalization of life (Bledstein, 1976; Haskell, 1977; Larson, 1977; Lasch, 1977, 1978). Just because counseling and psychotherapy can be used extensively over the life span does not mean that they should be. Each developmental stage places a new set of demands, challenges, and crises on everyone. Professionals, through their research, writings, and consultations, contribute enormously to our understanding of our developmental concerns and our ability to manage them. However, this does not mean that we should run to a professional whenever anything goes wrong. Haskell (1977) noted: "If modern man displays an alarming tendency to defer thoughtlessly to expert opinion, it is largely because alternative guides to conduct such as common sense and the customary ways of his local community have long since failed him in important areas of life" (p. 33). The answer to this is not a shrug of the shoulders but a refocusing of education to include the kinds of working knowledge and life skills that enable us to meet developmental and social challenges without becoming dependent on professionals (Egan & Cowan, 1979). Furthermore, extending formal helping processes into every nook and cranny of life is an economic absurdity. There are people who can afford to be in therapy all their lives, and they are free to do so. But this can be neither the norm nor the ideal. If helping is seen as a process to be applied everywhere, then everyone needs therapy and termination cannot be discussed sensibly.

Helpers need a working knowledge of the alternatives to one-to-one helping so that counseling and therapy can be restricted to clients with substantive problems in living, including blocked social-emotional growth and development. For instance, clients with relatively run-of-the-mill developmental concerns might be better served by a "lifestyle" group, while clients with more serious problems might get the help they need in a self-help group or a training program in problem management. These and other alternatives can have distinct advantages. Because they are group-based, they keep clients "in community." And, since their purpose is to empower clients to deal with issues, concerns, and problems using their own resources, including inner resources and family and friends, they promote self-responsibility. Therefore, a critical task for helpers is to determine right from the beginning what the best setting for *this* client is.

As suggested by Peake, Borduin, and Archer (1988), the interventions of helpers might be spread over the lifespan, at critical developmental points when growth and development are blocked or developmental crises bring to light other problems. Or helpers might provide lifestyle checkups for those who have symptoms of blocked growth and development and then, somewhat like a social-emotional nutritionist, help them design a regime to manage the blocks or problems discovered. Certainly the kind of helping described in these pages can be used to get rid of blocks to social-emotional growth or to restart the process. But it should then give way to normal growth and development processes in wider social settings and less expensive ones.

Principles Related to the Length of the Formal Helping Process

The following principles can be used to determine the length of the helping process when helping is defined as a special intervention in the lives of people who need or want help in managing their lives better and developing opportunities more effectively.

- Make sure that the values you espouse, such as respect, genuineness, pragmatism, and competence (as outlined in Chapter 3), permeate the entire helping process, from contract to termination.

- Long-term relationships belong in the everyday lives of clients, not in helping encounters. Subordinate the relationship to helping outcomes.
- To the degree possible, deal with the length of helping in the contract at the start of the helping process. Contract for blocks of sessions instead of making helping an open-ended process.
- Limit your help to those areas of a client's life that need remedial action. See the helping process in terms of outcomes that add value for the client.
- Keep in mind what the client wants to accomplish. If you think that the client needs more than he or she is stating, then explain what kind of help you think is called for and work out a mutually agreeable contract.
- If you move beyond remedial action to growth and development, strike a new contract with your client. Other things being equal, education/development experiences should take precedence over helping experiences. The less the client needs to be a client (much less a patient), the better. Help clients explore forums other than one-to-one helping that might be more compatible with their goals. These forums might include lifestyle groups, training programs, self-help groups, and the like.
- From the beginning help clients find in their everyday lives the resources they need to manage their problem situations and develop their unused opportunities. Optimize the use of resources that are closest to a client's life both physically (for instance, neighborhood) and psychologically (for instance, friends, family).
- In general, make sure that you have a set of principles related to the length of the helping process. Adapt the principles described here to the specific needs of each client.

If longer-term helping is required, then one-to-one helping might in time give way to community or small-group settings as close as possible to the client's everyday life. The picture might look something like this:

- One-to-one helping encounters as the principal intervention in the client's life are, for the most part, short-term.
- As soon as possible, one-to-one helping encounters are used in conjunction with group-focused help/education/support closer to the client's everyday life.
- This arrangement gives way to group-focused education/development with an occasional one-to-one helping encounter.
- Finally, group-focused and community-based education/development prevail, with choices being made independently by the client.

In this scenario, helpers would be hard at work as consultants, designing the kinds of group-focused and community-focused experiences needed to help people get on with their own growth and development. This approach is not typically taught in helper-education programs.

TERMINATION: BRINGING THE FORMAL HELPING RELATIONSHIP TO A CLOSE

Given the de facto time-limited nature of formal helping, Kanfer and Schefft (1988) pose the dilemma helpers may face in effectively bringing the helping process to a conclusion.

> The therapist is faced with the contradiction that treatment should be limited in time and limited to those segments of the client's life that require remedial action but that the data on treatment maintenance and generalization suggest that long and hard work may be necessary to integrate new behavior patterns into everyday life. The principle of minimum intervention suggests that the therapist must accept the inevitability of termination, even with a client who has made good progress but who remains short of perfection. (p. 275)

Many clients, though managing their lives better, will fall far short of perfection when they terminate. Since helping is not a substitute for living, there will always be compromises: "The ending of therapy usually represents a compromise between hoped for changes and limitations arising from waning motivation, the subjective discomfort of being in therapy, its cost, and a variety of other factors" (Zaro et al., 1982, p. 142).

Practitioners of some forms of helping, especially those with a pragmatic bent, pride themselves on a no-problem approach to termination. For instance, Grieger and Boyd (1980) claimed that termination was not a problem for those practicing rational-emotive therapy (RET).

> We find that termination of RET is really a fairly smooth, uneventful time for most of our clients. It could be that they find us so aversive [because of the amount of challenging that goes on] that leaving is a real treat. A more pleasing, and we think, more accurate explanation is that RET promotes client independence such that the severance of the on-going relationship is in no way traumatic. In successful RET, clients learn that they are responsible for their own problems; they learn what their problems are and how to go about giving up both these and future ones. . . . (p. 189)

The point is well made. Therapies and therapists that encourage dependence, however indirectly and covertly, must make a great deal of termination. In approaches to helping that promote independence and are short-term, much of what is written about termination (Bruckner-Gordon, Gangi, & Wallman, 1988, Chapters 10, 11; Kanfer & Schefft, 1988, pp. 275–294; Kramer, 1986; Kupers, 1988; London, 1982; Maholick & Turner, 1979; Ward, 1984) is either irrelevant or must be adapted to the short-term client.

The Role of Ongoing Monitoring and Evaluation in Termination

Throughout this book I have stressed the importance of monitoring and evaluating the helping process continually over its entire course. In general, monitoring provides answers to the questions "To what degree are we on track in terms of what we have contracted to do? Where do we stand as of now?" Monitoring includes making sure that only those parts of the helping model are used that the client needs to better manage his or her problems in living. Since helping is an organic process, it is impossible to see right from the beginning precisely what is needed. Ongoing monitoring is used in contracting with clients for the next block of helping sessions or in bringing the entire process to a close.

Initiative in Terminating the Helping Process

Ideally, termination comes about because client and therapist, sticking to the guidelines of the contract they are working from, review the accomplishment of objectives and conjointly agree to terminate the formal helping process. In reality, of course, either party can terminate the process unilaterally for good or bad reasons. Clients may terminate because they feel they have achieved what they came for, even if their helpers do not agree, or because they simply don't want to do the work that meaningful change demands. Similarly, helpers can terminate the process because they feel that the work has been done, even though their clients may disagree. Or they might terminate because they don't like their clients and want to be rid of them.

Bruckner-Gordon, Gangi, and Wallman (1988) suggest to clients that when thoughts of ending therapy arise, they should do three things: assess their progress, discuss ending therapy with the helper, and make a decision. They provide the following checklist for clients (pp. 171–172):

> I am considering ending therapy now because (check any statements that reflect your situation)
>
> _____ I have gotten a lot from my therapy and feel satisfied.
> _____ I keep thinking about leaving.
> _____ My friends and family want me to stop.
> _____ I (or my therapist) cannot continue because of outside circumstances.
> _____ Nothing much has happened in my therapy for quite a while.
> _____ My therapist and I are not working well together.
> _____ I think I've gotten all that I can from working with this therapist.
> _____ I think I've gotten most of what I want, and it doesn't seem worthwhile to continue.
> _____ My therapist suggested that I should think about leaving.
> _____ I don't have the time or money to continue.
> _____ or, _____

In longer-term helping, some clients do not like to bring up the issue of termination because they have become dependent on the helper or the helping process itself. If self-responsibility is a value for the helper, then he or she needs to challenge such clients. Even better, the helper should deal with dependency as it emerges.

A Client's Decision to Exit at Certain Steps or Stages of the Helping Process

At each stage and step of the helping process clients might think of terminating for good or bad reasons. For instance, a client who is challenged, even challenged well, might think of leaving because of hurt. Or challenging might be all that the client needed, and now he or she can go back and handle things without professional assistance. Other clients might leave after brainstorming strategies to accomplish some preferred-scenario goal. However, one might leave because he sees that the work involved in getting what he thought he wanted is just too much for him. Another might leave because once she sees the range of strategies that will get her to her goal, she no longer needs the help of the counselor. She picks the package of strategies she prefers, draws up a plan, and implements it. Again, if monitoring and evaluation are a part of the process, in most cases none of this will come as a surprise.

Kanfer and Schefft (1988) have pointed out signs indicating that the client is ready to terminate, including such things as missing appointments, having difficulty in finding substantive things to discuss, forgetting to carry out "homework" assignments, and showing signs of disengagement and boredom during helping interactions. Others have suggested similar cues. However, since such cues emerge over time, helpers should spot them early on and bring them front and center. I would prefer to see helping come to an end rather than "wind down." Helpers who, within reason, try to make every moment count would hardly let themselves become witnesses of such a winding-down process.

Premature Termination

For a variety of reasons, some clients leave a helping relationship or setting even though by objective criteria it would probably be in their own self-interest to stay. Yet theory and research on so-called premature termination is a rats' nest because of the many meanings that can be given to "premature" and because of the implication that helping is an open-ended process. One therapist defined "premature" to me in terms of his own expected economic return from his clients! Some definitions are so broad as to be meaningless: "In its broadest sense, premature termination refers to clients leaving treatment before their counselors believe they should"

(Mennicke, Lent, & Burgoyne, 1988, p. 458). Hardin, Subich, and Holvey (1988) note the problem and provide us with a narrower definition.

> "Premature termination" must be more clearly defined. Previous research has led to contradictory findings possibly arising from different definitions. We defined "premature termination" [in our research] as occurring when a client agreed to return for a second session, made an appointment, and still did not return. (p. 39)

Many clients drop out of the helping process along the way, no matter what approach to helping is used. If premature termination includes all clients whom helpers see as not having "finished" what needed to be done, then premature termination is probably the rule rather than the exception. Recall that Pekarik (1983) found that about 30% to 60% of all outpatient psychotherapy clients drop out of treatment prematurely. But in a further study (Pekarik & Wierzbicki, 1986) he found that clients expected (and attended) a relatively low number of sessions, while therapists expected a higher number of sessions. Thus, what is premature for one is not premature for the other. There is also some evidence that both helpers and clients know "in their hearts" how long the latter are going to stay around (Beck et al., 1987; Pekarik & Wierzbicki, 1986). Something is wrong with the contracting process here.

Kanfer and Schefft (1988) outline some of the reasons why clients terminate prematurely: clients feel that they have accomplished their goals; they believe that the helper's assistance is not longer needed even though goals have not yet been accomplished; they fear that they may be talked out of leaving; they are dissatisfied with their progress, or the helper's style, or the fit between their problems and the helping approach; they see the pain as too great for the outcomes produced; their lives have changed to such a degree that helping is no longer necessary. As suggested above, effective helpers pick up on these kinds of cues and use some form of immediacy to deal with them. Once more, ongoing monitoring and evaluation of the helping process should catch such cues early on.

Choosing the Appropriate Time to Terminate

Maholick and Turner (1979, pp. 588–589) suggested that helpers can use the following questions to help clients determine when it is time to terminate.

- Have initial problems or symptoms been reduced, eliminated, or managed?
- Has the original stress been dissipated or reduced?
- Is the client coping better with problems and concerns?
- Does the client understand himself or herself better?

- Has the client's self-esteem been increased?
- Is the client relating more effectively to others?
- Is the client going about the tasks of everyday life, including work, reasonably well?
- Is the client enjoying life more?
- Does the client feel that he or she can live effectively without further counseling?

If helping is short-term or is carried out in blocks of sessions, each block having its own specified outcomes, it is easier to determine when helping has fulfilled the role specified in the contract. Accordingly, it is much easier to determine the "best" time to terminate.

Principles of Effective Closure

Exactly how to bring the helping process to a close is a matter of individual case management. If helpers were to do eveything discussed in the literature on this subject, termination would be an extended process indeed. For example, Bruckner-Gordon, Gangi, and Wallman (1988) discuss four termination tasks for clients: exploring one's reactions to ending therapy, planning leave-taking, completing therapy, and saying goodbye. How long can this take? "If your therapy has been going for more than a year, you may spend months talking about leaving. If your therapy is longer term, proportionately longer time will be spent on ending" (pp. 193–194). Obviously, such extended time frames do not apply to the kind of helping discussed in this book.

Here are some hints, suggestions, and guidelines for bringing the helping process to a close that are more in keeping with the skilled-helper model.

- Build termination into the helping process right from the beginning. One way to do so is to contract for successive blocks of sessions (let us say, two or three at a time). Using this building-block technique helps to avoid an open-ended, "Well, let's see what happens" approach to helping and termination.
- Avoid self-indulgent and self-destructive dependency both on the part of the client and on your own part. If you make termination a natural part of the contract, it will not be abrupt or be seen by the client as a rejection. This is especially important with clients who have difficulties with relationships in their everyday lives.
- Work with the client to make every session count. Much of the helping literature talks about periods when "nothing seems to be happening." Work with the client to make things happen. Make helping not only humanly effective but also humanely efficient.

• Avoid making the relationship itself the central feature of the helping process (see Chapter 3). In this way termination will not be primarily the painful process of terminating a close or even dependent relationship. Monitor cues along the way that the relationship is becoming more important than the problem-management process it is meant to serve.

• If you are terminating helping because you think that the client has completed the work contracted for or refuses to take responsibility for the work involved in change, pause first and examine your motivation. It is not uncommon for helpers not to like their clients. This does not mean that they are unable to help them. It does mean that it will require self-control to do so. Do not abandon a client just because he or she is unappealing to you.

• Early in treatment decide with the client what degree of progress or change would be sufficient for termination of treatment.

• Constantly monitor goal achievement. End the process when it is clear to both you and your client that the contract has been fulfilled and the goals accomplished.

• In some cases it can be wise to take a gradual approach to termination by lengthening the time between sessions. During this period the helper becomes more of a consultant to work the client is doing. Longer periods between sessions give time for work to get done and to produce visible results.

• Provide for a final review of what the client has learned and how these learnings can be transferred to future problem situations. Include a review of the gains achieved in therapy, a discussion of ways the client can maintain or improve on what has been gained, and support for the client's future efforts.

• Discuss the possibility of some follow-up or booster sessions after official termination. Include here the conditions under which the client could return for such sessions.

• Respect a client's wish to terminate for whatever reason. However, an exit interview may include challenging, not so much the client's decision, but the reasoning behind the decision. If in your opinion the client is headed down a steep incline and needs further help, let this be part of your challenge. If you believe that the client is or will become a danger to others without further help, then you may have a duty-to-warn situation on your hands. In that case it is time to take counsel with colleagues and/or lawyers to determine the extent of your moral and legal obligations.

• If possible, get feedback on your style and performance if you have not done so on an ongoing basis through monitoring and evaluation of the helping process.

Once more, this is a set of principles, not formulas. Some may not apply to this or that client. All need to be adapted to the particular situation of each client.

FOLLOW-UP

In some cases the main work of helping is finished but some limited future work may be helpful. Follow-up can mean at least two things. First, it can mean a monitoring process intended to make sure that the goals have been accomplished. Second, it can refer to a kind of booster shot.

Once the helping sessions have ended, is follow-up in terms of monitoring necessary as part of evaluation? Nicholson and Berman (1983) reviewed the follow-up literature and discovered that follow-up often added little to what was already known by the end of therapy. They concluded that further monitoring is generally not needed: "The findings highlight the general durability of gains during psychotherapy, suggesting that costly follow-up procedures may be used more selectively" (p. 261). If your sessions with a client end in an unsettled way, however, then scheduling a follow-up monitoring session may be in order.

Follow-up in terms of booster-shot sessions is another matter. Kanfer and Schefft (1988) have suggested that booster shots can be included as part of the overall program: "'Booster' sessions can be arranged at intervals to provide additional consultation or to recapitulate and strengthen coping techniques or other self-regulatory skills that the client had learned during treatment and that had faded" (p. 287). These booster sessions can be contracted for at the end of the formal helping process on an as-needed basis. However, they should not be used as an excuse to prolong the helping relationship. The helping model as described in these pages is not about prolonged supportive therapy. Further support should come from settings much closer to the client's day-to-day life.

Epilog

This book outlines a model of helping that is rational, linear, and systematic. What good is that, you well might ask, in a a world that is often irrational, nonlinear, and chaotic? One answer is that rational models help clients bring much needed discipline and order into their chaotic lives. Effective helpers do not apologize for using such models.

More than intelligence is needed to apply the model well. The helper who understands and uses the model together with the skills and techniques that make it work might well be smart, but he or she must also be wise. Effective helpers understand the limitations, not only of helping models, but also of helpers, the helping profession, clients, and the environments that affect the helping process. One dimension of wisdom is the ability to understand and manage these limitations, which in sum, constitute what I call the arational dimensions, or the "shadow side," of life. Helping models are flawed; helpers are sometimes selfish, lazy, and even predatory, and they are prone to burnout. Clients are sometimes selfish, lazy, and predatory even in the helping relationship.

Indeed, if the world were completely rational, the pool of clients would soon dry up, since many clients cause their own problems. But there is no danger of that since, as Cross and Guyer (1980) note, people knowingly head down paths that lead to trouble. As Cross & Guyer go on to suggest, however, the popular view that people lacking foresight deserve what they get in life

> is itself based on the optimistic premise that human behavior is (or should be) determined by a goal-oriented intellectual process of evaluating alternative destinations and then following the path to the best one, rather than on the simpler and more direct procedure of permitting immediate rewards and punishments to dictate direction. (p. 41)

Life is not a straight road; often it is more like a maze. It often seems to be a contradictory process in which good and evil, the comic and the tragic, cowardice and heroism are inextricably intermingled.

The ancient Greeks said, "Know thyself." They understood that self-knowledge is one of the roots of wisdom. Knowing others in an undistorted way is another root. Jesus, we are told, "knew what was in men and women." While he loved deeply, he was no one's fool. Both of these—knowing both yourself and others in caring, reflective, unvarnished ways—will help you develop the wisdom that enables you to move beyond the technology of helping and the helping alliance to the kind of authenticity celebrated by Carl Rogers in *A Way of Being*. Experience can be either a teacher or a despot. The ability to befriend the shadow side of yourself, your clients, and the world without becoming its victim is not the fruit of raw experience. Experience needs to be wrestled with, reflected on, and learned from. Then it becomes your teacher and your friend. Wrestling with yourself, your colleagues, your intimates, your demons, and your God will provide you both pain and comfort and will go far in helping the skilled helper in you become the wise helper.

Bibliography

ABBEY, D. S., Hunt, D. E., & Weiser, J. C. (1985). Variations on a theme by Kolb: A perspective for understanding counseling and supervision. *Counseling Psychologist, 13,* 477–501.

ACKOFF, R. (1974). *Redesigning the future.* New York: Wiley.

ADKINS, W. R. (1984). Life skills education: A video-based counseling/learning delivery system. In D. Larson (Ed.), *Teaching psychological skills: Models for giving psychology away.* Pacific Grove, CA: Brooks/Cole.

AMERICAN PSYCHIATRIC ASSOCIATION COMMISSION ON PSYCHOTHERAPIES. (1982). *Psychotherapy research: Methodological and efficacy issues.* Washington, D.C.: American Psychiatric Association.

AMERICAN PSYCHOLOGICAL ASSOCIATION. (1987). *Casebook on ethical principles of psychologists.* Hyattsville, MD: Author.

AMERICAN PSYCHOLOGICAL ASSOCIATION. (1988). *AIDS: Abstracts of the psychological and behavioral literature 1983–1988.* Hyattsville, MD: Author.

AMERICAN PSYCHOLOGIST. (1988). Vol. 43 (11). Issue devoted to the psychology of AIDS.

ANDERSEN, B., & Anderson, W. (1985). Client perceptions of counselors using positive and negative self-involving statements. *Journal of Counseling Psychology, 32,* 462–465.

ANDERSON, C. M., & Stewart, S. (1983). *Mastering resistance: A practical guide to family therapy.* New York: Guilford Press.

ANSCOMBE, R. (1986). Treating the patient who "can't" versus the patient who "won't." *American Journal of Psychotherapy, 40,* 26–35.

ANTHONY, W. A., Pierce, R. M., & Cohen, M. R. (1979). *The skills of rehabilitation programming.* Amherst, MA: Carkhuff Institute of Human Technology.

ARGYRIS, C. (1957). *Personality and organization: The conflict between system and the individual.* New York: Harper & Row.

ARGYRIS, C. (1962). *Interpersonal competence and organizational effectiveness.* Homewood, IL: Dorsey Press.

ARGYRIS, C. (1964). *Integrating the individual and the organization.* New York: Wiley.

ARGYRIS, C. (1982). *Reasoning, learning, and action.* San Francisco: Jossey-Bass.

ASBURY, F. R. (1984). The empathy treatment. *Elementary School Guidance and Counseling, 18,* 181–187.

BACKER, T. E., & Richardson, D. (1989). Building bridges: Psychologists and families of the mentally ill. *American Psychologist, 44,* 546–550.

BAEKELAND, F., & Lundwall, L. (1975). Dropping out of treatment: A critical review. *Psychological Bulletin, 82,* 738–783.

BALDWIN, B. A. (1980). Styles of crisis intervention: Toward a convergent model. *Journal of Professional Psychology, 11,* 113–120.

BANDURA, A. (1977). Self-efficacy: Toward a unifying theory of behavioral change. *Psychological Review, 84,* 191–215.

BANDURA, A. (1980). Gauging the relationship between self-efficacy judgment and action. *Cognitive Therapy and Research, 4,* 263–268.

BANDURA, A. (1982). Self-efficacy mechanism in human agency. *American Psychologist, 37,* 122–147.

BANDURA, A. (1984). Recycling misconceptions of perceived self-efficacy. *Cognitive Therapy and Research, 8,* 257–262.

BANDURA, A. (1986). *Social foundations of thought and action: A social cognitive theory.* Englewood Cliffs, NJ: Prentice-Hall.

BANDURA, A., & Schunk, D. A. (1981). Cultivating competence, self-efficacy, and intrinsic interest through proximal self-motivation. *Journal of Personality and Social Psychology, 41,* 586–598.

BAYLESS, O. L. (1967). An alternative pattern for problem-solving discussion. *Journal of Communication, 17,* 188–197.

BECK, N. C., Lamberti, J., Gamache, M., & Lake, E. A. (1987). Situational factors and behavioral self-predictions in the identification of clients at high risk to drop out of psychotherapy. *Journal of Clinical Psychology, 43,* 511–520.

BECK, J. T., & Strong, S. R. (1982). Stimulating therapeutic change with interpretations: A comparison of positive and negative connotation. *Journal of Counseling Psychology, 29,* 551–559.

BECKHARD, R., & Harris, R. T. (1977). *Organizational transitions: Managing complex change* (1st ed.). Reading, MA: Addison-Wesley.

BECKHARD, R., & Harris, R. T. (1987). *Organizational transitions: Managing complex change* (2nd ed.). Reading, MA: Addison-Wesley.

BEIER, E. G., & Young, D. M. (1984). *The silent language of psychotherapy: Social reinforcement of unconscious processes* (2nd ed.). New York: Aldine.

BELKIN, G. S. (1987). *Contemporary psychotherapies* (2nd ed.). Pacific Grove, CA: Brooks/Cole.

BENJAMIN, A. (1981). *The helping interview* (3rd ed.). Boston: Houghton Mifflin.

BENNETT, M. I., & Bennett, M. B. (1984). The uses of hopelessness. *American Journal of Psychiatry, 141,* 559–562.

BENNIS, W., & Nanus, B. (1985). *Leaders.* New York: Harper & Row.

BERENSON, B. G., & Mitchell, K. M. (1974). *Confrontation: For better or worse.* Amherst, MA: Human Resource Development Press.

BERGER, D. M. (1984). On the way to empathic understanding. *American Journal of Psychotherapy, 38,* 111–120.

BERGER, P. L., & Neuhaus, R. J. (1977). *To empower people: The role of mediating structures in public policy.* Washington, D.C.: American Enterprise Institute for Public Policy Research.

BERNE, E. (1964). *Games people play.* New York: Grove Press.

BERNHEIM, K. F. (1989). Psychologists and the families of the severely mentally ill: The role of family consultation. *American Psychologist, 44,* 561–564.

BERNIER, M., & Avard, J. (1986). Self-efficacy, outcome, and attrition in a weight-reduction program. *Cognitive Therapy and Research, 10,* 319–338.

BLEDSTEIN, B. J. (1976). *The culture of professionalism.* New York: Norton.

BLOCHER, D. H. (1966). *Developmental counseling.* New York: Ronald.

BLOCK, P. (1981). *Flawless consulting: A guide to getting your expertise used.* Austin, TX: Learning Concepts.

BOHART, A. C. (1988). Empathy: Client-centered and psychoanalytic. *American Psychologist, 43,* 667–668.

BOOK, H. E. (1988). Empathy: Misconceptions and misuses in psychotherapy. *American Journal of Psychiatry, 145,* 420–424.

BRAMMER, L. (1973). *The helping relationship: Process and skills.* Englewood Cliffs, NJ: Prentice-Hall.

BRASWELL, M., & Seay, T. (1984). *Approaches to counseling and psychotherapy.* Prospect Heights, IL: Waverly.

BREHM, J. (1966). *A theory of psychological reactance.* New York: Academic Press.

BREIER, & Strauss, J. S. (1984). The role of social relationships in the recovery from psychotic disorders. *American Journal of Psychiatry, 141,* 949–955.

BROWN, J. E., & Slee, P. T. (1986). Paradoxical strategies: The ethics of intervention. *Professional Psychology: Research and Practice, 17,* 487–491.

BROWNELL, K. D., Marlatt, G. A., Lichtenstein, E., & Wilson, G. T. (1986). Understanding and preventing relapse. *American Psychologist, 41,* 765–782.

BRUCKNER-GORDON, F., Gangi, B. K., & Wallman, G. U. (1988). *Making therapy work.* New York: Harper & Row.

BRUHN, J. G., & Philips, B. U. (1984). Measuring social support: A synthesis of current approaches. *Journal of Behavioral Medicine, 7,* 151–169.

BUDMAN, S. H., & Gurman, A. S. (1988). *Theory and practice of brief therapy.* New York: Guilford Press.

BUGENTAL, J. F. T., & Bugental, E. K. (1986). A fate worse than death: The fear of changing. *Psychotherapy, 21,* 543–549.

BURKE, J. F. (1989). *Contemporary approaches to psychotherapy and counseling: The self-regulation and maturity model.* Pacific Grove, CA: Brooks/Cole.

BURKE, J. P., Haworth, C. E., & Brantley, J. C. (1980). Scientific problem-solver model: A resolution for professional controversies in school psychology. *Professional Psychology, 11,* 823–832.

CAPLAN, N., & Nelson, S. D. (1973). The nature and consequences of psychological research on social problems. *American Psychologist, 28,*199–211.

CARKHUFF, R. R. (1969a). *Helping and human relations: Vol. 1. Selection and training.* New York: Holt, Rinehart & Winston.

CARKHUFF, R. R. (1969b). *Helping and human relations: Vol. 2. Practice and research.* New York: Holt, Rinehart & Winston.

CARKHUFF, R. R. (1971a). *The development of human resources.* New York: Holt, Rinehart & Winston.

CARKHUFF, R. R. (1971b). Training as a preferred mode of treatment. *Journal of Counseling Psychology, 18,* 123–131.

CARKHUFF, R. R. (1985). *PPD: Productive program development.* Amherst, MA: Human Resource Development Press.

CARKHUFF, R. R. (1987). *The art of helping* (6th ed.). Amherst, MA: Human Resource Development Press.

CARKHUFF, R. R., & Anthony, W. A. (1979). *The skills of helping: An introduction to counseling.* Amherst, MA: Human Resource Development Press.

CATTELL, R. B. (1987). *Psychotherapy by structured learning theory.* New York: Springer.

CAVANAUGH, M. E. (1982). *The counseling experience.* Pacific Grove, CA: Brooks/Cole.

CAVELL, T. A., Frentz, C. E., & Kelley, M. L. (1986). Acceptability of paradoxical interventions: Some nonparadoxical findings. *Professional Psychology: Research and Practice, 17,* 519–523.

CENTER FOR CONSTRUCTIVE CHANGE. (1984). How intentional is your life? *Journal for Constructive Change, 6* (1), 16–17. The entire issue deals with intentionality.

CHAMBERLAIN, P., Patterson, G., Kavanagh, K., & Forgatch, M. (1984). Observations of client resistance. *Behavior Therapy, 15,* 144–155.

CHELUNE, G. (1977). Disclosure flexibility and social-situational perceptions. *Journal of Consulting and Clinical Psychology, 45,* 1139–1143.

CLAIBORN, C. D. (1982). Interpretation and change in counseling. *Journal of Counseling Psychology, 29,* 439–453.

CLEMENTS, C. (1985). The doctor and the lady: A reexamination of "humanistic" care. *American Journal of Psychiatry, 142,* 887–888.

CLIFFORD, J. S. (1983). Self-efficacy counseling and the maintenance of sobriety. *Personnel and Guidance Journal, 62,* 111–114.

COLE, H. P., & Sarnoff, D. (1980). Creativity and counseling. *Personnel and Guidance Journal, 59,* 140–146.

CONFER, W. N. (1987). *Intuitive psychotherapy: The role of creative therapeutic intervention.* New York: Human Sciences Press.

CONYNE, R. K. (1987). *Primary preventive counseling.* Muncie, IN: Accelerated Development.

CONYNE, R. K., & Clack, R. J. (1981). *Environmental assessment and design.* New York: Praeger.

COREY, G. (1986). *Theory and practice of counseling and psychotherapy.* Pacific Grove, CA: Brooks/Cole.

COREY, G., Corey, M. S., & Callanan, P. (1988). *Issues and ethics in the helping professions* (3rd ed.). Pacific Grove, CA: Brooks/Cole.

CORMIER, W. H., & Cormier, L. S. (1979). *Interviewing strategies for helpers: A guide to assessment, treatment, and evaluation.* Pacific Grove, CA: Brooks/Cole.

CORMIER, W. H., & Cormier, L. S. (1985). *Interviewing strategies for helpers: Fundamental skills and cognitive behavioral interventions* (2nd ed.). Pacific Grove, CA: Brooks/Cole.

CORMIER, W. H., & Cormier, L. S. (1986). Choice or change issues of clients and how to work with them. *Journal of Counseling and Human Service Professions, 1* (1), 88–99.

CORRIGAN, J. D., Dell, D. M., Lewis, K. N., & Schmidt, L. D. (1980). Counseling as a social influence process: A review [Monograph]. *Journal of Counseling Psychology, 27,* 295–331.

CORSINI, R., & Wedding, D. (1989). *Current Psychotherapies* (4th ed.). Itasca, IL: F. E. Peacock.

COWEN, E. L. (1982). Help is where you find it. *American Psychologist, 37,* 385–395.

COYNE, J. C., & DeLongis, A. (1986). Going beyond social support: The role of social relationships in adaptation. *Journal of Consulting and Clinical Psychology, 54,* 454–460.

COYNE, J. C., & Widiger, T. A. (1978). Toward a participatory model of psychotherapy. *Professional Psychology, 9,* 700–710.

CROSS, J. G., & Guyer, M. J. (1980). *Social traps.* Ann Arbor: University of Michigan Press.

CUMMINGS, N. A. (1979). Turning bread into stones: Our modern antimiracle. *American Psychologist, 34,* 1119–1129.

CYPERT, S. A. (1987). *Believe and achieve.* New York: Dodd, Mead.

DALY, M. J., & Burton, R. L. (1983). Self-esteem and irrational beliefs: An exploratory investigation with implications for counseling. *Journal of Counseling Psychology, 30,* 361–366.

DAVIS, G. A., & Manske, M. E. (1966). An instructional method of increasing originality. *Psychonomic Science, 6,* 73–74.

DEBORD, J. B. (1989). Paradoxical interventions: A review of the recent literature. *Journal of Counseling and Development, 67,* 394–398.

DEFFENBACHER, J. L. (1985). A cognitive-behavioral response and a modest proposal. *Counseling Psychologist, 13,* 261–269.

DEFOREST, C., & Stone, G. L. (1980). Effects of sex and intimacy on self-disclosure. *Journal of Counseling Psychology, 27,* 93–96.

DEGOOD, D. E. (1983). Reducing medical patients' reluctance to participate in psychological therapies: The initial session. *Professional Psychology: Research and Practice, 14,* 570–579.

DEMBO, R., Weyant, J. M., & Warner, J. (1982). The impact of intake experiences on clients' dropping out of treatment at a community mental health center. *Journal of Psychiatric Treatment and Evaluation, 4,* 345–353.

DENELSKY, G. Y., & Boat, B. W. (1986). A coping skills model of psychological diagnosis and treatment. *Professional Psychology: Research and Practice, 17,* 322–330.

DERLEGA, V. J., & Berg, J. H. (1987). *Self-disclosure: Theory, research, and therapy.* New York: Plenum.

DERLEGA, V. J., Lovell, R., & Chaikin, A. L. (1976). Effects of therapist self-disclosure and its perceived appropriateness on client self-disclosure. *Journal of Consulting and Clinical Psychology, 44,* 866.

DEUTSCH, M. (1954). Field theory in social psychology. In G. Lindzey (Ed.), *The handbook of social psychology* (Vol. 1). Cambridge, MA: Addison-Wesley.

DEVINS, G. M., & Edwards, P. J. (1988). Self-efficacy and smoking reduction in chronic obstructive pulmonary disease. *Behavior Research and Therapy, 26,* 127–135.

DIMOND, R. E., Havens, R. A., & Jones, A. C. (1978). A conceptual framework for the practice of prescriptive eclecticism in psychotherapy. *American Psychologist, 33,* 239–248.

DINKMEYER, D. C. (1970). *Developmental counseling and guidance.* New York: McGraw-Hill.

DIXON, D. N., & Glover, J. A. (1984). *Counseling: A problem-solving approach.* New York: Wiley.

DONLEY, R. J., Horan, J. J., & DeShong, R. L. (1989). The effect of several self-disclosure permutations on counseling process and outcome. *Journal of Counseling and Development, 67,* 408–412.

DORN, F. J. (1984). *Counseling as applied social psychology: An introduction to the social influence model.* Springfield, IL: Charles C Thomas.

DORN, F. J. (Ed.). (1986). *The social influence process in counseling and psychotherapy.* Springfield, IL: Charles C Thomas.

DOSTER, J. A., & Nesbitt, J. G. (1979). Psychotherapy and self-disclosure. In G. J. Chelune (Ed.), *Self-disclosure: Origins, patterns, and implications of openness in interpersonal relationships.* San Francisco: Jossey-Bass.

DREIKURS, R. (1967). Goals of psychotherapy. In A. Maher (Ed.), *The goals of psychotherapy.* New York: Appleton-Century-Crofts.

DRISCOLL, R. (1984). *Pragmatic psychotherapy.* New York: Van Nostrand Reinhold.

DRISCOLL, R. (1985). Commonsense objectives in paradoxical interventions. *Psychotherapy, 22,* 774–778.

DRYDEN, W., & Trower, P. (Eds.). (1988). *Developments in cognitive psychotherapy.* Newbury Park, CA: Sage Publications.

DUBRIN, A. J. (1987). *The last straw: How to benefit from trigger events in your life.* Springfield, IL: Charles C Thomas.

DYER, W. W., & Vriend, J. (1975). *Counseling techniques that work: Applications to individual and group counseling.* Washington, D.C.: APGA Press.

D'ZURILLA, T. J., & Goldfried, M. R. (1971). Problem solving and behavior modification. *Journal of Abnormal Psychology, 78,* 107–126.

D'ZURILLA, T. J., & Nezu, A. (1980). A study of the generation-of-alternatives process in social problem solving. *Cognitive Therapy and Research, 4,* 67–72.

EASTMAN, C., & Marzillier, J. S. (1984). Theoretical and methodological difficulties in Bandura's self-efficacy theory. *Cognitive Therapy and Research, 8,* 213–229.

EBERLEIN, L. (1987). Introducing ethics to beginning psychologists: A problem-solving approach. *Professional Psychology: Research and Practice, 18,* 353–359.

ECKERT, P. A., Abeles, N., & Graham, R. N. (1988). Symptom severity, psychotherapy process, and outcome. *Professional Psychology: Research and Practice, 19,* 560–564.

EGAN, G. (1970). *Encounter: Group processes for interpersonal growth.* Pacific Grove, CA: Brooks/Cole.

EGAN, G. (1976). *Interpersonal living: A skills-contract approach to human-relations training in groups.* Pacific Grove, CA: Brooks/Cole.

EGAN, G. (1977). *You and me: The skills of communicating and relating to others.* Pacific Grove, CA: Brooks/Cole.

EGAN, G. (1984). People in systems: A comprehensive model for psychosocial education and training. In D. Larson (Ed.), *Teaching psychological skills: Models for giving psychology away.* Pacific Grove, CA: Brooks/Cole.

EGAN, G. (1985). *Change agent skills in helping and human-service settings.* Pacific Grove, CA: Brooks/Cole.

EGAN, G., & Cowan, M. A. (1979). *People in systems: A model for development in the human-service professions and education.* Pacific Grove, CA: Brooks/Cole.

EISENBERG, N., & Strayer, J. (Eds.). (1987). *Empathy and its development.* New York: Cambridge University Press.

EISNER, E. (1979). *The educational imagination: On the design and evaluation of school programs.* New York: Macmillan.

EKMAN, P. (1982). *Emotion in the human face* (2nd ed.). New York: Cambridge University Press.

ELLIOTT, R. (1985). Helpful and nonhelpful events in brief counseling interviews: An empirical taxonomy. *Journal of Counseling Psychology, 32,* 307–322.

ELLIS, A. (1974). *Disputing irrational beliefs (DIBS).* New York: Institute for Rational Living.

ELLIS, A. (1979). *New developments in rational-emotive therapy.* Pacific Grove, CA: Brooks/Cole.

ELLIS, A. (1982). A reappraisal of rational-emotive therapy's theoretical foundations and therapeutic methods: A reply to Eschenroeder. *Cognitive Therapy and Research, 6,* 393–398.

ELLIS, A. (1984). Must most psychotherapists remain as incompetent as they are now? In J. Hariman (Ed.), *Does psychotherapy really help people?* Springfield, IL: Charles C Thomas.

ELLIS, A. (1985a). Expanding the ABCs of rational-emotive therapy. In M. Mahoney & A. Freeman (Eds.), *Cognition and psychotherapy.* New York: Plenum.

ELLIS, A. (1985b). *Overcoming resistance: Rational-emotive therapy with difficult clients.* New York: Springer.

ELLIS, A. (1987a). The evolution of rational-emotive therapy (RET) and cognitive-behavior therapy (CBT). In J. K. Zeig (Ed.), *The evolution of psychotherapy.* New York: Brunner/Mazel.

ELLIS, A. (1987b). Integrative developments in rational-emotive therapy (RET). *Journal of Integrative and Eclectic Psychotherapy, 6,* 470--479.

ELLIS, A. (1987c). The impossibility of achieving consistently good mental health. *American Psychologist, 42,* 364–375.

ELLIS, A., & Dryden, W. (1987). *The practice of rational-emotive therapy.* New York: Springer.

EMERY, E. E. (1987). Empathy: Psychoanalytic and client-centered. *American Psychologist, 42,* 513–515.

EPTING, F. R. (1984). *Personal construct counseling and psychotherapy.* New York: Wiley.

ERSKINE, R., & Moursund, J. (1988). *Integrative psychotherapy in action.* Newbury Park, CA: Sage Publications.

ESCHENROEDER, C. (1982). How rational is rational-emotive therapy? A critical appraisal of its theoretical foundations and therapeutic methods. *Cognitive Therapy and Research, 6,* 381–392.

EYSENCK, H. J. (1984). The battle over psychotherapeutic effectiveness. In J. Hariman (Ed.), *Does psychotherapy really help people?* Springfield, IL: Charles C Thomas.

FARRELLY, F., & Brandsma, J. (1974). *Provocative therapy.* Cupertino, CA: Meta Publications.

FERGUSON, M. (1980). *The aquarian conspiracy: Personal and social transformation in the 1980s.* Los Angeles: J. P. Tarcher.

FERGUSON, T. (1987a, January-February). Agreements with yourself. *Medical Self-Care,* pp. 44–47.

FERGUSON, T. (1987b, January-February). Toward self-responsibility for health. *Medical Self-Care,* pp. 67, 72.

FESTINGER, S. (1957). *A theory of cognitive dissonance.* New York: Harper & Row.

FINE, M. J. (1985). Intervention from a systems-ecological perspective. *Professional Psychology, 16*, 262–270.

FIRESTONE, R. W. (1988). *A psychotherapeutic approach to self-destructive behavior.* New York: Human Sciences Press.

FISCH, R., Weakland, J., & Segal, L. (1985). *The tactics of change: Doing therapy briefly.* San Francisco: Jossey-Bass.

FISHER, R., & Ury, W. (1981). *Getting to yes: Negotiating agreement without giving in.* Boston: Houghton Mifflin.

FORDYCE, M. W. (1983). A program to increase happiness: Further studies. *Journal of Counseling Psychology, 30*, 483–498.

FORDYCE, M. W. (1983). A program to increase happiness: Further studies. *Journal of Counseling Psychology, 30*, 483–498.

FORDYCE, W. E. (1976). *Behavioral methods for control of chronic pain and illness.* St. Louis: C. V. Mosby.

FOREST, J. J. (1988). Self-help books. *American Psychologist, 43*, 599.

FOX, R. E., & Barclay, A. (1989). Let a thousand flowers bloom or, weed the garden? *American Psychologist, 44*, 55–59.

FOXX, R. M., McMorrow, M. J., Bittle, R. G., & Fenlon, S. J. (1985). Teaching social skills to psychiatric patients. *Behaviour Research and Therapy, 23*, 531–537.

FRANCES, A., Clarkin, J., & Perry, S. (1984). *Differential therapeutics in psychiatry.* New York: Brunner/Mazel.

FRANK, J. D. (1973). *Persuasion and healing* (2nd ed.). Baltimore: Johns Hopkins University Press.

FREIRE, P. (1970). *Pedagogy of the oppressed.* New York: Seabury.

FRESE, M., & Sabini, J. (Eds.). (1985). *Goal directed behavior: The concept of action in psychology.* Hillsdale, NJ: Erlbaum.

GALBRAITH, J. K. (1979). *The nature of mass poverty.* Cambridge, MA: Harvard University Press.

GAMBRILL, E. (1984). Social skills training. In D. Larson (Ed.), *Teaching psychological skills: Models for giving psychology away.* Pacific Grove, CA: Brooks/Cole.

GARTNER, A., & Riessman, F. (1977). *Self-help in the human services.* San Francisco: Jossey-Bass.

GARTNER, A., & Riessman, F. (Eds.). (1984). *The self-help revolution.* New York: Human Sciences Press.

GAZDA, G. M. (1973). *Human relations development: A manual for educators.* Boston: Allyn & Bacon.

GAZDA, G. M. (1982). Life skills training. In E. K. Kurtz & P. D. Kurtz (Eds.), *Interpersonal helping skills: A guide to training methods, programs, and resources.* San Francisco: Jossey-Bass.

GAZDA, G. M. (1984). Multiple impact training: A life skills approach. In D. Larson (Ed.), *Teaching psychological skills: Models for giving psychology away.* Pacific Grove, CA: Brooks/Cole.

GELATT, H. B. (1962). Decision-making: A conceptual frame of reference for counseling. *Journal of Counseling Psychology, 9*, 240–245.

GELATT, H. B. (1989). Positive uncertainty: A new decision-making framework for counseling. *Journal of Counseling Psychology, 36*, 252–256.

GELATT, H. B., Varenhorst, B., & Carey, R. (1972). *Deciding: A leader's guide.* Princeton, NJ: College Entrance Examination Board.

GELSO, C. J., & Carter, J. A. (1985). The relationship in counseling and psychotherapy: Components, consequences, and theoretical antecedents. *Counseling Psychologist, 13*, 155–243.

GENDLIN, E. T. (1986). What comes after traditional psychotherapy research? *American Psychologist, 41*, 131–136.

GERBER, S. K. (1986). *Response therapy: A systematic approach to counseling skills.* New York: Human Sciences Press.

GIBB, J. R. (1968). The counselor as a role-free person. In C. A. Parker (Ed.), *Counseling theories and counselor education.* Boston: Houghton Mifflin.

GIBB, J. R. (1978). *Trust: A new view of personal and organizational development.* Los Angeles: The Guild of Tutors Press.

GILBERT, T. F. (1978). *Human competence: Engineering worthy performance.* New York: McGraw-Hill.

GILL, J. J. (1982). Empathy is at the heart of love. *Human Development, 3* (3), 29–41.

GOLDFRIED, M. R. (Ed.). (1982). *Converging themes in psychotherapy: Trends in psychodynamic, humanistic, and behavioral practice.* New York: Springer.

GOLDFRIED, M. R., & Wachtel, P. L. (1987). Clinical and conceptual issues in psychotherapy integration: A dialogue. *Journal of Integrative and Eclectic Psychotherapy, 6,* 131–144.

GOLDMAN, H. H., & Taube, C. A. (1988). High users of outpatient mental health services: 2. Implications for practice and policy. *American Journal of Psychiatry, 145,* 24–28.

GOLDSTEIN, A. P. (1980). Relationship-enhancement methods. In F. H. Kanfer & A. P. Goldstein (Eds.), *Helping people change: A textbook of methods* (2nd ed.). New York: Pergamon Press.

GOLDSTEIN, A. P., Gershaw, N. J., & Sprafkin, R. P. (1984). Structured learning therapy: Background, procedures, and evaluation. In D. Larson (Ed.), *Teaching psychological skills: Models for giving psychology away.* Pacific Grove, CA: Brooks/Cole.

GOLDSTEIN, A. P., Heller, K., & Sechrest, L. B. (1966). *Psychotherapy and the psychology of behavior change.* New York: Wiley.

GOLEMAN, D. (1985, August 2). Switching therapists may be best. *Indianapolis News,* p. 9.

GOODYEAR, R. K., & Bradley, F. O. (1980). The helping process as contractual. *Personnel and Guidance Journal, 58,* 512–515.

GORDON, T. (1970). *Parent effectiveness training.* New York: Wyden.

GOSLIN, D. A. (1985). Decision making and the social fabric. *Society, 22* (2), 7–12.

GOTTFREDSON, G. D. (1984). A theory-ridden approach to program evaluation. *American Psychologist, 39,* 1101–1112.

GOTTLIEB, B. H., & Schroter, C. (1978). Collaboration and resource exchange between professionals and natural support systems. *Professional Psychology, 9,* 614–622.

GREENBERG, L. S. (1986). Change process research. *Journal of Consulting and Clinical Psychology, 54,* 4–9.

GREENBERG, L. S., & Safran, J. D. (1989). Emotion in psychotherapy. *American Psychologist, 44,* 19–29.

GRIEGER, R., & Boyd, J. (1980). *Rational-emotive therapy: A skills-based approach.* New York: Van Nostrand Reinhold.

HALL, E. T. (1977). *Beyond Culture.* Garden City, NJ: Anchor Press.

HARCUM, E. R. (1988). The fractionary psychology we try to give away. *American Psychologist, 43,* 483–484.

HARDIN, S. I., Subich, L. M., & Holvey, J. M. (1988). Expectancies for counseling in relation to premature termination. *Journal of Counseling Psychology, 35,* 37–40.

HARE-MUSTIN, R., & Marecek, J. (1986). Autonomy and gender: Some questions for therapists. *Psychotherapy, 23,* 205–212.

HARE-MUSTIN, R. T., Marecek, J., Kaplan, A. G., & Liss-Levinson, N. (1979). Rights of clients, responsibilities of therapists. *American Psychologist, 34,* 3–16.

HARIMAN, J. (Ed.). (1984). *Does psychotherapy really help people?* Springfield, IL: Charles C Thomas.

HARRE, R. (1980). *Social being.* Totowa, NJ: Adams, Littlefield.

HARRIS, T. (1969). *I'm OK—You're OK: A practical guide to transactional analysis.* New York: Harper & Row.

HASKELL, T. L. (1977, October 13). Power to the experts. *New York Review of Books, 24* (16), pp. 28–33.

HAVENS, L. (1978). Explorations in the uses of language in psychotherapy: Simple empathic statements. *Psychiatry, 41,* 336–345.

HAWKINS, J. D., Catalano, R. F., & Wells, E. A. (1986). Measuring the effects of a skills training intervention for drug abusers. *Journal of Consulting and Clinical Psychology, 54,* 661–664.

HAYES, S. C., Nelson, R. O., & Jarrett, R. B. (1987). The treatment utility of assessment: A functional approach to evaluating assessment quality. *American Psychologist, 42,* 963–974.

HEATH, D. H. (1980a). The maturing person. In G. Walsh & D. Shapiro (Eds.), *Beyond health and normality.* New York: Van Nostrand Reinhold.

HEATH, D. H. (1980b). Wanted: A comprehensive model of healthy development. *Personnel and Guidance Journal, 58,* 391–399.

HEESACKER, M. (1986). Counseling pretreatment and the Elaboration Likelihood Model of attitude change. *Journal of Counseling Psychology, 33,* 107–114.

HELD, B. S. (1984). Toward a strategic eclecticism: A proposal. *Psychotherapy, 21,* 232–241.

HELLEKSON, C. J., Kline, J. A., & Rosenthal, N. E. (1986). Psychotherapy for seasonal affective disorder in Alaska. *American Journal of Psychiatry, 143,* 1015–1019.

HELLER, K., Swindle, R. W., & Dusenbury, L. (1986). Component social support processes: Comments and integration. *Journal of Consulting and Clinical Psychology, 54,* 466–470.

HENDRICK, S. S. (1988). Counselor self-disclosure. *Journal of Counseling and Development, 66,* 419–424.

HENDRICKS, M. N. (1986). Experiencing level as a therapeutic variable. *Person-Centered Review, 1,* 141–162.

HENIG, R. M. (1988, June 26). Less can be more. *The New York Times Magazine,* pp. 33–34.

HEPPNER, P. P. (1978). A review of the problem-solving literature and its relationship to the counseling process. *Journal of Counseling Psychology, 25,* 366–375.

HEPPNER, P. P. (1988). *The problem-solving inventory: Manual.* Palo Alto, CA: Consulting Psychologists Press.

HEPPNER, P. P. (1989). Identifying the complexities within clients' thinking and decision making. *Journal of Counseling Psychology, 36,* 257–259.

HEPPNER, P. P., & Anderson, W. P. (1985). The relationship between problem-solving self-appraisal and psychological adjustment. *Cognitive Therapy and Research, 9,* 415–427.

HEPPNER, P. P., & Dixon, D. N. (1981). A review of interpersonal influence process in counseling. *Personnel and Guidance Journal, 59,* 542–550.

HEPPNER, P. P., & Heesacker, M. (1982). Interpersonal influence process in real-life counseling: Investigating client perceptions, counselor experience level, and counselor power over time. *Journal of Counseling Psychology, 29,* 215–223.

HEPPNER, P. P., & Krauskopf, C. J. (1987). An information-processing approach to personal problem solving. *Counseling Psychologist, 15,* 371–447.

HEPPNER, P. P., Neal, G. W., & Larson, L. M. (1984). Problem-solving training as prevention with college students. *Personnel and Guidance Journal, 62,* 514–519.

HEPPNER, P. P., & Reeder, B. L. (1984). Problem-solving training with residence hall staff: Who's most satisfied? *Journal of College Student Personnel, 25,* 357–360.

HERMANSSON, G. L., Webster, A. C., & McFarland, K. (1988). Counselor deliberate postural lean and communication of facilitative conditions. *Journal of Counseling Psychology, 35,* 149–153.

HERR, E. L. (1989). *Counseling in a dynamic society: Opportunities and challenges.* Alexandria, VA: American Association for Counseling and Development.

HIGGINS, W., Ivey, A., & Uhlemann, M. (1970). Media therapy: A programmed approach to teaching behavioral skills. *Journal of Counseling Psychology, 17,* 20–26.

HIGHLEN, P. S., & Hill, C. E. (1984). Factors affecting client change in individual counseling: Current status and theoretical speculations. In S. D. Brown & R. W. Lent (Eds.), *The handbook of counseling psychology.* New York: Wiley.

HILL, C. E., Helms, J. E., Tichenor, V., Spiegel, S. B., O'Grady, K. E., & Perry, E. S. (1988). Effects of therapist response modes in brief psychotherapy. *Journal of Counseling Psychology, 35,* 222–233.

HILL, K. A. (1987). Meta-analysis of paradoxical interventions. *Psychotherapy, 24,* 266–270.

HILLS, M. D. (1984). *Improving the learning of parents' communication skills by providing for the discovery of personal meaning.* Doctoral dissertation, University of Victoria, British Columbia, Canada.

HILTONSMITH, R. W., & Miller, H. R. (1983). What happened to the setting in person-setting assessment? *Professional Psychology, 14,* 419–434.

HINES, M. H. (1988a). Whose problem is it? *Journal of Counseling and Development, 67,* 106.

HINES, M. H. (1988b). How to fail in private practice: Thirteen easy steps. *Journal of Counseling and Development, 67,* 253–254.

HOLTJE, H. F. (1988). Comment on Rosen. *American Psychologist, 43,* 600.

HOWARD, G. S., & Conway, C. G. (1986). Can there be an empirical science of volitional action? *American Psychologist, 41,* 1241–1251.

HOWARD, G. S., DiGangi, M., & Johnson, A. (1988). Life, science, and the role of therapy in the pursuit of happiness. *Professional Psychology, 19,* 191–198.

HOWARD, G. S., Nance, D. W., & Myers, P. (1987). *Adaptive counseling and therapy: A systematic approach to selecting effective treatments.* San Francisco: Jossey-Bass.

HOWARD, K. I., Kopta, S. M., Krause, M. S., & Orlinsky, D. E. (1986). The dose-effect relationship in psychotherapy. *American Psychologist, 41,* 159–164.

HOWELL, W. S. (1982). *The empathic communicator.* Belmont, CA: Wadsworth.

HUNSLEY, J. (1988). Conceptions and misconceptions about the context of paradoxical therapy. *Professional Psychology: Research and Practice, 19,* 553–559.

HURVITZ, N. (1970). Peer self-help psychotherapy groups and their implication for psychotherapy. *Psychotherapy: Theory, Research, and Practice, 7,* 41–49.

HURVITZ, N. (1974). Similarities and differences between conventional psychotherapy and peer self-help psychotherapy groups. In P. S. Roman & H. M. Trice (Eds.), *The sociology of psychotherapy.* New York: Aronson.

HUXLEY, A. (1963). *The doors of perception.* New York: Harper & Row.

IVEY, A. E. (1971). *Microcounseling: Innovations in interviewing training.* Springfield, IL: Charles C Thomas.

IVEY, A. E. (1983). *Intentional interviewing and counseling.* Pacific Grove, CA: Brooks/Cole.

IVEY, A. E. (1986). *Developmental therapy.* San Francisco: Jossey-Bass.

IVEY, A. E., & Authier, J. (1978). *Microcounseling* (2nd ed.). Springfield, IL: Charles C Thomas.

IVEY, A. E., & Matthews, W. J. (1984). A meta-model for structuring the clinical interview. *Journal of Counseling and Development, 63,* 237–243.

JACOBS, M. K., & Goodman, G. (1989). Psychology and self-help groups: Predictions on a partnership. *American Psychologist, 44,* 536–545.

JAMES, M., & Jongeward, D. (1971). *Born to win: Transactional analysis with Gestalt experiments.* Reading, MA: Addison-Wesley.

JANIS, I. L. (1983a). The role of social support in adherence to stressful decisions. *American Psychologist, 38,* 143–160.

JANIS, I. L. (1983b). *Short-term counseling: Guidelines based on recent research.* New Haven, CT: Yale University Press.

JANIS, I. L., & Mann, L. (1977). *Decision making: A psychological analysis of conflict, choice, and commitment.* New York: Free Press.

JANOSIK, E. H. (Ed.). (1984). *Crisis counseling: A contemporary approach.* Belmont, CA: Wadsworth.

JOHNSON, H., & Gelso, C. (1981). The effectiveness of time limits in counseling and psychotherapy. *The Counseling Psychologist, 9,* 70–83.

JOHNSON, W. C., Jr., & Heppner, P. P. (1989). On reasoning and cognitive demands in counseling: Implications for counselor training. *Journal of Counseling and Development, 67,* 428–429.

JONES, A. S., & Gelso, C. J. (1988). Differential effects of style of interpretation. *Journal of Counseling Psychology, 35,* 363–369.

JONES, E. E., Cumming, J. D., & Horowitz, M. J. (1988). Another look at the nonspecific hypothesis of therapeutic effectiveness. *Journal of Consulting and Clinical Psychology, 56,* 40–47.

JONES, R. A. (1986). Social psychological research and clinical practice. *Professional Psychology: Research and Practice, 17,* 535–540.

JOURNAL OF INTEGRATIVE AND ECLECTIC PSYCHOTHERAPY. (1987). Vol. 6(2). [This issue is devoted to the similarities and differences between systematic eclecticism and integration and to the search for a common language for psychotherapy.]

KAGAN, N. (1973). Can technology help us toward reliability in influencing human interaction? *Educational Technology, 13,* 44–51.

KANFER, F. H. (1980). Self-management methods. In F. H. Kanfer & A. P. Goldstein (Eds.), *Helping people change: A textbook of methods* (2nd ed.). New York: Pergamon Press.

KANFER, F. H., & Goldstein, A. P. (Eds.). (1986). *Helping people change: A textbook of methods* (3rd ed.). New York: Pergamon Press.

KANFER, F. H., & Schefft, B. K. (1988). *Guiding therapeutic change.* Champaign, IL: Research Press.

KANTER, R. M. (1983). *Change masters: Innovation for productivity in the American corporation.* New York: Simon & Schuster.

KATZ, J. H., & Torres, C. (1982). Couples contracting workshops: A proactive counseling strategy. *Personnel and Guidance Journal, 60,* 567–570.

KAZDIN, A. E. (1977). Assessing the clinical or applied importance of behavior change through social validation. *Behavior Modification, 1,* 427–451.

KELLY, J. A., St. Lawrence, J. S., Hood, H. V., & Brasfield, T. L. (1989). Behavioral intervention to reduce AIDS risk activities. *Journal of Consulting and Clinical Psychology, 57,* 60–67.

KIERULFF, S. (1988). Sheep in the midst of wolves: Person-responsibility therapy with criminals. *Professional Psychology: Research and Practice, 19,* 436–440.

KIMBLE, G. A. (1984). Psychology's two cultures. *American Psychologist. 39,* 833–839.

KIRSCHENBAUM, D. S. (1985). Proximity and specificity of planning. *Cognitive Therapy and Research, 9,* 489–506.

KIRSCHENBAUM, D. S. (1987). Self-regulatory failure: A review with clinical implications. *Clinical Psychology Review, 7,* 77–104.

KLEIN, J. G., & Friedlander, M. L. (1987). A test of two competing explanations for the attraction-enhancing effects of counselor self-disclosure. *Journal of Counseling and Development, 66,* 82–85.

KLEINMAN, A. (1988). *Rethinking psychiatry.* New York: Free Press.

KOHUT, H. (1978). The psychoanalyst in the community of scholars. In P. H. Ornstein (Ed.), *The search for self: Selected writings of H. Kohut.* New York: International Universities Press.

KOTTLER, J. A. (1986). *On being a therapist.* San Francisco: Jossey-Bass.

KNAPP, M. L. (1972). *Nonverbal communication in human interaction* (1st ed.). New York: Holt, Rinehart & Winston.

KNAPP, M. L. (1978). *Nonverbal communication in human interaction* (2nd ed.). New York: Holt, Rinehart & Winston.

KRAFT, R. G., Claiborn, C. D., & Dowd, E. T. (1985). Effects of positive reframing and paradoxical directives in counseling for negative emotions. *Journal of Counseling Psychology, 32,* 617–621.

KRAMER, S. A. (1986). The termination process in open-ended psychotherapy: Guidelines for clinical practice. *Psychotherapy, 23,* 526–531.

KUPERS, T. (1988). *Ending therapy: The meaning of termination.* New York: New York University Press.

KUTASH, I. L., & Wolf, A. (Eds.). (1986). *Psychotherapist's casebook: Theory and technique in the practice of modern principles.* San Francisco: Jossey-Bass.

LAMB, D. H., Clark, C., Drumheller, P., Frizzell, K., & Surrey, L. (1989). Applying *Tarasoff* to AIDS-related psychotherapy issues. *Professional Psychology: Research and Practice, 20,* 37–43.

LANDRETH, G. L. (1984). Encountering Carl Rogers: His views on facilitating groups. *Personnel and Guidance Journal, 62,* 323–326.

LANGER, E. (1989). *Mindfulness.* Reading, MA: Addison-Wesley.

LARKE, J. (1985). Compulsory treatment: Some methods of treating the mandated client. *Psychotherapy, 22,* 262–268.

LARSON, D. (Ed.). (1984). *Teaching psychological skills: Models for giving psychology away.* Pacific Grove, CA: Brooks/Cole.

LARSON, M. S. (1977). *The rise of professionalism.* Berkeley: University of California Press.

LASCH, C. (1977, November 24). The siege of the family. *New York Review of Books, 24* (19), pp. 15–18.

LASCH, C. (1978). *Haven in a heartless world: The family besieged.* New York: Basic Books.

LAUNGANI, P. (1984). Do psychotherapists meet clients' perceived needs? In J. Hariman (Ed.), *Does psychotherapy really help people?* Springfield, IL: Charles C Thomas.

LAZARICK, D., Fishbein, S., Loiello, M., & Howard, G. S. (1988). Practical investigations of volition. *Journal of Counseling Psychology, 35,* 15–26.

LAZARUS, A. A. (1976). *Multimodal behavior therapy.* New York: Springer.

LAZARUS, A. A. (1981). *The practice of multimodal therapy.* New York: McGraw-Hill.

LEAHEY, M., & Wallace, E. (1988). Strategic groups: One perspective on integrating strategic and group therapies. *Journal for Specialists in Group Work, 13,* 209–217.

LEBOW, J. (1982). Consumer satisfaction with mental health treatment. *Psychological Bulletin, 91,* 244–259.

LEE, C. (1983). Self-efficacy and behaviour as predictors of subsequent behaviour in an Assertiveness Training Programme. *Behaviour Research and Therapy, 21,* 225–232.

LEVINSON, D. J., with Darrow, C. N., Klein, E. B., Levinson, M. H., & McKee, B. (1978). *The seasons of a man's life.* New York: Knopf.

LEVY, L. H. (1968). Fact and choice in counseling and counselor education: A cognitive viewpoint. In C. A. Parker (Ed.), *Counseling theories and counselor education.* Boston: Houghton Mifflin.

LEVY, L. H. (1988). *Self-help groups.* Unpublished manuscript.

LEWIN, K. (1969). Quasi-stationary social equilibria and the problem of permanent change. In W. G. Bennis, K. D. Benne, & R. Chin (Eds.), *The planning of change.* New York: Holt, Rinehart & Winston.

LEWIS, J. D., & Magoon, T. M. (1987). Survey of college counseling centers' follow-up practices with former clients. *Professional Psychology: Research and Practice, 18,* 128–133.

LEWIS, W. A., & Evans, J. W. (1986). Resistance: A reconceptualization. *Psychotherapy, 23,* 426–433.

LIBERMAN, R. P., Mueser, K. T., & Wallace, C. J. (1986). Social skills training for schizophrenic individuals at risk for relapse. *American Journal of Psychiatry, 143,* 523–526.

LIEBERMAN, M. A. (1986). Social supports: The consequences of psychologizing: A commentary. *Journal of Consulting and Clinical Psychology, 54,* 461–465.

LIEBERMAN, M. A., Yalom, I. D., & Miles, M. B. (1973). *Encounter groups: First facts.* New York: Basic Books.

LINDAMAN, E. B., & Lippitt, R. O. (1979). *Choosing the future you prefer: A goal setting guide.* Washington, D.C.: Development Publications.

LIPOVSKY, J. A. (1988). Internship year in psychology training as a professional adolescence. *Professional Psychology: Research and Practice, 19,* 606–608.

LIVNEH, H. (1984). Psychiatric rehabilitation: A dialogue with Bill Anthony. *Journal of Counseling and Development, 63,* 86–90.

LLEWELYN, S. P. (1988). Psychological therapy as viewed by clients and therapists. *British Journal of Clinical Psychology, 27,* 223–237.

LOCKE, E. A., & Latham, G. P. (1984). *Goal setting: A motivational technique that works.* Englewood Cliffs, NJ: Prentice-Hall.

LOCKE, E. A., Shaw, K. N., Saari, L. M., & Latham, G. P. (1981). Goal setting and task performance: 1969–1980. *Psychological Bulletin, 90,* 125–152.

LONDON, M. (1982). How do you say good-bye after you've said hello? *Personnel and Guidance Journal, 60,* 412–414.

LONDON, P. (1986). Major issues in psychotherapy integration. *International Journal of Eclectic Psychotherapy, 5,* 211–216.

LOREFICE, L. S., & Borus, J. F. (1984). Consumer evaluation of a community mental health service: 2. Perceptions of clinical care. *American Journal of Psychiatry, 141,* 1449–1452.

LUBORSKY, L., Crits-Christoph, P., McLellan, A. T., Woody, G., Piper, W., Liberman, B., Imber, S., & Pilkonis, P. (1986). The nonspecific hypothesis of therapeutic effectiveness: A current assessment. *American Journal of Orthopsychiatry, 56,* 501–512.

LYND, H. M. (1958). *On shame and the search for identity.* New York: Science Editions.

MACDEVITT, J. W. (1987). Therapists' personal therapy and professional self-awareness. *Psychotherapy, 24,* 693–703.

MAGARO, P. (1985). Fourth revolution in the treatment of mental disorders: Rehabilitative entrepreneurship. *Professional Psychology: Research and Practice, 16,* 540–552.

MAHALIK, J. R., & Kivlighan, D. M. (1988). Self-help treatment for depression: Who succeeds? *Journal of Counseling Psychology, 35,* 237–242.

MAHOLICK, L. T., & Turner, D. W. (1979). Termination: That difficult farewell. *American Journal of Psychotherapy, 33,* 583–591.

MAHONEY, M. J. (1977). Reflections on the cognitive-learning trend in psychotherapy. *American Psychologist, 32,* 5–13.

MAHONEY, M. J., & Arnkoff, D. B. (1978). Cognitive and self-control therapies. In S. L. Garfield & A. E. Bergin (Eds.), *Handbook of psychotherapy and behavior change* (2nd ed.). New York: Wiley.

MAIER, N. R. F. (1970). *Problem solving and creativity in individuals and groups.* Pacific Grove, CA: Brooks/Cole.

MAIER, N. R. F., & Hoffman, L. R. (1964). Financial incentives and group decision in motivating change. *Journal of Social Psychology, 64,* 369–378.

MALTZMAN, I. (1960). On the training of originality. *Psychological Review, 67,* 229–242.

MARCH, J. G. (1982, November/December). Theories of choice and making decisions. *Society,* pp. 29–39.

MARGULIES, A. (1984). Toward empathy: The uses of wonder. *American Journal of Psychiatry, 141,* 1025–1033.

MARKS, S. E., & Tolsma, R. J. (1986). Empathy research: Some methodological considerations. *Psychotherapy, 23,* 4–20.

MARKUS, H., & Nurius, P. (1986). Possible selves. *American Psychologist, 41,* 954–969.

MARTIN, J., Martin, W., Meyer, M., & Slemon, A. (1986). Empirical investigation of the cognitive mediational paradigm for research on counseling. *Journal of Counseling Psychology, 33,* 115–123.

MARZIALI, E. A. (1987). People in your life: Development of a social support measure for predicting psychotherapy outcome. *Journal of Nervous and Mental Disease, 175,* 317–326.

MARZILLIER, J. S., & Eastman, C. (1984). Continuing problems in self-efficacy theory: A reply to Bandura. *Cognitive Therapy and Research, 8,* 257–262.

MASLOW, A. H. (1968). *Toward a psychology of being* (2nd ed.). New York: Van Nostrand Reinhold.

MASSON, J. F. (1988). *Against therapy: Emotional tyranny and the myth of psychological healing.* New York: Atheneum.

MAYEROFF, M. (1971). *On caring.* New York: Perennial Library (Harper & Row).

MAYS, D. T., & Franks, C. M. (Eds.). (1985). *Negative outcome in psychotherapy and what to do about it.* New York: Springer.

MCCARTHY, P. R. (1979). Differential effects of self-disclosing versus self-involving counselor statements across counselor-client gender pairings. *Journal of Counseling Psychology, 26,* 538–541.

MCKEE, J. E., Moore, H. B., & Presbury, J. H. (1982). A model for teaching counselor trainees how to make challenging responses. *Counselor Education and Supervision, 22,* 149–153.

MCNEILL, B. W., & Stoltenberg, C. D. (1988). A test of the Elaboration Likelihood Model for therapy. *Cognitive Therapy and Research, 12,* 69–79.

MEDEIROS, M. E., & Prochaska, J. O. (1988). Coping strategies that psychotherapists use in working with stressful clients. *Professional Psychology: Research and Practice, 19,* 112–114.

MEHRABIAN, A. (1970). *Tactics of social influence.* Englewood Cliffs, NJ: Prentice-Hall.

MEHRABIAN, A. (1971). *Silent messages.* Belmont, CA: Wadsworth.

MEHRABIAN, A., & Reed, H. (1969). Factors influencing judgments of psychopathology. *Psychological Reports, 24,* 323–330.

MEICHENBAUM, D. H. (1974). *Cognitive behavior modification.* Morristown, NJ: General Learning Press.

MEICHENBAUM, D. H. (1977). *Cognitive-behavior modification: An integrative approach.* New York: Plenum.

MEICHENBAUM, D., & Genest, M. (1980). Cognitive behavioral modification: An integration of cognitive and behavioral methods. In F. H. Kanfer & A. P. Goldstein (Eds.), *Helping people change: A textbook of methods* (2nd ed.). New York: Pergamon Press.

MEIER, S. T. (1989). *The elements of counseling.* Pacific Grove, CA: Brooks/Cole.

MENNICKE, S. A., Lent, R. W., & Burgoyne, K. L. (1988). Premature termination from university counseling centers: A review. *Journal of Counseling and Development, 66,* 458–465.

MILLER, G. A. (1969). Psychology as a means of promoting human welfare. *American Psychologist, 24,* 1063–1075.

MILLER, G. A., Galanter, E., & Pribram, K. H. (1960). *Plans and the structure of behavior.* New York: Holt, Rinehart & Winston.

MILLER, L. M. (1984). *American spirit: Visions of a new corporate culture.* New York: Morrow.

MILLER, M. J. (1989). A few thoughts on the relationship between empathy and counseling techniques. *Journal of Counseling and Development, 67,* 350–351.

MILLER, W. C. (1986). *The creative edge: Fostering innovation where you work.* Reading, MA: Addison-Wesley.

MISCHEL, W., & Patterson, C. J. (1976). Substantive and structural elements of effective plans for self-control. *Journal of Personality and Social Psychology, 34,* 942–950.

MONROE, J. E. (1988). Generalization and maintenance in therapeutic systems: Analysis and proposal for change. *Professional Psychology: Research and Practice, 19,* 449–453.

MORROW-BRADLEY, C., & Elliott, R. (1986). Utilization of psychotherapy research by practicing psychotherapists. *American Psychologist, 41,* 188–197.

MOWRER, O. H. (1968a). Loss and recovery of community: A guide to the theory and practice of integrity therapy. In G. M. Gazda (Ed.), *Innovations in group psychotherapy.* Springfield, IL: Charles C Thomas.

MOWRER, O. H. (1968b). New evidence concerning the nature of psychopathology. *University of Buffalo Studies, 4,* 113–193.

MOWRER, O. H. (1973a). Integrity groups today. In R-R. M. Jurjevich (Ed.), *Direct psychotherapy: Twenty-eight American originals* (Vol. 2). Coral Gables, FL: University of Miami Press.

MOWRER, O. H. (1973b). My philosophy of psychotherapy. *Journal of Contemporary Psychotherapy, 6* (1), 35–42.

MURPHY, K. C., & Strong, S. R. (1972). Some effects of similarity self-disclosure. *Journal of Counseling Psychology, 19,* 121–124.

MURRAY, C. (1988). *In pursuit of happiness.* New York: Simon & Schuster.

NAISBITT, J. (1982). *Megatrends: Ten new directions transforming our lives.* New York: Warner Books.

NEIMEYER, G. J., & Banikiotes, P. G. (1981). Self-disclosure flexibility, empathy, and perceptions of adjustment and attraction. *Journal of Counseling Psychology, 28,* 272–275.

NEIMEYER, G. J., & Fong, M. L. (1983). Self-disclosure flexibility and counselor effectiveness. *Journal of Counseling Psychology, 30,* 258–261.

NEWMAN, B. M., & Newman, P. R. (1984). *Development through life: A psychosocial approach* (3rd ed.). Homewood IL: Dorsey Press.

NEZU, A. M. (1987). A problem-solving formulation of depression: A literature review and proposal of a pluralistic model. *Clinical Psychology Review, 7,* 121–144.

NICHOLSON, R. A., & Berman, J. S. (1983). Is follow-up necessary in evaluating psychotherapy? *Psychological Bulletin, 93,* 261–278.

NILSSON, D. E., Strassberg, D. S., & Bannon, J. (1979). Perceptions of counselor self-disclosure: An analogue study. *Journal of Counseling Psychology, 26,* 399–404.

NORCROSS, J. C., & Prochaska, J. O. (1988). A study of eclectic (and integrative) views revisited. *Professional Psychology: Research and Practice, 19,* 170–174.

NORCROSS, J. C., Strausser, D. J., & Faltus, F. J. (1988). The therapist's therapist. *American Journal of Psychotherapy, 42,* 53–66.

O'LEARY, A. (1985). Self-efficacy and health. *Behavior Research and Therapy, 23,* 437–451.

OMER, H. (1985). Fulfillment of therapeutic tasks as a precondition for acceptance in therapy. *American Journal of Psychotherapy, 39*(2), 175–186.

ORGANIZATION DESIGN AND DEVELOPMENT. (1986). *The force field problem-solving model: Kurt Lewin.* Bryn Mawr, PA: Author.

ORR, D. W., & Adams, N. O. (1987). *Life cycle counseling.* Springfield, IL: Charles C Thomas.

OSBORN, A. F. (1963). *Applied imagination: Principles and procedures of creative problem solving* (3rd ed.). New York: Scribner's.

PAAR, D. W. (1988). Helping can hurt. *Journal of Counseling and Development, 67,* 107.

PANCOAST, D. L., Parker, P., & Froland, C. (Eds.). (1983). *Rediscovering self-help: Its role in social care:* Vol 6. *Social service delivery systems.* Beverly Hills, CA: Sage Publications.

PAQUIN, M. J. R. (1983). Beyond significant yet meaningless results in psychotherapy research. *Psychotherapy: Theory, Research, and Practice. 20,* 38–40.

PARLOFF, M. B., & Handlon, J. H. (1964). The influence of criticalness on creative problem-solving in dyads. *Psychiatry, 27,* 17–27.

PARNES, S. J. (1967). *Creative behavior guidebook.* New York: Scribner's.

PATTERSON, C. H. (1984). Empathy, warmth, and genuineness in psychotherapy: A review of reviews. *Psychotherapy, 21*, 431–438.

PATTERSON, C. H. (1985). *The therapeutic relationship: Foundations for an eclectic psychotherapy.* Pacific Grove, CA: Brooks/Cole.

PATTERSON, C. H. (1986). *Theories of counseling and psychotherapy* (4th ed.). New York: Harper & Row.

PATTERSON, C. H. (1988). The function of automaticity in counselor information processing. *Counselor Education and Supervision, 27*, 195–202.

PEAKE, T. H., Borduin, C. M., & Archer, R. P. (1988). *Brief psychotherapies.* Beverly Hills, CA: Sage Publications.

PEARSON, R. E. (1982). Support: Exploration of a basic dimension of informal help and counseling. *Personnel and Guidance Journal, 61*, 83–87.

PEARSON, R. E. (1983). Support groups: A conceptualization. *Personnel and Guidance Journal, 61*, 361–364.

PECA-BAKER, T. A., & Friedlander, M. L. (1987). Effect of role expectations on clients' perceptions of disclosing and nondisclosing counselors. *Journal of Counseling and Development, 66*, 78–81.

PECA-BAKER, T. A., & Friedlander, M. L. (1989). Why are self-disclosing counselors attractive? *Journal of Counseling and Development, 67*, 279–282.

PEKARIK, G. (1983). Follow-up adjustment of outpatient dropouts. *American Journal of Orthopsychiatry, 53*, 501–511.

PEKARIK, G., & Wierzbicki, M. (1986). The relationship between clients' expected and actual treatment duration. *Psychotherapy, 23*, 532–534.

PERLOFF, R. (1987). Self-interest and personal responsibility redux. *American Psychologist, 42*, 3–11.

PERRIN, D. K., & Dowd, E. T. (1986). Effect of paradoxical and nonparadoxical self-disclosure on counselor social influence. *Journal of Counseling Psychology, 33*, 207–210.

PETERSON, C., Seligman, M. E. P., & Vaillant, G. E. (1988). Pessimistic explanatory style as a risk factor for physical illness: A thirty-five-year longitudinal study. *Journal of Personality and Social Psychology, 55*, 23–27.

PHILLIPS, E. L. (1987). The ubiquitous decay curve: Service delivery similarities in psychotherapy, medicine, and addiction. *Professional Psychology: Research and Practice, 18*, 650–652.

PHILLIPS, E. L. (1988). Length of psychotherapy and outcome: Observations stimulated by Howard, Kopta, Krause, and Orlinsky. *American Psychologist, 43*, 669–670.

POLLIO, H. R. (1982). *Behavior and existence.* Pacific Grove, CA: Brooks/Cole.

POPE, K. S., Tabachnick, B. G., & Keith-Spiegel, P. (1988). Good and poor practices in psychotherapy: National survey of beliefs of psychologists. *Professional Psychology: Research and Practice, 19*, 547–552.

PROCHASKA, J. O., & Norcross, J. C. (1982). The future of psychotherapy: A Delphi poll. *Professional Psychology: Research and Practice, 13*, 620–627.

PROCHASKA, J. O., & Norcross, J. C. (1986). Exploring paths toward integration: Ten ways not to get there. *International Journal of Eclectic Psychotherapy, 5*, 136–139.

PROPST, R. L. (1987). *Psychotherapy in a religious framework.* New York: Human Sciences Press.

PS NEWS. (1982, No. 20). A sharing of ideas about problem solving.

PYSZCZYNSKI, T., & Greenberg, J. (1987). Self-regulatory perseveration and the depressive self-focusing style: A self-awareness theory of depression. *Psychological Bulletin, 102*, 122–138.

RAPPAPORT, J. (1981). In praise of paradox: A social policy of empowerment over prevention. *American Journal of Community Psychology, 9*, 1–26.

REDL, F. (1966). *When we deal with children.* New York: Free Press.

REICH, J., & Neenan, P. (1986). Principles common to different short-term psychotherapies. *American Journal of Psychotherapy, 40,* 62–69.

REISMAN, J. (1986). Psychotherapy as a professional relationship. *Professional Psychology: Research and Practice, 17,* 565–569.

RIDLEY, N. L., & Asbury, F. R. (1988, March). Does counselor body position make a difference? *The School Counselor,* pp. 253–258.

RIMLAND, B. (1979). Death knell for psychotherapy? *American Psychologist, 34,* 192.

RIORDAN, R. J., & Beggs, M. S. (1987). Counselors and self-help groups. *Journal of Counseling and Development, 65,* 427–429.

RIORDAN, R. J., Matheny, K. B., & Harris, C. W. (1978). Helping counselors minimize reluctance. *Counselor Education and Supervision, 18,* 6–13.

RITCHIE, M. H. (1986). Counseling the involuntary client. *Journal of Counseling and Development, 64,* 516–518.

ROBERTSHAW, J. E., Mecca, S. J., & Rerick, M. N. (1978). *Problem-solving: A systems approach.* New York: Petrocelli Books.

ROBINSON, M. D. (1988). *Meaningful counseling.* New York: Human Sciences Press.

ROGERS, C. R. (1957). The necessary and sufficient conditions of therapeutic personality change. *Journal of Consulting Psychology, 21,* 95–103.

ROGERS, C. R. (1961). *On becoming a person.* Boston: Houghton Mifflin.

ROGERS, C. R. (Ed.). (1967). *The therapeutic relationship and its impact.* Madison: University of Wisconsin Press.

ROGERS, C. R. (1980). *A way of being.* Boston: Houghton Mifflin.

ROGERS, C. R. (1986a). Reflection of feelings. *Person-Centered Review, 2,* 375–377.

ROGERS, C. R. (1986b). Rogers, Kohut, and Erikson. *Person-Centered Review, 2,* 125–140.

ROGERS, C. R., Perls, F., & Ellis, A. (1965). *Three approaches to psychotherapy 1* [Film]. Orange, CA: Psychological Films, Inc.

ROGERS, C. R., Shostrom, E., & Lazarus, A. (1977). *Three approaches to psychotherapy 2* [Film]. Orange, CA: Psychological Films, Inc.

ROOK, K. S. (1985). Promoting social bonding: Strategies for helping the lonely and socially isolated. *American Psychologist, 39,* 1389–1407.

RORER, L. G. (1983). "Deep" RET: A reformulation of some psychodynamic explanations of procrastination. *Cognitive Therapy and Research, 7,* 1–10.

ROSEN, G. M. (1987). Self-help treatment books and the commercialization of psychotherapy. *American Psychologist, 42,* 46–51.

ROSEN, S., & Tesser, A. (1970). On the reluctance to communicate undesirable information: The MUM effect. *Sociometry, 33,* 253–263.

ROSEN, S., & Tesser, A. (1971). Fear of negative evaluation and the reluctance to transmit bad news. *Proceedings of the 79th Annual Convention of the American Psychological Association, 6,* 301–302.

ROTHBAUM, F. M., Weisz, J. R., & Snyder, S. S. (1982). Changing the world and changing self: A two-process model of perceived control. *Journal of Personality and Social Psychology, 42,* 5–37.

RUBENSTEIN, E. A., & Parloff, M. B. (Eds.). (1959). *Research in psychotherapy.* Washington, D.C.: American Psychological Association.

RUDESTAM, K. E. (1980). *Methods of self-change: An ABC primer.* Pacific Grove, CA: Brooks/Cole.

RUSK, T. (1989, March 9–10). So you want to change: Helping people help themselves. Talk given at the 12th Annual Conference for Trainers, Consultants, and other HRD Professionals, sponsored by University Associates (San Diego), San Francisco.

RUSK, T., & Rusk, N. (1988). *Mind traps: Change your mind, change your life.* Los Angeles: Price, Stern, & Sloan.

RYAN, W. (1971). *Blaming the victim.* New York: Pantheon.

SCHIFF, J. L. (1975). *Cathexis reader: Transactional analysis treatment of psychosis.* New York: Harper & Row.

SCHMITT, J. P. (1985). Client-assumed responsibility: A basis for contingent and noncontingent therapeutic responding. *Professional Psychology: Research and Practice, 16,* 286–295.

SCHNEIDER, B. H., & Byrne, B. M. (1987). Individualizing social skills training for behavior-disordered children. *Journal of Consulting and Clinical Psychology, 55,* 444–445.

SCHWEBEL, R. S., Schwebel, A. I., & Schwebel, M. (1985). The psychological/mediation intervention model. *Professional Psychology, 16,* 86–97.

SCOTT, N. A. (1979). Beyond assertiveness training: A problem-solving approach. *Personnel and Guidance Journal, 57,* 450–452.

SEARIGHT, H. R., & Openlander, P. (1984). Systematic therapy: A new brief intervention model. *Personnel and Guidance Journal, 62,* 387–391.

SELBY, J. W., & Calhoun, L. G. (1980). Psychodidactics: An undervalued and underdeveloped treatment tool of psychological intervention. *Professional Psychology, 11,* 236–241.

SELIGMAN, M. E. P. (1975). *Helplessness: On depression, development, and death.* San Francisco: W. H. Freeman.

SELTZER, J., & Howe, L. W. (1987). Poor listening habits: Identifying and improving them. In *The 1987 annual: Developing human resources.* San Diego, CA: University Associates.

SELTZER, L. F. (1986). *Paradoxical strategies in psychotherapy.* New York: Wiley.

SHECTMAN, F. (1986). Time and the practice of psychotherapy. *Psychotherapy, 23,* 521–525.

SHOHAM-SALOMON, V., & Rosenthal, R. (1987). Paradoxical interventions: A meta-analysis. *Journal of Consulting and Clinical Psychology, 55,* 22–28.

SHURE, M. B., & Spivack, G. (1978). *Problem-solving techniques in childrearing.* San Francisco: Jossey-Bass.

SIDDALL, L. B., Haffey, N. A., & Feinman, J. A. (1988). Intermittent brief psychotherapy in an HMO setting. *American Journal of Psychotherapy, 42,* 96–106.

SIMONS, A. D., Lustman, P. J., Wetzel, R. D., & Murphy, G. E. (1985). Predicting response to cognitive therapy of depression: The role of learned resourcefulness. *Cognitive Therapy and Research, 9*(1), 79–89.

SIMONSON, N. R. (1976). The impact of therapist disclosure on patient disclosure. *Journal of Counseling Psychology, 23,* 3–6.

SMABY, M., & Tamminen, A. W. (1979). Can we help belligerent counselees? *Personnel and Guidance Journal, 57,* 506–512.

SMITH, M. L., Glass, G. V., & Miller, T. I. (1980). *The benefits of psychotherapy.* Baltimore: Johns Hopkins University Press.

SMITH, T. W. (1982). Irrational beliefs in the cause and treatment of emotional distress. A critical review of the rational-emotive model. *Clinical Psychology Review, 2,* 505–522.

SNYDER, C. R. (1984, September). Excuses, excuses. *Psychology Today,* pp. 50–55.

SNYDER, C. R., & Higgins, R. L. (1988). Excuses: Their effective role in the negotiation of reality. *Psychological Bulletin, 104,* 23–35.

SNYDER, C. R., Higgins, R. L., & Stucky, R. J. (1983). *Excuses: Masquerades in search of grace.* New York: Wiley.

SPIER, M. S. (1973). Kurt Lewin's "force-field analysis." In J. W. Pfeiffer & J. E. Jones (Eds.), *The 1973 annual handbook for group facilitators.* San Diego: University Associates.

SPINKS, S., & Birchler, G. (1982). Behavioral-systems marital therapy: Dealing with resistance. *Family Process, 21,* 169–185.

SPIVACK, G., Platt, J. J., & Shure, M. B. (1976). *The problem-solving approach to adjustment: A guide to research and intervention.* San Francisco: Jossey-Bass.

SPIVACK, G., & Shure, M. B. (1974). *Social adjustment of young children: A cognitive approach to solving real-life problems.* San Francisco: Jossey-Bass.

STADLER, H. A., & Rynearson, D. (1981). Understanding clients and their environments: A simulation. *Counselor Education and Supervision, 21,* 153–162.

STANDAL, S. (1954). *The need for positive regard: A contribution to client-centered theory.* Unpublished doctoral dissertation, University of Chicago.

STARKER, S. (1988a). Do-it-yourself therapy: The prescription of self-help books by psychologists. *Psychotherapy, 25,* 142–146.

STARKER, S. (1988b). Self-help treatment books: The rest of the story. *American Psychologist, 43,* 599.

STEIN, B. A. (1980). *Quality of work life in context: What every practitioner should know.* Unpublished manuscript.

STENSRUD, R., & Stensrud, K. (1981). Counseling may be hazardous to your health: How we teach people to feel powerless. *Personnel and Guidance Journal, 59,* 300–304.

STERN, E. M. (Ed.). (1984). *Psychotherapy and the abrasive patient.* New York: Haworth Press.

STEWART, A. J., & Healy, J. M., Jr. (1989). Linking individual development and social changes. *American Psychologist, 44,* 30–42.

STRAUSS, J., & Ryan, R. M. (1987). Autonomy disturbances in subtypes of anorexia nervosa. *Journal of Abnormal Psychology, 96,* 254–258.

STRAVYNSKI, A., Grey, S., & Elie, R. (1987). Outline of the therapeutic process in social skills training with socially dysfunctional patients. *Journal of Consulting and Clinical Psychology, 55,* 224–228.

STREAM, H. S. (1985). *Resolving resistances in psychotherapy.* New York: Wiley.

STROHMER, D. C., & Newman, L. J. (1983). Counselor hypothesis-testing strategies. *Journal of Counseling Psychology, 30,* 557–565.

STRONG, S. R. (1968). Counseling: An interpersonal influence process. *Journal of Counseling Psychology, 15,* 215–224.

STRONG, S. R., & Claiborn, C. D. (1982). *Change through interaction: Social psychological processes of counseling and psychotherapy.* New York: Wiley.

STRUPP, H. H. (1986). Psychotherapy: Research, practice, and public policy (how to avoid dead ends). *American Psychologist, 41,* 120–130.

SWEENEY, J. A., Clarkin, J. F., & Fitzgibbon, M. L. (1987). Current practice of psychological assessment. *Professional Psychology: Research and Practice, 18,* 377–380.

TAMMINEN, A. W., & Smaby, M. H. (1981). Helping counselors learn to confront. *Personnel and Guidance Journal, 60,* 41–45.

TAUBE, C. A., Goldman, H. H., Burns, B. J., & Kessler, L. G. (1988). High users of outpatient mental health services: 1. Definition and characteristics. *American Journal of Psychiatry, 145,* 19–24.

TAUSSIG, I. M. (1987). Comparative responses of Mexican Americans and Anglo-Americans to early goal setting in a public mental health clinic. *Journal of Counseling Psychology, 34,* 214–217.

TENNOV, D. (1975). *Psychotherapy: The hazardous cure.* New York: Abelard-Schuman.

TESSER, A., & Rosen, S. (1972). Similarity of objective fate as a determinant of the reluctance to transmit unpleasant information: The MUM effect. *Journal of Personality and Social Psychology, 23,* 46–53.

TESSER, A., Rosen, S., & Batchelor, T. (1972). On the reluctance to communicate bad news (the MUM effect): A role play extension. *Journal of Personality, 40,* 88–103.

TESSER, A., Rosen, S., & Tesser, M. (1971). On the reluctance to communicate undesirable messages (the MUM effect): A field study. *Psychological Reports, 29,* 651–654.

THASE, M., & Page, R. A. (1977). Modeling of self-disclosure in laboratory and nonlaboratory interview settings. *Journal of Counseling Psychology, 24,* 35–40.

THOMPSON, A. P., & Mountain, M. A. (1987). Effects of an orientation videotape for newly admitted psychiatric patients. *Professional Psychology: Research and Practice, 18,* 619–623.

TINSLEY, H. E., Bowman, S. L., & Ray, S. B. (1988). Manipulation of expectancies about counseling and psychotherapy: Review and analysis of expectancy manipulation strategies. *Journal of Counseling Psychology, 35,* 99–108.

TROTTER, R. J. (1987, February). Stop blaming yourself. *Psychology Today,* pp. 30–39.

TROWER, P., Casey, A., & Dryden, W. (1988). *Cognitive-behavioral counseling in action.* Newbury Park, CA: Sage Publications.

TYLER, F. B., Pargament, K. I., & Gatz, M. (1983). The resource collaborator role: A model for interactions involving psychologists. *American Psychologist, 38,* 388–398.

TYLER, L. E. (1969). *The work of the counselor* (3rd ed.). New York: Appleton-Century-Crofts.

URBAIN, E. S., & Kendall, P. C. (1980). Review of social-cognitive problem-solving interventions with children. *Psychological Bulletin, 88,* 109–143.

VAN DAM-BAGGEN, R., & Kraaimaat, F. (1986). A group social skills training program with psychiatric patients: Outcome, drop-out rate, and prediction. *Behaviour Research and Therapy, 24,* 161–169.

VANDECREEK, L., & Angstadt, L. (1985). Client preferences and anticipations about counselor self-disclosure. *Journal of Counseling Psychology, 32,* 206–214.

VAN DEURZEN-SMITH, E. (1988). *Existential counseling in practice.* Newbury Park, CA: Sage Publications.

WACHTEL, P. L. (1980). What should we say to our patients? On the wording of therapists' comments. *Psychotherapy: Theory, Research, and Practice, 17,* 183–188.

WACHTEL, P. L. (Ed.). (1982). *Resistance: Psychodynamic and behavioral approaches.* New York: Plenum.

WAGMAN, M. (1979). Systematic dilemma counseling: Theory, method, research. *Psychological Reports, 44,* 55–72.

WAGMAN, M. (1980a). PLATO DCS: An interactive computer system for personal counseling. *Journal of Counseling Psychology, 27,* 16–30.

WAGMAN, M. (1980b). Systematic dilemma counseling: Transition from counselor mode to autonomous mode. *Journal of Counseling Psychology, 27,* 171–178.

WARD, D. E. (1984). Termination of individual counseling: Concepts and strategies. *Journal of Counseling and Development, 63,* 21–25.

WASIK, B. H., & Fishbein, J. E. (1982). Problem solving: A model for supervision in professional psychology. *Professional Psychology, 13,* 559–564.

WATKINS, C. E., Jr., & Schneider, L. J. (1989). Self-involving versus self-disclosing counselor statements during an initial interview. *Journal of Counseling and Development, 67,* 345–349.

WATSON, D. L., & Tharp, R. G. (1989). *Self-directed behavior* (5th ed.). Pacific Grove, CA: Brooks/Cole.

WEICK, K. E. (1979). The social psychology of organizing (2nd ed.). Reading, MA: Addison-Wesley.

WEIGEL, R. G., Dinges, N., Dyer, R., & Straumfjorn, A. A. (1972). Perceived self-disclosure, mental health, and who is liked in group treatment. *Journal of Counseling Psychology, 19,* 47–52.

WEINER, M. F. (1979). *Therapist disclosure: The use of self in psychotherapy.* Boston: Butterworth.

WEINSTEIN, G., & Alschuler, A. S. (1985). Educating and counseling for self-knowledge development. *Journal of Counseling and Development, 64,* 19–25.

WEISZ, J. R. (1983). Can I control it? The pursuit of veridical answers across the life span. In P. B. Baltes & O. G. Brim (Eds.), *Life span development and behavior* (Vol. 5). New York: Academic Press.

WEISZ, J. R., Rothbaum, F. M., & Blackburn, T. C. (1984). Standing out and standing in: The psychology of control in America and Japan. *American Psychologist, 39,* 955–969.

WESTCOTT, M. R. (1988). *Psychology of human freedom.* New York: Springer-Verlag.

WESTERMAN, M. A., Frankel, A. S., Tanaka, J. S., & Kahn, J. (1987). Client cooperative interview behavior and outcome in paradoxical and behavioral brief treatment approaches. *Journal of Counseling Psychology, 34,* 99–102.

WHEELER, D. D., & Janis, I. L. (1980). *A practical guide for making decisions.* New York: Free Press.

WILLIAMS, R. (1989, January-February). The trusting heart. *Psychology Today,* pp. 36–42.

WILLIAMS, R. L., & Long, J. D. (1988). *Toward a self-managed life style* (4th ed.). Boston: Houghton Mifflin.

WITMER, J. M., & Young, M. E. (1985). The silent partner: Uses of imagery in counseling. *Journal of Counseling and Development, 64,* 187–189.

WOLBERG, L. R. (1954). *The technique of psychotherapy.* New York: Grune & Stratton.

WOLLERSHEIM, J. P., McFall, M. E., Hamilton, S. B., Hickey, C. S., & Bordewick, M. C. (1980). Effects of treatment rationale and problem severity on perceptions of psychological problems and counseling approaches. *Journal of Counseling Psychology, 27,* 225–231.

WRIGHT, R. M., & Strong, S. R. (1982). Stimulating therapeutic change with directives: An exploratory study. *Journal of Counseling Psychology, 29,* 199–202.

ZARO, J., Barack, R., Nedelman, D., & Dreiblatt, I. (1982). *A guide for beginning psychotherapists.* Cambridge: Oxford University Press.

ZDENEK, M. (1987). *Inventing the future.* New York: McGraw-Hill.

ZINS, J. E. (1984). A scientific problem-solving approach to developing accountability procedures for school psychologists. *Professional Psychology, 15,* 56–66.

ZWICK, R., & Attkisson, C. C. (1985). Effectiveness of a client pretherapy orientation videotape. *Journal of Counseling Psychology, 32,* 514–524.

Name Index

Abbey, D S., 163
Abeles, N., 8
Ackoff, R., 263
Adams, N. O., 19
Adkins, W. R., 24
Alschuler, A. S., 163
American Psychiatric Association Commission on Psychotherapies, 10
American Psychological Association, 22, 74, 75
American Psychologist, 22
Andersen, B., 224
Andersen, W., 224
Anderson, C. M., 168
Anderson, W. P., 102
Angstadt, L., 220, 224
Anscombe, R., 190
Anthony, W. A., 224, 384
Archer, R. P., 397, 399
Argyris, C., 85, 186
Arnkoff, D. B., 15
Asbury, F. R., 109, 136
Attkisson, C. C., 83
Authier, J., 218, 224
Avard, J., 99

Backer, T. E., 275
Baekeland, F., 67
Baldwin, B. A., 250
Bandura, A., 20, 72, 99, 100, 238, 311
Banikiotes, P. G., 223
Bannon, J., 222
Barclay, A., 17
Batchelor, T., 208
Bayless, O. L., 333
Beck, J. T., 194
Beck, N. C., 404
Beckhard, R., 270, 372
Beggs, M. S., 105
Beier, E. G., 199, 203, 205, 230, 241
Belkin, G. S., 13

Benjamin, A., 142
Bennet, M. B., 97
Bennet, M. I., 97
Bennis, W., 214, 235
Berenson, B. G., 64, 235, 238
Berg, J. H., 156
Berger, D. M., 131
Berger, P. L., 78
Berman, J. S., 407
Berne, E., 199, 227
Bernheim, K. F., 275, 276
Bernier, M., 99
Birchler, G., 168
Blackburn, T. C., 93, 374
Bledstein, B. J., 398
Blocher, D. H., 19
Block, P., 242
Boat, B. W., 338
Bohart, A. C., 123
Book, H. E., 139
Borduin, C. M., 397, 399
Borus, J. F., 12
Bowman, S. L., 83
Boyd, J., 97, 401
Bradley, F. O., 80
Brammer, L., 257
Brandsma, J., 73, 184, 241
Brantley, J. C., 15
Braswell, M., 13
Brehm, J., 168
Breier, A., 387
Brown, J. E., 230, 232, 233
Brownell, K. D., 376, 377
Bruckner-Gordon, F., 83, 401, 402, 405
Bruhn, J. G., 387
Budman, S. H., 397
Bugental, E. K., 172
Bugental, J. F. T., 172
Burgoyne, K. L., 404
Burke, J. P., 15
Burke, J. F., 13, 19

431

Subject Index